Why Be Moral?

SUNY series in Chinese Philosophy and Culture

Roger T. Ames, editor

Why Be Moral?

Learning from the
Neo-Confucian Cheng Brothers

YONG HUANG

Cover Calligraphy: Peimin Ni

Published by State University of New York Press, Albany

For information, contact State University of New York Press, Albany, NY
www.sunypress.edu

Production by Diane Ganeles
Marketing by Michael Campochiaro

Library of Congress Cataloging-in-Publication Data

Huang, Yong.
    Why be moral? : learning from the neo-Confucian Cheng Brothers / Yong Huang.
        pages cm. — (SUNY series in Chinese philosophy and culture)
    Includes bibliographical references and index.
    ISBN 978-1-4384-5291-3 (hardcover : alk. paper)
    1. Ethics—China. 2. Neo-Confucianism. 3. Cheng, Yi, 1033–1107. 4. Cheng, Hao, 1032–1085. I. Title.

BJ1185.C5H828 2014
170.951—dc23   2013040988

10 9 8 7 6 5 4 3 2 1

To Qinfang

Contents

Acknowledgments

This book is long in process. I began to have a serious interest in neo-Confucianism and a strong desire to write something about it following two graduate seminars I took, on ZHU Xi and LIU Zongzhou respectively, with Professor TU Weiming. It was at the time I was conceiving my dissertation topic on the debate between liberalism and communitarianism on which is prior: (religious and metaphysical conception of) the good or (political conception of) the right. I had a sense that something could be developed from neo-Confucianism, particularly ZHU Xi's philosophy, to reconcile these two sides and thus had an itch to bring it into my dissertation. My dissertation committee, directed by Professor Francis Fiorenza and including Cornel West and the late Gordon Kaufman, wisely dissuaded me from doing it, not because they thought neo-Confucianism is unimportant or irrelevant to this topic, but because the project would grow too big to be manageable. They suggested that I focus on the liberal and communitarian debate in my dissertation and work on ZHU Xi afterward.

This proved to be one of the most prudent pieces of advice I have ever received and taken. I was able to finish my dissertation in a timely fashion, without losing my preliminary thoughts about the relevance of ZHU Xi's philosophy to this debate, which is summarized in "ZHU Xi on Humanity and Love: A Neo-Confucian Solution to the Liberal-Communitarian Problematic" (*Journal of Chinese Philosophy*, 23.2 [1996]: 213–235; it is among my earliest publications in English). Moreover, luckily, my dissertation became one of the two annually selected, out of about a dozen each year from Harvard's two doctoral programs in religious studies, the Divinity School ThD and the Graduate School of Arts and Sciences PhD, for publication in *Harvard Theological Studies*, a book series that also includes faculty publications. It was eventually published a few years later, in 2001, entitled *Religious Goodness and Political Rightness: Beyond the Liberal-Communitarian Debate*. The most wonderful thing about inclusion in this series, at least for me and at least at that time, was that it would be published without a need for any revision, thus allowing me to immediately start my project on Zнu Xi.

So I began to read Zнu Xi right after I finished my dissertation. However, almost every time I was excited about a brilliant idea in the reading, Zнu Xi would quote the Cheng brothers, particularly Cнeng Yi, attributing the idea to him. I guess that was the reason why "plagiarism" was not part of the ancient Chinese vocabulary; if anything, the problem back then was perhaps the reverse. Not only were people not in the habit of putting their names on their writings; there were people who put other people's (Confucius's, for example) names on what they wrote, so that we contemporary scholars, luckily, get a little extra job security: if we cannot, or do not want to, be philosophers ourselves, we can try to be appraisers or connoisseurs of the authenticity of some classical works.

In any case, that was the reason I shifted the focus of my project from Zнu Xi to the Cheng brothers. By 2008, I thought I was done with the book, as I had all chapters written, with a number of them already published or accepted for publication in various journals. However, since these different chapters were written over a long span of years, when I reread them for publication as a book, I was no longer satisfied with most of them, partly because by then I started to become self-conscious of the somewhat unique methodology I had so far only unconsciously employed. As I explain in more detail in the introduction of this book, all chapters are written with an eye to show how the Cheng brothers could help Western philosophers better answer their (the Western philosophers') own questions or how Western philosophers could learn something from the Cheng brothers. Thus, I started to revise or, rather, rewrite most chapters, and it took me another four or five years to finish. As a result, the book in its current form is very different from what it looked like five years ago. For example, "Cheng Brothers' Neo-Confucian Virtue Ethics: The Identity of Virtue and Nature" (*Journal of Chinese Philosophy* 30 [2003]3–4: 451–467) was supposed to be chapter 2 of this book, but not a single paragraph from that paper can be found in this chapter now. For another example, "Confucian Love and Global Ethics: How Cheng Brothers Would Help Respond to Christian Criticism" (*Asian Philosophy* 15 [2005] 1: 35–60) was originally written as chapter 4 of this book, but it is also hard to trace anything in the latter from the former. Still, I would like to thank the editors and the publishers of these two journals for providing me with the opportunities to try out these initial thoughts.

In addition to these two, part of the introduction is used in "How to Do Chinese Philosophy in a Western Philosophical Context: Introducing a Unique Approach to Chinese Philosophy" (*Chinese Studies* 漢學研究 31 [2013] 2: 117–151); an earlier and much short version of chapter 1 is published as "Why be Moral? The Cheng Brothers' Neo-Confucian Answer" (*Journal of Religious*

Ethics 36 [2008] 2: 321–353); an early version of chapter 2 is published as "The Cheng Brothers on Virtue: Is a Virtuous Person Self-Centered?" (*Journal of Sino-Western Communications* 2 [2010] 2: 12–50); chapter 3 uses materials from both "How Is Weakness of the Will Not Possible? CHENG Yi on Moral Knowledge" (*Educations and Their Purposes: A Philosophical Dialogue among Cultures*, edited by Roger Ames, Honolulu: University of Hawaii Press, 2008) and "Virtue Ethics and Moral Responsibility: Confucian Conception of Moral Praise and Blame" (*Journal of Chinese Philosophy* 40 [2013]: 381–399); a small part of chapter 4 is published as "Between Generalism and Particularism: The Cheng Brothers' Neo-Confucian Virtue Ethics" (*Confucianism and Virtue Ethics*, edited by Stephen Angle and Michael Slote, Routledge, 2013); an early version of chapter 5 is published as "Government by Propriety: Why the Political Is Also Personal" (*The Kingly Culture, Social Renovation, and the Sustained Development in a Global Age* 全球化時代的王道文化, 社會創新 與永續發展, edited by LIN Jianfu, National Taiwan University Press, 2013); a remote ancestor of chapter 6 appeared as "Cheng Brothers' Onto-theological Articulation of Confucian Values" (*Asian Philosophy* 17 [2007] 3: 187–211); an early version of chapter 7 was published as "CHENG Yi's Neo-Confucian Ontological Hermeneutics of Dao" (*Journal of Chinese Philosophy* 27 [2000] 1: 69–92); and the appendix is a shortened version of "Neo-Confucian Hermeneutics at Work: CHENG Yi's Philosophical Interpretation of *Analects* 8.9 and 17.3" (*Harvard Theological Review* 101 [2008] 1: 169–201). I would like to thank the editors and publishers of the above publications for their permissions for me to reuse materials first published there. Most of these papers have also been translated and published in Chinese, and I will take the opportunity to thank their translators, editors, and publishers when (and if) this book appears in Chinese.

As the book has been long in process, I have also accumulated many other debts. While I am clearly aware that I am going to take the risk of missing ten thousands by every one mention (*guayilouwan* 掛一漏萬), I cannot help but list those who come to my mind at this moment. Until I left for Hong Kong in the summer of 2013, I was co-chair of the University Seminar on Neo-Confucian Studies at Columbia University. It was a very congenial group. In addition to two formal presentations of materials developed into this book, I shared informally many other ideas from this book in the seminar. For their comments, criticisms, and encouragements, I would like to thank particularly its regular participants: Ari Borrell, CHANG Chung Yue, Ted de Bary, JUNG Hwa Yol, KIM Yongkun, JIANG Tao, NG On-Cho, Conrad Schirokauer, Deborah Sommer, SOEK Bongrae, and Richard Stickler.

I used the manuscript of this book as materials for an intensive summer course at Shanghai Normal University in 2010, for which I would like to thank

Professors CHEN Weiping and LE Xiaojun; at Huafan University in Taipei in 2011, for which I would like to thank President JUE Jien-Ming and, particularly, Professor CHEN Jen-kuen; and then at East China Normal University in 2012, for which I would like to thank Professors YANG Guorong, YU Zhenhua, YAN Qingshan, FANG Xudong, CAI Zhen, GE Siyou, LIU Liangjian, and CHEN Qiaojian. I used materials of this book for a series of three talks at Wuhan Universityin 2010, for which I would like to thank Professors GUO Qiyong, WU Genyou, DING Sixin, HAO Changchi, WEN Bifang, LIU Junping, and HU Zhihong. I would also like to give thanks to the following for inviting me to give talks using materials from this book, Professors SUN Xiangchen, WU Zhen, ZHANG Rulun, WANG Tangjia, BAI Tongdong, and GUO Xiaodong at Fudan University in Shanghai; Professors LI Xianghai, WANG Xinsheng, and CHEN Jianhong at Nankai University in Tianjin, Professor ZHANG Zailin at Xi'an Jiaotong University in Xi'an; Professors LEE Ming-heui and LIN Yuehui at the Institute of Chinese Literature and Philosophy of Academia Sinica in Taipei; and Professors ISHII Tsuyoshi, NAKAJIMA Takahiro, and Kevin Lam of University of Tokyo, among many others.

I have also benefited from many other long-time friends, either from their comments on a part of an earlier version of this book or through informal discussions related to the book's topics. These include Roger Ames, Steve Angle, CHEN Weigang, CHENG Chung-ying, the late Antonio Cua, Warren Frisina, FAN Ruiping, Paul Goldin, HUANG Chun-chieh, P. J. Ivanhoe, LI Chenyang, John Lizza, LIU Xiaogan, John Makeham, NI Peimin, the late Richard Rorty, Vincent Shen, SHUN Kwong-loi, Michael Slote, XIAO Yang, Justin Tiwald, TONG Shijing, WANG Qingjie, YAO Xinzhong, YU Jiyuan, and YU Wujin.

Finally, I would like to thank Professor Roger Ames for his enthusiasm for including this book into the series he is editing, Laurel Delany for going through my manuscript before I submitted it to SUNY Press, and Nancy Ellegate for overseeing the review process and accepting this book for publication. I am most grateful to the two anonymous reviewers, whose absolutely positive review reports not only allow me to publish the book essentially as it was submitted but also infuse in me a strong dose of confidence that I badly need. The methodology adopted in this book is unconventional and the conclusion reached in each chapter is controversial to say the least, and yet in their detailed review reports, they not only carefully detected but also expressed their appreciation for these controversial conclusions. I treat them as my true *ziyin* 知音, even though I don't know who they are and I am sure they don't fully agree with me. I would also like to thank Jenn Dum for preparing the list of index terms as well as the bibliography, Diane Ganeles for overseeing the production process, Camille Hale for copyediting, and Sue Morreale for typesetting and proofreading.

Introduction

1. Introduction

This is a book about the neo-Confucian brothers Cheng Hao 程顥 and Cheng Yi 程伊; it takes an approach of comparative philosophy; and it focuses on issues related to ethics. In this sense, it is a fairly conventional book. However, in a different sense, it is quite unconventional. Unlike most books on the Cheng brothers (while this is only the second book-length study of the Cheng brothers in English, a few dozens monographs on them in Chinese, to say nothing about numerous journal articles and book chapters, have appeared in the last a few decades), this book does not aim to provide a comprehensive coverage of their philosophy; unlike most books in comparative philosophy, it does not aim either to find the similarities and differences between the Cheng brothers and some particular philosopher(s) in a different philosophical tradition or to bring them into a dialogue so that they can enlighten each other; and unlike most books in ethics, it does not aim to construct a system of moral ideas or explore some topics that have not received their deserved attentions so far. What, then, is unique about this book, and what potential contributions does it aim to make to the relevant field(s)? The best way to explain this is to introduce the unique methodology of comparative philosophy this book adopts (section 3). Before I do that, however, it is necessary to make a case for comparative philosophy in general, since there are some doubts about its feasibility (section 2). The balance of this introduction will provide a short biography of the Cheng brothers (section 4) and a synopsis of each of the following chapters (section 5), before it concludes (section 6).

2. Possibility of Comparative Philosophy

The most common type of comparative philosophy is what Kwong-loi SHUN
calls "direct comparison," which

> engages in explicit and direct comparison of thinkers, texts,
> movements, concepts, or themes from two different traditions,
> with a . . . goal of helping us understand the perspective of one
> or the other of the two traditions. Examples include comparative
> studies of Confucius and Aristotle, Confucian and Kantian ethics,
> the Confucian notion of *chi* [恥] and the contemporary Western
> notion of shame, or the Confucian and contemporary Western
> perspectives on the relation between self and society. Often, such
> a comparative study involves a discussion of similarities and dif-
> ferences between traditions, though it may also go beyond such a
> discussion. (Shun 2009, 468)

Such a way of doing comparative philosophy has to meet two challenges, which
are of course not necessarily unsurmountable. The first, most clearly voiced
by Alasdair MacIntyre, involves the idea of incommensurability. For example,
between Confucianism and Aristotelianism, while there are some similarities
and differences, MacIntyre claims that "there are indeed no shared standards
and measures, external to both systems and neutral between them. The two
systems of thought and practice are incommensurable in the sense made
familiar to us by Thomas Kuhn" (MacIntyre 1991, 109). Although the two
systems may be about one and the same subject matter, "in their characterizations of and questions about that subject matter [they] employ, to a large and
significant degree, concepts whose applicability entails the nonapplicability, the
vacuousness, of the conceptual scheme or schemes employed by their rivals";
and this is because "the standard or standards which determine how the true-
false distinction is to be applied are not the same. And there is . . . no higher
standard yet available to judge between these rival standards" (MacIntyre 1991,
110). By incommensurability of two theories, Kuhn originally "intended only
to insist that there was no common language within which both could be fully
expressed and which could therefore be used in a point-by-point comparison
between them" (Kuhn 1976, 190–91). So MacIntyre may be right that there
are no common measures between two different philosophers from two different philosophical traditions. However, does this mean that we therefore
cannot compare these two philosophers? The answer, as Richard Bernstein

points out, is "no": "Kuhn never intended to deny that paradigm theories can be compared—indeed *rationally* compared and evaluated. In insisting on incommensurability, his main point was to indicate the ways in which paradigm theories *can* and *cannot* be compared" (Bernstein 1991, 81). The reason incommensurable theories can be compared is that, when we compare two philosophers from two different philosophical traditions, for example, we do not compare each of the two with a common measure and then see how each of the two stands with this common measure. Such a comparison is, by definition, impossible, if there is indeed no (and it is difficult to prove that there is one) common measure between and among different philosophical traditions. Rather, what we do is to compare the two directly with each other. This is similar to translation. As Jeffrey Stout points out, when we translate one language (the source language) into another (the target language), we do not first translate the source language, language A, into a third, supposedly neutral, language, language C (such as Esperanto), which serves as a common measure for both the source language and the target language, language B, and then translate this neutral language into the target language, language B. Even if there is no such neutral common language, we can still translate between different languages, as we translate them directly into each other (Stout 1988, 63). Similarly even if there is no common measure between two different philosophical traditions, we can still do comparisons between philosophers belonging to these philosophical traditions, because we are comparing them directly with each other.

The second challenge of doing comparative philosophy is what David Wong, a good comparative philosopher himself, regards as "the most obvious sin": "assimilating another tradition to one's own by unreflectively importing assumptions, frameworks, and agendas into one's reading of that other tradition" (Wong 2009, §4). If the first challenge is about the tool a comparativist uses to do comparative study, this second challenge is related to that comparativist. In normal cases, what a comparativist does is to compare something in his or her home tradition to something in a different tradition. In this sense, the comparativist is not neutral: he or she, consciously or unconsciously, tends to use the terms and categories familiar to him or her and to his or her audience in the home tradition to explain things in the alien tradition. What happens in such a comparison is best captured by the Chinese term *geyi* 格義, often translated as "meaning-matching," to describe the effort of the early Chinese Buddhists to use existing Chinese philosophical concepts to introduce alien Buddhist ideas to a Chinese audience.[1] It should be noted that *geyi* is done not to intentionally distort the alien tradition but to make the "best" sense of it, at least for its intended audience; moreover, as David Wong points out, it may be done by someone who "is a dissident from the main trends in one's home tradition" in order to "find another tradition that 'got it right'" (Wong 2009, §4). For whatever purpose, however, the danger here is the possible distortion of another tradition as a consequence if not as an intention.

This second challenge seems to be more daunting, as it is indeed the case that a comparativist often compares his or her home tradition with another tradition, and, as Gadamer's hermeneutics teaches us so well, it is unreasonable to expect a comparativist to become presuppositionless when understanding and interpreting the other tradition. For that matter, the potential danger of distorting the target tradition(s) cannot be avoided even by a comparativist who compares two traditions other than his or her own, for example, a comparativist, whose home tradition is Chinese, comparing Western philosophy and Indian philosophy. This comparativist may be even-handed with the two traditions he or she compares but may distort both by, perhaps unconsciously, imposing the framework, concepts, and issues of his or her home tradition upon the two foreign traditions he or she compares.[2] However, a number of perceptive comparativists have recently proposed ways to minimize if not entirely avoid this potential danger. Here I would like to mention just three examples that seem to me rather promising.

The first is to apply the principle of charity, particularly the version corrected by the principle of humanity, when we interpret an alien philosophical tradition, as advocated by David Wong himself and Chad Hansen. According to the version of principle of charity formulated by Quine and adopted by early Davidson, when we interpret a philosopher of an alien tradition, we ought to aim at the "maximal" agreement between us, the interpreters, and the philosopher, the interpretee. When we are not able to make sense of what the philosopher says, we should not simply disregard it as false or nonsense; rather we should realize that perhaps we have not fully interpreted the philosopher correctly, and we cannot claim that we understand the philosopher correctly until we reach the maximum agreement with the philosopher.

The importance of this principle in comparative philosophy is that it enjoins us to take the philosopher(s) from the alien tradition seriously. However, as Chad Hansen points out, the principle of charity

> poses a danger, since in practice, it foists upon users of that language a body of truths which we (with a completely different scientific and cultural background) accept. So they proposed that we maximize reasonableness rather than truth. . . . The principle

of humanity thus allows us to attribute philosophical doctrines that are different from any we adopt now or have historically adopted. Our interpretive theory must simply explain why, given people's other beliefs, they accept the belief in question. That it now seems (or ever seemed) true to us is not crucial. (Hansen 1992, 10–11)

In other words, to follow the principle of charity, an interpreter may run the risk of making the interpretee look too much like the interpreter. For this reason, this principle should be corrected by the principle of humanity, originally developed by Richard Grandy as an alternative to the principle of charity. According to the principle of humanity, "If a translation tells us that the other person's beliefs and desires are connected in a way that is too bizarre for us to make sense of, then the translation is useless for our purposes. So we have, as a pragmatic constraint on translation, the condition that the imputed pattern of relations among beliefs, desires, and the world be as similar to our own as possible" (Grandy 1973, 443).

In appearance, this does not sound much different from the principle of charity, but what Grandy wants to emphasize is that our interpretees, like any humans, tend to err, and when they actually err, we should not interpret them, out of charity, as not erring. He uses the example of a person, Paul, attending a party, and making a claim that "the man with a martini is a philosopher" when he saw a man who, not a philosopher, was actually drinking water from a martini glass, and yet there was indeed a philosopher at the party, whom Paul didn't see, drinking a martini. Now Grandy says that the principle of charity may dictate that we interpret what Paul says as true, while his principle of humanity will recognize Paul's statement as false. For this reason, the principle of humanity allows an interpreter to attribute false beliefs to the interpretee where the principle of charity does not allow. The basic idea of the principle was later incorporated by Davidson into his revised version of principle of charity, which emphasizes *optimal* agreement instead of *maximal* agreement and thus also allows us to interpret others as making mistakes. In his application of the revised version of principle of charity in comparative philosophy, David Wong claims that, in interpreting others, "charity directs us to 'optimize' agreement between them and ourselves wherever it is plausible to do so. The idea is to make them 'right, as far as we can tell, as often as possible'" (Wong 2006, 13). This, however, does not prohibit us from attributing mistakes to our interpretees, if we can identify them. Still, if we find others believing something different from what we believe, but we cannot identify the mistakes they make, in David Wong's view, we should construe them as making no mistakes but as taking a different path from the one we are taking, perhaps a path that we could have taken ourselves.

The second is Aaron Stalnaker's bridge concepts. Bridge concepts are not imposed from the comparativist's home tradition upon another tradition, nor are they concepts common to the traditions being compared, nor are they imported from the alien tradition to our home tradition. Rather, as pointed out by Mark A. Benson, "the cross-cultural comparativist is, in many cases, forced to come up with terms from outside both traditions and languages to act as 'bridge concepts,' for if the terms come from one of the traditions or thinkers being studied, the comparison will be driven in a biased way" (Benson 2005, 295). They are thus concepts that bridge the traditions being compared. To serve this function, they "can be given enough content to be meaningful and guide comparative inquiry yet are still open to great specification in particular cases" (Stalnaker 2006, 17). Apparently, such bridge concepts at the beginning of the comparison are vague, and in this sense they are merely thin concepts,[3] not necessarily corresponding to particular terms in the traditions being compared. It is in this sense that they are ad hoc concepts. However, this does not mean that "they are thereby purely neutral, but they are articulated in order not to prejudice the comparison so that one side is rendered in glowing terms, while another is presented as foolish. Bridge concepts, in other words, are designed to facilitate comparative description and analysis of the concepts" (Lewis, et al. 2005, 213). The task of comparison in this approach is thus to fill in the details of these thin bridge concepts from the traditions being compared so that they become thick. However, since different traditions have different details to fill in such originally thin bridge concepts, the result of the comparative work is that each single thin bridge concept at the beginning of the comparison becomes two thick concepts at the end of the comparison.

The third is Edward Slingerland's conceptual metaphor. Just as Stalnaker develops his bridge concept as a *via media* between a local concept from one of the traditions under comparison and the universal concepts reflecting the deep structure of both traditions being compared, Slingerland develops his conceptual metaphor also as a *via media*, this time between individual words and philosophical theories. In other words, when comparing two traditions or parts thereof, on the one hand, a comparativist should not start with individual linguistic signs from his home tradition and then look for its counterpart in the target tradition (which he calls the word fetishism approach, an approach that pays exclusive attention to the same words used in both traditions),[4] for example "human nature" in the West and *xing* 性 in Confucianism. Such words, despite their lexical similarity, may have significantly different meanings in their respective traditions. However, the comparativist should not take a particular philosophical theory from his or her home tradition and compare it with a particular philosophical theory in the target tradition (which Slingerland regards as the theory-based approach), as there can hardly be a perfect fit between philosophical theories from the two traditions compared (which is then regarded as evidence of cognitive incommensurability). In contrast, Slingerland claims that, when we do comparisons, we should look at the level of conceptual metaphor, which "is more general than any individual linguistic sign but also more basic than a theory" (Slingerland 2004b, 13). Drawing on contemporary cognitive sciences, Slingerland argues that conceptual metaphors, understood broadly to also include simile and analogy, arise as our embodied mind adapts to our environment. Conceptual metaphors are important to comparative studies, because, on the one hand, as "human bodies are quite similar the world over, and the types of environments human beings face are also shared in most important respects, one would expect to find a high degree of similarity with regard to conceptual metaphors across human cultures and languages, especially with regard to primary metaphor" (Slingerland 2004a, 327); on the other hand,

> the recognition that these structures are contingent on bodies and the physical environment, that no self of conceptual schemas provided access to the "things in themselves," and that some degree of cultural variation in schemas is to be expected allow us to avoid the sort of rigid universalism. . . . Ideally, at least, the methods of cognitive linguistics give scholars in the humanities access to a shared conceptual grammar that can allow them to engage in genuine conversation with other cultures. (Slingerland 2004a, 336)

It is not my purpose here to assess the strengths and weaknesses of such strategies. I only want to show that the second challenge facing a comparativist, not to impose concepts, frameworks, and issues from one's home tradition to the target tradition, may also be adequately met.

3. How to Do Comparative Philosophy

If it is possible to do comparative philosophy, the next question is how to do it, which is closely connected to the question regarding the purpose of doing it. For Aaron Stalnaker, it is for historical contextualization: the "insightful interpretation that recreates as closely as possible the initial conditions for a text's reception, and thus perhaps as well authorial intention" (Stalnaker 2006, 15). He contrasts comparative philosophy with this goal with comparative philosophy with a goal of "creative, emblematic generalization" represented, in his view, by the collaborative work on Confucianism done by David Hall and Roger Ames, which, in Stalnaker's view,

> is most profitably interpreted . . . as a creative attempt to articulate a form of "New Confucianism" that draws heavily on American pragmatism. Thus Confucius serves as the emblem and "launch pad" for their [Ames and Hall's] own creative philosophizing in a Confucian vein. The main potential virtue of this strategy is the development of novel approaches to familiar material. . . . The danger of the emblematic generalization, then, is of losing touch with the historical sources that provoked one's efforts in the first place. (Stalnaker 2006, 15–16)

The contrast between these two different goals and therefore two different types of comparative philosophy has been stressed by many others. In his article published in the inaugural issue of *Dao: A Journal of Comparative Philosophy*, entitled "Two Forms of Comparative Philosophy," Robert Neville designates them as the objectivist and normative approaches respectively:

> The objectivist approach treats the positions to be compared as finished objects, takes up a perspective of distance upon them, and measures its comparative judgments in empirical ways over against the evidence of the positions. The normative approach centers first on addressing contemporary philosophical problems and looks to the historical positions as resources for contemporary thinking, bringing them into comparative perspective against the contemporary background. (Neville 2001b, 2)

More recently Kwong-loi SHUN contrasts these two types of comparative philosophy as textual studies and philosophical construction. The former "engages in explicit and direct comparison of thinkers, texts, movements, concepts, or themes from two different traditions, with a . . . goal of helping us understand the perspective of one or the other of the two traditions. . . . Often, such a comparative study involves a discussion of similarities and differences between traditions"; the latter is directed to building an account of our ethical life that engages our own experiences and is of appeal to us. Though not as commonly found in the literature, there can be a kind of study that discusses issues in ethics in a way that draws on insights from two different ethical traditions, though without necessarily mentioning, or with only incidental references to, these two traditions. . . . In doing so, one might not have made any direct reference to these two traditions, though one might have included footnote references to acknowledge the sources of one's ideas. (Shun 2009, 467–68)

This is because in this activity, "we are no longer constrained by textual and historical considerations, and are instead guided by criteria of excellence pertaining to this philosophical excellence" (Shun 2009, 454–56). Similarly, Liu Xiaogan distinguishes between two orientations in doing Chinese philosophy: historical and objective study and innovative development of ideas. In his view, "in the studies oriented toward historical objectivity, of course, one can also borrow or make reference to Western perspectives, concepts, and methodology, but it is not so necessary, and the room for such a borrowing is not so big" (Liu 2009, 441); in contrast, in theoretical innovation,

one does not have to borrow the fully developed Western philosophical concepts and definitions to interpret Chinese philosophical terms, but one can borrow the problematic, theoretical dimensions, thesis, and concepts to deepen the ideas in ancient Chinese philosophy. Through transplantation, development, modification, criticism, or renovation, one can create Chinese philosophical theories, concepts, and theses to meet the challenges we are facing in the contemporary world and enrich and substantiate traditional Chinese thought. (Liu 2009, 443)

In this context, it is easier to see in what sense and to what extent the comparative philosophy undertaken in this study is unconventional. Clearly, as a comparative study of Chinese and Western philosophy, while on the Chinese side, this study focuses exclusively on the Cheng brothers, no corresponding counterparts in Western philosophy are fixed. This is closely related to an important feature of this comparative study. As we have seen, what type of comparative philosophy one does is at least partially determined by the goal one attempts to reach by doing it, and the goal one attempts to reach is at least partially affected by the audience one has in mind. This book on the

Cheng brothers is written in English and is addressed to Western philosophers. The first question that we have to ask is why Western philosophers ought to know anything about Chinese philosophy in general and the Cheng brothers in particular. There are of course many intelligible ways to answer this question and therefore many ways to do comparative studies of Chinese and Western philosophy. However, I think one of the plausible answers to this question is that Western philosophers have something important to learn from Chinese philosophy. With this goal in mind, and focusing on ethics just to make this study more manageable, I shall identify a number of important and controversial moral issues in the West to see what representative positions on each of these issues are, what problems there may be with each of these positions, and whether and how the Cheng brothers can have anything, not only new but also better, to say on these issues. Such an approach demands a significant amount of patience from the comparativist, not only because it requires a comparativist to engage both traditions deeply, but also because the comparativist may often feel it necessary to abandon a project of comparative study after some initial work is done, either because the views developed in the Western philosophical traditions are already very much satisfactory or at least more satisfactory than anything that can be found in Chinese philosophy, or, if not satisfactory, Chinese philosophers have nothing better to say.

This can at least partially explain the two apparent defects of this book. The first is its unsystematic nature, in two related senses. As a book on the Cheng brothers, it does not cover every important aspect of their philosophy; as a book of ethics, it does not include all important issues in ethics in the Western tradition. Both can be explained by the main goal of this book: to suggest to philosophers in the West what they may learn from the Cheng brothers on the very issues they (Western philosophers) have regarded as important and have passionately engaged themselves with. Thus, I only select those issues in Western philosophy on which I believe that the Cheng brothers have views that are not only different from but also better than those developed in the Western philosophical tradition. On the one hand, thus, the aspects of the Cheng brothers' philosophy not discussed in this book are not necessarily without value. Some of them may be extremely important. They are not discussed because they do not connect to the issues raised in the Western philosophical traditions in any significant ways. On the other hand, it is also important to keep in mind that moral issues not discussed in this book are not necessarily insignificant. Some of them may be as important as, if not more important than, those discussed in this book. However, on some of them, Western philosophers have already provided convincing arguments or at least more convincing arguments than those we can find in the Cheng brothers; and on some others, while I found the representative positions developed in the history of Western philosophy unsatisfactory or problematic, the Cheng brothers do not have anything better to say. I have thus dropped both types of issues from the scope of this book, however significant they are in their own light.

The second apparent defect of this approach is its asymmetric nature, in two opposite directions. On the one hand, this books seems to contribute to what Kwong-loi Shun regards as the problematic asymmetry in the comparative study of Chinese and Western philosophy: "to approach Chinese thought from a Western philosophical perspective, by reference to frameworks, concepts, or issues found in Western philosophical discussions" and not the other way round (Shun 2009, 47). Shun listed seven different ways in which such an asymmetry is exhibited, and my study may be guilty of the fourth and/or the fifth ways. The fourth way "focuses on certain questions raised in Western philosophical discussions, and considers how Chinese thinkers would view and address such questions" (Shun 2009, 470); and the fifth way, like the fourth way, "also focuses on certain questions raised in Western philosophical discussion, but instead of just considering how Chinese thinkers might view the relevant questions differently, also attempts to address the questions in a way that draws on the insight of Chinese thought" (Shun 2009, 469–70). If there is anything special in my approach that is not fully captured by Shun's characterization of these two ways, it is my attempt to argue that Chinese thinkers' views on these Western philosophical questions are superior to those found in the history of Western philosophy itself. However, precisely because of this, my approach may be guilty of an opposite asymmetry: instead of being even-handed, showing both strengths and weaknesses of both Chinese and Western philosophers under comparison, on each issue discussed in this book, for reasons mentioned above, I attempt to show that the Cheng brothers' neo-Confucian position is superior to the representative views in the Western philosophical tradition, to the extent that I might be mistaken by some as a (neo-)Confucian fundamentalist. It is true that Shun's point is not about the symmetry to be maintained in any individual study of Chinese philosophy but about the symmetry of overall studies of Chinese philosophy. (There are overwhelmingly more Western-centered studies than Chinese-oriented studies.) Still, it is my hope that the two asymmetries in opposite directions simultaneously present in this study can themselves somehow balance each other, resulting in a special kind of symmetry between the Chinese side and the Western side in this project: while I let Western philosophy dictate what issues to talk about, I let Chinese philosophy have the final say on each of these issues.

As I mentioned, I take this approach primarily because I am writing in English and addressing a Western audience. The basic idea is that, if I want to introduce to Western philosophers a Chinese philosopher they are not familiar with, it is pointless to show them how ridiculous (some of) this Chinese philosopher's ideas are or how inferior these ideas are to those found in their (Western philosophers') own tradition, other than providing them with a dose of confidence in their own tradition, which they hardly need. Instead, I believe what they would most like to know is what interesting and important things this Chinese philosopher has to say on the philosophical issues with which they are concerned. For that reason, if I am writing in Chinese and addressing a Chinese audience, my approach may go in an opposite direction. I will try to see on what important and yet controversial issues in Chinese philosophy Western philosophers have something better to say. In other words, I will let Chinese philosophy dictate what issues to discuss and let Western philosophy have its final say on each of the issues under investigation.[5]

We can examine where this way of doing comparative philosophy stands between the two contrasting models of comparative philosophy outlined above. Clearly, it is not a textual study. The primary purpose of this study is not to provide a new interpretation of the Cheng brothers but to see how the Cheng brothers can help Western philosophers better deal with their (the Western philosophers') questions. Moreover, according to Shun's characterization, in textual studies, whether the ideas are philosophically appealing to us from a contemporary perspective should not affect the process (Shun 2009, 455), while in this study, I have left out precisely those aspects of the Cheng brothers' ethics that are not philosophically appealing to us in the sense that they are not conducive to solutions to issues in Western philosophy.[6] However, this study does not fit well with the category of philosophical construction either. On the one hand, it is not my intention in this book to create *my* philosophical theory on any philosophical issues. What I am trying to do is rather see how Chinese philosophers, the Cheng brothers in this case, can help Western philosophers answer their (Western philosophers') own questions. In the sense that this book provides new answers to a number of old questions in Western philosophy, there is philosophical construction involved. However, this is so only if we look at the thing within the context of Western philosophy: something new comes up, yet this something new is really not new, as it has already been present in the Cheng brothers' philosophy. So if there is any philosophical construction, it is not done by the comparativist, the author of this book, although clearly this comparativist fully endorses it. On the other hand, comparative philosophy aiming at philosophical construction tends to downplay the importance of textual studies, at least as characterized by some. For example, Stalnaker states that "such an approach should be judged as their [comparativists'] own creation not as interpretation of the classics," as it has the danger of losing touch with the historical sources that provoked one's efforts in the first place (Stalnaker 2006, 16). Shun also states that, in taking this approach, "we are no longer constrained by textual and historical considerations, and are instead guided by criteria of excellence pertaining to this philosophical exercise" (Shun 2009, 455–56). In this sense, this approach differs from philosophical construction. What I as a comparativist am doing in this study is presenting the Cheng brothers' answers to a number of important issues of ethics in the Western tradition, even though the Cheng brothers may not have these issues in mind when they develop the ideas that I present in this study. Of course, since I myself also endorse these ideas, their views on these issues can also be seen as my views, but they are not the views that I develop myself merely with some inspiration from the Cheng brothers (even though sometimes I do draw further implications of their views that they may or may not endorse). Thus it is important for me to make sure that the views I present here are indeed the Cheng brothers' views, which can only be done through careful textual studies. For this reason, while this study itself is not a textual study, in a number of places, I do challenge some prevalent interpretations of the Cheng brothers' philosophy. Of course, it is possible that I may have misunderstood some aspects of their work, and if this is the case, then such misunderstandings should be corrected by further textual studies instead of being excused or even defended for their philosophical utilities.[7]

4. The Neo-Confucian Cheng Brothers

This study draws primarily on the thought of two Chinese philosophers, CHENG Hao 程顥 (1032–1085), also known as CHENG Mingdao 程明道, and his younger brother CHENG Yi 程頤 (1033–1107), also known as CHENG Yichuan 程伊川, from the Song dynasty. The two brothers, normally addressed together in Chinese scholarship as Two Chengs (*Er Cheng* 二程), are identified with the group known as the Five Masters of the (Northern) Song period (the other three being ZHOU Dunyi 周敦頤 [1016–1073], ZHANG Zai 張載 [1020–1077], and SHAO Yong 邵庸 [1011–1077]), pioneers of the neo-Confucian movement. In one common, although not unquestionable, classification, neo-Confucianism in the Song and Ming (and sometimes also Qing) dynasties is regarded as the second epoch of the development of Confucianism, with pre-Qin classical Confucianism as the first and contemporary Confucianism as the third. One of the main goals of neo-Confucianism is to restore the orthodox status of Confucianism after a long Buddhist dominance in Chinese history; and one of the chief tools neo-Confucians used to achieve this goal is to draw insight from Buddhism, and Daoism integrated with it, particularly its metaphysical dimensions, to provide what I regard as an ontological articulation, as I shall argue in chapter 6, of the classical Confucian values. The result is the development of a sophisticated Confucian moral metaphysics, centered on the most fundamental idea of *li* 理, commonly but not unproblematically translated as "principle" in both its metaphysical and normative senses, so that the neo-Confucianism emerging in this period is most frequently referred to in Chinese scholarship as the learning of *li* (*lixue* 理學).

It is in this sense that the two Cheng brothers can be truly regarded as the founders of neo-Confucianism. On the one hand, of the earliest five masters of the neo-Confucian movement, while Taiji 太極, the ultimate, is central to ZHOU Dunyi, *qi* 氣, the physical-psychic force, to ZHANG Zai, and the number (*shu* 數) to SHAO Yong, it is in the Cheng brothers that *li* for the first time in Chinese history is regarded as the ultimate reality of the universe. The Chengs' unique understanding of this ultimate reality is that it is not a particular thing but the life-giving activity of the ten thousand things, which strikes a similar tone with Martin Heidegger's Being of beings (see Heidegger, 26), almost a millennium later. Assuming the identity of *li* and human nature, they further argue that human nature is good, since what is essential to human nature is humanity (*ren*), also the cardinal virtue in Confucianism, and this is nothing but this life-giving activity. A person of *ren* is one who is in one body with ten thousand things and therefore can feel their pains and itches just as one can feel them in one's own body. Thus, in comparison with classical Confucian philosophy, neo-Confucian philosophy has a more fully developed metaphysics, although moral life is still the central concern for neo-Confucians as for classical Confucians. The metaphysics they develop is to provide an ontological articulation of classical Confucian values, so it is essentially a moral metaphysics.

On the other hand, it is not an exaggeration to say that the later development of neo-Confucianism in its various forms can be traced, to a significant extent, back to one or another emphasis in the Cheng brothers, largely through the lineages of their various students. While the two brothers share fundamentally similar views, and most of their students learned from both, different students noticed and sometimes exaggerated their different emphases, and thus different neo-Confucian schools emerged. Among their students, XIE Liangzuo 謝良佐 (1050–1103) and YANG Shi 杨時 (1053–1135)

are the most distinguished. While YANG Shi transmitted CHENG Yi's teaching through his student LUO Congyan 羅從彥 (1072–1135) and the latter's student LI Tong 李侗 (1093–1163) to ZHU Xi 朱熹 (1130–1200), the synthesizer of the *lixue* 理學 (the learning of principle, understood in a narrow sense) school of neo-Confucianism, XIE Liangzuo transmitted CHENG Hao's learning through a few generations of students such as WANG Ping 王蘋 (1082–1153) and ZHANG Jiucheng 張九成 (1092–1159) to LU Jiuyuan 陸九淵 (1139–1193) and eventually to WANG Yangming 王阳明 (1472–1529), the culminating figure of the *xinxue* 心學 (the learning of heart/mind) school of neo-Confucianism. Sometimes a third school of neo-Confucianism, *xingxue* 性學 (learning of human nature), is identified, whose most important representative is HU Hong 胡宏 (?–1161). HU Hong continued the learning of his father, HU Anguo 胡安国 (1074–1138), who in turn was also influenced by XIE Liangzuo, one of the Chengs' most distinguished students. In this sense, the Cheng brothers left their marks on all three main schools of neo-Confucianism (all recognized, in Chinese scholarship, as *lixue*, learning of principle, understood in the broad sense).

While the later development of the neo-Confucian movement is obviously beyond the Cheng brothers' vision, they were certainly conscious of what they were aiming at. As is well known, HAN Yu (768–824), an important Tang dynasty Confucian, established a lineage of the Confucian tradition (*daotong* 道統) from Yao, Shun, Yu, Tang, King Wen, King Wu, Duke of Zhou, Confucius, and Mencius and claimed that, after Mencius, this lineage was interrupted. CHENG Yi accepted this Confucian *daotong* and claimed that his brother CHENG Hao was the first to continue this lineage after Mencius (Cheng and Cheng, *Wenji* 11; 640).[8] While there may be some exaggeration in such a claim, particularly as it is in the tomb inscription he wrote for CHENG Hao, there is also some truth in it.

The two brothers, only one year apart, were from a family of several generations of middle-level officials. They were both born in Huangpi 黃陂 in present-day Hubei 湖北 Province, where their father, CHENG Xiang, served as a local official (*xianwei* 縣尉). When young, the two brothers moved quite often as their father's official appointment changed. In 1046, while serving a position in Nan'anjun 南安軍, in present-day Jiangxi Province, CHENG Xiang became acquainted with ZHOU Dunyi, one of the so-called five masters in the Northern Song, who also had an official position in the same place. Impressed by Zhou's learning and personality, CHENG Xiang sent his two sons to study with Zhou, which lasted for about a year. Partially due to this encounter, the two brothers set it as the goal of their life to become sages. In 1056, the Cheng brothers followed their father back to their home town, the capital city Luoyang 洛陽,

and began scholarly exchanges with their uncle ZHANG Zai and neighbor SHAO Yong, the other two of the five masters.

Of the two brothers, CHENG Hao largely continued his family tradition, serving at various middle-level offices. Soon after passing the examination for the degree of Jinshi 進士, he was appointed as the registrar of the Hu 鄠 county of the present Shanxi 陝西 Province in 1057 and then of the Shangyuan 上元 County of the present Jiangsu 江蘇 Province in 1060. In 1064, he was appointed as the chief of Jincheng 晋城 County of the present Shanxi 山西 Province. In these offices, CHENG Hao was known as efficient in carrying out things, fair in deciding cases, intelligent in solving problems, and, most importantly, caring to common people. In 1069, CHENG Hao was appointed in the central government, participating at WANG Anshi's 王安石 reform movement. However, in less than a year, he resigned as his advice received no hearing from the emperor, and he began to disagree with Wang and became an opponent of the latter's reform movement. In all these years, CHENG Hao had to spend his time mostly on his governmental affairs. The only notable scholarly activity was his exchange of letters with ZHANG Zai on stabilizing human nature (*dingxing* 定性), which turned out to be one of his main philosophical essays. From 1071 until his death, however, although he continued to serve at a number of different positions, he devoted most of his energy to scholarly and educational activities. Most of his philosophical ideas, including his view of *tianli* 天理, which he claims to be his own despite his acknowledged indebtedness to others on many other issues, his famous discourse on humanity (*Shiren Pian* 識仁篇), and his view of human nature as identical to *dao* and as the life-giving activity (*sheng* 生), were developed during this period of time.

In contrast, CHENG Yi had a largely scholarly career, perhaps due to an early disappointment at a political career and an early success in his scholarly endeavor. On the one hand, in 1050, when he was only eighteen, he wrote a letter to the emperor disclosing the prevalent social problems with his suggested solutions; the emperor never replied. Although he received a number of offers of official positions later in life, he mostly declined them. He expressed his political views largely through drafting documents, including letters to emperors, for officials. On the other hand, in 1056, CHENG Yi wrote "What Learning Yanzi Loves," as an student essay in the imperial college, which greatly impressed the chief examiner HU Yuan 胡瑗, who offered him a teaching position. CHENG Yi taught his first group of students while in his twenties. In 1067, he exchanged his views with a recluse on the *Book of Change*, commentary on which is one of his life-long projects; in 1068, he began to exchange letters with ZHANG Zai, who then came to Luoyang to meet and discuss a wide range of philosophical issues with the two brothers in 1077. In 1086, CHENG Yi was appointed to a high-level teaching position in the imperial college, with the opportunity to teach the young emperor. However, this position lasted for only one year, largely because CHENG Yi was too strict with the emperor. In 1097, CHENG Yi completed his long-term project, a commentary on the *Book of Change*. He then devoted most of his time to private teaching and writing commentaries on other Confucian classics, such as the *Analects*, the *Mencius*, the *Book of Rites*, and the *Spring and Autumn Annals*, in his later years.

The Chengs' philosophical ideas are largely developed in conversations with students, many of whom recorded their sayings. In 1168, ZHU Xi edited some of these recorded sayings in *Chengs' Surviving Sayings* (*Yishu* 遺書) in twenty-five chapters, in which four chapters are attributed to CHENG Hao and eleven chapters to CHENG Yi. The first ten chapters are sayings by the two masters, as in most cases it is not clearly indicated which saying belongs to which brother. In 1173, ZHU Xi edited *Chengs' Additional Sayings* (*Waishu* 外書) in twelve chapters, including those recorded sayings circulated among scholars and not included in *Yishu* (in most cases, it is not indicated which saying belongs to which brother). As ZHU Xi himself acknowledged that the authenticity of sayings in this second collection is mixed, one should be cautious. Before ZHU Xi edited these two works, YANG Shi, one of the students common to the two Chengs, rewrote some of these sayings in a literary form in *The Purified Words of the Two Chengs* (*Cuiyan* 粹言), although it mostly represents CHENG Yi's sayings. CHENG Hao's own writings, mostly official documents, letters, and poetry, are collected in the first four chapters of *Chengs' Collected Writings* (*Wenji* 文集). In addition, CHENG Hao wrote a correction of the *Great Learning*, which is included in the *Chengs' Commentary on Classics* (*Jingshuo* 經說). CHENG Yi's writings are collected in the eight chapters (chapters 5–12) of the *Chengs' Collected Writings* (*Wenji*), in CHENG Yi's *Commentary on the Book of Change* (*Yizhuan*), and in the Chengs' *Interpretation of the Classics* (*Jingshuo*) (except part of chapter 5, which was authored by CHENG Hao, and chapter 8, whose authorship is not indicated). All these are now conveniently collected in the two-volume edition of *The Works of the Two Chengs* (*Er Cheng Ji*) by Zhonghua Shuju in Beijing. It consists of the following: (1) *Yishu*, ten chapters of sayings by the two Chengs' (chapters 1–10); four chapters of CHENG Hao's sayings (chapters 11–14); eleven chapters of CHENG Yi's sayings (chapters 15–25), plus a number of appendices; (2) *Waishu*, in twelve chapters; (3) *Wenji*, including four chapters of CHENG Hao's writings, eight chapters of CHENG Yi's writings, one chapter of CHENG Yi's posthumous writings, and an appendix; (4) *Zhouyi Chengshi Zhuan*, in four chapters and two prefaces; (5) *Jingshuo* in eight chapters; and (6) *Cuiyan*, in two chapters, with five sections in each chapter.

Naturally, it is unlikely that the two brothers hold the exact same philosophical views on all issues. However, any attempt to make a clear distinction between the two is futile. This is not only because the majority of their sayings, the main source of their philosophical views, are recorded without indicating whom they belong to, but also because their views expressed in those clearly marked sayings as well as their own writings are largely similar, mostly with some differences in emphasis. It is true that one of the brothers may have said something that the other brother had not said, which is particularly the case of the younger brother, CHENG Yi, as he lived much longer, but this should not be considered to be an indication of their disagreement, as CHENG Yi made it clear that he fundamentally shared his view with his brother in the tomb inscription that CHENG Yi wrote for CHENG Hao. It is perhaps true that that ZHU Xi and WANG Yangming, the greatest representatives of the two most important neo-Confucian schools respectively, may each have been primarily indebted to one of the Cheng brothers, but this should not be regarded as evidence for philosophical disagreement between the two brothers, as there has been an exaggeration of the differences between ZHU Xi and WANG Yangming in the first place and, more importantly, it is quite easy to find in CHENG Hao what ZHU Xi emphasizes and in CHENG Yi what WANG Yangming emphasizes. In any case, due to the nature of this study, I shall not endeavor to present a textual and philosophical analysis of the differences between the two brothers. Instead, in most cases, I shall discuss their views together. In a few chapters, I primarily draw on CHENG Yi only because he has more to say on the issues of concern in these chapters.

5. Looking Ahead

In chapter 1, I discuss the question that has long troubled moral philosophers: "Why be moral?" I first argue against a number of philosophers who dismiss this question too quickly as either tautological or self-contradictory. For the former, the question really asks why one ought to be (do) what one ought to be (do), since to be moral is to be (do) what one ought to be (do) (Stephen Toulmin); for the latter, the question really asks what good it serves you to be moral, in other words, what selfish reasons one has to be unselfish, or what immoral reasons one has to be moral (F. H. Bradley). In contrast, I argue that, in the extended form of the question, "Why ought I to be (do) what I ought to be (do)?" the first "ought" does not involve the issue of moral justification but the issue of moral motivation: the person who asks this question knows that one ought to be moral but lacks a motivation to be so. Then I examine a number of the most representative answers to the question found in Western philosophy, particularly those in connection with Gyge's ring in Plato's *Republic*, the irresponsible fool in Thomas Hobbes's *Leviathan*, and the sensible knave in David Hume's *An Inquiry Concerning the Principles of Morals*, as well as the idea of *summum bonum* in Immanuel Kant. I argue that each of these answers suffers its unique problems. In this context, I present the answer to the question by the Cheng brothers, which I argue is not only more convincing than any of those mentioned above but can also avoid some problems in the answer developed by Aristotle, which bears a great resemblance with the one provided by the Cheng brothers. According to the Chengs, one should be moral because it is a joy to be moral. Sometimes one finds it a pain, instead of joy, to be moral only because one lacks the necessary genuine moral knowledge, which is available to every common person, as long as one makes an effort to learn. The reason one ought to make an effort to learn such knowledge to seek joy in being moral is that to be moral is a distinguishing mark of being human. Here this neo-Confucian answer does seem to be egoistic, as its conception of motivation for morality is still based on self-interest: to seek one's own joy. However, since it emphasizes that one's true self-interest is to seek joy in things uniquely human, which is to be moral, self-interest and morality become identical: the more a person seeks one's self-interest, the more moral the person is, and vice versa.

Such an answer relates to the self-centeredness objection to virtue ethics, which is the topic of the second chapter. Virtue ethics is sometimes differentiated from utilitarianism and deontology, the two dominant ethical theories in modern and contemporary philosophy, in this way: while a utilitarian says that a person ought to be moral in order to increase the total amount of happiness, and a deontologist says that a person ought to be moral because it is the requirement of moral principles, a virtue ethicist says that a person ought to be moral in order to become a virtuous person. The virtue ethicist's view, in comparison to the utilitarian view and deontological view, seems to be self-centered: one does moral things only in order for the agent to become a virtuous person, while morality is supposed to be primarily concerned with others. As David Solomon points out, while in appearance this is an objection very easy to respond to: a person cannot be virtuous without being concerned with the welfare of others, the objection goes much deeper. While a virtuous person is indeed concerned with the well-being of others, that person is concerned with their external and material well-being. In contrast, a virtuous person is concerned about his or her character. Since in the Aristotelian tradition, the most important representative of virtue ethics, one's character is more important than one's external well-being, a virtuous person is still self-centered. While Solomon thinks that there is no better response to the self-centeredness objection to virtue ethics in this deeper sense than the partners-in-crime argument (by charging utilitarianism and deontology of the same problem), there are some important Aristotelian scholars, such as Julia Annas, Richard Kraut, Dennis McKerlie, and Christopher Toner, who argue that Aristotelian virtue ethics is not guilty of the self-centeredness problem. In this chapter, after showing why such scholars fail to defend Aristotelian virtue ethics from this objection, I argue that the Cheng brothers' neo-Confucian virtue ethics is clearly not self-centered in the deeper sense, since a virtuous person for the Chengs is virtuous precisely because he or she is concerned not only with other people's external well-being but also with their character traits. In other words, for the Chengs, a person cannot be regarded as virtuous if the person is only concerned about his or her being virtuous without trying to make others virtuous. Indeed one cannot make oneself virtuous unless one also makes others virtuous, for part of what it means to be virtuous is to make others virtuous.

If one ought to be moral, then we must answer another question: Can one be moral? This question is related to the issue of weakness of the will, the focus of my discussion in chapter 3. In his essay, "How Is Weakness of the Will Possible?" Donald Davidson defines weakness of the will as a phenomenon in which an agent intentionally does something when he or she believes that he or she can do something better. Davidson argues that weakness of the will is possible because the person may be irrational. However, if weakness of the will is possible, morality may become impossible, at least for some people. Just as a person may know it is bad to smoke and yet still smokes, a person may know it is bad to be immoral and yet still do immoral things. In this chapter, I examine the Cheng brothers' (particularly CHENG Yi's) distinction between knowledge merely from one's intellect, which is superficial and therefore not genuine knowledge, and knowledge also from one's heart, which is profound and therefore genuine knowledge. The crucial difference between these two types of knowledge is that, while a person who has knowledge from intellect about being moral does not necessarily do moral things, a person who has knowledge from heart about being moral will never fail to be moral. Moreover, knowledge from heart, unlike advanced scientific knowledge, is available to everyone who makes an effort to acquire it. Thus one with so-called weakness of will is really negligent and is responsible for that negligence and failure to act morally. This view of the Cheng brothers regarding weakness of the will is thus both similar and superior to those of Socrates and Aristotle, who also deny (or so I shall argue) the possibility of weakness of the will. Socrates's view that a "weak-willed" person is really a near-sighted person and Aristotle's view that a "weak-willed" person is really an ignorant, or at least not fully knowledgeable, person fail to distinguish (for example) a person who knows it is bad to smoke and still smokes and a person who does not know it is bad to smoke and smokes. From the Cheng brothers' view, while neither person has knowledge from heart, knowledge from the intellect is present in the former but not in the latter. This difference is not insignificant, because for the Chengs, knowledge of intellect can be transformed into knowledge from heart.

With the questions of "Why be moral?" and "Can one be moral?" answered, in chapter 4, I proceed to discuss the question of how to be moral. Since I have been taking a virtue ethics approach, one of the unique features of virtue ethics is its emphasis on particularities. Thus I start with an examination of the ethics of commonality and its problems. As examples of such ethics of commonality I discuss the popular Golden Rule present in many religious and cultural traditions; Kant's moral philosophy, which is critical of the Golden Rule; and even the morality of "banal" commonalities of Richard Rorty, for whom Kant is a villain. They all emphasize human commonalities and fail to realize or simply ignore important differences. On the other end of the spectrum, there is an antitheoretical or particularist approach in contemporary ethics. The most outspoken representative of this approach is Jonathan Dancy, according to whom moral situations are so radically different or particular that one's past moral experiences can help a person act morally in a new situation only in a formal sense (sharpening one's faculty of moral perception) but not materially (providing actual guidance about how to act). It is in this context that, as a *via media*, I present the Cheng brothers' interpretation of the idea of love with distinction in classical Confucianism through their neo-Confucian framework of "one principle with many differences" (*li yi fen shu* 理一分殊). In such an interpretation, love with distinction primarily does not mean that one loves one's parents more than others as has often been interpreted; rather it means that one loves different people equally but differently, in ways that take their differences into consideration. However, while there is not an abstract love other than concrete love for one's parents, children, spouse, friends, enemies, and so on, they are all loves. Thus one's past love experiences can not only formally but also materially help one find the appropriate way of love in a new situation. For example, one's love experiences with one's parents are materially helpful for one to find the appropriate way to love one's neighbor's parents, and one's love experiences with one's children are materially helpful for one to find the appropriate way to love one's neighbor's children, even though in both cases one does not simply transport one's love in the former situation to the latter, since there are still differences between my parents and my neighbor's parents and between my children and my neighbor's children.

The questions that I have been discussing so far all belong to the so-called personal ethics in contrast to social ethics, which I use interchangeably with political philosophy. There is a quite widespread view that Confucianism is strong in personal ethics but deficient as political philosophy. So in chapter 5, I explore how the Cheng brothers' neo-Confucianism can contribute to contemporary political philosophy by debunking the very dichotomy between the political and the personal, on which liberalism is predicated. According to this political philosophy dominating the modern and contemporary West, on the one hand, the political is not personal, in the sense that government is only concerned with the fairness of rules of the games that people play and not concerned with the characters of people who play the games; on the other hand, the personal is not political in the sense that government is not to regulate personal matters. Many feminist thinkers have challenged the second aspect of this liberal personal-political dichotomy by claiming that some personal matters, particularly things taking place within the family, should belong to the legitimate sphere of political influence. However, they leave the first aspect of the dichotomy intact; as a matter of fact, the very measures they propose to bring family into the political sphere have enforced the dichotomy. It is in this context that I suggest that we turn our attention to the Cheng brothers' neo-Confucianism, according to which the political is also personal in the sense that anything that government does to regulate interactions among individuals is not neutral with respect to the characters of these individuals. The legal system of punitive laws that the modern West takes pride in, for the Chengs, tends to make people, including those law-abiding ones, less virtuous if they are originally virtuous, more difficult to become virtuous if they are not, and more vicious if they are already vicious. In order to make people virtuous, the Cheng brothers claim that a society should be governed by rules of propriety (*li* 禮), which sages create according to human emotions arising from human nature. So rules of propriety serve not only an interpersonal function—to ensure the harmony or peace of society—but also an intrapersonal function—to cultivate virtuous individuals.

In contemporary studies of ethics, particularly in the Anglo-Saxon tradition, there is a noticeable naturalist, empirical, and even experimental turn, and an increasing collaboration between ethicists and empirical scientists in psychology, biology, sociology, anthropology, and economics among others.

Correspondingly, moral metaphysics becomes discredited, and there is an immediate skepticism about, if not distrust for, any moral philosopher who decides to go metaphysical. This puts the Cheng brothers' neo-Confucianism in an uncomfortable position, as one of the unique features of neo-Confucianism, in contrast to classical Confucianism, is precisely its moral metaphysics. Indeed, anyone who attempts to first establish a metaphysics, which consists of a priori principles and is entirely independent of empirical data, and then tries to derive moral obligations from it will be regarded as naïve. However, the moral metaphysics that the Cheng brothers construct is different in two crucial aspects. First, instead of constructing a metaphysics from which to derive moral values, the Cheng brothers start from empirical moral emotions (*qing* 情) and then try to see what metaphysical ground (*xing* 性) constitutes such emotions as moral. In this sense, their moral metaphysics is similar to Charles Taylor's ontological articulation of modern values. Second, instead of acting as the first premise from which moral principles are deduced as conclusions, the Cheng brothers' moral metaphysics appears like a summary of moral experiences. While such summary helps us take a moral stance in particular situations we have not previously encountered, it cannot trump our moral experiences. In this sense, the relationship between moral metaphysics and moral experience in the Cheng brothers is similar to that between general principles of justice and particular moral intuitions in John Rawls. Therefore, in both cases, they should be situated in a reflective equilibrium. In chapter 6, I discuss the Cheng brothers' moral metaphysics, and I argue that such a moral metaphysics not only is congenial to the naturalistic turn in ethics but is also indispensable to it.

In contrast to Western philosophers who typically claim the originality of their philosophical system, philosophers in Chinese history have notoriously disowned their originality. Instead they tend to claim that they merely provide an interpretation of classics, which contain all that they have to say. In this respect, the Cheng brothers are not an exception. For this reason, hermeneutics has always been in the forefront of Chinese philosophy, so it would be interesting to see what unique contributions the Cheng brothers can make to contemporary hermeneutics, particularly in its ethical dimension. This is what I will do in the last chapter, with a focus on CHENG Yi. As a self-conscious reflection upon our interpretational experiences, hermeneutics in its strict sense did not emerge in Western philosophy until Schleiermacher, usually considered to be the father of modern hermeneutics (see Schleiermacher 1986; Huang 1996). Even so, hermeneutics remained marginal in philosophy. It was Hans-Georg Gadamer's *Truth and Method* (Gadamer 1993) that brought hermeneutics into the heart of philosophy. However, contemporary hermeneutics still has much to learn from CHENG Yi's neo-Confucian hermeneutics. First, the central debate in contemporary Western hermeneutics revolves around the question of whether a correct interpretation should aim at the objective meanings of classics independent of both their authors and readers; at the original intentions of the authors beyond both classics and readers; or at the pre-understanding of readers independent of both authors and texts. CHENG Yi, however, unified the three by means of *dao*, since for him (Confucian) classics are carriers of *dao*, sages wrote classics with an intention to illuminate *dao*, and readers project upon classics a preunderstanding of *dao*. Second, Western hermeneutics has been basically focused on the interpretation of classical texts, religious or secular. Even the so-called ontological turn of hermeneutics initiated by Heidegger simply means a hermeneutics of human existence. Hermeneutics in CHENG Yi, however, is nothing but ontology, since for him hermeneutics is essentially hermeneutics of *dao*, the ultimate reality of the universe. Third, and most important, Western hermeneutics basically aims at understanding. In this respect, even Gadamer's hermeneutics, which claims to be a practical philosophy, is not an exception, since it is still only interested in understanding, even though this involves not merely readers' understanding of the text or of the author, but also of themselves, their self-understandings. CHENG Yi's hermeneutics, however, unifies understanding *dao* and practicing *dao*. In his view, it is a self-contradiction to say that one understands *dao* and yet is unable to practice it. In this sense, his hermeneutics is a more genuine practical philosophy.

To see how CHENG Yi's hermeneutics actually works, in the appendix, I examine his unique interpretation of two passages in the *Analects*, 8.9 and 17.3, that have given commentators headaches throughout history. The two *Analects* passages in question are: (1) "Common people can (or: are permitted to) be made to follow it [*dao*, the Way] but cannot (or: are not permitted to) be made to know it" (8.9); and (2) "only the wise above and the stupid below do not change" (17.3). Critics of Confucius, particularly during the anti-Confucius campaign during the Cultural Revolution of the 1970s, often regard these two passages as evidence that Confucius advocated a policy of keeping people in ignorance (*yumin* 愚民), while his defenders, particularly during the Confucian revival in Mainland China today, usually argue that the passages are merely Confucius's lamentation over the fact that people are ignorant (*minyu* 民愚). So it seems that both critics and defenders of Confucius agree that Confucius regarded common people as ignorant, differing only over whether he held that people are originally ignorant (*minyu*) or that they are made ignorant (*yumin*). In CHENG Yi's view, however, neither interpretation captures the true meaning of these two passages because both are content with providing a literal interpretation without an understanding of the normative principles embodied by the Confucian classics. In this appendix, I shall contrast CHENG Yi's philosophical interpretations of these two passages with more conventional interpretations and show that the former are superior to the latter, not as an apology for Confucianism but as a significant development thereof.

6. Conclusion

In addition to a brief account of the Cheng brothers as pioneers of the Neo-Confucian movement and an equally brief summary of the chapters that are to follow, the main purpose of this introduction is to present a unique methodology of doing Chinese philosophy in the Western context, which is employed throughout this book. According to this methodology, the way one does Chinese philosophy should at least be partially determined by the type of audience one intends to address. Since one who does Chinese philosophy in the Western context must address (at least also) Western philosophers, an important question one has to keep in mind is why they ought to care about Chinese philosophy. I believe that they will hardly be interested in learning how inferior or even absurd some philosophical views developed in the Chinese tradition are; they may be slightly more interested and sometimes are even surprised to learn that some Chinese philosophers have developed positions very similar to those in their own tradition, sometimes much earlier although often less systematic; however, they will perhaps be most interested in being shown that they can learn things from Chinese philosophy or that Chinese philosophers have better things to say on the very issues they have been dealing with. I do not claim that this is the only way to do Chinese philosophy in the Western context, but I do think it is at least one of the legitimate ways of doing Chinese philosophy in the Western context, although I also wish to further claim that it is perhaps a more interesting, important, and fruitful way of doing it.

Chapter 1

Joy (*le* 樂)

"Why Be Moral?"

1. Introduction

The question "Why be moral?" has long troubled moral philosophers. The question is puzzling, because it does not ask, Why should *we* be moral? which is relatively easy to answer. For example, we can use Thomas Hobbes's argument: if we are not moral to each other, we will be living in the state of nature, in which everyone is at war against everyone else. The question is, Why should *I* be moral? Put more concretely, it is, Why should I be moral to others, particularly if my not being moral to others will not cause them to be equally or even more immoral to me? Obviously, this is a question raised by an egoist who is first of all concerned with his or her self-interest.[1] To such a question, we might be tempted to answer: If everyone, just like you, acts immorally to others, thinking that acting immorally will not cause others to be equally immoral, then everyone will act immorally to each other; as a result you will also be treated immorally by others; so you should be moral to others. However, such an answer is obviously not convincing to the person who poses the question: even if this were the case, since at least my being moral to others cannot guarantee that others will be moral to me, why should I be moral to them? It would certainly be much worse to me if I am moral to others while they are immoral to me.[2] In this chapter, I first examine the legitimacy of the question (section 2) and the inadequacy of some representative answers to the question in the West (section 3). I then devote the rest of this chapter to presenting what seems to me a more adequate answer to the question provided by the Cheng brothers (sections 4–7). I conclude this chapter with a brief summary of this neo-Confucian answer.

2. The Question of "Why Be Moral?

As absurd as it might appear, this question has been repeatedly posed, rather seriously, in the history of Western philosophy. In the form of "Why should I be just," it was put most sharply by Glaucon and his brother Adimantus, as devil's advocates, in Plato's *Republic*. Glaucon presents his famous example of Gyges's ring, a ring that one can use to make oneself visible or invisible at will. Suppose that there are two such rings, with one for a just person and one for an unjust person. On the one hand, the unjust person uses the ring to make himself invisible when doing unjust things and visible when doing just things. This is because, in Glaucon's example, the unjust person is not someone who consistently does unjust things or does nothing but unjust things. Rather,

> the unjust man must act as clever craftsmen do. . . . The unjust man who attempts injustice rightly must be supposed to escape detection if he is to be altogether unjust, and we must regard the man who is caught as a bungler. For the height of injustice is to seem just without being so. To the perfectly unjust man, then, we must allow him, while committing the greatest wrongs, to have secured for himself the greatest reputation for justice, and if he does happen to trip, we must concede to him the power to correct his mistakes by his ability to speak persuasively if any of his misdeeds come to light. (Plato 1963b, 361a–b)

On the other hand, the just person uses the ring to turn himself invisible when doing just things and visible when not doing just things. This is because

> if he [the just man] is going to be thought just he will have honors and gifts because of that esteem. We cannot be sure in that case whether he is just for justice' sake or for the sake of the gifts and the honors. So we must strip him bare of everything but injustice and make his state the opposite of his imagined counterpart. Though doing no wrong he must have the repute of the greatest injustice, so that he may be put to the test as regards justice through not

softening because of ill repute and the consequences thereof. But let him hold on his course unchangeable even unto death, seeming all his life to be unjust though being just. (Plato 1963b, 361c)

In short, if an unjust or immoral person can have the appearance of being just or moral, and a just or moral person can have the appearance of being unjust or immoral, an egoist will ask, "Why should I be just or moral?" Here, as Glaucon's brother, Adimantus, points out, it seems that injustice pays much better than justice: "[T]he consequences of my being just are, unless I likewise seem so, not assets, they say, but liabilities, labor, and total loss, but if I am unjust and have procured myself a reputation for justice, a godlike life is promised" (Plato 1963b, 365b).

This same question was later raised again by Thomas Hobbes's "irresponsible fool" and David Hume's "sensible knave." In Hobbes's *Leviathan*, unsatisfied with their life in the state of nature, in which no one has security, people as rational beings will follow some general rules of reason or laws of nature. The first law is that people ought to endeavor to make peace, and the second law is that they ought to make covenants with each other, in which they mutually agree to lay down some of their natural rights or liberties. It is at this stage that the "irresponsible fool" comes to the scene. He "hath said in his heart there is no such thing as justice, and sometimes also with his tongue, seriously alleging that every man's conservation and contentment, being committed to his own care, there could be no reason why every man might not do what he thought conduced thereunto; and therefore also to make or not make, keep or not keep, covenants was not against reason when it conduced to one's benefit" (Hobbes 1998, 15.4). The question the fool has is whether he should honor the covenant he has made with others or whether it is irrational for him not to honor it. His answer is that it is rational for him to honor as well as break the covenant, as long as the action he takes in either case conduces to his benefit, since the "reason," as the fool understands it, "dictates to every man his own good; and particularly then when it conduces to such a benefit as shall put a man in a condition to neglect not only the dispraise and revilings, but also the power, of other men" (Hobbes 1998, 15.4). Here the fool's reasoning is this: since it is reasonable to seek one's own good, what reason do I have to (why should I) keep the covenant (be moral)?

Hume argues for moral virtues from self-interest or self-love (see Baldwin 2004): virtues are beneficial to those who possess them, while vices are harmful to those who are inflicted by them. For example, Hume argues that "avarice, ambition, vanity, and all passions vulgarly, though improperly, comprised under the denomination of *self-love* are here excluded from our theory concerning the origin of morals, not because they are too weak, but because they have not a proper direction for that purpose" (Hume 1957, 92–93). In other words, they are considered vices not because they are expressions of *self-love*, but precisely because they cannot serve the purpose of self-love. Just like such "monkish virtues" as celibacy, fasting, penance, mortification, self-denial, humility, silence, and solitude, which Hume thinks should be placed in the catalogues of vices, they "serve to no manner of purpose; neither advance a man's fortune in the world, nor render him a more valuable member of society; neither qualify him for the entertainment of company, nor increase his power of self-enjoyment[.] We observe, on the contrary, that they cross all these desirable ends, stupefy the understanding and harden the heart, obscure the fancy and sour the temper" (Hume 1957, 91).

He goes on to argue that "the immediate feeling of benevolence and friendship, humanity and kindness is sweet, smooth, tender, and agreeable, independent of all fortune and accidents. . . . What other passion is there where we shall find so many advantages: an agreeable sentiment, a pleasing consciousness, a good reputation?" (Hume 1957, 102). So he thinks that it is superfluous to prove that "the virtues which are immediately *useful* or *agreeable* to the person possessed of them are desirable in a view to self-interest" (Hume 1957, 100). Hume regards such virtues as natural in contrast to justice and fidelity, which he regards as artificial. The main distinction between natural and artificial virtues is that, while one immediately feels that the former are beneficial to oneself, one does not have such a feeling of the latter. For example, a person who borrowed money from others does not feel naturally that it serves his self-interest to return the money. So in the case of artificial virtues, "'tis certain, that self-love, when it acts at its liberty, instead of engaging us to honest actions, is the source of all injustice and violence; nor can a man ever correct those vices, without correcting and restraining the *natural* movements of that appetite" (Hume 1978, 480). To make such correction and restraining, Hume argues that such artificial virtues are not only "absolutely necessary to the well-being of mankind" (Hume 1957, 121), but also to the well-being of each individual. To show this, he makes an interesting analogy: "[T]he same happiness, raised by the social virtue of justice and its subdivisions, may be compared to the building of a vault where each individual stone would, of itself, fall to the ground; nor is the whole fabric supported but by the mutual assistance and combination of its corresponding parts" (Hume 1957, 121). Here, by being part of the building, each stone not only contributes to support the vault but is also being supported by other stones making up the vault. By analogy, by being just, an individual not only contributes to the well-being of mankind but also serves his or her own well-being. It is in this sense that Hume thinks that the artificial virtues ultimately can also be justified by self-love.

It is also here, however, that Hume conceives the possibility of a sensible knave, who, "in particular incidents, may think that an act of iniquity or infidelity will make a considerable addition to his fortune, without causing any considerable breach in the social union and confederacy. That *honesty is the best possible policy* may be a good general rule, but is liable to many exceptions; and he, it may perhaps be thought, conducts himself with most wisdom, who observes the general rule, and takes advantage of all the exceptions" (Hume 1957, 102). In other words, the sensible knave agrees that acts of justice and fidelity generally contribute to both the well-being of mankind and that of himself. However, there are exceptions. On the one hand, as Hume himself acknowledges, sometimes justice does not contribute to the well-being of mankind. For example, "riches inherited from a parent are in a bad man's hand the instrument of mischief. The right of succession may, in one instance, be hurtful" (Hume 1957, 121). On the other hand, similarly, sometimes violation of justice may better contribute to one's fortune, especially when such violations are done wisely so that they will not be found out. So the sensible knave will be just only when it serves his self-interest but will take all opportunities of injustice when such injustices better serve his self-interest.

Understood this way, the question "Why be moral?" has often been regarded as absurd and can be safely ignored. Stephen Toulmin, for example, thinks that this question reaches "the limits of ethical reasoning—that is, the kind of occasion on which questions and considerations of an ethical kind can no longer arise" (Toulmin 1964, 160). In his view, "ethical reasoning may be able to show why we ought to do this action as opposed to that, or advocate this social practice as opposed to that," but "there is no room *within* ethics for" the question "why ought one to do what is right." To be moral is to do what I should do; and to ask, "Why should I be moral?" is to ask, "Why should I do what I should do?" which is "on a level with the question 'Why are all scarlet things red?'" (Toulmin 1964, 162). In other words, for Toulmin, the question "Why should I be moral?" just like the question "Why are all scarlet things red?" is a tautological question. To answer this question, we can only ask a rhetorical question, "What else 'ought' one to do?" (Toulmin 1964, 162), just like the answer to the question "Why are scarlet things red?" can only be a rhetorical question: "[W]hat else can scarlet things be?"[3]

While Toulmin regards this question as illegitimate because it is tautological, F. H. Bradley considers it unreasonable because it is self-contradictory:

morality asks us to be not self-interested, but the person who asks the question "Why should I be moral?" is apparently looking for some self-interested reasons for being not self-interested. In his view, when we ask the question of why be moral, we are regarding morality as a means to some further end, but morality is the end in itself. He argues that "to take virtue as a mere means to an ulterior end is in direct antagonism to the voice of the moral consciousness. That consciousness, when unwarped by selfishness and not blinded by sophistry, is convinced that to ask for the Why? is simply immorality; to do good for its own sake is virtue, to do it for some ulterior end or object, not itself good, is never virtue; and never to act but for the sake of an end, other than doing well and right, is the mark of vice" (Bradley 1935, 61–62).[4]

Is then the question "Why should I be moral?" indeed an unreasonable one? Here, morality tells one what one should do. When we ask people to be moral, we are essentially saying that "you should follow morality"; in other words, we are saying that "you should do what you should do." So when someone asks the question "Why should I be moral?" the person is indeed asking "Why should I do what I should do?" However, this is not a tautological question. Kai Nielsen makes an important distinction between the moral and nonmoral uses of the word "should." While the second "should" is indeed used in the moral sense, the first is used in a nonmoral sense. Thus, Nielsen points out:

> When I ask, "Why should I be moral?" I am not asking . . . "What moral reason or reasons have I for being moral?" That indeed is like asking "Why are all scarlet things red?" Rather I am asking, can I, everything considered, give a reason sufficiently strong—a non-moral reason clearly—for my always giving an overriding weight to moral considerations, when they conflict with other considerations, such that I could be shown to be acting irrationally, or at least less rationally than I otherwise would be acting, if I did not give such pride of place to moral considerations? (Nielsen 1989, 286–87)

In other words, the question "Why should I be moral?" asks "whether it is rational for me to be moral," assuming it is a good thing to be moral. However, if this is the case, does this mean that the question "Why should I be moral" is indeed a self-contradictory question? In appearance it is. Bill Shaw and John Corvino agree with Nielsen's distinction between moral and nonmoral uses of the word "should." In their view, when people ask, "Why should I be moral?" they are not asking "Why (morally) ought I to do what I (morally) ought to do?" Such a question clearly would be circular. Rather, they are asking, "Why is it in my interest to do what I (morally) ought to do?," "What (non-moral) reasons are there for acting morally?" or "Why should moral claims have any purchase on me in the first place?" ("should" is used here in a non-moral sense). Put in these ways, the question is quite intelligible. (Shaw and Corvino 1996, 374)

According to Shaw and Corvino, the first "should" asks what *self-interested* reasons I have to do what I ought to do. Since what I ought to do is something not self-interested, the question "Why should I be moral?," that is, "What self-interested reasons do I have to be not self-interested?" becomes a self-contradictory question. David Copp, however, disagrees. In his view, to ask, "What self-interested reasons do I have to be moral (to be not self-interested)?" is to ask, "Does morality override self-interest? Or does self-interest override morality?" Here, Copp assumes that "there are possible cases in which the overall verdicts of morality and self-interest conflict" and claims that "the conflict between morality and self-interest in conflict cases is therefore a normative conflict; it is conflict between the overall verdicts of different normative standpoints. I take it that the question of whether morality overrides self-interest is the question of whether the verdicts of morality are *normatively more important* than the verdict of self-interest" (Copp 1997, 86). I agree with Nielsen and Copp that the question "Why should I be moral" is neither tautological nor self-contradictory. It is a legitimate question. However, given the simple fact that whoever asks the question does not have the inclination to be moral, I shall emphasize the distinction between moral justification and moral motivation. In its extended form, "Why should I do what I should do (follow a moral principle)?" the first "should" is not intended to provide a justification for the second "should" (the moral principle). Otherwise, the moral principle would become something merely instrumental. Instead, the question "Why should I be moral?" or the first "should" in its extended form, really concerns the issue of moral motivation. The person who asks the question is not a moral skeptic. She knows clearly that she should be moral but lacks the motivation to be so. A person who is motivated to be moral will never ask the question "Why should I be moral?" Understood this way, the question really asks, "What motivation(s) do or can I have to be moral?" and this seems to me a perfectly legitimate question.

3. Representative Answers in
Western Philosophy and Their Inadequacies

In the history of Western philosophy, many attempts have been made to provide a satisfactory answer to the question of why be moral. As the question was raised in Plato, Hobbes, and Hume by their respective antagonists, it is most fruitful to see how they, as protagonists, try to answer this question respectively.

First, let us take a look at the answer Plato provides to Glaucon's question in his *Republic*. From our above discussion, it is clear that, in posing the question "Why should I be just?" Glaucon knows that a person should be just; what he is concerned with is that the person is not necessarily motivated to be just. In response, Plato argues that it pays to be moral or just. This response starts with a definition of justice in a person, which is based on his analogy with justice in a state. Just as a state has three classes—economic, military, and governing—one's soul also has three parts—appetitive, spirited, and rational. Here to the appetitive belongs the desire for the pleasures of nutrition and generation (Plato 1963b, 436a). Sometimes one desires something and yet refuses to have the desire satisfied, which shows that our soul has something that masters such desires. This is its rational part, by which the soul reckons and reasons (Plato 1963b, 439d). To the spirited belongs one's feeling of anger, which becomes an ally of reason when reason is in conflict with desires (Plato 1963b, 440b). Now, just as justice in a state means that each class does and does only its respective job, Plato argues that "each of us also in whom the several parts within him perform each their own work—he will be a just man" (Plato 1963b, 441e).

With such a conception of justice in hand, Plato continues to argue why justice pays or in what sense a just person is happier than an unjust person. In relation to the three aspects of the soul, Plato mentions that there are three kinds of pleasure: (1) when the appetitive part controls the soul (which is injustice, as it should obey the rational part), there is a pleasure of profit, in comparison with which "the pleasures of the honor or of learning are of no value except in so far as they produce money" (Plato 1963b, 581d); (2) when the spirited part controls the soul (which is also injustice, as it should assist reason to control desires), there is only the pleasure of honor, in comparison with which the pleasure of profit is vulgar and low, while "that of learning, save in so far as the knowledge confers honor, [is] mere fume and moonshine" (Plato 1963b, 581d); (3) when the rational part controls the soul (which is justice, as this is its proper job), "the other pleasures compared with the delight of knowing the truth and the reality" are regarded as "far removed from true pleasure" and are called "literally the pleasures of necessity" (Plato 1963b, 581e). Now among these three pleasures, Plato argues that the last pleasure, the pleasure from a just person, is the genuine pleasure, because

> all our actions and words should tend to give the man [reason]
> within us complete domination over the entire man and make
> him take charge of the many-headed beast [the other parts of the
> soul]—like a farmer who cherishes and trains the cultivated plants
> but checks the growth of the wild—and he will make an ally of
> the lion's nature, and caring for all beasts alike will first make
> them friendly to one another and to himself, and so foster their
> growth. (Plato 1963b, 589a–b)

However, pleasures of injustice are not genuine pleasure, as by accepting such pleasures, one "enslaves the best part of himself to the worst . . . the most divine part of himself to the most despicable and godless part" (Plato 1963b, 589d–e).

David Sachs argues that there is a serious problem with Plato's argument. In his view, even if a just person in Plato's sense is indeed a happy person, it is not clear whether such a just person, a person the several parts of whose soul perform their respective tasks, is a just person in the common or vulgar sense, which Glaucon has in mind (Plato 1963b, 442d–443b): a person who does not perform such acts as temple robbing, kidnapping, swindling, embezzling, stealing, betraying, behaving sacrilegiously, breaking promises, committing adultery, neglecting parents. For this reason, Sachs claims that Plato's argument commits a fallacy of irrelevance. In his view, in order to establish his thesis that justice pays to counter Glaucon's thesis that injustice pays, first, Plato "has to prove that his conception of the just man precludes behavior commonly judged immoral or criminal; that is, he must prove that the conduct of his just man also conforms to the ordinary or vulgar canons of justice. Second, he has to prove that his conception of the just man applies to—is exemplified by—every man who is just according to vulgar conception" (Sachs 1963, 12–153). Sachs argues that Plato "met neither requirement; nor is it plausible to suppose that he could have met either of them" (Sachs 1963, 153).[5]

Here I agree with many other Plato scholars (see Vlastos, Mahoney, Dahl, and Demos) that Plato does argue that a just person in his sense must also be a just person in the vulgar sense, although he does not provide a watertight proof for it. For example, immediately after he presents his conception of justice as harmonious function of the tripartite soul in book 4, Plato relates it to its "commonplace and vulgar" definition and argues that a just person in his sense would not, when entrusted with a deposit of gold or silver, "withhold it and embezzle it," would "be far removed from sacrilege and theft and betrayal of comrades in private life or of the state in public," "would not be in any way faithless either in the keeping of his oaths or in other agreements," and would have nothing to do with "adultery . . . and neglect of parents and of the due service of the gods" (Plato 1963b, 442e–443a). At the end of this list, Plato makes it clear that the cause of all these is "to be found in the fact that each of the principles within him does its own work in the matter of ruling and being ruled" (Plato 1963b, 443b). In other words, one's being just in the vulgar sense is due to one's being just in the Platonic sense.[6] Moreover, at the end of book 9, Plato has a more direct counterargument to Glaucon's claim that injustice pays. He argues that it does not pay for a person to escape detection in wrongdoing as "he who evades detection becomes a still worse man, while in the one who is discovered and chastened the brutish part is lulled and tamed and the gentle part liberated, and the entire soul, returning to its nature at the best, attains to a much more precious condition in acquiring sobriety and righteousness together with wisdom" (Plato 1963b, 591B).

The problem with Plato's answer lies elsewhere. Assume that it is true that Plato thinks that a just person in his sense is also a just person in the common sense; also assume that Plato has provided a convincing argument for this. We are left with the question: How can one be a just person in Plato's sense, that is, how can one achieve a harmonious soul? Richard Kraut argues that this right psychological condition "consists in a receptivity to the valuable objects that exists independently of oneself" (Kraut 1992, 329). By such valuable objects Kraut means "forms—those eternal, changeless, imperceptible, and bodiless objects the understanding of which is the goal of the philosopher's education . . . [I]t is precisely because of the philosopher's connection with these abstract objects that the philosophical life is superior to any other" (Kraut 1992, 317). In other words, philosopher is "the paradigm of the just person" (Kraut 1992, 332). If this is the case, then to be just requires one to be a philosopher. The question is then whether everyone can become a philosopher, as we expect everyone to be just. It is here that we have a problem with Plato. As Vlastos points out, "if Plato thought psychic harmony a necessary condition of a morally just disposition, he must have thought the latter attainable only by the people of his ideal state and, in the present world, by Platonic philosophers and their moral dependents; and this would cut out the vast majority of our fellow-men, all of whom are expected to be justly" (Vlastos 1987, 138). This is precisely what Plato has repeatedly argued for. For example, he claims that a nature "for the perfect philosopher is a rare growth among men and is found in only a few" (Plato, 491a–b) and that "philosophy, then, as the love of wisdom, is impossible for the multitude" (Plato 1963b, 494a). Moreover, in Plato's view, this is not a problem to which education or environment alone can provide a solution, for philosophers must not only be well bred but also well born (Plato 1963b, 496b). If this is the case, then Plato cannot be thought as having provided an appropriate answer to Glaucon's question "Why should I be just?" as the person who asks the question is obviously not a philosopher and is unlikely to become one and therefore can never enjoy the pleasure the Platonic just person can.

Next, let us take a look at Hobbes's response to the irresponsible fool. At the end of the paragraph of his description of the fool's argument, Hobbes says that the fool's "specious reasoning is nevertheless false" (Hobbes 1998, 15.4). While the fool thinks it is reasonable for him to break the covenant as long as doing so is to his benefit, Hobbes thinks that it is against reason. As a matter of fact, Hobbes discusses the fool's argument in his attempt to establish the third natural law, "men perform their covenants made" (Hobbes 1998, 15.1). Since his natural law is the law that humans will naturally follow in light of their reason, if it is the light of reason to perform the covenants made, it must be against reason to break it. In Rosamond Rhodes's view, Hobbes here makes a distinction between "reason" and "Reason." When the fool argues that it is reasonable to break the covenants, it is the lowercase "reason"; while when Hobbes argues that it is Reasonable to perform the covenants, it is the uppercase "Reason." I think this is an important distinction, similar to the one between "rational" ("reason") and "reasonable" ("Reason") made by John Rawls (see Rawls 1996, 48–54). It is rational (in the sense of a means adequate for an end) for the fool to break the covenant, but it is reasonable (in the sense of considering others' interests) for people to perform the covenants. However, Hobbes tries to argue that the fool's not performing the covenants made is not only unreasonable (against Reason) but also irrational (against reason). While Rhodes thinks that Hobbes succeeds in making this argument (see Rhodes 1992), I shall argue that he fails to do so.

First, Hobbes argues that "when a man doth a thing which notwithstanding anything can be foreseen and reckoned on tends to his destruction, howsoever some accident which he could not expect, arriving may turn to his benefit, yet such events do not make it reasonably or wisely done" (Hobbes 1998, 15.5). Here Hobbes thinks that the fool, in breaking the covenants made, is knowingly doing something that can be foreseen to tend to his own destruction, although by accident it may bring him benefits. For this reason, the fool is not reasonable or wise. This argument is certainly weak, for not only does the fool not think that, by not performing the covenants made, he is doing something that tends to his destruction, but as a matter of fact, as Bernard Boxill has powerfully argued, one's immoral action more often than not does bring him benefits (see Boxill 1980). Second, Hobbes argues,

> in a condition of war, wherein every man to every man, for want of a common power to keep them all in awe, is an enemy there is no man who can hope by his own strength or wit to defend himself from destruction without the help of confederates; where every one expects the same defence by the confederation that any one else also does; and therefore he which declares he thinks it reason to deceive those that help him can in reason expect no other means of safety than what can be had from his own single power. (Hobbes 1998, 15.5)

Here, Hobbes's argument fails too. Apparently, Hobbes argues that the fool is "unReasonable" in the sense that he only expects help from others but does not want to help others; instead he wants to cause harm to them. However, the fool holds an instrumental conception of rationality and so it is "reasonable" (with lower "r") or rational (in Rawls's sense) for him to get help from those whom he deceives, as long as he can (i.e., his means serve his ends).

Hobbes provides another reason to argue that the fool is not only "unReasonable" but also "unreasonable" or "irrational" in his not performing covenants made:

> He therefore that breaks his covenant, and consequently declares that he thinks he may with reason do so, cannot be received into any society that unite themselves for peace and defence but by the error of them that receive him; nor, when he is received, be retained in it without seeing the danger of their error; which errors a man cannot reasonably reckon upon as the means of his security; and therefore, if he be left or cast out of society, he perishes, and if he lives in society, it is by the errors of other men which he could not foresee nor reckon upon, and consequently against the reason of his preservation; and so, as all men that contribute not to his destruction, forbear him only out of ignorance of what is good for themselves. (Hobbes 1998, 15.5)

Hobbes's main argument here is that the fool's success (that his means [breaking the covenants] can serve his goal [conducing to his benefits]) entirely relies upon his not being found breaking the covenants. In Hobbes's view, here the fool overestimates his ability to deceive others and underestimates others' ability to detect his deception, and this is irrational: They are

> prone to all such Crimes, as consist in Craft, and in deceiving of their neighbors; because they think their designes are too subtle to be perceived. These I say are effects of a false presumption of their own wisdome. . . . Those that deceive upon hope of not being observed, do commonly deceive themselves (the darkness in which they believe they lye hidden, being nothing else but their own blindnesse) and are no wiser than Children, that think all hid, by hiding their own eyes. (Hobbes 1998, 27.16)

Of course, if the fool will do nothing but immoral things and still hope that they will not be found, he is indeed not only unReasonable but also irrational. However, the fool obviously does not always break the covenants he made. He does so only when he is quite sure that he will not be found.

Let us now examine Hume's answer to the sensible knave. At the beginning, Hume seems to think that the question raised by the sensible knave is not worthy of responding: "[I]f a man think that this reasoning much requires an answer, it would be a little difficult to find any which will to him appear satisfactory and convincing. If his heart rebel not against such pernicious maxims, if he feel no reluctance to the thoughts of villainy or baseness, he has indeed lost a considerable motive to virtue" (Hume 1957, 102–03). However, he does provide several answers. First, Hume argues that knaves, "with all their pretended cunning and abilities, [are] betrayed by their own maxims; and while they purpose to cheat with moderation and secrecy, a tempting incident occurs, nature is frail, and they give into the snare; hence they can never extricate themselves, without a total loss of reputation, and the forfeiture of all future trust and confidence with mankind" (Hume 1957, 103). This answer is weak, to say the least. As we have seen, sensible knaves follow moral principles in general cases and only take exceptions when they are doing immoral things. These exceptions are obviously the occasions where the sensible knave finds it safe to be immoral, so it will not cause "any considerable breach in the social union and confederacy." It is thus unlikely that he will lose reputation or trust by others. Hume's reply assumes that whenever one does something unjust, one will be found out, but this is obviously not the case.[7]

What we say here also applies to Hume's second criticism of sensible knaves. In Hume's view, sensible knaves

> themselves are, in the end, the greatest dupes, and have sacrificed the invaluable enjoyment of a character, with themselves at least, for the acquisition of worthless toys and gewgaws. How little is requisite to supply the necessities of nature? And in a view to pleasure, what comparison between the unbought satisfaction of conversation, society, study, even health and the common beauties of nature, but above all the peaceful reflection on one's own conduct; what comparison, I say, between these and the feverish, empty amusements of luxury and expense? These natural pleasures, indeed, are really without price; both because they are below all price in their attainment, and above it in their enjoyment. (Hume 1957, 103)

Here, Hume tries to argue that, in comparison with satisfaction of conversation, society, study, even health and the common beauties of nature, and peaceful reflection on one's own conduct, what the sensible knave can get by being immoral are simply worthless toys and gewgaws and feverish, empty amusement of luxury and expense. This argument is also problematic. On the one hand, what the sensible knave gains through his immoral actions are certainly not what Hume regards as worthless, as otherwise they would not be motivated to be immoral. On the other hand, since the sensible knave keeps his immoral actions secret and so still has an appearance of being moral, he may still be able to have all the valuable things Hume thinks a moral person can have, except perhaps the last item, the "peaceful reflection on one's own conduct," which I will discuss in relation to Hume's next criticism.

Hume sees a third problem with the sensible knave: "[I]n all ingenuous natures, the antipathy to treachery and roguery is too strong to be counterbalanced by any views of profit or pecuniary advantage. Inward peace of mind, consciousness of integrity, a satisfactory review of our own conduct; these are circumstances, very requisite to happiness, and will be cherished and cultivated by every honest man, who feels the importance of them" (Hume 1957, 103).[8] Here, Hume makes another list of good things requisite to happiness but unavailable to someone who performs immoral things: peace of mind, consciousness of integrity, satisfactory review of one's own conduct. They are indeed significantly different from the things on the list of Hume's second criticism. As we have seen, by hiding his immoral actions and presenting an appearance of being moral, the sensible knave can still obtain things on the previous list. In contrast, the things listed here are not available to the sensible knave, since they are all related to his inner life. While the knave can hide his immoral actions from others, he cannot hide them from himself. It is in this sense that I disagree with Postema, who argues that the successful knave can also enjoy these things (Postema 1988, 34). In my view, the problem with Hume's criticism here lies rather in his assumption that the sensible knave cares about such things. A person will care about these things only if he still has some conscience. However, as Hume himself acknowledges, the sensible knave does not have a heart that rebels against pernicious maxims, so he feels no reluctance to the thoughts of villainy or baseness.

In addition to Plato, Hobbes, and Hume, of course, many other philosophers have tried to answer the same question of "Why be moral?" either directly or indirectly. Among them Aristotle and Kant are most representative. I shall discuss the Aristotelian answer in section 6. In the remainder of this section, I shall briefly examine the one provided by Kant. Moral motivation or, rather, motivation for morality, is a particularly pressing issue for Kant. He makes a clear distinction between morality and inclination, whose satisfaction happiness is (Kant 1956a, 75–76). In his view, the moral worth of an action is entirely independent of one's inclination. Thus he claims that

> there are many spirits of so sympathetic a temper that . . . they find an inner pleasure in spreading happiness around them and can take delight in the contentment of others as their own work. Yet I maintain that in such a case an action of this kind, however right and however amiable it may be, has still no genuinely moral worth; suppose that the mind of this friend of man were overclouded by sorrows of his own which extinguished all sympathy with the fate of others, but that he still had power to help those in distress, though no longer stirred by the need of others because sufficiently occupied with his own; and suppose that, when no longer moved by any inclination, he tears himself out of this deadly insensibility and does the action without any inclination for the sake of duty alone; then for the first time his action has its genuine moral worth. (Kant 1956b, 66)

Kant provides two pictures of actions in consistence with duty: one is the person who acts from a natural inclination but not from a sense of duty; the other is the person who acts from a sense of duty but not from an inclination. Since he claims that only the action from the sense of duty has moral value, it is clear that the moral value comes from one's sense of duty and not from one's inclination. Of course Kant also allows an action both from one's inclination and one's duty to have moral value, although, even in this case, the moral value still comes from the sense of duty and not from the inclination. What the coincidental inclination adds is merely the delight one may have in performing the moral action.[9]

So, in Kant's case, for those spirits of sympathetic temper, the issue of moral motivation does not exist: whatever they are inclined to do is precisely what they morally ought to do. However, for most people, what they morally ought to do is often not what they are inclined to do, and what they are inclined to do is often not what they morally ought to do. For such people, "Why should I be moral" becomes a very natural question. If this question is not answered, even if people know what they ought to do, they will not be motivated to do what is moral. For this reason, Kant developed the idea of the highest good (*summum bonum*), which includes both morality and happiness (satisfaction of inclination). However, since morality does not imply happiness, nor does happiness imply morality, either synthetically or analytically, Kant has to postulate the existence of God to cause the harmony between happiness and morality and an immortal soul through which such harmony can be maintained. About this, Kant says very clearly that "without a God and without a world invisible to us now but hoped for, the glorious ideas of morality are indeed objects of approval and admiration, but not springs of purpose and action" (Kant 1965, 640).[10]

Kant's answer is unsatisfactory. As many philosophers have seen, one problem lies in his problematic postulation of God. In this respect, Kai Nielsen makes the most vehement criticism:

> It is increasingly difficult for an educated modern even to believe in God, to say nothing of making him such a *deau ex machine*. . . . Yet for the sake of the argument let us assume . . . that we have an appropriate sense of "God" and let us assume that we have some evidence that there is an X such that X is God. Even making these assumptions, it does take the utmost vanity and the epitome of self-delusion to believe that such a Being could be so concerned with our weal and woe. And to postulate God *because* of his practical necessity or to postulate immortality to try to insure a justification of morality is just too convenient. (Nielsen 1989, 177)[11]

However, it seems to me that a more serious problem with Kant's answer is that, even in his idea of "highest good," happiness and morality are still two separate things: a person who does moral things may still feel unhappy and may still have to overcome his contrary inclination. Here it remains a question whether, for a person who does not have the inclination to be moral, a future reward of happiness is a strong enough motivation to be moral.

In the above, we have examined some representative answers to the question "Why be moral?" Having seen that none of them is adequate, it is tempting to claim that the question, while a legitimate one, is simply unanswerable. Meldon, for example, argues that "for a thoroughly amoral intelligence, nothing in principle can serve as a reason for *inducing* him to accept any moral responsibilities. Metaphysical elaborations, logical arguments, empirical generalizations and data and, finally, all moral discourse with its lavish, complex, and ingenious devices of persuasion are wholly inadequate. No reasons are possible" (Meldon 1948, 455). Copp agrees on this. As we have seen, in Copp's view, the question "Why be moral?" is really a question about self-interest and morality. However, he points out, "neither morality nor self-interest overrides the other. . . . There is no standpoint that can claim normative priority over all other normative standpoints and render a definitive verdict on the relative significance of moral and self-interested reason" (Copp 1997, 86–87). Although Nielsen tries very hard to show that the question "Why be moral?" is a legitimate one, at the end, he is also pessimistic about an adequate answer to it: "We have not been able to show that reason requires the moral point of view or that all rational persons, unhoodwinked by myth or ideology, not be individual egoists or classist amoralists. Reason doesn't decide here" (Nielsen 1989, 299). Instead, he claims that it all depends upon one's existential decision. In the remainder of this chapter, however, I shall present the Cheng Brothers' neo-Confucian answer, which I believe is more promising.

4. The Chengs' Neo-Confucian Answer: Joy in Being Moral

Confucianism is a learning of moral self-cultivation. However, the highest goal of such self-cultivation is joy (*le* 樂). The very first two sentences of Confucius's *Analects* are related to it: "What a joy it is to learn and practice what one learns from time to time! What a joy it is to have a friend coming from afar!" (*Analects* 1.1). The neo-Confucianism initiated by the Cheng brothers is sometimes also called the learning of *dao* (*daoxue* 道學). Feng Youlan 馮友蘭, a renowned historian of Chinese philosophy, is right in saying that "the learning of *dao* is not merely a kind of knowledge; it is also an enjoyment" (Feng 1995, 131). For example, a superior person (*junzi* 君子) is an exemplary person in the Confucian tradition. However, for CHENG Yi, the younger brother, "[W]ithout joy, one is not qualified as a superior person" (Cheng and Cheng 2004, *Yishu* 17; 181). Similarly, the goal of Confucian self-cultivation is to become a sage, and one of the Chengs says that "when one's learning reaches the level of cultivating what one gets so that one finds joy in it, it becomes clear, bright, lofty, and far-reaching" (*Cuiyan* 1; 1189). Thus CHENG Hao claims that "learning is complete only when one feels joy. A person with firm belief and love for learning still does not have the joy of self-getting. The person who loves something is like one who visits someone else's garden, while the person who feels joy in something does not make distinction between oneself and the other" (*Yishu* 11; 127). The question then is how to find joy. The Cheng brothers relate to us that they "once studied under ZHOU Maoshu 周茂叔, who asked us to look for things in which Yanzi and Confucius found joy" (*Yishu* 2a; 16). Thus, the Chengs make a special effort to understand, through their own inner experiences, what is meant by such sayings as "he does not allow his joy to be affected [by hardship] (*bu gai qi le* 不改其樂)" and "joy also lies in them (*le zai qizhong* 樂在其中)" in the *Analects*, as well as "there is no greater joy (*le mo da yi* 樂莫大亦)" in the *Mencius*.

"He does not allow his joy to be affected" appears in a passage in which Confucius praises Yanzi: "How virtuous is YAN Hui! With a single bamboo dish of food, a single gourd dish of unboiled water, and living on a shabby lane, while all others cannot endure the hardship, only he does not allow his joy to be affected. YAN Hui, how virtuous he is indeed!" (*Analects* 6.11). To live a poor life on a shabby lane is normally considered painful. Why does Yanzi feel joy in it, and why does Confucius praise Yanzi for finding joy in it? According to CHENG Yi: "Yanzi's joy is not caused by his eating a single bamboo dish of food, drinking a single gourd dish of unboiled water, and living on a shabby lane. The reason that Confucius regards him as virtuous is that he does not allow his poverty to burden his heart/mind and affect his joy" (*Jingshuo* 6; 1141). In another place, Cheng says that "Yanzi does not find the poverty joyful; he simply forgets it in joy" (*Yishu* 6; 88). This shows that Yanzi is no different from anyone else as poverty cannot make him, or anyone else, feel joy. Yanzi is joyful for some other reason, and what is praiseworthy is that his living in poverty does not diminish the joy he has found elsewhere. CHENG Hao agrees: poverty "has nothing to make Yanzi joyful, but he has reason for his joy. Here 'his reason' has profound meaning and we should try to understand it" (*Yishu* 12; 135). Then exactly what is the reason for Yanzi's joy? In Cheng's view, it is *ren* (humanity), the highest Confucian virtue: "realizing *ren* within oneself, what do you have to worry about?" So, living in poverty, "while other people would be worried, only Yanzi can find joy. This is because of his *ren*" (*Waishu* 1; 352). The Chengs' understanding of this *Analects* passage is confirmed by the other passage in which "joy also lies in them" appears.

"Joy also lies in them" refers to an *Analects* passage in which Confucius talks about his own joy: "[W]ith coarse grain to eat, with unboiled water to drink, and with my bended arm as pillow—my joy lies right in them. Riches and honors not acquired in the right way seem to me a floating cloud" (*Analects* 7.16). In this passage, Confucius makes a clear connection between joy and moral rightness. The meaning of this passage can be better understood in connection with another *Analects* passage: "Riches and honor are what every person desires. However, if they are obtained in violation of moral principles, they cannot be kept. Poverty and humble station are what every person dislikes. However, if they can be avoided only in violation of moral principles, they should not be avoided" (*Analects* 4.5). Obviously, Confucius feels joy in his poverty because, by not avoiding it, he is able to abide by moral principles. In his *Interpretation of the Analects*, CHENG Yi states that Confucius is still joyful "even though he has only coarse grain to eat and unboiled water to drink. This is what he means by 'joy also lies in them.' It does not mean that he has joy because he eats coarse grain and drinks unboiled water" (*Jingshuo* 6; 1145). In Cheng's view, what gives Confucius joy is his being in accord with morality. Although Confucius says that his joy lies in eating coarse grain and drinking unboiled water, it does not mean that coarse grain and unboiled water themselves are good things. The real source of one's joy comes from one's being in accord with morality, which will be violated if he wants to avoid poverty in this particular case. As long as one is in accord with morality, one can find joy in anything one encounters. In his reply to a student's question about Mencius's statement that "there is a better way to nurture one's heart/mind than having fewer desires" (*Mencius* 7b35), CHENG Yi tells us that "this is easy to understand, but what most deserves our appreciation is his statement that 'the principle and rightness pleases (*yue* 悅) my heart/mind just as meat pleases my palate.' However, what is important is [for the heart/mind] to really experience the pleasure in being in accord with moral principle and rightness as for the palate to be so in tasting meat" (*Waishu* 12; 425). Immediately before the quoted sentence from the *Mencius*, it is also claimed that "all palates have the same preference in taste, all ears have the same preference in sound, and all eyes have the same preferences in beauty. How can heart/minds alone be different? In what are all heart/minds the same? It is principle and rightness"

(*Mencius* 6a7). Here CHENG Yi emphasizes that Confucian joy comes from one's heart/mind nurtured by moral principle and not from our sense organs affected by their preferred objects. Thus, in another place commenting on the same passage of Mencius, he states that "in investigating the principle, one should know how to apply one's heart/mind according to greater or lesser urgency. If one exerts force on it hard without finding joy, how can he nourish the heart/mind?" (*Yishu* 3; 67). So what is important is not only to do things according to moral principles, but to find joy in doing so.

In addition to the joy of Confucius and Yanzi (the so-called *kong yan zhi le* 孔顏之樂), the Chengs were fascinated by Mencius's saying, "There is no greater joy," which appears in the following passage: "Ten thousand things are all here in me. There is no greater joy than finding that I have realized myself through self-reflection (*fan shen er cheng* 反身而誠)" (*Mencius* 7a4). About this, in his famous passage later recognized as "Discourse on Humanity (*ren shuo* 仁說)," which starts with the claim that "a learner should first understand *ren*, as a person of *ren* is in one body with all things," CHENG Hao explains that

> if one cannot realize oneself in self-reflection, then some opposition exists between oneself and others. In this case, one tries to suit oneself to the other but can never get unified with the other. If so, how can one have joy? . . . "Never do things with expectation. Let the mind not forget its objective, but let there be no artificial effort to help it grow" [*Mencius* 2a2]. The way to preserve *ren* is not to exert slightest effort. When *ren* is preserved, the harmony between oneself and others is obtained. This is because our original *ren* and our ability to know *ren* have never been lost. . . . If we practice it and feel joy in it, we do not need to worry about losing it. (*Yishu* 2a; 17)

Here I translate the Chinese character *cheng* 誠 as "realization," in its double meaning in English. On the one hand, through self-examination, one realizes (knows) oneself or, rather, the nature (*xing* 性) or principle (*li* 理) within oneself; on the other hand, one realizes (fulfills or completes) one's self-nature. Since in Cheng's view, the nature or principle within oneself is the same nature or principle within the ten thousand things, to realize oneself is at the same time to realize (bring to completion) the ten thousand things. In contrast, CHENG Hao claims, "if one cannot realize oneself, one is in opposition to all things and feels uneasy with everything" (*Yishu* 11; 129). In his view, it is in this sense that Mencius says that there is no joy greater than realization of oneself. In this aspect, CHENG Yi completely agrees. When asked how he thinks about the statement that "to fulfill the human *dao* is *ren*, while to fulfill the heavenly *dao* is sagely," CHENG Yi replies, "How can one know the human *dao* without knowing the heavenly *dao*? There is only one *dao*. How can the human *dao* be merely the human *dao*, while the heavenly *dao* is only the heavenly *dao*?" Then he cites the following passage from the *Doctrine of the Mean* to support his view: "Those who can fully develop their nature can develop the nature of other humans; those who can fully develop the nature of human beings can develop the nature of things; those who can fully develop the nature of things can assist in the transforming and nourishing process of heaven and earth" (*Yishu* 18; 182–83).

Here it is important to see how joy as the highest goal of Confucian self-cultivation is both similar to and different from joy in our common sense; in other words, it is important to see whether this neo-Confucian answer also commits the fallacy of irrelevance that David Sachs claims Plato commits in his answer to the same question. On the one hand, what do Confucians mean by joy? For the Cheng brothers, first of all, joy means to be without doubt and worry. CHENG Yi exclaims: "What a joy it is to be without any hesitancy in interaction with other human beings" (*Yishu* 18; 193). For this reason, he repeatedly speaks very highly of a saying by the Han Confucian DONG Zhongshu 董仲舒, "While everyone else under heaven worries, I alone do not worry; while everyone else under heaven is doubtful, I alone am not doubtful" (*Yishu* 18; 220). In Cheng's view, a joyful person is one who has reached the realm of no worry or doubt. Second, to have joy is to act naturally, without exerting any artificial effort. We should find joy in rightness and principle, but one of the Chengs asks, "Why are there people today who have set their mind in rightness and principle and yet cannot feel joy in their heart/mind? This is because they try to help them grow. One indeed need preserve them in one's heart/mind. However, if one exerts too much artificial effort, one is not doing things naturally but is trying to change the natural cause" (*Yishu* 2a; 42). In other words, if you need to exert any special effort to do something, you will not feel joy. Only when you act naturally and spontaneously can you feel joy. In the former, it is as if you are using a stick to pick up something and so inevitably you will feel something unnatural, while in the latter, it is as if you are using your own hand to pick up something and there is nothing uneasy (see *Yishu* 2a; 22).

It is in this sense that, in Confucianism, joy (*le*) and music (*yue*) are closely related. While pronounced differently, *le* and *yue* share the same Chinese character. In the *Analects*, Confucius states that one's morality "is to be stimu-lated by poetry, established by rules of proprieties, and perfected by music" (*Analects* 8.8). Here, among poetry, rules of propriety, and music, Confucius ranks music as the highest. To explain this, one of the Chengs points out that "when 'stimulated by poetry and established by rules of proprieties,' one needs to make efforts, while when 'perfected by music,' there is no effort involved" (*Yishu* 1; 5). The reason that one does not need to exert any effort is that music brings one joy, which is made clear by Mencius: "The essence of music (*yue* 樂) is to enjoy (*le* 樂) the two [*ren* and rightness], naturally resulting in joy (*le* 樂). As soon as joy arises, it cannot be stopped. One cannot help but dance with feet and wave with hands" (*Mencius* 4a27). CHENG Hao thus brings the passage in the *Analects* 8.8 and this passage in the *Mencius* together. After explaining stimulation by poetry and establishment by proprieties, he claims that

> it is through music that one obtains virtue, which brings one joy. As soon as joy arises, it cannot be stopped. Because it cannot be stopped, one cannot help but dance with feet and wave with hands. When one is in joy, one is calm, to be calm is to be with heaven, and to be with heaven is to be divine. Heaven is trusted without saying anything, and divinity is awed without being angry. This is even greater than dancing with feet and waving with hands. (*Yishu* 11; 128)

It is thus clear that joy in Confucianism means the same thing as in our common sense: to act without hesitation, without impediment, spontane-ously, and naturally. However, it is also clear that in terms of what makes one joyful, Confucians hold a very different view from the common conception of joy. It is in this sense that CHENG Yi states that "people today often find joy in things they should not and cannot find joy in things they should; love things they should not and do not love things they should. This is all because they do not know what is important and what is not important" (*Yishu* 25; 317). Normally wealth brings people joy, while poverty causes people pain. However, while Confucians do not deny wealth as a source of joy, one's joy cannot come from one's immoral action; in contrast, the primary source of joy is moral action, and such joy should not be affected by one's poverty or wealth. As a matter of fact, to perform moral action often requires one to endure certain physical pain or even sacrifice of life. Thus, in the famous passage in which he talks about a farmer who has genuine knowledge of how a tiger is hurtful, CHENG Yi states that one should have the heart/mind that "has a feeling of being in hot water when seeing something evil." If so, a person will be truly different. . . . Virtue is something one gets from one's inner heart/mind. When one is virtuous, there is no need for any forced effort, although a learner does need to exert such effort. In ancient time, there were people who are willing to sacrifice their bodies and lives. If they do not have the genuine knowledge, how could they do it? One needs to truly understand that righteousness is more important than life. (*Yishu* 15; 147)

Of course, as we have seen, poverty and sacrifice of life are not the things that bring joy to people. They cause pain to Confucian sages as well as common people. However, if such poverty and sacrifice can be avoided only by being immoral, for Confucian sages it is more painful to avoid them. In contrast, one will feel joy in enduring poverty and sacrifice if this is necessary for one to be moral. In this sense, Confucian joy is very different from joy in our common sense. What is crucial is that, in such a view, as stated by McDowell, "no payoff from flouting a requirement of excellence, however desirable . . . can count as a genuine advantage; and conversely, no sacrifice necessitated by the life of excellence, however desirable what one misses may be . . . can count as a genuine loss" in circumstances (McDowell 1998b, 17). Here McDowell emphasizes "circumstances": in different circumstances such advantage or loss may be genuine. For example, "to starve in the normal circumstance is a genuine loss; however, if to avoid starving will involve flouting a virtue, it is not a genuine loss" (McDowell 1998b, 17)[12]

5. Joy and Knowledge

So why should I be moral? For the Cheng brothers, to be moral brings one joy. However, to those who ask the question, apparently this is not an appropriate answer. While a Confucian sage or superior person can find it a joy to be moral, this is perhaps not true of all people, many of whom do not and cannot find joy in being moral. If so, does this (neo-)Confucian answer have the similar problem that Postema thinks Hume's answer has: it sounds implausibly high-minded and so can do nothing to those who lack the motivation to be moral, as they lack the motivation precisely because they cannot find joy in being moral. Here it is crucial to understand why a person cannot find joy in being moral. From the last quotation of the previous section, we can see that, for CHENG Yi, one does not feel joy and instead feels pain in being moral because one does not have genuine knowledge. Because one does not have genuine knowledge, one will necessarily feel reluctant in doing moral things if one does them at all. So "a learner must seek genuine knowledge. As soon as one knows what is right, one will naturally act" (*Yishu* 18; 188). As I shall devote chapter 3 to a discussion of the Cheng brothers', particularly CHENG Yi's, view of moral knowledge, here I shall simply focus on their view of the relationship between genuine knowledge that inclines us to act and the joy such action brings to us.

In our analysis of the question "Why be moral?" we have assumed that those who pose this question know not only what is moral but also that they should be moral. They only lack the motivation to be moral.[13] So it seems that knowledge does not have the power that the Chengs think it has to motivate people to be moral. In the Chengs' view, the knowledge in question here is only common knowledge (*changzhi* 常知), shallow knowledge (*qianzhi* 淺知), or knowledge of hearing and seeing (*wenjian zhizhi* 聞見之知), while the knowledge needed for moral actions is genuine knowledge (*zhenzhi* 真知), profound knowledge (*shenzhi* 深知), or knowledge of/as virtue (*dexing zhizhi* 德性之知). To obtain common knowledge, one only needs to exercise the intellectual function of *xin* 心 as mind, while to obtain knowledge of/as virtue, one must also rely on the affective function of *xin* 心 as heart.

In the Chengs' view, as soon as one obtains genuine knowledge, one will naturally feel inclined to be moral. Commenting on one of the famous passages in the *Mencius* (7a21), CHENG Yi points out that "if one gets it from one's heart/mind, this is called virtue, naturally, which 'is rooted in his heart, and manifests itself in his face, giving it a sleek appearance. It also shows in his back and extends to his limbs, rendering their message intelligible without words.' How can there be any reluctance in action?" (*Yishu* 15, 147). Of course, Cheng does not mean that one cannot do moral things or cannot refrain from immoral actions before one obtains knowledge of/as virtue. The crucial thing is whether one can find joy in being moral or in not being immoral. Without knowledge of/as virtue, one may still be able to perform moral actions or refrain from performing immoral actions by following some external rules of propriety or law. Since from their inner heart they are not inclined to do it, they do not find joy in doing so; instead, they may feel pain. Thus, CHENG Yi points out that "a learner of course need exert some unusual effort. However, if one does not have knowledge, how can one act? If one acts only reluctantly, how can it last? Only when one is illuminated by *li* (principle) can one naturally find joy in following it (*le xunli* 樂循理)"

(*Yishu* 18, 187–188). In the Chengs' view, without genuine knowledge, one acts as if one is using the sages' teaching as an external measuring rod. Thus, to a certain extent, one is forced to act and so feels unhappy in acting morally. When asked whether one can find joy by being ruler or minister, father or son, husband or wife, younger or elder brother, and friend according to propriety, CHENG Yi replies: "Of course. However, the question is how one can find joy. If one is forced to do things, one cannot get joy. One needs first to have knowledge and only then can one find joy. That is why one should first know before acting" (*Yishu* 18, 187).

To better understand the relationship between knowledge and joy in being moral, we can take a look at the distinction Cheng makes between ordinary people, superior people, and sages, according to the respective depths of their knowledge:

> Ordinary people know that one ought not to do what is against rules of propriety, but they follow them reluctantly, although they know that one ought not to steal and can avoid stealing without reluctance. This shows that knowledge can be deep or shallow. Ancient people told us that those who find joy in following moral principles are superior persons. If one does something only reluctantly, one may only be able to follow moral principles but is not joyful. When one is truly joyful, one is joyful in following moral principles and is not joyful in not following them. So why should one suffer from not following moral principles? Here there is no reluctance at all. Sages are even more superior in the sense that they can get to the target without trying and can understand without thinking. (*Yishu* 18; 186)

Here, Cheng first describes ordinary people, who do not need to exert any strong effort to refrain from stealing (and perhaps can even find joy in not stealing); yet they are reluctant to follow rules of propriety. Thus, they may follow these rules, but they may feel it burdensome to do so; they wish that they could do things contrary to them, even though they do not actually do so. As we all know, from the Kantian point of view, such people may be considered typical moral people, as they are able to overcome their inner inclinations and follow moral principles. However, for CHENG Yi, this shows that their knowledge is shallow: they know, perhaps from sages, that they ought to follow moral principles, but they do not know why they should follow them and what good it does to follow them. He next describes superior persons. Not only can they find joy in following moral principles, but they are also pained for not following them. Thus, when they follow moral principles, they do so without any reluctance. This shows that their knowledge is deeper: they know not only that they ought to follow moral principles but also why they ought to do so and what good it does to do so. Finally, Cheng describes sages. A sage, of course, does nothing against propriety and feels joy in doing whatever he does. However, strictly speaking, the sage is not *following* moral principles. It is in this sense that CHENG Hao emphasizes the Mencian distinction between "practicing humanity and rightness" (*xing ren yi* 行仁義) and "acting from humanity and rightness" (*you ren yi xing* 由仁義行) (*Yishu* 3; 61; see *Mencius* 4b19). In the former, humanity and rightness are still something external to the person who practices them; in the latter, they are something internal to the agent. Mencius says that "to be great and transformed by the greatness (*da er hua zhi* 大而化之) is sage" (*Mencius* 7b25). According to CHENG Yi, " 'to be great and transformed by this greatness' means nothing but to be one with the principle. A person who has not been thus transformed is like a person who uses a measuring rod to measure things, and so can not help but feel somewhat uneasy. A person who has been thus transformed is like a person who himself is the measuring rod or the measuring rod is he himself" (*Yishu* 15; 156). In another place, instead of a measuring rod, Cheng uses the analogy of a weighing scale: "If one does not have the weighing scale, one can not know what is heavy and what is light. However, a sage does not need the weighing scale to know what is heavy and what is light, because the sage himself is the weighing scale" (*Waishu* 6; 384). The reason that CHENG Yi can claim that the sage is the measuring rod and weighing scale is that, for him, "sages and the principle are identical" (*Yishu* 23; 307).[14]

Here, it is important to see that, for the Chengs, the knowledge that motivates a person to be moral is different from scientific, historical, and mathematical knowledge. In one sense, it is indeed more difficult for one to acquire moral knowledge than scientific knowledge, as the former requires both heart and mind to function, while the latter only needs the function of the mind. At the same time, however, it is easier to acquire moral knowledge than scientific knowledge, as not everyone has an inborn ability to grasp complicated scientific knowledge, but everyone is endowed with the ability to have moral knowledge. Thus, while it is obviously impossible for everyone to become Einstein, for example, the Chengs claim that everyone can become a sage. In their view, in terms of abilities to acquire moral knowledge, there is no difference between superior persons and inferior persons:

Only superior persons can apprehend and practice it [the principle]. People do not apprehend it in their own heart/mind only because they give themselves up. Thus Mencius says that "with the four beginnings [of humanity, righteousness, propriety, and wisdom] fully developed, one can take under one's protection the whole realm within the four seas, but if one fails to develop them, one will not be able even to serve one's parents." Whether to develop them or not is entirely dependent upon oneself. (*Yishu* 25; 321)

In other words, the difference between superior persons and inferior persons is only that the former make an effort to acquire moral knowledge through their own heart/mind, while the latter do not make such an effort. Moreover, there is such a difference not because superior persons are endowed with the ability that inferior persons do not have. Rather it is because inferior persons give up on themselves. Thus, in his commentary on the *Book of Change*, when asked why there are people who cannot be transformed, CHENG Yi replies:

If one cultivates oneself to become good, there is no one who cannot be changed. Even those who are extremely unintelligent can also gradually make moral progress. Only those who lack self-confidence and do not trust themselves (*zibao* 自暴) and those who abandon themselves and do not want to make any effort (*ziqi* 自棄) cannot be transformed to enter the Way even if they are surrounded by sages. These are what Confucius refers to as the stupid below. (*Zhouyi Chengshi Zhuan* 4; 956)

So in Cheng's view, *zibao* and *ziqi* are the two greatest enemies in moral cultivation. For the Chengs, not only will one find it a joy to be moral if one has the necessary moral knowledge, but everyone can have such moral knowledge as long as one is willing to make an effort.

Before we pursue the Chengs' Confucian answer any further, let us stop to reflect upon a potential Kantian objection to it. The Chengs' answer to the question is that it is one's inborn natural inclination to perform moral actions, satisfaction of which brings one joy. As we have seen, from the Kantian point of view, the moral worth of an action cannot be dependent upon one's natural inclination, for the inclination one is born with is merely a natural accident. One's inborn temperament, sympathy for example, in terms of its moral worth, is no different from any other inborn temperament, envy for example. However, the Chengs' Confucian answer, it seems to me, can avoid this problem. On the one hand, following the Mencian tradition, the Chengs believe that human nature is good. In other words, everyone is born with a moral heart/mind. One's having the inclination to be good is not an accident. On the other hand, just like Mencius, the Cheng Brothers believe that one's inborn inclination to do good may be beclouded by one's selfish desires. This is the reason why they put so much emphasis on making an effort to acquire genuine knowledge, which helps one fully develop one's natural inclination or recover it if lost. Strictly speaking, the inclination a superior person follows is not the inclination that one is born with (of which one is without self-consciousness) but the one the superior person cultivates with genuine knowledge (of which one is self-conscious), even though this cultivated inclination is not qualitatively different from the one that one is born with. Such an effort to acquire moral knowledge and cultivate one's inborn natural inclination is obviously neither accidental nor morally irrelevant.

6. To Be Moral and to Be Human

Let us collect what we have gained so far. To answer the question "Why be moral?" the Chengs tell us that it is a joy to be moral; the reason that some people do not or cannot find joy in being moral is that they do not have the necessary knowledge; and the reason they do not have the necessary knowledge is that, instead of lacking sufficient intelligence, they gave up on themselves and are not willing to make any effort to learn. Is this answer now enough to motivate those who pose the question "Why be moral" to be moral? In one sense, it is: it is certainly rational to make an effort to acquire moral knowledge, which is within everyone's ability, since such knowledge is necessary to be moral; and it is entirely rational to be moral, since it is a joy to do so. In another sense, however, it is not. The person who poses the question may say: yes, through moral self-cultivation I can feel joy in being moral; however, I can also feel joy in being immoral without going through the process of self-cultivation. So the question remains: "Why should I be moral?" In other words, when I can find joy in satisfying my desires for riches, honors, and other nonmoral and even immoral things, why do I have to seek joy in being moral?

Not advocating asceticism, Confucianism is not opposing people seeking joy in nonmoral things. As we have seen, Confucius says that "riches and honor are what every person desires" (*Analects* 4.5). Mencius also says that life that everyone wants is good and death that everyone desists is bad (*Mencius*

6a10). There is no problem seeking joy in such things as long as one will not thereby violate morality. In the *Analects*, there is a famous passage in which Confucius asks his students about their ambitions. They respond by expressing their desires, respectively, to administer an invaded big state, endowing its people with courage and correct principles; to be a ruler of a small state, making people sufficient in their livelihood; to be a junior assistant, serving at an ancestral temple and conferences of feudal lords. One of his students, ZENG Dian, however, playing the zither, expresses his rather different desire: "in a late Spring, wearing the Spring dress, I would go with five or six grownups and six or seven children to bathe in the Yi River, enjoy the breeze from the Rain Dance Altar and then return home singing." After listening to them all, Confucius says, somewhat surprisingly, "I agree with ZENG Dian (*wu yu dian ye* 吾與點也)" (*Analects* 11.26). Later Confucians have taken delight in talking about Confucius's "*wu yu dian ye*." In this connection, CHENG Hao also relates to us: "Since I saw uncle Mao 茂 [ZHOU Dunyi], I have been singing of the moon and wind and had quite a feeling of *wu yu dian ye*" (*Yishu* 3; 59). The problem occurs only when one's seeking joy in nonmoral things leads to the violation of morality or when one's seeking joy in being moral frustrates one's desires for nonmoral things. As we have seen, in such situations, Confucius clearly prizes the joy in being moral over the joy in doing nonmoral things (*Analects* 4.5). Cheng agrees: "As long as [moral] principle and rightness are not violated, one feels joy even being poor; If they are violated, one feels uneasy without any joy" (*Waishu* 3; 369). An egoist will ask: if it is rational for us to seek joy, why should we follow Confucius and Mencius to prefer joy in being moral to other joy when the two come into conflict?

The Chengs' neo-Confucian answer to this question is surprisingly simple: to be moral is characteristic of being human. CHENG Yi says, "What makes superior persons different from animals is that they have the nature of humanity and rightness. So if one loses the heart/mind and does not want to get it back, the person is not different from an animal" (*Yishu* 25; 323). This view, of course, is very consistent with Mencius's view: "[W]hoever is devoid of the heart of compassion is not human; whoever is devoid of the heart of shame is not human, whoever is devoid of the heart of courtesy and modesty is not human, and whoever is devoid of the heart of right and wrong is not human" (*Mencius* 2a6). In another place, Mencius says that "the distinction between humans and beasts is very little. Inferior persons abandon it, while superior persons preserve it" (*Mencius* 4b19). When a student asks whether Mencius means that the difference between superior persons and inferior persons lies precisely in preserving or abandoning this little difference between

humans and beasts, CHENG Yi replies affirmatively: "Indeed. Humans have the
heavenly principle only. If one cannot preserve it, how can one be a human?
SUN Mingfu has a poem: 'human being is only one of the things between
heaven and earth, and so always needs to eat when hungry and drink when
thirsty. If there is no principle of *dao* filled within, how can they be different
from beasts?" (*Yishu* 18; 214–15). Immediately after this, a student asks about
the Tang dynasty Confucian HAN Yu's 韓愈 following alleged comment: if one
has a snake-like body, cow-like head, and beak-like mouth but a distinctive
heart, how can we regard the person as nonhuman? On the other hand,
even if there is someone with a rosy face aglow, with a human appearance
but the heart of beast, how can it be regarded as human? Although CHENG Yi
says that he cannot remember this passage clearly, he agrees that "the only
thing a human being need do is to preserve the heavenly principle" (*Yishu* 18;
215); when this heavenly principle "is lost to a small extent, one becomes a
barbarian; when it is lost to a great extent, one becomes a beast" (*Yishu* 17;
177). In Cheng's view, it is "in case that humans will degenerate into beasts
that sages established very strict rules of propriety in the Spring and Autumn
period" (*Yishu* 2a; 43).

So here is the Chengs' final answer to the question "Why should I be
moral?": because you are a human being. It is rational for a human being to
seek joy. It is true that joy can be sought either by following moral principles
or by doing immoral things. However, since the distinctive mark of being
human is a moral heart, and a human being is essentially a moral being, one
should seek joy in being moral.[15]

It is in this context that we can make a fruitful comparison and contrast between this Confucian answer and the Aristotelian one. The similarity
between the Cheng brothers and Aristotle is quite striking. First, just like the
Cheng brothers, Aristotle argues that we cannot identify human happiness with
mere pleasure, as it fails to distinguish between humans and beasts (Aristotle,
1095b15–20). Instead, happiness, as the chief goal, is "the activity of the soul
in accordance with virtue" (Aristotle 1915, 1098a16–17). In his view, "no one
would choose to live with the intellect of a child throughout his life, however
much he were to be pleased at the things that children are pleased at, nor to
get enjoyment by doing some most disgraceful deed, though he were never to
feel any pain in consequence" (Aristotle 1915, 1174a1–4).

Second, just like the Cheng brothers, Aristotle is not an ascetic, thinking that pleasure is a bad thing; instead, pleasure as unimpeded activity is
necessary for a happy life:

If certain pleasures are bad, that does not prevent the chief good
from being some pleasure. . . . Perhaps it is even necessary, if each
disposition has unimpeded activities, that, whether the activity (if
unimpeded) of all our dispositions or that of some one of them
is happiness, this should be the thing most worthy of our choice,
and this activity is pleasure. Thus the chief good would be some
pleasure, though most pleasure might perhaps be bad without
qualification. And for this reason all men think that the happy life
is pleasant and weave pleasure into their ideal of happiness—and
reasonably too; for no activity is perfect when it is impeded, and
happiness is a perfect thing. (Aristotle 1915, 1153b8–18)

So in Aristotle's view, happiness, as the chief good of human life, has mingled
with it pleasures marvelous for their purity and enduringness (Aristotle 1915,
1177a23–28). What is important is to realize that each animal, horse, dog,
and man has a proper pleasure that corresponds to its proper activity. Since
the chief good of human life is happiness, and happiness is the activity of the
soul in accordance with virtue, the pure pleasure proper to human beings
must be related to virtuous activities. Thus, just like the Cheng brothers,
Aristotle argues that virtuous actions are pleasant to virtuous people: "[N]ot
only is a horse pleasant to the lover of horses, and a spectacle to the lover
of sights, but also in the same way just acts are pleasant to the lover of
justice and in general virtuous acts to the lover of virtue" (Aristotle 1915,
1099a9–12).

Third, like the Cheng brothers, Aristotle argues that such virtuous actions
are not only pleasant to virtuous people, but are pleasant in themselves:

Now for most men their pleasures are in conflict with one another
because these are not by nature pleasant, but the lovers of what
is noble find pleasant the things that are by nature pleasant; and
virtuous actions are such, so that these are pleasant for such men
as well as in their own nature. . . . The man who does not rejoice
in the noble actions is not even good; since no one would call a
man just who did not enjoy acting justly, nor any man liberal who
did not enjoy liberal actions; and similar in all other cases. If this
is so, virtuous actions must be in themselves pleasant. (Aristotle
1915, 1099a13–20)

In other words, for Aristotle, since virtuous actions are pleasant in themselves, they are not only pleasant to virtuous people but should also be so to all human beings.[16]

Finally, in Aristotle's view, just as in the Chengs' view, people who find bad things pleasant and good things painful prefer the taste of beast and so are no different from beasts. It is for this reason that Aristotle argues that "we ought to have been brought up in a particular way from our very youth . . . so as both to delight in and to be pained by the things they ought; for this is the right education" (Aristotle 1915, 1104b8–13). A good person is thus one who both takes delight in and is pained by the things they ought to take delight in and be pained by. In his view, such a person "does many acts for the sake of his friends and his country, and if necessary dies for them; for he will throw away both wealth and honours and in general the goods that are objects of competition, gaining for himself nobility; since he would prefer a short period of intense pleasure to a long one of mild enjoyment, a twelvemonth of noble life to many years of humdrum existence, and one great and noble action to many trivial ones" (Aristotle 1915, 1169a18–25).[17]

We have so far seen an Aristotelian account very similar to the Chengs' Confucian one. One may seek joy in doing good things or in doing bad things, but one should seek joy in doing good things, as the activity of the soul in accordance with virtue is a distinctive mark of being human.[18] However, Aristotle adds, "if happiness is activity in accordance with virtue, it is reasonable that it should be in accordance with the highest virtue; and this will be that of the best thing in us. . . . The activity of this in accordance with its proper virtue will be perfect happiness. That this activity is contemplative we have already said" (Aristotle 1915, 1177a11–18). For Aristotle, the rational soul that is unique to human beings has its practical as well as theoretical parts, with their respective virtues: moral virtues and intellectual virtues. Here he makes it clear that the intellectual virtues in relation to the activity of contemplation are the highest: "The activity of reason, which is contemplative, seems both to be superior in serious worth and to aim at no end beyond itself, and to have its pleasure proper to itself. . . . [I]t follows that this will be the complete happiness of man" (Aristotle 1915, 1177b18–24). For Aristotle, there are several reasons:

> Firstly, this activity is the best (since not only is reason the best thing in us, but the objects of reason are the best of knowable objects); and, secondly, it is the most continuous, since we can contemplate truth more continuously than we can *do* anything. And we think happiness has pleasure mingled with it, but the

activity philosophic wisdom is admittedly the pleasantest of virtuous activities; at all events the pursuit of it is thought to offer
pleasures marvelous for their purity and their enduringness, and
it is to be expected that those who know will pass their time more
pleasantly than those who inquire. And the self-sufficiency that is
spoken of must belong most to the contemplative activity. . . . Just
man needs people toward whom and with whom he shall act justly,
and the temperate man, the brave man, and each of the others
is in the same case, but the philosopher, even when by himself,
can contemplate truth, and the better the wiser he is. (Aristotle
1915, 1177a20–35)

For these three reasons, the best, the most continuous, and the most self-
sufficient, Aristotle thinks that the life according to reason is the happiest.
In contrast, only "in a secondary degree" can "the life in accordance with the
other kind of virtue [be] happy; for the activities in accordance with this befit
our human estate. Just and brave acts, and other virtuous acts, we do in relation to each other, observing our respective duties with regard to contracts
and services and all manner of actions and with regard to passions; and all of
these seem to be typically human" (Aristotle 1915, 1178a5–14).

Scholars do not agree on how to interpret Aristotle's view about the relationship between moral virtues and intellectual virtues. Richard Kraut adopts
a monist interpretation, according to which philosophical contemplation is the
single aim of a happy life; every other good is good and worth choosing only
for contemplation's sake (Kraut 1989, 202–203, 211–213). In contrast, Irwin
and Ackrill hold an inclusive interpretation, according to which the highest goal
of human life contains a set of goods, including philosophical contemplation
and virtuous actions (see Irwin 1991; Ackrill 1980). Gabriel Richardson Lear
criticizes these two interpretations, arguing that the monistic interpretation
cannot explain Aristotle's claim that one should choose virtuous actions for
their own sake (as well as for the sake of contemplation), while the inclusiv-
ist interpretation cannot explain Aristotle's claim that contemplation is the
highest good. In their stead, Lear proposes an approximation interpretation,
according to which moral actions are choiceworthy for the sake of philosophical contemplation, as the former teleologically approximates and imitates the
latter (Lear 2004, chapter 5).

It is not my intention to join the debate. However, it seems to me that,
whatever interpretation we adopt, we cannot interpret away the fact that Aristotle himself says most clearly that philosophical contemplation is the highest

goal of human life, while virtuous actions can have only a secondary place. In other words, while virtuous actions are indeed also unique to humans (and therefore should be pursued for their own sake as well), what ultimately sets human beings apart from other animals is philosophical contemplation. Such a position, as a response to the question "Why should I be moral?" is doubly problematical. (Of course, Aristotle does not have this question clearly in his mind when he develops his theory of virtue.) On the one hand, in order to be a true human being, what one really needs is philosophical contemplation and not virtuous (moral) activities; and since philosophical contemplation is most self-sufficient, it seems that one can do philosophical contemplation without doing virtuous things: the better a philosopher can do that, the wiser the philosopher is (Aristotle 1915, 1177a34–35). As a matter of fact, although Aristotle acknowledges that the philosopher "perhaps can do so better if he has fellow workers" (Aristotle 1915, 1177a35–1177b1), which might be interpreted as saying that one can do philosophy better if he is virtuous in his relationship to fellow workers, Aristotle makes it clear that virtuous activities are unleisurely, while philosophical contemplation depends upon leisure. This could be interpreted as saying that virtuous activities are even detrimental to philosophical contemplation. If this is the case, Aristotle cannot provide us with an appropriate answer to the question "Why be moral?": if I do not try to distinguish myself from other animals, I can seek bodily pleasures and so I do not have to be moral; if I want to be an authentic human being, I must pursue philosophical contemplation in leisure and so I do not have to be moral (or even cannot be moral, as to be moral is unleisurely).[19] On the other hand, even if we can ignore the potential tension between philosophical contemplation and virtuous actions, Aristotle's idea of human happiness seems to suffer the same problem as Plato's: despite Aristotle's emphasis that human happiness must be achievable by all human beings, it is apparently impossible or at least impractical for all human beings to be happy in Aristotle's sense: how many people have the intellectual ability for Aristotle's philosophical contemplation? Even if every human being does have the needed ability, how many people have the leisure that is necessary for philosophical contemplation?

It is here that we can see the advantage of the Chengs' neo-Confucian approach, which avoids the double problems of the Aristotelian approach. As we have seen, in the Chengs' view, a human being is essentially a moral rather than an intellectual being. In other words, the distinguishing mark of being human is being moral. So in order to be an authentic human being, one has to be moral. At the same time, while they acknowledge that different human beings may be endowed with different intellectual and other nonmoral abilities, they are all equally endowed with moral ability.[20] A moral person with higher intellectual abilities is of course able to do more moral things than a moral person with lower intellectual abilities. However, the former is not any more moral than the latter. They are equally authentic human beings. Similarly, an immoral person with high intellectual abilities is able to do more immoral things than an immoral person with low intellectual abilities. However, the latter is not any less immoral than the former: they are equally beast-like. Again an immoral person may have higher intellectual abilities than a moral person and so can do more immoral things than a moral person can do moral things. However, precisely because the person is immoral, he or she is not a human being as the moral person is.

7. Conclusion

In the above, I have presented the Cheng brothers' neo-Confucian answer to the question "Why should I be moral?" which I claim is a question concerning motivation for morality. I have argued that this answer is superior to the most representative answers to the same question developed in the West, including those by Plato, Aristotle, Thomas Hobbes, David Hume, and Immanuel Kant. According to the Chengs, one should be motivated to be moral, because it is a joy to be moral. Sometimes one finds it painful rather than joyous to be moral or finds it joyous rather than painful to be immoral only because one lacks the necessary genuine moral knowledge. However, such genuine knowledge, unlike advanced scientific and mathematical knowledge or abstract philosophical knowledge, which may be beyond the intellectual abilities of many people, is accessible to every common person, as long as one makes an effort to learn, to experience it from one's own heart/mind. The reason one should make the effort to learn such knowledge in order to feel joy in performing moral actions, instead of seeking joy in performing immoral actions, is that to be moral is a distinguishing mark of being human. It is here that the Chengs' neo-Confucian approach becomes particularly unique, as in the West, humans are distinguished from animals often in terms of rationality. Here the Chengs' answer to the question does seem to be egoist, as its conception of motivation for morality is still based on self-interest: to seek one's own joy. In the next chapter, I shall discuss the Cheng brothers' response to their ethics as egoistic in the context of contemporary discussion of virtue ethics.

Chapter 2

Virtue (*de* 德)

Is a Virtuous Person Self-Centered?

1. Introduction

In the first chapter, we examined the Cheng brothers' answer to the question "Why be moral?" The Chengs believed that one should be moral because it is joyful, and it is joyful because morality is a distinguishing mark of being human. To be moral is to realize one's own true nature. In this sense, the Cheng brothers' neo-Confucian ethics is fundamentally a virtue ethics, a type of ethics that focuses on the development of one's character traits instead of moral principles that constrain one's actions, which is the main focus of this chapter. I shall start with a brief discussion of the main features of virtue ethics, particularly its contrast to alternative ethical theories, with an eye to align Confucianism to virtue ethics (section 2). However, the main task of this chapter is to explore the unique contribution the Cheng brothers can make to contemporary virtue ethics by providing a more adequate response to one of the central objections to virtue ethics: virtue ethics is self-centered. I shall argue that the Cheng brothers can relatively easily respond to this objection, at least on the first level, by showing that the self that a virtuous person is centered on is personal virtue, which requires that person to be centered on others (section 3). While this response is also available to Aristotelian virtue ethics, the main school of virtue ethics in the West, I shall argue that the Cheng brothers provide a better account of virtue than Aristotelians and so can better explain why a characteristic human being should possess other-regarding virtues (section 4). I examine this self-centeredness objection to virtue ethics on two deeper levels: (1) a virtuous person, in being virtuous, is concerned only with the less important external material interests when the well-being of others is involved but with the more important internal traits of character when his or her own well-being is involved; and (2) the virtuous person is concerned with this well-being, whether external or internal, ultimately because the person wants to develop his or her own virtue. I argue that, while Aristotelians are ill-equipped to provide an adequate response to the objection on these two deeper levels, the Cheng brothers' neo-Confucian virtue ethics not only can avoid such objections but also show why virtue ethics is better than alternative theories of ethics (sections 5–6). I shall conclude this chapter with a brief summary (section 7).

2. Virtue Ethics and Confucian Ethics

In the last few decades, there has been an impressive revival of virtue ethics as an alternative to deontology and consequentialism, which dominate modern and contemporary moral discourses. Virtue ethics comes in a variety of forms. While most contemporary virtue ethicists are neo-Aristotelians, there are others who get their primary inspirations from the Stoics, David Hume, Nietzsche, and John Dewey. What is unique about virtue ethics and common to its various forms is its focus on the character of agents, in contrast to deontology and consequentialism, which focus on the nature of actions. So while virtue ethics does not always disagree with deontology and consequentialism in moral evaluations, even when it issues the same moral approval or disapproval, its judgment is based on something different from those for deontology and consequentialism. To illustrate this, we can use Rosalind Hursthouse's example. The three types of ethics may well agree that I should help someone in need, but they disagree on why: "A utilitarian will emphasize the fact that the consequences of doing so will maximize well-being, a deontologist will emphasize the fact that, in doing so, I will be acting in accordance with a moral rule such as 'Do unto others as you would be done by,' and a virtue ethicist will emphasize the fact that helping the person would be charitable or benevolent" (Hursthouse 1999, 1).

To say that virtue ethics focuses on the virtue of the agent in contrast to the rightness of the action does not mean that deontology and consequentialism are antivirtue, just as it does not mean that virtue ethics is necessarily antirightness. For example, consequentialism can allow virtue to have a prominent place in it. This is particularly true of the so-called motive utilitarianism and, more directly, character utilitarianism. According to Robert

Merrihew Adams, the most important advocate of motive utilitarianism, motives are "principally wants and desires, considered as giving rise or tending to give rise to actions" (Adams 1976, 467). Although he sees the distinction between a desire and a trait of character, he does think that "a desire, if strong, stable, and for a fairly general object . . . may perhaps constitute a trait of character" (Adams 1976, 467). According to his motive utilitarianism, "the morally perfect person . . . would have the most useful desires, and have them in exactly the most useful strengths; he or she would have the most useful among the patterns of motivation that are causally possible for human beings" (Adams 1976, 470). Since what the morally perfect person in motive utilitarianism has is not merely desires or motivations, but *patterns* of such desires and motivations, such a person can be regarded as a virtuous person. However, motive or character utilitarianism is still different from virtue ethics, because the virtuous character is not intrinsically but only instrumentally good: it is good only because it is useful to produce the desired consequence.[1]

Similarly, deontology, particularly the Kantian one, can also have a prominent place for virtue, so much so that some Kantian scholars even claim that Kant himself is a virtue ethicist. For example, Onora O'Neill, in an article originally published in 1984, focuses on Kant's idea of maxims, which, according to her, "are underlying principles that make sense of an agent's varied specific intentions," so they "can have little to do with the rightness or wrongness of acts of specific types, and much more to do with the underlying moral quality of a life, or aspects of a life. . . . To have maxims of a morally appropriate sort would then be a matter of leading a certain sort of life, or being a certain sort of person" (O'Neill 1989, 152). While duties indeed occupy a central place in Kant's ethics, O'Neill argues that they are "duties to act out of certain maxims, that is, to structure our moral lives along certain fundamental lines, or to have certain virtues" (O'Neill 1989, 153). However, we must keep in mind that maxims in Kant's ethics are not the most fundamental concepts. Sometimes one has to refrain from acting on certain maxims, and sometimes one has to act on certain maxims that one is reluctant to accept. It is the moral principle that tells us on which maxims we should act.[2] So in a "Postscript" to this article written fifteen years later, O'Neill herself realizes that her earlier characterization of Kant as offering an ethics of virtue is misleading, acknowledging that "Kant's fundamental notion is that of the morally worthy principle that provides guidelines not only for matters of outward right and obligation, but for good characters and institutions as well" (O'Neill 1989, 162). In short, virtuous characters are good only with the guidelines of the moral principle.

Thus, in both consequentialism and deontology, virtues can have very important instrumental value to help promoting good consequences or acting on moral rules, while in virtue ethics, virtue is inherently good. While there are radical or extreme virtue ethicists, the so-called replacement virtue ethicists (see Anscombe 1958), who consider the notion of the rightness or wrongness of acts as unintelligible and want to replace it with the idea of virtue or vice of agents, most virtue ethicists writing today are reductionists. They do not necessarily deny the appropriateness of the notions of the rightness or wrongness of actions that deontologists and consequentialists are concerned with, but they think that such notions can be reduced to or derived from judgments about the moral characters of agents. For example, Hursthouse thinks that it is wrong to say that "virtue ethics does not concern itself at all with right action, or what we should do" (Hursthouse 1999, 26); for according to virtue ethics, "an action is right iff it is what a virtuous agent would, characteristically, do in the circumstances" (Hursthouse 1999, 31). In other words, in order to know what the right action is, we need to do what a virtuous agent would do. In this sense, although Michael Slote claims that his agent-based virtue ethics, in contrast to merely agent-prior and agent-focused virtue ethics, is the most radical form of virtue ethics, it is still a virtue ethics of reduction rather than replacement. According to Slote, the agent-based virtue ethics "treats the moral or ethical status of acts as entirely derivative from independent and fundamental aretaic (as opposed to deontic) ethical characterizations of motives, character traits, or individuals" (Slote 2001, 5). So Slote here does not consider the rightness of action as an unintelligible idea. He only thinks that the rightness of action has to be derived from virtuous characters. The reason he claims that his virtue ethics is more radical than the more familiar types of virtue ethics, including the Aristotelian one, is that, in the agent-based virtue ethics, the character trait from which rightness of action is derived is itself the most fundamental and not derived from anything else, including Plato's health of the soul and Aristotle's eudaimonia.

So, with regard to virtue, the distinction between virtue ethics on the one hand and deontology and consequentialism on the other is that virtue is inherently good for the former, while it is merely instrumentally good for the latter. Between these two positions, Thomas Hurka develops a recursive account of virtue. This account starts with what he calls a base clause about goods such as "pleasure, knowledge, and achievement are intrinsically good" (Hurka 2001, 12), and one about evils such as "pain, false belief, and failure in the pursuit of achievement are intrinsically evil" (Hurka 2001, 15), where such actual states of affairs that count as intrinsic goods or evils may be replaced by others. The account then adds a recursion clause about the intrinsic goodness of certain attitudes to what is good and evil and one about the intrinsic badness of certain other attitudes to what is good and evil. Since some states of affairs are intrinsically good and others are intrinsically evils, then the attitude of loving the former and hating the latter must also be intrinsically good, and the attitude of hating the former and loving the latter must also be intrinsically bad. Then finally the account defines virtues as precisely such attitudes to goods and evils (i.e., loving intrinsic goods and hating intrinsic evils) that are intrinsically good and, accordingly, vices as precisely such attitudes to goods and evils (i.e., loving evils and hating goods) that are intrinsically evil (Hurka 2001, 20). Since virtues are intrinsically good attitudes, they are intrinsically good; and since vices are intrinsically evil attitudes, they are intrinsically bad. However, Hurka argues that, since virtues are intrinsically good only because it is an attitude of loving what is intrinsically good or hating what is intrinsically evil, such intrinsically good attitudes to goods and evils, the virtuous attitudes or, simply, virtues, can be either good or bad instrumentally, just as intrinsically bad attitudes to goods and evils, the vicious attitudes or, simply, vices, can be either bad or good instrumentally. He illustrates this point in the following way: "*B* tries benevolently to promote *A*'s pleasure but through no fault of his causes *A* pain. *B*'s benevolent action, though intrinsically good, is instrumentally evil, and if the pain it causes *A* is sufficiently great, it can be all things considered evil. Similarly, if a malicious attempt to cause *A* pain in fact gives *A* pleasure, it can be instrumentally and even all things considered good" (Hurka 2001, 21).

In this chapter, I shall focus on the virtue ethicists' understanding of virtue. According to this understanding, virtuous character is more fundamental than right action, and to be virtuous is to be a characteristically human being. Thus a virtuous person performs virtuous actions " 'naturally,' without having to fight with emotions, inclinations or traits of character, without being in any conflict between 'spirit' and 'body,' or 'reason' and 'passion' " (Statman 1997, 16). In other words, virtuous persons take delight in doing virtuous things. It is in this sense that we can claim that Confucian ethics is primarily a virtue ethics. As we have seen in the previous chapter, for Confucianism, a moral person does moral things because doing moral things brings joy to the person, and it brings joy to the person because the person has the moral knowledge that to be moral is indispensable to being an authentic human being. Thus there is no wonder that effort abounds to relate Confucianism to virtue ethics, and the most stunning achievements of such an effort are the almost simultaneous publication of three comparative studies: Bryan Van

Norden's *Virtue Ethics and Consequentialism in Early Chinese Philosophy* (2007), Yu Jiyuan's *The Ethics of Confucius and Aristotle* (2007), and May Sim's *Remastering Morals with Aristotle and Confucius* (2007).[3] While such comparisons have been almost exclusively focused on classical Confucians, in this chapter, I shall focus on the neo-Confucian Cheng brothers. More importantly, my interest is not in exploring the similarities and differences between Confucianism and virtue ethics in the West as these comparative studies primarily aim to do, but in seeking the possibility of any possible contributions Confucianism can make to contemporary virtue ethics. While the revival of virtue ethics is impressive, there have been serious objections to it. Some of these—particularly the objection regarding uncodifiability, that is, the inability of virtue ethics to provide people with practical action guides—have been persuasively responded to by leading virtue ethicists today. However, one of the central objections to virtue ethics, the so-called self-centeredness objection, particularly on its deeper levels, has not been adequately responded to and, it seems to me, can hardly be responded to adequately if we are limited to drawing on resources available in Western philosophical traditions. In contrast, I shall argue, a philosophically significant response to this objection can be found in the Cheng brothers' neo-Confucianism.

3. The Self-Centeredness Objection: The First Level

The self-centeredness objection, as summarized by David Solomon,

> alleges that an EV [ethics of virtue] tends to focus too much attention on the agent. . . . Such theories demand a focus on the character of the individual agent. What gives the point to the task of acquiring the virtues is that one supposes that one should become a person of a particular kind. . . . This view demands that the moral agent keep his or her own character at the center of his or her practical attention . . . [while] the point of moral reflection essentially involves a concern for others. (Solomon 1997, 169)

Solomon himself does not specify who raises this objection, but he thinks that this objection, or at least its spirit, can be found in Kant and contemporary Kantian philosophers. For example, we do find Kant stating that "all material principles, which place the determining ground of choice in the pleasure or displeasure to be received from the reality of any object whatsoever, are entirely of one kind. Without exception they belong under the principle of self-love or one's own happiness" (Kant 1956b, 22). In another place, Kant argues,

> Of the ancient Greek schools, there were only two opposing each other on this issue. But so far as the definition of the concept of the highest good is concerned, they followed one and the same method, since neither held virtue and happiness to be two different elements of the highest good, but seeking the unity of principle under the rule of identity. But again they differed in that each selected a different principle as the fundamental one. The Epicurean said: To be conscious of one's maxims as leading to happiness is virtue. The Stoic said: To be conscious of one's virtue is happiness. To the former, prudence amounted to morality; to the latter, who chose a higher term for virtue, morality alone was true wisdom. (Kant 1956b, 111)

In short, for Kant, both Epicureans and Stoics regard morality as identical to happiness, which seems to him a self-centered conception of morality.[4]

This criticism, in appearance, is also applicable to the Cheng brothers' neo-Confucianism. As we have seen in the first chapter, their answer to "Why be moral?" is apparently self-regarding instead of other-regarding: one should be moral because one can take delight in it. In other words, it is in one's own interest, or it pays, to be moral. As a matter of fact, as an admirer of the Golden Age, Confucius claims that "ancient learners were for the sake of themselves (*weiji* 為己), while present learners are for the sake of others (*weiren* 為人)" (*Analects* 14.24). It is important, however, to see what Confucius means by "for the sake of oneself" and "for the sake of others." In the Chengs' view, by "for the sake of oneself," Confucius means to cultivate one's inner virtues, while by "for the sake of others," Confucius means to decorate oneself with fine scholarship in front of others. In the above statement, Confucius does not mean that "ancient learners" that he admires were only concerned with their own interests and ignore the interests of others, nor does he mean that "present learners" that he looks down upon are only concerned with the interests of others while ignoring their own interest; otherwise he would give his praise to the "present learners" instead of "ancient learners."

These two different senses of "for the sake of oneself" and "for the sake of others" are brought out most clearly when one of the Chengs contrasts learners (*xuezhe* 學者) and officials (*shizhe* 仕者). This is particularly illuminating, as there is a saying in the *Analects* through the mouth of Confucius's student

Zixia 子夏 that "the good learners should become officials" (*Analects* 19.13). After quoting "ancient learners were for the sake of themselves, while present learners are for the sake of others," Cheng makes a parallel statement: "Ancient officials were for the sake of others, while present officials are for the sake of themselves" (*Yishu* 6; 90; see also *Cuiyan* 1; 1214). Obviously Cheng here uses the two phrases "for the sake of oneself" and "for the sake of others" in two different senses in relation to learners and officials; otherwise we cannot understand why learners should be for themselves, while officials should be for others. In Cheng's view, learners should aim at cultivating themselves, not displaying their scholarship in front of others; and officials should be concerned with the interest of others and not merely with their own interest. Here it is important to see that the ancient learners' "for the sake of themselves" is on par with the ancient officials' "for the sake of others," and present learners' "for the sake of others" is no different from the present officials' "for the sake of themselves." To cultivate oneself (to be for the sake of oneself), in this Confucian tradition, means to develop one's inborn tendencies to be concerned with others' interests. Therefore, the more one is for the sake of oneself, the more one is for the sake of others. However, to show off one's scholarship in front of others (to be for the sake of others) is to be concerned with one's own interest (in fame). So the more one is for the sake of others in this sense, the more one is for the sake of oneself. It is in this sense that CHENG Yi says that "ancient learners were for the sake of themselves but ended up bringing the goodness of others to completion" (*Yishu* 25; 325; see also *Cuiyan* 1; 1197).[5] In contrast, "present learners are for the sake of others and end up losing their own selves" (*Yishu* 25; 325; see also *Cuiyan* 1; 1197). In other words, if learners focus their attention on showing off their scholarship and neglect self-cultivation, their inborn moral heart/mind will be lost.

From this we can see that, since for the Chengs, virtuous agents are for the sake of themselves, this neo-Confucian position may be characterized as self-centered. However, there are two things distinctive about such a self-centeredness. First, while this Confucian response also says that it is to one's self-interest to be moral, this self-interest is not something extraneous to one's moral action as the term "self-interest" is commonly understood. In contemporary business ethics, LaRue Tone Hosmer, for example, asks, "[W]hat shall we say to a modern Gyges active in management?" (Hosmer 1994, 191), referring to the mystic ring in Plato's *Republic*, which can make one invisible when doing immoral things. Hosmer's answer is that "acting in ways that can be considered to be 'right' and 'just' and 'fair' is absolutely essential to the long-term competitive success of the firm" (Hosmer 1994,

192). Here disregarding some criticisms of such an approach as ineffective,[6] we can see that the reason it pays to be moral is that such a moral action will, sooner or later, bring material benefits to the business person. In such situations, the business person does not find it a joy to be moral. As a matter of fact, the person may be pained by doing moral things. He or she nevertheless chooses to be moral in order to seek the benefits that may come with his or her moral actions. In other words, one performs moral actions not for the sake of moral actions but for the sake of benefits likely to accompany such actions. One performs moral actions only for prudential reasons. Similarly, in contemporary virtue ethics, Rosalind Hursthouse argues that virtue benefits its possessor in a similar sense. Hursthouse acknowledges that virtue does not always benefit the agent, enabling her to flourish,[7] so she agrees that virtue is neither necessary nor sufficient for the flourishing of the agent: "[I]t is not necessary, since it is generally acknowledged that the wicked may flourish like the green bay tree. And it is not sufficient because of those nasty cases that came up in consideration of the particular question" (Hursthouse 1999, 172). Even so, Hursthouse still thinks that by and large virtue benefits its possessor. She makes an analogy. While following medical advice is neither a sufficient nor a necessary condition for being healthy, following it is one's best bet for being healthy. Similarly, although being virtuous is neither necessary nor sufficient for one's flourishing, it is one's best bet for flourishing (Hursthouse 1999, 173).[8] If the Cheng brothers mean the same thing as Hosmer and Hursthouse when they claim that it is a joy to be moral, then the claim is indeed self-centered. However, as we have seen, in the Cheng brothers' Confucian view, the self-interest one seeks by performing moral actions is inherent in these actions: one feels joy in being moral not because it can serve one's interest in gaining fame, praise, wealth, and so on, that may result; rather it is because one realizes one's self-nature—as a moral being—by being moral.

Second, while the familiar version of self-interest by itself is in conflict with morality (although in some situations one's self-interest may motivate one to be moral and one's being moral may be conducive to one's self-interest), in Confucianism, there is no such conflict. Although the Cheng brothers claim that one should be moral because it brings one joy, they do not mean that one should do whatever brings one joy. In other words, while one should be moral because it is in one's own interest to be moral, one should not do whatever is in one's self-interest. Here one must first be clear about what one's genuine interest is: to find the uniquely human joy, which is precisely to do virtuous things. Here the conflict between self-interest and morality disappears, since one's proper self-interest is precisely to be concerned with others' interest. In this sense, the better one serves one's self-interest, the more moral the person is. Here, as Richard Kraut states, a virtuous person "first proposes a concrete conception of the good, and then urges each of us to maximize our own good, so conceived. . . . It does not claim that one should seek one's own good, come what may for others; rather, by arguing that acting virtuously and acting well coincide, it seeks to undermine the common assumption that at bottom the self must come into conflict with others" (Kraut 1998, §4).

The essence of the Cheng brothers' view above is summarized by Robert Solomon, who thinks that the self-centeredness objection to virtue ethics can be responded to, at least on this level, if we take

> account of an important distinction between two features of an EV [ethics of virtue]. There is, first, the feature that the objector notices: the central place that one's own character plays in the practical thinking associated with an EV. But there is also within an EV the set of virtues that each agent aims to embody in his character. While the first feature of an EV may appear to render it excessively self-centered, the second feature is surely able to counteract that danger. The particular virtues characteristic of an EV may be as other-regarding as one might wish. While each agent may be expected to devote primary practical attention to the development of his or her own character, the attention may be required to turn the agent into a person fundamentally concerned with the wellbeing of others. (Solomon 1997, 171–72)

In other words, while the virtue ethical reasons for actions may appear to be self-regarding: to cultivate your own virtues, the very virtues (or at least some of them) you need to possess are other-regarding. One cannot cultivate one's virtue without taking care of the interest of the others. The virtuous person, as stated by Bernard Williams, "desires, quite often, to do various virtuous things," and one may claim that "anything motivated by desires is directed toward pleasure, and the pursuit of the pleasure is egoistic" (Williams 1985, 49). However, as Williams also points out, it is important to see that "some of my desires aim at states of affairs that do not involve me at all. . . . There are self-transcending desires" (Williams 1985, 50). In other words, we cannot claim that a virtuous person is self-centered simply because he or she always tries to satisfy his or her own desires. We need to see what desires this person wants to satisfy. As a virtuous person, the desires he or she typically wants to satisfy are desires of helping others. In this sense, the virtuous person is not self-centered at all.[9]

In this respect, the Cheng brothers' neo-Confucianism is quite consistent with the Aristotelian view. We have seen that Hursthouse has made a controversial argument that virtue benefits its possessor, which may well be subject to the self-centeredness objection. However, as a good Aristotelian, she emphasizes that this argument is only part of her entire argument and so must be understood in combination with her other argument, that virtue makes its possessor a characteristic human being. In this argument, virtuous people do virtuous things not because they believe that this is the best bet for their getting more material and external benefits. In contrast, when they do virtuous things, they do so for the sake of others. For this reason, they often sacrifice their own material interest and even their own life. Virtuous people's self-interest is served by serving the interest of others, as they take delight in their actions of making others happy. This is made most clear by Aristotle's idea of true self-lovers. In Aristotle's view, true lovers of self are not those "who assign to themselves the greater share of wealth, honours, and bodily pleasures" (Aristotle 1915, 1168b15–16), but those who are always anxious that they "should act justly, temperately, or in accordance with any other of the virtues" and in general "try to secure for themselves the honourable course" (Aristotle 1915, 1168b26–28). A person of the latter type "assigns to himself the things that are noblest and best, and gratifies the most authoritative element in himself . . . ; and therefore the man who loves this and gratifies it is most of all a lover of self" (Aristotle 1915, 11168b29–33). Then he reaches exactly the same conclusion as the Cheng brothers: "Therefore the good man should be a lover of self (for he will both himself profit by doing noble acts, and will benefit his fellows), but the wicked man should not; for he will hurt both himself and his neighbours, following as he does evil passions" (Aristotle 1915, 1169a12–15).

4. Virtue and Human Nature

From the above, we have seen that both Confucian and Aristotelian virtue ethics can have an appropriate initial response to the self-centeredness objection. A virtuous person is indeed concerned with his or her own characters. However, the characters that a virtuous person is concerned with are virtues, which are typically if not exclusively other-regarding.[10] The more one is concerned with oneself (one's own virtues), the more one is concerned with others. Thus, crucial to this initial response to the self-centeredness objection is what determines a character as virtue instead of vice. For example, why is benevolence a virtue rather than a vice, and why is greediness a vice and not a virtue? Obviously, if benevolence is a vice, and greediness is a virtue, then the virtue ethics would be unable to respond to the self-centeredness objection. So any virtue ethics must have a theory or at least an account of virtue: what makes a character trait virtuous? It is here that I think Aristotelian virtue ethics faces a problem that the Confucian virtue ethics can avoid. Although both Confucianism and Aristotelianism appeal to human nature to explain virtue, they have very different conceptions of human nature. Hursthouse provides a prudential argument for virtue as something that benefits its possessor, which, as I have argued in the previous section, is problematic and clearly subject to the self-centeredness objection to virtue ethics. However, as we have also mentioned, she makes it clear that this prudential argument is inseparable from the argument that virtue makes its possessor a good human being. This is related to Aristotle's famous function argument. According to Aristotle, the good and the "well" of anything that has a function or activity must reside in the function. So the good and the "well" of human beings must also reside in the human function, which is characteristic of human beings or, to use McDowell's term, which it is the business of human beings to perform. Aristotle identifies this human function as the "active life of the element that has a rational principle" (Aristotle 1915, 1098a3). Thus virtue is what makes a person a good human being, a human being who performs rational activities, or lives a rational life, excellently.

This account of virtues, particularly the moral virtues that concern us here, has several problems. We will quickly bypass two of them so that we can focus on the third one, which is most relevant to the issue discussed here. First, since Aristotle distinguishes between practical reason and intellectual reason in a hierarchical order, with the latter being higher than the former, it is not clear whether a good human being must be morally virtuous, since one can have a well-, if not better, functioning reason in contemplation without being moral. Second, even if moral virtues are necessary for the good functioning of human reason, it is not clear whether the Aristotelian ethics can be properly regarded as a virtue ethics. As we have seen, virtue ethics regards virtue as central, which contrasts it to other types of ethics that allow virtue only a secondary place in their systems. However, if virtue serves reason in Aristotle, then it is not much different from the virtue that serves the greatest good in utilitarianism and the virtue that serves duty in deontology.[11] In other words, virtue with such a secondary function will not make the ethics virtue ethics.

However, the more serious problem in this Aristotelian virtue ethics is with the relation between moral virtues and reason. While most people agree with Aristotle's view of rationality as characteristic of human beings as well as his substantive view of moral virtues,[12] there have been serious challenges, yet to be met adequately, about whether Aristotle's virtues can be derived from his conception of human nature as rational. Bernard Williams, for one, has consistently doubted the possibility of deriving the former from the latter. In an early work, he claims that "if it is the mark of a man to employ intelligence and tools in modifying his environment, it is equally a mark of him to employ intelligence in getting his own way and tools in destroying others" (Williams 1971, 73–74).[13] In his major work, *Ethics and the Limits of Philosophy*, Williams continues to think that there is a gap between Aristotle's account of human nature and that of virtue: "[I]t is hard to believe that an account of human nature—if it is not already an ethical theory itself—will adequately determine one kind of ethical life as against others" (Williams 1985, 52). In a long article, Martha Nussbaum tries to respond to Williams's challenge on behalf of Aristotle. Since in the above quoted passage, Williams adds the conditional, "if it is not already an ethical theory itself," one of Nussbaum's goals is to show that Aristotle's account of human nature is not morally neutral, and, in her analysis of Aristotle's function argument, she comes to the conclusion that "since no life will count as a good life for us unless it is first of all a life for *us*, and since a life for us must be a life organized, in some fashion, by practical reason, in which all functions are informed and infused by reason's organizing activity, then *eudaimonia* must be sought within the group of such lives, not in a life totally given over to bodily pleasure without reason, not in the sleeper's life of non-guided digestive functioning" (Nussbaum 1995, 116). However, with such an account, a life without the guidance of reason indeed cannot be regarded as a human life, as Nussbaum claims; yet it does not show a vicious life must be a life without the guidance of reason and so must also be regarded as not a human life. Naturally Williams is not convinced: "As Nussbaum points out, however, the life of a wicked or self-indulgent person is equally a certain kind of life structured by reason; it is also a distinctive kind of *human* life. So far we still wait for the considerations that may move the idea of a life 'structured by reason' in the specific direction of life of moderation" (Williams 1995, 199).[14]

Williams's suspicion is shared by John McDowell. In an essay on Aristotle's *eudaimonia*, McDowell first imagines a debate between a person, X, who thinks that a human being should exercise certain virtues, including those other-regarding ones, and another person, Y, who thinks that the virtuous life is suitable only for contemptible weaklings and that a real man, who looks out for himself, does not practice those other-regarding virtues. Then McDowell looks at Aristotle's famous passage in the function argument, concluding that this passage "can be read in such a way that the conclusion is (so far) neutral, as between Aristotle's own substantive view [of virtues] and, say, a view of *eudaimonia* corresponding to the position of Y in the dispute" (McDowell 1998b, 12). In McDowell's view, "the thesis that man's *ergon* [function] consists in rational activity obviously excludes what might otherwise have been a conceivable view of *eudaimonia*, namely, a life of unreflective gratification of appetite; in the spirit of the *ergon* argument, we might say that that embodies no recognizable conception of a distinctively human kind of excellence. But no other likely candidate is clearly excluded by the eliminative argument for that thesis" (McDowell 1998b, 13). In a different essay, on Aristotle's moral psychology, McDowell further explains the kinds of life that may be excluded and the kinds of life that cannot be excluded by Aristotle's function argument:

> In fact there are only two substantive points on which Aristotle suggests that facts about human nature constrain the truth about a good human life. . . . First, a good human life must be an active life of that which has *logos* (*N.E.* 1098a3–4); this excludes, for instance, the ideal of uncontrolled gratification of appetite with which Socrates saddles Callics, in Plato's *Gorgias*. Second, human beings are naturally social (*NE* 1097b11, 1069b18–19); this excludes a solitary life. Obviously these two points fall a long way short of purporting to afford a validation of Aristotle's ethic in full. (McDowell 1998b, 35–36)

To further illustrate his point that rationality does not necessarily lead to virtue, in yet another essay arguing against Aristotelian naturalism, McDowell imagines a rational wolf. Without reason, the wolf would find it natural for him to play his part in the co-operative activity of hunting with the pack. However, "Having acquired reason, he can contemplate alternatives; he can step back from the natural impulse and direct critical scrutiny at it . . . and frame the question 'why should I do this?' . . . wondering whether to idle through the hunt but still grab his share of the prey" (McDowell 1998b, 171). In McDowell's view, even if the wolf by its nature does what virtue might require it to do, the addition of reason may cause it to question its natural behavior. Then, McDowell draws the lesson that "even if we grant that human beings have a naturally based need for the virtues, in a sense parallel to the sense in which wolves have a naturally based need for co-operativeness in their hunting, that need not cut any ice with someone who questions whether virtuous behaviour is genuinely required by reason" (McDowell 1998b, 173).

One might wonder whether Williams and McDowell do not have a proper view of rationality, and rationality, when properly understood, would necessarily require moral virtues. Thomas Hurka, another critic of the view that rationality necessitates moral virtue, however, argues that this is not the case. In Hurka's view, Aristotle's function argument basically says that (1) human flourishing consists in the development of what is fundamental to human nature, (2) rationality is what is fundamental to human nature, and (3) moral virtues instantiate rationality because they "exercise practical reason in different domains of action and are therefore essential to a flourishing life" (Hurka 2001, 236). Hurka's problem is with (3), not necessarily because it is false but because it is misleading. To see this, Hurka invites us to consider our definition of rationality. In his view, rationality can be either defined formally or substantively. The formal account of rationality "says that actions express practical rationality to a higher degree when they involve better-justified beliefs that they will achieve their goals and when their goals are more extended and arranged in more complex means-end hierarchies" (Hurka 2001, 237). Hurka argues that there are two problems with this formal definition. First, virtues are valued here not as virtues but as tools to the development of the agent's rationality. Second, and more importantly, "the criteria do not successfully distinguish virtuous actions from neutral and even vicious ones; playing chess and torturing can also extend a person's goal and involve complex means-end reasoning" (Hurka 2001, 237). Hurka then asks us to imagine two situations. In one, a person can either save another's life or continue with a theoretical activity. In another, one's saving a life will distract her from some more challenging and complex activity such as chess playing or even torturing (see Hurka 2001, 238). In Hurka's view, this formal account of rationality cannot show that a rational person will perform the morally virtuous action of saving a person's life, as the alternative activities in these two situations can better extend the agent's rationality than the morally virtuous actions. If so, Hurka argues that we may need to accept a more substantive account of rationality, according to which rationality "involves reasoning about, identifying, and successfully pursuing what is good. As truth is the proper aim of belief, so goodness is the proper aim of desire, and practical rationality is directed to this aim. As so directed, it is instantiated especially by virtue" (Hurka 2001, 238). If the formal account makes virtues serve reason, this substantive account makes reason serve virtues. If so, moral virtues, instead of rationality, both practical and theoretical, would become central to human flourishing. This, of course, is not consistent with the Aristotelian view. However, I shall argue, this is precisely the view argued for in the Cheng brothers' neo-Confucianism.

The Cheng brothers' Confucian account of virtue is also closely connected with its conception of human nature, so virtue makes its possessor a good human being. However, because it is based on a different conception of human nature, it can avoid the Aristotelian gap between virtue and human nature. As we saw in chapter 1, what distinguishes human beings from beasts is not rationality but morality: human nature is virtuous, and human virtues are natural. In other words, virtues are virtues of human nature (*xing zhi de* 性之德), and human nature is always virtuous nature (*de xing* 德性). Here, CHENG Hao tells us, "we talk about 'virtuous nature' in order to show the nobility of human nature, which is equivalent to saying that human nature is good; we talk about 'virtues of human nature' to indicate what human nature possesses" (*Yishu* 11; 125). By virtuous nature, the Chengs mean that it is "natural endowment and natural asset" (*Yishu* 2a; 20). Because human nature is virtuous, and human virtues come from human nature, Confucians often talk about natural virtue (*tian de* 天德). CHENG Hao tells us that

> the reason that sages and the worthy talk about natural virtues is that they are all things originally complete in us by nature. If they are not corrupted, we only need to straightly practice from them. When some minor defects appear, we need to fix them with reverences so that their original status can be restored. We can restore their original status precisely because we are originally complete with them. (*Yishu* 1; 1)

It is well known that humanity, rightness, propriety, wisdom, and faithfulness are central Confucian human virtues. For the Chengs, "these five cardinal Confucian virtues . . . are also human nature. Humanity is like the whole body, while the other four are like the four limbs" (*Yishu* 2a; 14). In another place, CHENG Yi claims that "in human nature, we need to make a distinction among these five: humanity, rightness, propriety, wisdom, and faithfulness" (*Yishu* 15; 168). This view of identity between human nature and human virtue is of course closely related to the Confucian view of human nature as good. Thus CHENG Yi states,

> all actions from one's human nature are good. Because of the goodness of human nature, sages name it by humanity, rightness, propriety, wisdom, and faithfulness. Because their applications are

different, these five different names are used. Whether viewed as
a unity or viewed separately, however, they are all *dao*. When one
acts in violation of these five, one is in violation of *dao*. There are
people who think that human nature, *dao*, is different from these
five. This is only because they lack the knowledge: they have not
experienced their own human nature; they have no idea of where
dao lies. (*Yishu* 25; 318)

Here, what CHENG Yi means by *dao* is the *dao* by which human beings relate
to each other. So in another place he tells us: "Confucius says that 'the *dao*
governing the father-son relationship is one's innate nature (*tian xing* 天性).'
Here Confucius is talking about filial piety, and therefore he says that [this
dao governing] father and son is one's innate nature. However, what about the
dao governing the relationships between rulers and ministers, between older
and younger brothers, between hosts and guests, and among friends? Is not
it also one's innate nature?" (*Yishu* 18; 234).

This Confucian account of human nature as virtuous or of human virtues
as natural is significant. As we have seen, the Aristotelian virtue ethicists
want to claim, as Hursthouse does, that "the virtues make their possessor a
good human being. (Human beings need the virtues in order to live well, to
flourish *as* human beings, to live a characteristically good, *eudaimon*, human
life.)" (Hursthouse 1999, 167). However, because they hold that what is
characteristically human is the rational activity of the soul, they have trouble
not only in maintaining that Aristotelian ethics is a virtue ethics (since virtues
are good in their ethics only to serve the function of rational activity) but
also in showing that a characteristically good human life necessitates virtues
or that virtues will make its possessor a characteristically good human. The
Confucian view of human nature as virtuous can avoid this problem. Here,
virtues are good also because they benefit their possessor as a human being,
but the nature of human being itself is defined by virtue. So in Confucian
ethics, virtue is inherently and not merely instrumentally good. At the same
time, since human nature is virtuous, virtue naturally makes its possessor a
good human being. It is in this sense that the Chengs' neo-Confucian ethics
can also avoid what Gary Watson regards as the dilemma of ethics of virtue.
The dilemma in question is that "either the theory's pivotal account of human
nature (or characteristic human life) will be morally indeterminate, or it will not
be objectively well founded" (Watson 1997, 67). Hursthouse states this version
of the dilemma in a clearer way: "[E]ither we speak from the neutral point of
view, using a scientific account of human nature—in which case we won't get

very far [in getting virtues from human nature]—or we speak from within an acquired ethical outlook—in which case we will not validate our ethical beliefs, but merely re-express them" (Hursthouse 1999, 193).[15] Hursthouse herself tries to argue that the Aristotelian naturalism is able to avoid this dilemma, while our argument above shows that, as an objective, well-founded, and neutral view of human nature, it is morally indeterminate in the sense that to be a characteristically human being in terms of rationality does not determine one to be a morally virtuous person.

So if the Aristotelian ethics falls onto one of the horns of Watson's dilemma (being objective in accounting human nature but unable to derive virtue from such an objective account), we need to see whether the Cheng brothers' Confucian ethics, by avoiding this horn, falls into the other. In other words, by avoiding this problem of moral indeterminacy, does it merely re-express virtues and therefore become objectively not well founded? The answer is "no." The Cheng brothers regard human nature as virtuous. This, however, does not mean that this view is merely internal and not objective. For the Cheng brothers, we know that human nature is virtuous because we can experience the four moral feelings, both in ourselves and in others. For example, "it is from the feeling of commiseration that we know that human nature possesses the virtue of humanity" (*Yishu* 15; 168). Similarly, from the feeling of shame we know that human nature possesses the virtue of rightness, from the feeling of courtesy that of propriety, and from the feeling of right and wrong that of wisdom. A possible objection to such a view of human nature is that, if so, there would be no vicious human beings. As a matter of fact, Confucianism in general and Cheng brothers' neo-Confucianism in particular do claim that there are no vicious *human* beings, because those who have lost their original virtuous human nature are no longer regarded as human beings. However, it also claims that, unlike beasts, those who have lost their originally virtuous human nature can still get it back and become human beings again. To understand this, we need to see that the Confucian explanation of virtue is neither merely external (or "neutral" in Hursthouse's words) nor entirely internal (or from "an acquired ethical view" in Hursthouse's words). Rather, to use David Wong's term, it is internal to human nature (so that all and only human beings can be virtuous) but is not necessarily internal with respect to any given individual agent (so that there can be individuals who are not virtuous) (Wong 2006, 188).[16] Such virtues, to use Christopher Toner's term, are natural norms.[17] They are natural, since all human beings and only human beings can have them, although not every individual human being actually has them. In this sense, this Confucian account of virtues also has an objective basis and therefore does not merely re-express the normative virtues. At the same time, however, they are norms, since not everything that humans naturally have is recognized as a virtue. Not only many things that all human beings naturally share with animals (such as the desire to exploit [see Toner 2008, 236]), but even some things that are uniquely human, such as rationality and being social, are not recognized as virtues in Confucianism. For this reason, the Confucian account of virtue, while based on nature, is not morally indeterminate.

5. The Self-Centeredness Objection: The Second Level

In the above, we have seen that a virtuous person, while self-concerned, is concerned with being virtuous, and virtuous characters, particularly those other-regarding ones, make the virtuous person concerned with the interest of others. In this sense, virtue ethics is not self-centered in the morally condemnable sense. However, this response to the self-centeredness objection to virtue ethics, as David Solomon points out, may allow the objection to arise at a deeper level, at which,

> the objection points to an asymmetry that arises between an agent's regard for his own character and his regard for the character of others. The question raised here has this form: Since an EV [ethics of virtue] requires me to pay primary attention to the state of my own character, doesn't this suggest that I must regard my own character as the ethically most important feature of myself? But, if so, and if I am suitably concerned about others, shouldn't my concern for them extend beyond a mere concern that their wants, needs and desires be satisfied, and encompass a concern for *their* character? Shouldn't I indeed have the same concern for the character of my neighbour as I have for my own? (Solomon 1997, 172)

Solomon uses the example of a Christian's view of love or charity as a primary virtue. This person will make it a goal to become someone who exhibits this virtue toward others, but this virtue does not require others to be virtuous: "Christian love requires me to attend to the wants, needs and desires of others. But doesn't this suggest that I regard others as less morally important than myself? Satisfying their needs is good enough for them, but I require of myself that I become a loving person" (Solomon 1997, 172).

As this objection may sound somewhat strange, one might wonder who would raise such an objection. Solomon himself does not state it clearly except that it is also traceable to some versions of Kantianism. This is perhaps true. However, the closest example of this objection I can find is in Bernard Williams, hardly a Kantian. As we have seen, Williams argues against the view of virtue ethics as egoistic in the sense that virtuous persons desire pleasure in performing virtuous actions, as the actions they perform are other-regarding. However, he argues that even when we get rid of this misconception, "there may still seem to be something left to the charge of egoism," which "involves the agent's *thinking about* these dispositions themselves and relating them to a life of well-being. Even if the dispositions are not themselves directed toward the self, it is still his own well-being that the agent in Socratic reflection will be considering. Egoism seems to be back again" (Williams 1985, 50). The type of egoism that Williams has in mind is clearly what Solomon calls the self-centeredness of virtue ethics on the deeper level: the virtuous person is exclusively focused on the external well-being of others but is primarily concerned with the internal well-being of his or her self, when he or she clearly realizes that internal well-being is far more important and constitutive of human being than external well-being. This becomes most clear when he tries to expose the problem of Socrates' view that "the good man cannot be harmed" (one can harm his body but not his soul, which is his true self): "[I]n describing moral motivations, it takes a very spirited view of one's own interests, but the subject matter of ethics requires it to give a less spiritual view of other people's interests. If bodily hurt is not real harm, why does virtue require us so strongly not to hurt other people's body?" (Williams 1985, 34). (Here it might be added: if bodily pleasure is not real pleasure, why does virtue require us so strongly to bring such pleasures to others?) Aristotle does not think that bodily harm and pleasure are not real harm and pleasure, but he still regards them as less important than the harm and pleasure of the soul. Yet, precisely with regard to the harm and pleasure of the soul, Aristotle's virtuous person is only concerned with himself. Moreover, the virtuous person acquires the pleasure and avoids the harm of his own soul largely by providing others with bodily pleasure and eliminating or decreasing their bodily harm. Thus, Williams states, "when Aristotle seems most removed from modern ethical perceptions, it is often because the admired agent is disquietingly concerned with himself" (Williams 1985, 35).

What Williams has in mind must be Aristotle's argument about the virtuous person as a true self-lover as we mentioned earlier in this chapter. Aristotle makes a contrast between such true self-lovers and self-lovers in the common sense. The latter are "people who assign to themselves the greater share of wealth, honours, and bodily pleasures" (Aristotle 1915, 1168b15–17). Such self-lovers are to be reproached. However, a true self-lover is the one who is "always anxious that he himself, above all things, should act justly, temperately, or in accordance with any other of the virtues"; such a person is a true self-lover because "at all events he assigns to himself the most authoritative element in himself and in all things obeys this" (Aristotle 1915, 1168b25–30). Such a true self-lover is obviously not self-centered in the sense that, when he performs virtuous acts and therefore benefits his fellows, he does so "for the sake of his friends and his country, and if necessary dies for them" (Aristotle 1915, 1169a19–20). However, the Aristotelian self-lover is self-centered on a deeper level in David Solomon's sense. Although people's virtuous acts will benefit themselves and their fellows at the same time, there is an asymmetry between these two kinds of benefit: the benefit their fellows get from their virtuous actions is wealth, honor, and bodily pleasures, while the benefit they get themselves from their virtuous actions is nobility; and Aristotle makes it clear that nobility is much more important than wealth, honor, and bodily pleasure: the true self-lover "will throw away both wealth and honours and in general the goods that are objects of competition, gaining for himself nobility" (Aristotle 1915, 1169a20–21). Here the self-centeredness objection to virtue ethics is precisely this: while the Aristotelian virtuous agents do care for others for their own sake, they only care about their external goods, not their more important internal goods (virtue or nobility); while they sacrifice their own external goods, they do so, at least partially, in order to acquire their own internal goods.

Solomon, himself an advocate of virtue ethics, acknowledges that the self-centeredness objection at this deeper level is ineliminable within virtue ethics. In his view, the only reasonable response to such an objection is to find partners in crime (if it is indeed a crime, he adds), that is, to indicate that the major rivals to virtue ethics, particularly deontology and utilitarianism, commit the same crime. For example, Kantian ethics requires an agent to act from the sense of duty but does not require the agent to try to cause others to also act from the sense of duty. Kant thinks that we have imperfect duty to promote our moral perfection and to advance others' happiness, but we do not have the corresponding imperfect duty to promote our happiness and others' moral perfection; for the former, because we do not have a duty to do what we always automatically wish to do; and for the latter, because "the perfection of another man, as a person, consists precisely in *his own* power to adopt his end in accordance with his own concept of duty; and it is self-contradictory to demand that I do (make it my duty to do) what only the other person himself can do" (Kant 1964a, 44). So, in Solomon's view, "the Kantian slogan here might be, 'rightness for me, happiness for you'" (Solomon 1997, 172).[18] The case of utilitarianism is slightly more complicated, as Solomon acknowledges that classical utilitarianism requires that an agent ought not only become benevolent but also attempt to make others benevolent. However, the asymmetry is still there: while the agent's concern for others' benevolence is only of instrumental concern (to maximize human happiness), the agent's concern for benevolence is not merely of instrumental concern. The benevolence of the agent "is, as it were, the perspective from which the benevolence of others attains a kind of (instrumental) moral significance, but his [the agent's] own benevolence cannot, itself, attain moral significance from this perspective, because it *is* the perspective. It is in this way that even for a utilitarian one's own character has a special status that is denied to others" (Solomon 1997, 173).

Still, some Aristotle scholars try to go beyond this partners-in-crime argument by showing that Aristotle's eudaimonism can avoid the self-centeredness objection on this deep level.[19] The strongest evidence for them is a passage in which Aristotle discusses what they regard as moral competitions: "those, then, who busy themselves in an exceptional degree with noble actions all men approve and praise; and if *all* were to strive towards what is noble and strain every nerve to do the noblest deeds, everything would be as it should be for the common weal, and everyone would secure for himself the goods that are greatest, since virtue is the greatest of goods" (Aristotle, 1169a6–12). Richard Kraut, for example, argues that Aristotle here is talking about the moral competition among virtuous agents. Such competition "differs from other forms of competition in precisely this respect: normally, when people try to outdo one another, one person's gain is another's loss; but when virtuous individuals 'compete for the fine' then everyone benefits in some way or other" (Kraut 1989, 117). To illustrate this, Kraut uses the analogy of a competition among solo musicians: "The better each plays, the more likely he is to win, but at the same time, everyone else benefits by the fact that each is striving to do his best" (Kraut 1989, 117).

The idea is that my playing to my best will cause others to play to their best, as we all want to win the competition. So in this moral competition among virtuous persons, the more I try to develop my own virtuous characters, the more I do to develop the virtuous characters of others. Julia Annas makes a similar point. In her view, since Aristotle has redefined self-love as love of one's virtuous character,

it is not surprising that the competition between true self-lovers
is also redefined, and turns out to be wholly different from the
common understanding of competition. Normally competition is
for a limited good, and hence is at others' expense; if I get more
you will get less. But when people "compete to be virtuous" what
they do is not at the others' expense, for Aristotle insists that *each*
person gets the greatest good, since "virtue is that kind of thing."
Virtue is an inexhaustible good; if I have more this does not leave
less for you. (Annas 1993, 297)

So although neither Kraut nor Annas clearly states it, the significant difference
between the moral competition and other forms of competition is perhaps that,
while in the latter there is normally only one winner, in the former everyone
can be a winner, as if the referee of the competition had a different criterion
from the one used in other forms of competition. In a normal race, for example,
the winner is the fastest runner. However, in the Aristotelian race, the winner
is the one who does his best. Thus, while it is possible that the winner runs
slower than others (as those who run faster than the winner may have not
done their best), it is also possible that everyone is a winner (if everyone does
his best). It is perhaps in this sense that Kraut claims that "when Aristotelian
agents compete with one another to be best, each places far more emphasis on
doing as well as he can than on doing better than others" (Kraut 1989, 119).

This is indeed an interesting interpretation. However, as a response to
the self-centeredness objection, there are at least three serious problems. First,
to what degree can we make sense of the moral competition among virtuous
persons? To show what I mean, let us look at a couple of examples used by
Aristotelian scholars to explain the following passage of Aristotle in the context
of moral competition: the true self-lover, among other things, will "sacrifice
actions to his friend, since it may be finer to be responsible for his friends'
doing the action than to do it himself. In everything praiseworthy, then, the
excellent person awards himself what is fine" (*NE* 1169a33–36). Christopher
Toner illustrates this self-lover's self-sacrifice of virtuous action by such a
scenario: two of us are friends and fellow members of a platoon engaged in
a dangerous reconnaissance. One volunteer is needed to be the first to cross
an open area. I am moved to volunteer, but I recall that you have unfairly
acquired a reputation for cowardice and wanted to clear this reputation. So I
remain silent so that you can be the first (see Toner 2006, 611). Richard Kraut
provides a similar illustration: Suppose that I think my friend is capable of
supervising major civic projects, but that he has had too few opportunities to

show his worth. So I persuade public officials who oversee such projects to secure the opportunity for him (Kraut 1989, 126).

In each example, the virtuous person sacrifices a virtuous action so that a friend can perform them. In this case, the virtuous person awards herself what is fine, while her friend has the chance to perform the virtuous actions. However, there is something wrong here. In both cases, the virtuous person's friend is already virtuous. In Toner's example, the courageous friend just has a bad reputation of being a coward, and the virtuous person's sacrifice of the courageous action helps this friend to restore personal honor. However, this does not make the friend more virtuous, as for Aristotle, honor belongs to the same category as money and wealth, things that the self-lovers in the vulgar sense love. A truly virtuous person is only concerned with being virtuous, not with being known for being virtuous. As a matter of fact, as Thrasymachus in Plato's *Republic* says of the perfectly virtuous (just) person, "though doing no wrong, he must have the repute of the greatest injustice, so that he may be put to the test as regards justice through not softening because of ill repute and the consequences thereof. But let him hold on his course unchangeable even unto death, seeming all his life to be unjust though being just" (Plato 1963b, 361c). In Kraut's example, the virtuous person sacrifices his virtuous action for his friend so that the friend can have an opportunity to show his worth. This assumes that a person who has more opportunities to perform virtuous actions is more virtuous than a person who has fewer opportunities to do so. This assumption is wrong. It focuses too much on actions. A virtuous person is simply one who does virtuous things whenever such circumstances arise. Moreover, as Hurka has pointed out, "though a person can certainly act virtuously, she can also have virtuous desires and feelings that never issue in action—for example, compassion for someone whose pain she is unable to relieve" (Hurka 2001, 8). After all, Aristotle himself also claims that virtue is related to both action and feeling.

Second, as shown in both Toner's and Kraut's examples, those who are in the moral competition must already be somehow virtuous persons or true self-lovers. Only virtuous persons are willing to join the moral competition, and virtuous persons compete with only virtuous persons. This causes an immediate problem. The self-centeredness objection to virtue ethics is precisely about the virtuous agent's lack of interest in making others virtuous. While there is no need for a virtuous person to be concerned about the character of another virtuous person, we need to know whether a virtuous person in the Aristotelian sense is also concerned or able to make nonvirtuous persons virtuous. On the one hand, in his discussion of friendship, Aristotle makes it clear that this is friendship of characters, that is, friendship among virtuous people.[20] Moreover, as pointed out by Kraut, if a virtuous friend turns out to be bad, the virtuous person who breaks off such a friendship would seem to be doing nothing strange (1165b13–21; see Kraut 1989, 111). This shows that the Aristotelian virtuous person is not concerned with the character of nonvirtuous persons. On the other hand, the Aristotelian virtuous person's action is unable to make nonvirtuous persons virtuous. Suppose that the person to whom the virtuous person in Toner's example sacrifices his action is indeed a coward. Will the virtuous person's sacrifice in this particular situation make the friend courageous? A coward is so not because of a lack of opportunities to encounter dangerous situations, but because this person is too scared to act whenever he encounters dangerous situations. So, if anything, the virtuous person's refraining from performing the courageous action would only make the person not feel guilty of being a coward, as he would see no one doing anything differently: those who are cowards just like him, as cowards, will not move forward, and those who, unlike him, have the virtue of courage would decide to sacrifice their courageous actions to those cowards. If a courageous (virtuous) person can make a coward (vicious person) become courageous (virtuous) by sacrificing courageous (virtuous) actions to the coward (vicious person), then a coward (vicious person) can also perform this function, as a coward (vicious person) naturally makes such "sacrifices" for others. Moreover, if such a negative sacrificing (withdrawing from virtuous actions) is useful to make a vicious person virtuous, we might even have to endorse such positive actions, which otherwise are considered vicious, as virtuous. For example, continuously harassing a person may be useful to cultivate in the person harassed the virtue of endurance. This of course is absurd, as it implies that vicious persons are really virtuous persons, as they "selflessly" not only give opportunities to others but even create them for others to perform virtuous actions.[21]

Third, even in the moral competition among somehow already virtuous persons, one's effort to develop one's own virtues as fully as possible may indeed cause competitors to make a similar effort to develop their own virtues as fully as possible. However, this looks like the invisible hand justification of individual greediness in competition in a well-ordered market economy: the more one strives for one's own interest, the more the person contributes to others' welfare. In such competitions, it is true that everyone's self-centered actions benefit others in the competition as a consequence, but one joins the competition for one's self-interest and not for the benefit of others. Some Aristotle scholars disagree about this. They think that virtuous persons not only make others virtuous as a by-product of their being virtuous but also intend to make others virtuous. However, this view is often supported by problematic inferences from some ambiguous passages in Aristotle. For example, Kraut infers that virtuous "friends help each other develop in character and correct each other" (Kraut 1989, 121) from Aristotle's claims that "a certain training in virtue arises also from the company of the good" (Aristotle 1915, 1170a11–12) and that "the friendship of good men is good, being augmented by their companionship; and they are thought to become better too by their activities and by improving each other; for from each other they take the mould of the characteristics they approve" (Aristotle 1915, 1172a12–14). Obviously, what Aristotle says in these passages about the improvement of virtues can also be read in such a way that is entirely compatible with the invisible hand argument.

Dennis McKerlie makes some similar inferences. Aristotle says that the good man "is related to his friend as to himself" (Aristotle 1915, 1166a31–32). From this McKerlie infers that, for Aristotle, "in this kind of friendship we should feel a concern for another person that does not differ importantly in its nature from the concern we feel for ourselves. . . . [W]e should care about the friend's realizing *eudaimonia* in much the same way that we care about realizing it ourselves. So the friend's *eudaimonia* should be almost as fundamental a goal as our own *eudaimonia*" (McKerlie 1991, 88). Aristotle also says that "as his own being is desirable for each man, so, or almost so, is that of the friend" (Aristotle 1915, 1170b7–8). For McKerlie, this passage "could mean that the good man values the friend's existence to almost the same extent that he values his own existence, or that he values the friend's existence in almost the same way or manner in which he values his own existence. . . . [T]he key to the argument is the thought that the friend is another self. . . . I should care about the friend's *eudaimonia* in the way that I care about my own *eudaimonia*" (McKerlie 1991, 96–97). However, in both cases, Aristotle can also be understood as saying that a virtuous person should only make friends with virtuous persons.

I do not deny the possibility of making such inferences to show that Aristotle's virtuous person is interested in the virtues of others (though these "others" are clearly limited to those who are already somehow virtuous) so that the self-centeredness objection to virtue ethics may be responded to by Aristotelian virtue ethicists. However, when we turn to the Cheng brothers' neo-Confucianism, we are presented with a much clearer, more direct, and brighter picture. In the Chengs' view, a person is superior or virtuous (*junzi* 君子) not simply because he or she has the disposition to provide material and external comforts to people in need, but also because he or she has the disposition to make others virtuous. This is most clear in their interpretation of the beginning sentences of the *Great Learning*: "the way of great learning is to *ming ming de* 明明德, *xin min* 新民, and *zhi shan* 至善." Particularly relevant to our concern here are *ming ming de* and *xin min*. According to common interpretation, *ming ming de* and *xin min* are two different items. The former is related to oneself: to brighten one's own originally bright virtue. The latter is related to others: to love (here *xin* 新 is interpreted as *qin* 親, love) people. Thus understood, it may also be subject to the self-centeredness objection to virtue ethics on the deeper level, particularly if we understand loving people in the normal sense of providing people with material and external goods. However, in the Chengs' interpretation, "to *ming ming de* and *xin min* cannot be separated. They are both things necessary for one to become virtuous" (*Yishu* 6; 84). In their view, "*ming ming de* is to understand the *dao*, and *xin min* is to let people transform themselves with this *dao*" (*Yishu* 2a; 22). A person is not virtuous or does not understand *dao* if the person is not interested in letting others transform themselves with this *dao* so that they can also become virtuous.

For this reason, the Chengs make frequent references to Mencius's claim that those who are awake first should wake those who are not awake yet (*Mencius* 5a7). In the Chengs' view, a virtuous person is like the person who is awake, that is, understands *dao*, first. Thus, CHENG Yi claims that "the learning of superior persons is that those who understand *dao* first should enlighten those who have not understood it yet, and those who are awake first should wake up those who are not awake yet. In contrast, according to Laozi, instead of enlightening others, [those who understand *dao* first] should keep others ignorant" (*Yishu* 25; 322). In CHENG Yi's view, those who claim to have obtained knowledge and therefore fulfilled their nature and yet are not interested in enlightening others are "destroying their own nature" (*Yishu* 25; 322). In other words, the very meaning of being awake implies being disposed to wake up those who are not yet awake, and the very meaning of fulfilling one's own nature implies fulfilling the nature of others. A person who appears to be awake and yet does not proceed to wake up others is not really awake, and a person who appears to be virtuous and yet does not proceed to make others virtuous is not really virtuous. Thus, for the Chengs, "how could a person who is awake not wake up others?" (*Yishu* 1; 5). In another place, interpreting *Analects* 14.42, CHENG Yi also states that "if one thinks that it is enough to have oneself ordered, one is not a sage yet" (*Yishu* 15; 169).

So in the Chengs' view, a person cannot be regarded as virtuous unless the person also has the disposition to make others virtuous. One's self-cultivation and moral cultivation of others are one and the same process: "One's heart/mind possesses the heavenly virtue. When one's heart/mind is not fully realized, the heavenly virtue is not fully realized. When one tries to fully realize one's own heart/mind, one is also fully realizing [the heart/mind] of other people and things" (*Yishu* 5; 78). In other words, to fully realize one's virtue and to realize the virtue of others, to make oneself virtuous and to make others virtuous, are one and the same thing. For example, CHENG Hao claims that "to arouse people and cultivate their virtue" is the way a superior person cultivates himself and others (*Yishu* 14; 140). Clearly, CHENG Hao does not regard cultivating the virtue in others as something a superior person can or should do only after cultivating his or her own virtue. Instead, to cultivate the virtue in others is inherent in one's cultivating the virtue in oneself. In other words, a virtuous person cannot *not* be concerned with the virtue of others. This claim of the Chengs was objected to as providing an unrealistic short cut: when one becomes virtuous, everyone becomes virtuous automatically (see *Yishu* 10, 115). What the Chengs mean, however, is that a person cannot become virtuous without being concerned about the virtue of others. Thus in his interpretation of the *Zhongyong*, CHENG Yi states that "if one wants to bring one's own goodness to completion, one will necessarily think how to bring the goodness of others to completion" (*Jingshuo* 8; 1161), and "as soon as one cultivates oneself, one knows how to cultivate others" (*Jingshuo* 8; 1157).[22]

It is important, however, to point out that, in their interpretation of *xin min* in the *Great Learning*, what they say is, instead of transforming people with this *dao*, "to make people to transform themselves with this *dao*" (*shi ren yong ci dao yi zi xin* 使人用此道以自新). Similarly, in their interpretation of *Mencius* 5a7, where a virtuous person (one who is already awake) enlightens those who are not virtuous yet (wake up those who are not awake yet), it is emphasized that "this is not to take something out of me [virtuous person] to give it to you [one who is not virtuous yet], for you yourself also possess the moral principle (*yili* 義理); only that I am aware of it [and you are not yet]" (*Yishu* 1; 5). While a virtuous person can try to help others become aware of the moral virtue, the former cannot force it upon others. For the Chengs, a person can become virtuous ultimately by oneself. Virtue as moral knowledge cannot be taught to others in the same way scientific knowledge is taught, because moral knowledge is not acquired merely through intellectual understanding but, more importantly, through inner experience. For this reason, the Chengs put great emphasis on self-getting (*zi de* 自得). At the same time, however, this does not mean that virtue as moral knowledge cannot be taught at all, and a person should only care about personal virtue. Thus, when Wang

Yanlin 王彥霖, one of the Chengs' students, says that "a person can become good only when the person himself or herself is willing to become virtuous. We cannot force a person to be virtuous," CHENG Hao replies, "While it is true that a person need be willing to be good himself or herself, we cannot therefore leave him or her alone. There is a need for education" (*Yishu* 1, 2). Although CHENG Yi states that "in relation to others, superior persons look for merits in their faults, instead of looking for faults in their merits" (*Yishu* 21a, 272), he does not mean that we should do nothing with people infected with vice. When one of his students asks, "When I see a person I live with has some fault, I feel uneasy in my heart/mind. Yet what to do if I point this out and the person is unwilling to accept?" Cheng replies, "To live with the person and yet not to point out his or her fault is not *zhong* 忠. The important thing is to be sincere with the person before talking to him or her. Then he or she will trust what you say" (*Yishu* 4; 74). He also says that "the way to demand goodness [from others] is to have more than enough sincerity and less than enough talking" (*Yishu* 4; 75).[23]

However, the most important way a virtuous person is concerned with the virtue of others, in the Chengs' view, is to set a personal example, to be a virtuous person. Thus, CHENG Yi points out, "The way superior persons cultivate people is to teach them to improve themselves in aspects in which they are not as good as others so that they can be as good as others. In order to cultivate people, one need cultivate oneself through *zhong* 忠 and *shu* 恕. To demand one's sons to be filial, one first realizes how deficient one is to serve one's parents. The same is the case with one's demands upon one's subordinate, one's younger brother, and one's friend" (*Cheng Shi Jingshuo* 8; 1155). It is in this sense that Cheng emphasizes Mencius's idea of "great people" (*da ren* 大人) as those who make themselves upright so that others will be upright [by themselves]" (*Mencius* 7a19) (*Yishu* 9, 105; see also *Yishu* 11; 119). So in the hypothetical situation imagined by Toner, a virtuous person in the Confucian tradition will not "selflessly" yield to others the opportunity to perform the courageous action, as only by setting a good example by being courageous in such a dangerous situation can the virtuous (courageous) person move others to act in the same way in similar future situations. Thus, to be virtuous oneself of course implies that one does all appropriate things to provide material and external comfort to others in need. However, in the Chengs' view, a virtuous person does so not merely for the sake of such material and external comfort for others, but also to move others to be virtuous as well. Thus, CHENG Yi claims that "sincerity can [morally] touch people (*dong ren* 動人). The reason that there is [moral] transformation wherever a superior person passes is nothing but this exemplary moving power" (*Yishu* 18; 203; see also *Yishu* 18; 185).[24] The Chengs believe in the moving power of such moral education. CHENG Yi, for example, in his interpretation of the sentence at the very beginning of the *Analects*, "What a joy it is to have friends to visit from afar," points out that this is because a virtuous person's "goodness touches others, who become morally converted; and this brings joy to the virtuous person" (*Jingshuo* 6; 1133).

6. The Self-Centeredness Objection: The Foundational Level

We have now examined the Cheng brothers' Confucian response to the self-centeredness objection to virtue ethics on both the surface level and the deeper level as discussed by David Solomon, an advocate of virtue ethics himself. A virtuous person desires to do virtuous things and feels happy when such a desire is satisfied. This, however, does not mean that this person is self-centered. First, the things that the virtuous person desires to do are virtuous things, things that require concern about the interest and welfare of others. Second, the interest and welfare of others that a virtuous person is concerned with are not limited to their external and material benefits but also include their characters. As we have seen, while both Confucianism and Aristotelianism have resources for the former, clear evidence for the latter can only be found in Confucianism.

However, the self-centeredness objection goes even deeper than anticipated by Solomon. What I have in mind is Thomas Hurka's objection that virtue ethics is foundationally egoistic. This objection agrees that a virtuous person is concerned with the interest of others; it would agree with Confucians that the interest of others the virtuous person is concerned with includes their character; and it would even agree that the virtuous person is concerned with the good, whether external or internal, of others for their own sake and not merely for the sake of the virtuous agent. However, it claims that virtue ethics is still self-centered or egoistic, for the virtuous person is concerned with the interest of others, including their characters, for their sake, ultimately because the person is concerned with fully realizing his or her virtue. In Hurka's view, virtue ethics

> presupposes an egoistic theory of normative reasons whereby all a
> person's reasons for action derive from his flourishing. The resulting
> virtue-ethical theory need not be egoistic in its substantive claims
> about action; it can tell people to promote others' pleasure and

knowledge [and, we may add, virtue] even at the expense of their own. Nor need it be egoistic about motivation: it can say that to act virtuously, they must care about others' pleasure and knowledge [and virtue] for its own sake. But it is what I will call foundationally egoistic, insisting that their reasons to act and be motivated in these ways derive *ultimately* from their own flourishing. (Hurka 2001, 232; emphasis added)

This further objection of Hurka is partially a response to Julia Annas's defense that virtue ethics is not self-centered or egoistic. In her response, Annas makes a distinction between self-centeredness in content and self-centeredness in form. She thinks that a virtuous person is not self-centered in content but can be regarded as self-centered in form:

What I have to develop, in order successfully to achieve my final good, are the *virtues*. . . . [B]ut all virtues are dispositions to do the right thing, where this is established in ways that are independent of my own interest. Thus the fact I aim at my own final end makes ancient ethics formally agent-centered or self-centered, but does not make it self-centered in content. . . . [A]chieving my final good, happiness, whatever that turns out to be, will involve respecting and perhaps furthering the good of others. (Annas 1993, 223)

Annas insists that a virtuous person is committed by being virtuous to respecting and furthering the good of others for their sake and not merely as instrumental to his or her own good or end. Still, Annas agrees that virtue ethics is self-centered in form, as a virtuous person respects and furthers the good of others in an effort to achieve his or her final good. This, in Hurka's view, means "that they [virtue theories] connect all of a person's reasons for action to his own flourishing. Assuming his flourishing is a state of him, this makes the theories egoistic in my foundational sense" (Hurka 2001, 232–33 note 28). While Hurka can agree that a virtuous person respects and furthers the good of others for the sake of others, the virtuous person does it in such a way that it is ultimately self-beneficial. In other words, a virtuous person is concerned with his or her own good, but due to the special nature of this good (virtue), the virtuous person has to be concerned with the good of others, and to be so for their sake. To use Richard Kraut's terms, it is for one's own sake that a virtuous person should benefit others for their sake. While Kraut himself finds it unintelligible to talk about "benefit[ing] others for their sake for your own sake" (Kraut 1989, 136), we can see the point that Hurka tries to make. On one level, the virtuous person, in contrast to a prudential person, does benefit others for their sake. If the person benefits others for self-gain, whether externally or internally, the person is not a virtuous person. However, on a higher level, the virtuous person does so for his or her own sake: to be a virtuous person. Now, according to Hurka, it is "not virtuous—it is morally self-indulgent—to act primarily from concern for one's own virtue. Someone motivated by the theory's claims about reasons will therefore be motivated not virtuously but in an unattractively self-indulgent way" (Hurka 2001, 246).[25]

One way to respond to this self-centeredness objection to virtue ethics on the foundational level is that the virtuous person is fundamentally, ultimately, or simply foundationally other-regarding. It is true that the virtuous person seeks his or her goal, but that goal is to respect and further the good of others. In this sense, a virtuous person seeks his or her goal only to realize the goal of respecting and furthering the good of others.[26] In other words, a virtuous person is concerned with the good of others. Only in the sense that the goal of respecting and furthering the good of others is the virtuous person's goal and not anyone else's goal, the virtuous person is virtuous for his her own sake. However, no one can seek a goal other than one's own. When one seeks the goals of others, one regards such goals as one's own. So to imitate what Richard Kraut says, it is perhaps to benefit others for my sake for their sake. Kraut would certainly regard it as also unintelligible, but the implied idea here is that, while (as Julia Annas says) the virtuous person aims at her own flourishing "just in the sense that she is living her life and not mine" (Annas 2006, 522), the life she lives is to respect and further the good of others. Thus, the virtuous person is essentially other-regarding. If the self-centeredness objection claims that virtue ethics reduces the good of others to the good of the agent, this reply to the objection seems to claim that the good of the virtuous agent is reduced to that of others. However, in this sense, Hurka claims that, instead of self-indulgence, virtue ethics then turns out to be self-effacing: virtue ethicists

> can say that to flourish or express virtue, a person must act from genuinely virtuous motives, such as a desire for another's pleasure for its own sake. If she instead aims at her own flourishing or virtue, she does not act from the required motives and so does not achieve the flourishing or virtue that is her goal. This requires the theories to be what Parfit calls *self-effacing*, telling agents not to be motivated by or even to think of their claims about the source of their reasons. (Hurka 2001, 246)

This, Hurka claims, is ironic, because "some partisans of virtue ethics have been vocal critics of the self-effacingness of consequential theories . . . but their own theories have the same feature, if anything in a more disturbing way" (Hurka 2001, 246).

To avoid this dilemma between self-indulgence and self-effacingness, a correct understanding of the nature of virtue, particularly Confucian virtues, is not to see it as either foundationally self-indulgent (for the sake of oneself) or as foundationally self-effacing (for the sake of others); it is rather both "to benefit others and to benefit oneself." Moreover, it is not to see them as two independent reasons, as Kraut says (Kraut 1989, 137), as if a virtuous person can have one without having the other or can have one before the other; it is rather to see them as two sides of one and the same reason. As we have seen, a virtuous person in the Confucian tradition cannot be an altruist (serving the interests of others) without taking good care of one's own great body, to use Mencius's terms. In this sense, an altruist has to be an "egoist"; however, one cannot be an "egoist" (taking care of one's own great body) without serving the interests of others. In this sense, an "egoist" has to be an altruist. Thus, the two apparently antithetical ideas, egoism and altruism, or self-regarding and other-regarding, are combined. Moreover, they are combined not in such a way that a virtuous person is partially egoistic and partially altruistic, but in a way that the person is completely "egoistic" and completely altruistic: a virtuous person acts entirely for the sake of one's true self and so is completely egoistic; however, this is only because the virtuous person realizes his or her true self as one concerned with the good of others and so is entirely altruistic. It is not correct to say that the virtuous person is primarily or foundationally an "egoist" as if he takes care of the interests of others only as a means to serve the interest of his own true self, just as it is not correct to say that the virtuous person is primarily or foundationally an altruist as if he takes care of his own true self only as a way to serve others. Rather, altruism and egoism here completely overlap. As illustrated by the figure used by Wittgenstein in his *Philosophical Investigations*, which looks like a duck in one way and a rabbit in another (Wittgenstein 1958, 194), a virtuous person looks like an egoist in one way (working toward his or her goal) and an altruist in another way (working to serve the interest of others).

In this sense, it is wrong to ask, as a Kantian may well be tempted to, whether a virtuous person does a virtuous thing because he or she thinks it is to his or her interest or because the person thinks it is really the right thing to do. In the Kantian view, if the former, the person does the virtuous thing for a wrong reason; and only if the latter can the person's action have any genuine moral value. In Confucian virtue ethics, however, to be self-interested and to be concerned with others are not only not contradictory; they are even not two things that happen to coincide perfectly: they are actually one and the same thing. When one seeks one's true self-interest, one must be doing virtuous things; and when one does virtuous things, one must be seeking one's true self-interest. Thus, we can say that a person seeks the interest of others (is other-regarding) precisely in order to seek one's own interest (be self-regarding); and we can also say that a person seeks one's own interest (is self-regarding) precisely in order to seek the interest of others (be other-regarding). To be self-interested in this sense is identical to being interested in others. The very action that promotes the interest of others, precisely when and because it promotes the interest of others, promotes one's self-interest, as one's self-interest is precisely to promote the interest of others. Thus, the more virtuous (more concerned with the interest of others) a person is, the better his or her self-interest is served, and vice versa.

In this connection, I think Harry Frankfurt's analysis of love is quite interesting. According to Frankfurt, there are two aspects of love. On the one hand, "the inherent importance of loving is due precisely to the fact that loving consists essentially in being devoted to the well-being of what we love. The value of loving to the lover derives from his dedication to his beloved. As for the importance of the beloved, the lover cares about what he loves for its own sake"; on the other hand, "what he loves necessarily possesses an instrumental value for him, in virtue of the fact that it is a necessary condition of his enjoying the inherently important activity of loving it" (Frankfurt 2003, 59). These two aspects are so closely interwoven that, for Frankfurt, it is foolish to ask whether I love someone for the sake of the beloved or for the sake of my own enjoyment in loving the person. He uses the following example to make his point: "Consider a man who tells a woman that his love for her is what gives meaning and value to his life . . . [T]he woman is unlikely to feel that what the man is telling her implies that he does not really love her at all, and that he cares about her only because it makes him feel good. From his declaration that his love for her fulfills a deep need of his life, she will surely not conclude that he is making use of her" (Frankfurt 2003, 60).[27] So what is most distinctive about virtue ethics in general and Confucian virtue ethics in particular is that, when a virtuous person takes care of the interest of others, that person does not have to overcome the inclination. Instead one takes delight in being concerned with others, because, by being concerned with others, one satisfies one's desire, achieves one's goal, realizes one's true self, and therefore feels happy. This is indeed one of the unique features of virtue ethics.

However, it might be asked why it is not enough for one simply to be moral but one must take delight in being so. This is perhaps also what is behind the self-centeredness objection to virtue ethics. When asked why a virtuous person should benefit others, the virtue ethics explains, in the end, that "this will make his life better or admirable, but that is, intuitively, not the right explanation. The right explanation is that it will make the other's life better" (Hurka 2001, 249). It is is obvious that the moral life recommended by virtue ethics must be a better life for the agent than the lives recommended by alternative theories of ethics. For example, Michael Stocker asks, "[W]hat sort of life would people live who did their duties but never or rarely wanted to?" (Stocker 1997, 67). Obviously, whether such a life is good for others for whom one performs moral duties, this cannot be a good life for the moral agent, as the agent has to make a great effort to overcome his or her natural inclination in order to perform moral actions and therefore cannot take delight in doing so. This is made most clear by Kant's separation of morality from happiness. Of course, critics of virtue ethics think that whether a moral life is good to the agent is at least not the most important thing we need to keep in mind when we are talking about morality; what matters is whether it is good for moral patients. However, contrary to what we may normally think, moral actions recommended by nonvirtual ethical theories are not necessarily good for moral patients either. This point is made most clear by Michael Stocker's following hypothetical scenario:

> Suppose you are in a hospital, recovering from a long illness. You are very bored and restless and at loose ends when Smith comes in once again. You are now convinced more than ever that he is a fine fellow and a real friend—taking so much time to cheer you up, traveling all the way across town, and so on. You are so effusive with your praise and thanks that he protests that he always tries to do what he thinks is his duty, what he thinks will be best. . . . [T]he more you two speak, the more clear it becomes that. . . . it is not essentially because of you that he came to see you, not because you are friends, but because he thought it his duty . . . or simply because he knows of no one more in need of cheering up and no one easier to cheer up. (Stocker 1997, 74)

This example shows clearly that only when and because a virtuous person's action benefiting others makes the person's life better can it make the lives of others better.

7. Conclusion

In this chapter, I claim that Confucianism in general and the Chengs' neo-Confucianism in particular are examples of virtue ethics, a type of ethical theory that has emerged or, rather, revived in the Western philosophical world in the last few decades. However, my interest is not to justify this claim but to explore the possible contribution that Confucianism can make to contemporary virtue ethics. With this in mind, I focus on the self-centeredness objection to virtue ethics. The objection states that, since virtue ethics recommends that we be concerned with our own virtues or virtuous characters, it is self-centered. In response, I argue that, for the Chengs, the self that a virtuous person is concerned with is precisely such virtues that incline that person to be concerned with the good of others. While such an answer is also available to the Aristotelian eudaimonistic virtue ethics, I argue that the Chengs' neo-Confucianism can better respond to the objection. First, Aristotelian virtue ethicists claim that virtue makes its possessor a characteristically human being and a characteristic human being is one with rational activity. However, they fail to show that a rational being has to be morally virtuous. In contrast, the Chengs' neo-Confucianism claims that a characteristic human being is a virtuous being. Thus it shows in a more convincing way that virtue can make its possessor a characteristic human being. Second, the self-centeredness objection goes a step further, claiming that, while a virtuous person, as in the eudaimonistic virtue ethics, is concerned with the external and material goods of others, he or she is concerned with his or her own character. Since virtue ethics thinks that one's character is more important than the material benefit, virtue ethics is self-centered in this deeper sense. I argue that a virtuous person in the Chengs' neo-Confucianism, unlike one in Aristotelianism, is virtuous because the person takes care of not only the material well-being but also the character traits of others. Third, the Chengs' neo-Confucianism can even respond to the self-centeredness objection on Hurka's foundational level: a virtuous person promotes the good, both internal and external, of others, ultimately for the sake of his or her own good. I argue that, in the Chengs' neo-Confucianism, one's concern with oneself and one's concern with others are inseparable and therefore one cannot say which is more foundational or ultimate.[28]

Chapter 3

Knowledge (*zhi* 知)

How Is Weakness of the Will (*akrasia*) *Not* Possible?

1. Introduction

Chapter 1 provides an answer to the question "Why should I be moral?": because you are a human! Chapter 2 argues that such a virtue ethical answer is not self-centered. Assuming that this is an appropriate answer, we can now proceed to discuss a related question: "Can I be moral?" Although our discussion in previous chapters has already touched upon this issue, we will discuss it in more detail in relation to the issue of *akrasia* or weakness of the will. While the issue of *akrasia* belongs to a broader theory of action, our concern in this chapter is primarily with its moral aspect. Often we hear it said that "I know what is moral, but I just cannot do it" or "I know it is wrong, but I just cannot help but do it." The purpose of this chapter is to provide an adequate response to such claims and to show that (1) if one has genuine moral knowledge, one cannot fail to act according to such knowledge; and (2) if one makes an effort, one will be able to acquire such genuine knowledge.

In 1970, Donald Davidson published an influential article, "How Is Weakness of the Will Possible?" reviving and reversing an ancient discussion on the issue of *akrasia*. In addition to "weakness of the will," the Greek term *akrasia* has also been translated as "incontinence" and "unrestraint." According to Davidson's definition, "in doing *x* an agent acts incontinently if and only if: (*a*) the agent does *x* intentionally; (*b*) the agent believes there is an alternative

99

action y open to him; and (c) the agent judges that, all things considered, it would be better to do y than to do x" (Davidson 1969, 22). For example, if one knows that, all things considered, it is better to refrain from smoking, which one believes one can, and yet still smokes intentionally, this person then acts incontinently. Philosophers since ancient times have tried to understand whether weakness of the will is possible, and if possible, how it is possible; or, if it is not possible, how to explain the apparent cases of people knowing without acting in everyday life.

To bring this issue into a sharper focus, it is important to understand how weakness of the will, thus defined, is different from some similar situations. Michael Smith distinguishes weakness of the will from (a) recklessness or intemperance and (b) compulsion. He uses an example of a particular woman intentionally taking a drink that she ought not to have because she will then be unfit to fulfill some of her obligations: "In (1) [recklessness or intemperance] the woman knows what she is doing but accepts the consequences. Her choice is to get drunk or risk getting drunk. She acts in accordance with her judgement. In (2) [weakness of the will] the woman knowingly takes the drink contrary to her (conscious) better judgement; the explanation for this lack of self-control is that she is weak-willed. In (3) [compulsion], she knowingly takes the drink contrary to her better judgement, but she is the victim of a compulsive (irresistible) desire to drink" (Smith 2003, 17–18). R. M. Hare further distinguishes weakness of the will from (c) hypocrisy, in which case a person does (or does not do) what she says she ought not to (or ought not to) do, but does not say sincerely what she actually thinks (see Hare 1963, 82–83). In addition to these, I think it also helpful if we further distinguish weakness of the will from the following phenomena: (d) Ignorance. In this case, a man, for example, smokes because he does not know that smoke is bad and that he ought not to smoke; (e) Negligence, which is related to (d) in the sense that the person also acts from ignorance, but the ignorance in this case is caused by the person's negligence: he or she could and ought to know what he or she is doing and whether he or she ought to do it; (f) Rational choice, which can best be explained by an example: a person may know smoking is unhealthy; at the same time, the person also knows that smoking is pleasant. So the person faces a dilemma: either to live a longer, less satisfying life without smoking or live a shorter but more exciting life and smoke. After some deliberation, this person chooses the former.

Now all these phenomena (a–f) are easily understandable, and nobody would ask whether they are possible, as we can certainly find many examples of each in our daily life. However, the issue of weakness of the will is different.

It is supposed to describe a situation in which one does intentionally what one believes sincerely one could and ought not to do (or does not do intentionally what one believes sincerely one could and ought to do). For this reason, many ancient philosophers argue that not only is there no weak-willed person in this sense, but weakness of the will is simply impossible. Any case considered as weakness of will is nothing but one of the above six phenomena in disguise. Thus, whoever thinks that weakness of the will is possible (or even actual) must bear the burden of proof to show how it is possible. In the following, I shall first briefly introduce the problem of the weakness of the will in the Western philosophical discussion (section 2); I shall then discuss the Cheng brothers' (particularly CHENG Yi's) related conceptions of (1) the relationship between knowledge and action (section 3) and (2) the distinction between the two types of knowledge (knowledge from hearing and seeing and knowledge of/as virtue) (section 4). Through these two conceptions, the Chengs show not only that weakness of the will is not possible but also how it is not possible. This view is diametrically opposite to the dominant view in contemporary Western philosophy, largely influenced by Donald Davidson and, accordingly, is obviously similar to the view of Socrates and Aristotle. However, I argue that, in a number of important aspects, the Chengs' view on weakness of the will is not only different from but also superior to those of Socrates and Aristotle (sections 5 and 6); I shall conclude with a brief general comment (section 7).

2. The Problem of Weakness of the Will in Western Philosophy

Socrates, in Plato's *Protagoras*, is perhaps the first philosopher to discuss the issue of weakness of the will directly, and he makes it clear that weakness of the will is impossible: "[N]o one who either knows or believes that there is another possible course of action, better than the one he is following, will ever continue on his present course when he might choose the better. To 'act beneath yourself' is the result of pure ignorance; to 'be your own master' is wisdom" (Plato 1963a, 358b–c). In our example of smoking, in Socrates's view, one knows that one ought not to smoke because it will be harmful in the future but decides to smoke because it will bring pleasure now. If one indeed knows that one's future and long-term happiness are more important than the current, momentary pleasure, one will not smoke, so weakness of the will is not possible. Of course, one may choose to smoke, but in this case one must be thinking, mistakenly, that current, momentary pleasure is more important than future, long-term happiness. Now Socrates thinks that, while such mistaken judgment is easily understandable, this shows that one is ignorant of the truth, not that one is weak-willed. He uses this analogy: "The same magnitudes seem greater to the eye from near at hand than they do from a distance. . . . And sounds of equal loudness seem greater near at hand than at a distance" (Plato 1963a, 356c–d). So in Socrates's view, the so-called weakness of the will is really ignorance or misjudgment and falls into category (d), mentioned earlier, in disguise.[1]

Later this issue is taken up by Aristotle, particularly in book 7, chapter 3 of his *Ethica Nicomachea*. Aristotelian scholars disagree among themselves about whether Aristotle intends to argue against or merely explain Socrates's position. I myself tend to think that Aristotle holds a view fundamentally similar to that of Socrates. At the beginning of his discussion, Aristotle mentions Socrates's view and then immediately says that "this view plainly contradicts the observed facts" (Aristotle 1915, 1145b27). This has become the strongest evidence for those who think that Aristotle is setting the stage to argue against Socrates (see Dorter 1997, 313). However, I think they have ignored several important things. First, the Greek word, here translated as "observed facts," is *phainomena*, which can also be translated as "common opinion." Thus understood, Aristotle only says that Socrates's view is against the common opinion about weakness of the will and not against the fact about weakness of the will.[2] Second, immediately after he says that Socrates's view is plainly against common opinion, Aristotle argues that "we must inquire about what happens to such a man [*akrate*]; if he acts by reason of ignorance, what is the manner of his ignorance?" (Aristotle 1915, 1145b27–30). So here he seems to accept Socrates's view that such a man acts by reason of ignorance; and what he wants to do is simply explain the manner of such ignorance (it is noteworthy that he does not add another "if": "If he does not act by reason of ignorance . . ."). Third, and most important, at the very end of his explanation in this chapter, Aristotle maintains that "the position that Socrates sought to establish actually seems to result; for it is not in the presence of what is thought to be knowledge proper that the affection of incontinence arises (nor is it this that is 'dragged about' as a result of the state of passion), but in that of perceptual knowledge"; and he finally concludes that "this must suffice as our answer to the question of action with and without knowledge, and how it is possible to behave incontinently with knowledge" (1147b15–19).

So in my view, Aristotle's main task in this concentrated discussion of *akrasia* is basically to explain the manner of ignorance that Socrates talks about. He first makes it clear that the so-called *akrates* definitely do not have practical wisdom, since it is absurd to say that "the same man will be at once practically wise and incontinent. . . . It has been shown before that the man of practical wisdom is one who will act" (Aristotle 1915, 1146a5–9). However, if so, what exactly happens to such a man? Aristotle provides two explanations. The first is related to the distinction he makes between knowledge in the sense of possession and knowledge in the sense of using.[3] About this distinction, he says that a man asleep, mad, or drunk has knowledge in the first sense but not in the second sense; he may still be able to utter scientific proof and verses of Empedocles, but obviously he is not using such knowledge. With this analogy in mind, Aristotle claims that "this is just the condition of men under the influence of passions; for outbursts of anger and sexual appetites and some other such passions, it is evident, actually alter our bodily condition, and in some men even produce fits of madness. It is plain, then, that incontinent people must be said to be in a similar condition to men asleep, mad, or drunk. The fact that men use the language that flows from knowledge proves nothing" (Aristotle 1915, 1147a14–19). If we accept this interpretation, weakness of the will does not exist; it is really a case of phenomenon (*b*) mentioned at the beginning of this chapter: compulsion. The second explanation Aristotle provides is related to his practical syllogism. Aristotle is not clear on this issue, so scholars have tried to figure out what exactly he wants to say. What seems to be clear is that, from Aristotle's view, the so-called *akrate* lacks the minor premise of the practical syllogism. For example (not Aristotle's own example), a person may know that he or she ought not to steal (major premise), but does not know that the action he or she is going to take belongs to the category of stealing (minor premise), and so does not know that he or she ought not to take this action (conclusion) (see Aristotle 1915, 1146b5–1147a9).[4] According to this interpretation, again there is no weakness of will; what we have here is instead phenomenon (*d*), as the person who acts this way does not have all the knowledge necessary for the action in question to take place.[5]

After Aristotle, the Stoics, Augustine, Aquinas, Descartes, Leibniz, Spinoza, Locke, and Hume all discuss, directly or indirectly, the issue of weakness of the will. With the exception of Augustine and to a lesser degree Hume,[6] all of them hold a position either clearly in line with the Socratic/Aristotelian view or not far from it. Just a few years before the publication of Davidson's article, the English moral philosopher R. M. Hare again argues that weakness of the will is impossible, although his argument is largely from his normative ethics point of view. According to Hare, the word "ought," unlike the word "want," has the dimension of both universality and prescriptivity. It functions like Kant's categorical imperative. So if someone knows, for example, that he

ought not to smoke, he will not smoke; if he does, he does not really know
that he *ought* not to smoke (see Hare 1963, 67–85).

From this context, we can better appreciate the significance of Davidson's
article, "How Is Weakness of the Will Possible?" In this article, after rejecting
many attempts to explain away weakness of the will, he affirms clearly that
weakness of the will is possible. His main task in this article is to explain *how*
it is possible. To show that there are two practical syllogisms going on in the
mind of a weak-willed person as Aristotle indicates, Davidson uses Aquinas's
example of fornication in his (Aquinas's) attempt to make sense of Aristotle
(see Aquinas 1952, part 1 of Second Part Q. 77 art. 2; and Aquinas 1993, book
7, lecture 3). On the one hand, the person thinks: "No fornication is lawful;
this is an act of fornication; so this act is not lawful." On the other hand, the
person thinks: "[P]leasure is to be pursued; this act is pleasure; and so this
act is to be pursued" (see Davidson 1969, 33). Here the weak-willed person
faces two contradictory conclusions from two different practical syllogisms.
According to Davidson's definition of weakness of the will, we may consider
this person weak willed if he takes the action of fornication intentionally, while
he believes that he can refrain from this action and that, all things considered,
it would be better to refrain from this action. How is this possible? Davidson
introduces a distinction between absolute judgment and all things considered
judgment. Thus an incontinent person "does x for a reason r, but he has a
reason r' that includes r and more, on the basis of which he judges some
alternative y to be better than x" (Davidson 1969, 40). Here r is reason for
absolute judgment, while r' is all things (including r) considered judgment.
An incontinent or weak-willed person takes the action (fornication) according to his absolute reason (the act is pleasant), and so he does not act from
ignorance, but he should have acted according to his all things considered
judgment (although it is pleasant, it is unlawful, and it is more important to
avoid unlawful actions than to seek pleasant actions), since this also includes
his absolute reason. So in Davidson's view, "what is wrong is that the incontinent man acts, and judges, irrationally, for this is surely what we must say
of a man who goes against his own best judgment" (Davidson 1969, 41). In
other words, for Davidson, weakness of the will is made possible by the person's irrationality. In a later article, he further explains such irrationality by
appealing to the idea of mind partitioning: for the weak-willed person, there
are "two semi-autonomous departments of the mind, one that finds a certain
course of action to be, all things considered, best, and another that prompts
another course of action" (Davidson 1982, 300).

Davidson's 1970 article reignites the interest in the issue of weakness
of the will among contemporary philosophers; and a significant amount of

literature has been produced on this issue since then. However, with very few exceptions (see Watson 1977; Pugmire 1982, for example),[7] most authors have agreed with Davidson that weakness of the will is possible and even factual, although many have tried to provide different explanations about how it is possible.[8] Some go much further than Davidson on this issue. For example, although Davidson thinks that weakness of the will is possible, he still regards it as irrational. Alison McIntyre, however, argues that it is not necessarily irrational. The reason we regard someone as weak willed is that the person intentionally does something different from what she has better reason to do, but McIntyre thinks that we need to make a distinction between reasons a person *believes* she has and the reasons she actually *has*: "If an agent is not necessarily clear-sighted about what reasons she has on a particular occasion to act in one way rather than another, then when she deliberates, taking into account all the reasons she sees as relevant, the practical judgments that she arrives at will express what she *believes* that she has most reason to do, but they might fail to express what she actually *has* most reason to do or what it would be most rational for her to do" (McIntyre 1990, 386). In such cases, McIntyre argues, a person who does not do what she has the best reasons to do does not necessarily act irrationally (see also Audi 1990). In addition, Davidson's discussion of weakness of the will is limited to action. Robert Audi argues that weakness of will has a broad spectrum: it "manifests itself not just in action but at the level of intending and wanting" (Audi 1979, 185). In other words, if I have intentions or desires that I think I could and should not have, then I have also suffered from weakness of the will.

3. Knowledge and Action:
Why Is Weakness of the Will *Not* Possible?

As we have seen, what distinguishes weakness of the will from other related phenomena mentioned at the beginning of this chapter is that the agent is supposed to *know*, at the very moment of performing an action, that he ought not to, and is able not to, perform it. So central to the issue of weakness of will is the relationship between knowledge and action, and central to the idea of possibility of weakness of the will is the claim that one's knowledge does not necessarily lead one to action. It is in this context that it becomes fruitful to bring the Confucian tradition to our discussion of the issue of weakness of will. Although technically this issue does not arise for Confucians, the relation of knowledge and action is the central concern of the Confucian tradition, and one typical Confucian view on this issue is that knowledge leads to action. If asked whether weakness of the will is possible, the Confucian answer is "no." Confucianism holds a view very similar to that of Socrates: a person who cannot act must be nearsighted. For example, Mencius describes the immoral person as nearsighted or even stupid: as someone who abandons a comfortable home and proper road: "Humanity (*ren*) is the comfortable home and rightness is the proper road. How lamentable it is to abandon the comfortable home and divert from the proper road!" (*Mencius* 4a10); as one who cares to look for lost chickens or dogs but not one's own lost heart/ mind: "When one's chickens and dogs go astray, one cares to get them back; and yet when one's heart/mind goes astray, one does not care to get it back" (*Mencius* 6a11);[9] as someone who knows that trees need to be taken care of but not that she should be taken care of: "[E]ven with a *tong* or *zhi* tree one or two spans thick, anyone who wishes it to be alive knows that it needs to be taken care of. However, when it comes to one's own person, one does not know that it also needs to be taken care of. Does not one love one's person less than one's trees? This is unthinking to the highest degree!" (*Mencius* 6a13); as someone "who tends the ordinary trees while neglecting the valuable ones" (*Mencius* 6a14); and as someone who cares about his or her finger more than his or her heart/mind: "Now if one's third finger is bent and cannot stretch straight, although this does not cause any pain nor hinder one's use of it, if there is someone who can straighten it, one will not care about the distance [to seek the cure]. This is because one's finger is not as good as the finger of others'. When one's finger is not as good as others', one knows to dislike it; however, when one's heart/mind is not as good as others, one does not know to hate it" (*Mencius* 6a12).

In the following, I shall focus on the Cheng brothers, particularly CHENG Yi, who held a view of knowledge as prior to and implying action, which effectively denies the possibility of weakness of will. I shall argue that this position, while similar to that of Socrates and Aristotle in the Western tradition in its denying the possibility of weakness of will, can better address the concern of those contemporary Davidsonian philosophers who insist that weakness of the will is not only a logical possibility but also an actual reality.

In the view of the Cheng brothers, knowledge is prior to action. First, knowledge comes before action. CHENG Yi argues that "after all, one can act only after one obtains knowledge" (*Yishu* 18; 187). The reason is that, for CHENG Yi, knowledge serves as a light that shows us the way ahead. Thus, he points out, "knowledge has to be before action, as when walking, one has to have light to lead" (*Yishu* 3; 67); and "if there is no light from Sun, Moon, or candle, one cannot move forward. Thus a superior person values knowledge. One should study hard to apprehend the principle (*li* 理), and then one's knowledge becomes bright, so that one will not be confused" (*Cuiyan* 1; 1190). Of course, he does not mean that one can never act before one has knowledge. However, without knowledge, one's action is either blind as walking in the darkness, which is dangerous, or forced as being dragged around, which cannot be long lasting. About the danger of blind action, CHENG Yi points out that "today there are people who may attempt to act, but because their knowledge is not enough to see what to do, they become heretics, getting away from the right path without knowing the need to get back. They do not know what is good or evil inside and what is right or wrong outside. Thus, even if they have Weisheng's 尾生 virtue of trust and Zengsen's 曾參 virtue of filial piety, I do not value them" (*Yishu* 25; 320). About the problem of forced action, CHENG Yi states that "after all, one needs first to know before one can act. If one does not know, one can only observe Yao 堯 and imitate his action. However, without the great deal of Yao's wisdom and knowledge, how can one maintain one's composure and action in consistence with propriety as Yao does?" (*Yishu* 18, 187).

A question arises here: if one needs to know first before one can act, where does one's knowledge come from? It is true that both Chengs, following Mencius, accept the idea of innate knowledge (*liangzhi* 良知). For example, CHENG Hao claims that one's *liangzhi* "is given by heaven and has nothing to do with human" (*Yishu* 2a; 20). In other words, it is something that one is born with and not something that one later acquires. CHENG Yi also claims that "what is to be known is something inherent in everyone" (*Yishu* 25; 316). However, there are two things we need keep in mind. First, the innate knowledge is only moral knowledge, that is, the knowledge of what is right and wrong and what is good and evil. No one, including sages, is born with knowledge of particular affairs in the world. For example, in Cheng's view, even the Duke of Zhou (*Zhou Gong* 周公), one of Confucius's heroes, did not have foreknowledge of GUAN Shu 管叔 before he rebelled (*Yishu* 4; 71). Similarly, Confucius was regarded as a sage born with knowledge. However, as CHENG Yi points out, Confucius still "needed to ask Laodan 老聃 about particular rules of propriety and Tanzi 郯子 about names of official positions" (*Yishu* 15; 152). Second, although everyone is born with moral knowledge, except for sages, people are not aware of it, just as people asleep are not aware of what they know when they are awake. This is because the innate moral knowledge is blocked by one's private desires, just as the sun is blocked by clouds. When the clouds are cleared, however, the full sun is over there. Similarly, when one's private desires are cleared, one's innate knowledge is completely there, and nothing needs to be added to it (*Yishu* 2a; 32).

So in order to recover the innate moral knowledge, the Chengs emphasize the importance of learning. In this respect, CHENG Yi argues: "to read books in order to be clear about principles, to discuss about people and events in history and contemporary world in order to know what is right and what is wrong; to deal with human affairs in order to be appropriate: all these are ways to grasp the principle" (*Yishu* 18; 188); and "in order to learn something, one does not have to resort to discourses on *dao* in classics. One also ought to get it from one's behavior and action in consistence with proprieties" (*Waishu* 10; 404). In this passage, while he does not think that action is the only source for us to gain knowledge, CHENG Yi does regard actions according to propriety as one of the many ways to understand the principle. He even goes so far as to emphasize the importance of action for knowledge: "Only through practice can one know *li*. If you do not apply it to practice, you can never know it" (*Yishu* 3; 65).[10] Here, however, we seem to be presented with a circular argument: on the one hand, Cheng says that knowledge must come before action; on the other, he says that knowledge also comes from action. In order to makes sense of it, PANG Wanli 龐萬里 argues that in CHENG Yi, learning is clearly divided into two stages: knowing and acting. In the first stage practice is for and centered around knowledge, while in the second stage knowledge is for and centered around practice (Pang: 169–70; see also 151). While it is still unclear whether such a procedure solves the perceived circularity in Cheng's view, it is certainly not Cheng's view that in the first stage (if there are such two clearly marked stages for Cheng), the only function of action is to gain knowledge. It is of course better to act with knowledge, and everyone is able to gain the necessary knowledge to perform the action. However, in Cheng's view, there are always people who fail to make the effort to gain the necessary knowledge. For such people, it is still important to act according to proprieties established by sages. It is not self-conscious action, to be sure, but it is still better than not to act according to, or even to act against, such proprieties. It is in this context that we can better appreciate Cheng's very creative interpretation of an otherwise controversial statement in the *Analects* 8.9. The statement is normally interpreted and translated as "the people may be made to follow the path of action, but they may not be made to understand it." According to CHENG Yi: "It is not that sages do not want people to know it. Sages establish rules of propriety only to let everyone know them. . . . However, while sages can only make everyone under heaven to follow them, how can they make everyone fully understand them? This is something that sages are unable to do. This is what is meant by 'sages cannot make everyone understand it'" (*Yishu* 18; 220). Whether this is the original meaning of the *Analects* or not, Cheng's interpretation is significant in two counts for our discussion here (see appendix for detail). First, sages know that they cannot make people understand *propriety*, but still establish it for people to follow. This shows that obtaining knowledge is not the only reason sages encourage people to follow propriety. After all, to act according to propriety, even reluctantly and blindly, is still better than to not act or to act against propriety. Second, and more importantly, why can sages make their teachings known to everyone and make everyone follow them yet not be able to make them understand their teachings? As we shall see in the next section, for CHENG Yi, this is not because people are stupid. It is rather because knowledge here is the type that can incline one to act, knowledge of/as virtue (*dexing zhi zhi* 德性之知)[11] in contrast to knowledge from hearing and seeing (*wenjian zhizhi* 聞見之知). While sages can let people have knowledge from hearing and seeing, they cannot let them have knowledge of/as virtue, which, by definition, can only be obtained by oneself.

Second, CHENG Yi argues that to know is both more important and more difficult than to act, a claim apparently in contradiction, which he is clearly aware of, with what is said in the Confucian classic, the *Book of Documents*. On this, he states,

> Thus, if one wants to act, one has to know first. Not only is it dif-
> ficult to act; it is also difficult to know. The *Shangshu* 尚書 states
> that "to know is not hard; only to act is hard." It is true that it
> is hard to act, but it is also hard to know. For example, if one
> wants to go to the capital, one first needs to know which gate to
> take to exit and which road to take in order to get there. If one
> does not know, even if one has the desire to go there, how can
> one succeed? From ancient time people who can try hard to act
> are not rare; however, few people can understand *dao*. This shows
> that to know is also a difficult thing. (*Yishu* 18; 187)

Here, on the one hand, CHENG Yi makes it clear that knowledge is more important than action, as without knowledge, we will have no idea of what action
to take, how to take the action, and why to take it. It is in this sense that
he argues that "knowledge is the most fundamental of all learning; only after
this come making friends, acting, and speaking" (*Yishu* 25, 324); and "superior
persons take knowledge as the root and action as something secondary" (*Yishu*
25, 320). On the other hand, he also claims that to know is more difficult than

to act. In this passage, Cheng apparently makes a moderate claim that, while it is difficult to act, it is no easier to know. It is clear that he does so only not to make a claim directly contradictory to the statement in this Confucian classic. As a matter of fact, however, since he says that there are fewer people having knowledge than people able to act, he obviously thinks that to know is more difficult than to act. We can see this more clearly in another passage: "For those of you here, it is really not hard to make some effort to act, but it is difficult to gain knowledge and insight" (*Yishu* 17; 181). Without knowledge, one can still act as long as there are laws and rules of propriety, or as long as they have some particular intentions. Thus CHENG Yi claims that "today it is not that there are no people of filial piety and brotherly love; but they cannot manifest their nature and fulfill their mandate, all because they lack knowledge" (*Yishu* 18; 225). In other words, people who have no knowledge of filial piety can still perform actions of filial piety either because of some external pressures for such actions or because of some selfish intentions (such as to get praise from the community). Thus, knowledge is more difficult than action because one can have a forced and reluctant action, but one cannot have a forced or reluctant knowledge. His above interpretation of the Confucian statement, "common people may be made to follow the path of action, but they may not be made to understand it," actually also shows that knowledge is more difficult to achieve than action: sages can make people perform actions, but they are unable to make them have knowledge.

Third, knowledge will necessarily lead to action. In CHENG Yi's view, while there are people who can act without knowing, there is no one who knows and yet cannot act. Thus, while one should not refrain from acting before one knows, "one's forced (*mianqiang* 勉強) action cannot be long lasting" (187). So what is important is to acquire knowledge: "When knowledge is profound, action will be thorough. No one ever knows without being able to act. If one knows without being able to act, the knowledge is superficial. Because they know the danger, people do not eat poisonous herbs when hungry, and do not tread on water and fire. People do evil things simply because they lack knowledge" (*Yishu* 15; 164). CHENG Yi here holds the view that all those who do not act appropriately lack the proper knowledge, and all those who have the proper knowledge will necessarily act appropriately. It is a contradiction, in his view, to claim that one knows and yet is unable to act: "So if one knows what is immoral and still does it, this is not true knowledge. If this is true knowledge, one will certainly not do the immoral thing" (*Yishu* 2a; 16).[12] CHENG Hao holds the same view in this regard. He argues that "when one obtains *dao* from one's own heart/mind, this knowledge will be displayed in one's four limbs" (*Yishu* 2a; 20). Because "it is what one gets (*de* 得) from one's heart/mind, it is called virtue (*de* 德). Naturally, it 'will be manifested in one's face, shown in one's back, and extended to one's four limbs, rendering its message intelligible without words.' What is the need for any forced actions?" (*Yishu* 15; 147). Here CHENG Hao is not merely playing on a pun. The Chinese character for virtue, *de* 德, is closely related to the Chinese character for "to get," *de* 得. The main difference is that the character for virtue has the character of heart/mind, *xin* 心, in it. So CHENG Hao claims that what one gets from one's own heart/mind is virtue. Since this is the virtue, it will naturally be displayed in one's action, as described by Mencius in the passage that CHENG Hao cites in the above quote (see *Mencius* 7a21).

This view of the Cheng brothers, the view that one who knows what is good will necessarily do good, and people do evil only because they do not know, seems to go against our common sense, as it seems quite common that a person knows what is right and yet fails to do it. In this respect, even the prominent historian of Chinese philosophy, FENG Youlan (FUNG Yulan) 馮友蘭, thinks that such a view "has something that is theoretically incoherent and practically infeasible," as "it is one thing to increase one's objective knowledge of concrete things, and another to elevate one's subjective realm of spirit. While there is something overlapping between the two, they are fundamentally two different things" (Feng 1995, 177–78). Here, Feng raises two questions. On the one hand, the apparent theoretical incoherence is related to the issue of weakness of the will. For example, we can easily imagine a person who has a perfect understanding that it is wrong to lie and yet still lies. The familiar explanation is that one has two different faculties functioning here: the intellect decides what something is, and the will decides what is to be done. So it is possible that one may have perfect knowledge of something and yet decide to not act according to this knowledge or even to act against this knowledge. On the other hand, the so-called practical infeasibility is related to the idea of moral responsibility. We can hold a person responsible for an action only because we assume that the person knows what is the right thing to do and yet decides not to do it. We do not hold animals, the insane, and sleepwalkers responsible for what they do because they lack the necessary knowledge. Thus if CHENG Yi is correct, it seems that we cannot hold people responsible for their actions, because those who do immoral things do not have the required knowledge. In the next two sections, I shall explore how CHENG Yi deals with the first apparent difficulty, and in section 6, I shall discuss the second apparent difficulty.

4. Knowledge of/as Virtue versus Knowledge from
Hearing and Seeing: How Is Weakness of the Will *Not* Possible?

We have seen that the Cheng brothers' view that knowledge will necessarily lead
to action is a clear rejection of weakness of the will as something impossible.
In order to explain many apparent counterexamples in our everyday life that
seem to suggest the existence of such a phenomenon, CHENG Yi distinguishes
between two senses of knowledge, in three different ways. First, he distinguishes between profound knowledge and shallow knowledge. For example,
he argues that "it is not that people do not know. The reason that one is not
willing to act is that the knowledge is shallow and belief is not firm" (*Yishu*
23; 305). So here he acknowledges the possibility of someone who knows and
yet does not act according to this knowledge. However, in his view, this is a
shallow knowledge; it is not something one firmly believes in. When knowledge is profound, and one firmly believes in it, one cannot fail to act upon
this knowledge. For CHENG Yi, such shallow knowledge cannot be regarded as
knowledge in its proper sense.

Second, he makes a distinction between genuine knowledge (*zhen zhi*
真知) and ordinary knowledge (*chang zhi* 常知):

> Genuine knowledge is different from ordinary knowledge. There
> was a farmer who had been hurt by tiger. When hearing that tiger
> was hurting people, nobody was not scared, but the farmer's com-
> posure was different from everyone else's. Tigers can hurt people;
> this is something that even children know, but they do not have
> genuine knowledge. Genuine knowledge is the one that the farmer
> has. Therefore a person who knows that something is not good
> and still does it does not have genuine knowledge. Had the person
> had genuine knowledge, he or she would have not done it. (*Yishu*
> 2a; 16; see also *Yishu* 18; 188)

This distinction between genuine knowledge and common knowledge is the
same distinction between profound knowledge and shallow knowledge. Thus,
in another place where CHENG Yi uses the same example of the tiger, he first
says that "knowledge is all different. While some is profound, some is shallow"; then, after telling the story of tiger and farmer, he concludes that this
farmer "has genuine knowledge of tiger. The profound knowledge of a learner
is similar. . . . A learner ought to seek genuine knowledge; only then can one
claim to have the knowledge and act naturally. When I was twenty years old,

I could interpret classics without much difference from the way I am doing today. However, what I get from classics today is very different from what I got then" (*Yishu* 18; 188). As CHENG Yi often uses this story of tiger and farmer to illustrate genuine knowledge, scholars often think that his distinction between genuine knowledge and ordinary knowledge is one between knowledge from direct experience and that from indirect experience.[13] However, in Cheng's view, while genuine knowledge must be from direct experience, not all knowledge from direct experience is genuine knowledge. Genuine knowledge is one from a special kind of direct experience: the inner experience. This is clear from Cheng's discussion above about a learner's genuine knowledge and his own experience with the interpretation of classics. It is only in this sense of knowledge that he claims that "with genuine knowledge, no one will fail to act" (*Waishu* 6; 388).

However, the most important and also most controversial distinction that CHENG Yi makes is the one we mentioned in the previous section: between knowledge of/as virtue and knowledge from hearing and seeing: "knowledge from seeing and hearing is not knowledge of/as virtue. It results from the contact between one thing and another thing and therefore is not internal. The knowledge of those erudite and skillful persons belongs to this. Knowledge of/as virtue does not rely upon hearing and seeing" (*Yishu* 25, 317). Here CHENG Yi explains more clearly what he means by "genuine knowledge" or "deep" knowledge by using ZHANG Zai's 張載 idea of knowledge of/as virtue in contrast to knowledge from seeing and hearing. In this distinction, while knowledge from seeing and hearing is external knowledge (whether from direct experience or indirect experience), knowledge of/as virtue is internal knowledge coming from inner experience. Thus, Cheng claims that "learning, generally speaking, cannot be obtained by knowledge from hearing. One can obtain it only by its being apprehended in one's own heart/mind (*mo shi xin tong* 默識心通). If a learner wants to learn something, the learner has to be sincere in seeking the illumination from the principle. The best way to get it is the sudden enlightenment" (*Yishu* 17; 178). Because it is internal, it is important to get it by oneself (*zide* 自得) and not to be imposed upon from the outside, as it cannot be communicated by words (*Cuiyan* 2; 1253).[14]

So *zide* becomes an important idea for the Cheng brothers.[15] This is an idea they took from Mencius, who says that "superior persons explore deeply into *dao* in order to get it by themselves. When they get it by themselves, they will be at ease in it; when they are at ease with it, they can draw deeply upon it; when they can draw deeply upon it, they can rely on it to deal with everything properly. For this reason, superior persons want to get it by themselves" (*Mencius* 4b14). Cheng uses this Mencian idea of getting *dao* by oneself to explain the idea of knowledge of/as virtue. Sages can of course teach us about moral principles, but unless we really grasp it from our own heart/mind, it is for us (although not for sages) merely knowledge of hearing and seeing, which will not be able to motivate us to act according to such moral principles. Therefore, in his view, "nothing is more important in learning than to get it by oneself. Because one does not get it from outside, it is called self-getting" (*Yishu* 25; 316). CHENG Hao also claims that "the key to learning is *zide*," because "only when one gets it oneself can it become one's own" (*Yishu* 11; 122). It is through this idea of *zide* that he explains *Analects* 5.13, in which it is said that one cannot hear Confucius's talk about human nature and heavenly *dao*: "One cannot know human nature and the heavenly *dao* unless through self-getting. It is for this reason that it is said that one cannot hear Confucius's talk about human nature and heavenly Dao" (*Wai-shu* 2; 361). It is also through the idea of *zide* that CHENG Hao explains why Confucius says that finding joy in *dao* is higher than merely knowing or even loving dao (*Analects* 6.20): "Learning is perfected when it reaches the level of joy . . . When one loves it, one is like taking a tour of someone else' garden; when one takes joy in it, the garden is one's own" (*Yishu* 11; 127).

    Zide is thus important but requires one's active effort of inner experience. CHENG Yi claims that "it is easy to learn but difficult to know; it is easy to know, but it is difficult to know by one's inner experience" (*ti er de zhi* 體而得之) (*Yishu* 25; 321). Here the word *ti* 體, through which one can get knowledge of/as virtue by oneself, is extremely important in the Cheng brothers in particular and in Confucianism in general. In recent years, TU Weiming has written extensively on the conception of *tizhi* 體知, knowledge or knowing through *ti* 體 (see various articles in Tu 2002, vol. 5). While literally the word *ti* means "body," as Tu correctly points out, its meaning cannot be adequately expressed by this English word. Of course, knowledge of/as virtue will necessarily be manifested in body, which has been pointed out by Mencius (*Mencius* 7a21); this is also what CHENG Yi has in mind when he states that "whatever one gains inside will necessarily be manifested out' (*Yishu* 18; 185). However, this is still related to Cheng's view that one who has knowledge will necessarily act upon the knowledge. What we are concerned with here is the *ti* through which one's knowledge is gained in the first place. Here, TU Weiming points out that "recognition through *ti* (*tiren* 體認), awareness through *ti* (*ticha* 體察), justification through *ti* (*tizheng* 體證), understanding through *ti* (*tihui* 體會), tasting through *ti* (*tiwei* 體味), appreciation through *ti* (*tiwan* 體玩), inquiry through *ti* (*tijiu* 體究), and knowledge through *ti* (*tizhi* 體知) are all very different from knowledge, observation, verification, taste, and understanding in general sense" (Tu 2002, 5: 331–32). Here, Tu correctly warns us against understanding *knowledge* from *ti* as something one gets from one's body. However, he does not clearly tell us what this *ti* means. In my view, in the Cheng brothers, the word *ti* is used as both a noun and a verb. First, as a noun, it refers to *xin* 心 (one's heart/mind), which Mencius calls *dati* 大體, literally, "the great body," in contrast to our external body, which he calls *xiaoti* 小體, literally, "the small body" (*Mencius* 6a15).[16] That is why CHENG Yi says in the previously quoted passage that "one can obtain it only by its being apprehended in one's own heart/mind (*mo shi xin tou* 默識心通)." In his commentary on *The Doctrine of Mean*, he contrasts knowledge of/as virtue and knowledge from hearing and seeing, as the latter "is not what one gets from *xin* (heart/mind)" (*Jingshuo* 8; 1154). Second, as a verb, *ti* refers to the activity of the heart/mind. It is extremely important to understand the "heart" part of the *xin* in its role in getting knowledge of/as virtue. Knowledge from hearing and seeing is not merely something one gets from one's sense organs. It also requires the "mind" part of the *xin* to play its role, as it is something that one needs to understand, justify, and prove. However, only when knowledge is grasped also by the "heart" part of the *xin* can it become knowledge of/as virtue, the knowledge that one not only possesses but is also ready to act upon.[17]

5. Cheng Brothers versus Socrates and Aristotle

From our discussion above, deep knowledge, genuine knowledge, or knowledge of/as virtue is knowledge one gains through one's inner experience, understood by one's mind, grasped by one's heart, and therefore knowledge that inclines one to act accordingly, while shallow knowledge, common knowledge, or knowledge from hearing and seeing is knowledge one gains through external experience. Even if knowledge is understood by the mind, it is not grasped by the heart and therefore does not incline one to act accordingly. The so-called *akrate* or weak-willed person, in this view, is one who has knowledge only in the latter sense. Since knowledge in the latter sense, strictly speaking, cannot be called knowledge, we can say that the so-called weak-willed person acts from ignorance. It is in this sense that the neo-Confucian position represented by the Cheng brothers here is diametrically opposite to the dominating view in contemporary Western philosophy, largely influenced by Donald Davidson and thus, as observed by several scholars, is similar to the view of Socrates and Aristotle.[18] However, I would like to make a stronger claim that the Chengs provide a better solution to the problem of weakness of the will than Socrates and Aristotle. This can be seen in four different aspects. I shall discuss the first three in the remaining part of this section and the fourth one in the next section.

First, the Chengs' idea of getting knowledge by oneself (*zide*) is philosophically significant. As we have seen, it provides a creative interpretation of Confucius's otherwise problematic statement that people can be made to act but cannot be made to understand. Since knowledge that inclines one to act, the profound and genuine knowledge of/as virtue is the knowledge that one has to get from one's own heart/mind, even sages cannot make people have such knowledge, although they can let them have knowledge from hearing and seeing. This idea is also important in solving the apparent paradox that Socrates mentions at the end of *Protagoras*: on the one hand, Socrates claims that virtue is knowledge, and on the other hand, he states that virtue is not teachable. Usually virtue is considered as different from knowledge, and in this sense it can be said that it cannot be taught. However, knowledge is teachable, and since virtue is knowledge according to Socrates, why is it not teachable? Socrates does not provide us with a convincing answer, at least not as convincing an answer as the Cheng brothers can provide. For the Chengs, knowledge of/as virtue (or virtue as knowledge) is different from knowledge from hearing and seeing. The latter is teachable, but the former is not. One has to get it with one's own heart/mind.

Second, according to Aristotle, weakness of the will is caused by one's temporary loss of knowledge, which can be found later. Thus he states that "the explanation of how the ignorance is dissolved and the incontinent man regains his knowledge, is the same as in the case of the man drunk or asleep and is not peculiar to this condition; we must go to the students of natural science for it" (Aristotle 1915, 1147b6–9). Such an interpretation is problematic. It seems to imply that the knowledge that a "weak-willed" person has and then loses is no different from the knowledge a virtuous person has. The only difference between them seems to be that the weak-willed person would lose knowledge when it is needed while a virtuous person will not; moreover, as soon as the weak-willed person regains the lost knowledge, that person ceases to be different from the virtuous person, just as a drunkard will be no different from normal people when sober. If this is the case, we need to know why the same knowledge will always get lost for some people but not for others. Here the Chengs' distinction between knowledge from hearing and seeing and knowledge of/as virtue provides a better solution. In the Chengs' view, the difference between "weak-willed" persons and virtuous persons is not that the former lose their knowledge while the latter do not; it is rather the difference between the types of knowledge they have respectively. The reason one will forget knowledge when it is needed shows that the knowledge is merely knowledge from hearing and seeing and not knowledge of/as virtue, which, once obtained, will never be lost. So the solution is not to help the person regain the lost knowledge from hearing and seeing, but to encourage the person to make an effort to gain the knowledge of/as virtue personally.[19]

Third, the reason that many people (including many contemporary philosophers who have done significant work on the issue of weakness of will) think that Socrates's solution is too simplistic and against our common sense is that, when he claims that virtue is knowledge and that one cannot do good only because one is ignorant, he fails to make a distinction between two types of persons: one (for example) smokes without knowing that smoke is harmful, while another smokes with such knowledge. In Socrates's view, there is no difference between these two types of persons: as long as one smokes, we can be sure that this person is ignorant about the danger of smoking. However, our common sense and intuition seem to tell us that there must be some difference between these two types of persons. I think this is the main reason why most contemporary philosophers tend to reject Socrates's solution. However, the Chengs' distinction between knowledge from hearing and seeing and knowledge of/as virtue maintains the Socratic position that the "weak-willed" person acts from ignorance, while at the same time appropriately addresses the concerns of those Davidsonian philosophers, who believe that weakness of the will is possible. In the Chengs' view, what is common to both types of persons is that they lack knowledge of/as virtue; since knowledge of/as virtue is the only genuine knowledge, we can say, as Socrates does, that they are both ignorant. However, what distinguishes these two persons from each other is that the one has knowledge from hearing and seeing, while the other lacks that knowledge. Here we may think that, since knowledge from hearing and seeing is not genuine knowledge, whether one has this knowledge or not does not seem to make much difference. In the above, we have focused on Cheng's view of the distinction between these two types of knowledge, but he also thinks that there are some connections between them. As this view of his is quite complicated, and scholars cannot agree on what Cheng actually says, I shall devote the rest of this section to this issue.

As we have seen, CHENG Yi, following ZHANG Zai, thinks that knowledge of/as virtues does not rely upon hearing and seeing. From this, it is sometimes believed that, for Cheng, these two types of knowledge are "mutually exclusive and there is no connection between the two" (Cai 1996, 111). However, in my view, it is at least not clear whether Cheng indeed thinks that knowledge from hearing and seeing has nothing to do with knowledge of/as virtue, and, if he does think so, we need to know in what sense knowledge of/as virtue does not rely upon knowledge from hearing and seeing. It is worth noting that, in the passage in which he contrasts knowledge from hearing and seeing and knowledge of/as virtue, Cheng is largely paraphrasing ZHANG Zai, who first made the distinction that "knowledge from hearing and seeing is knowledge resulting from the contact between one thing and another thing. It is not knowledge of/as virtue. Knowledge of/as virtue does not originate from hearing and seeing" (Zhang 2000: 144). It is of course beyond doubt that Cheng fundamentally agrees with Zhang. However, in order to understand the nuances he puts on this thesis, we need to understand it in light of Cheng's discussions in related passages. Most obviously, for Cheng, knowledge from hearing and seeing is not limited to those that result from one's direct experience, the contact of one thing (one's sense organ) with another thing (an external thing); it also includes knowledge resulting from one's indirect experience, which one learns from reading classics or conversing with other people. This is clear in the passage quoted earlier, where Cheng, while basically repeating Zhang, adds that "the knowledge of those erudite and skillful persons" belongs to knowledge from hearing and seeing. Here, those erudite people have their knowledge at least partially from reading books. About knowledge from hearing and seeing in this sense, CHENG Yi points out that "if one just hears something from other people, one does not really get it from one's heart/mind" (*Yishu* 15; 147).

More importantly, while it is true that, for CHENG Yi, knowledge of/as virtue does not have to use hearing and seeing, knowledge from hearing and seeing, in both senses (direct and indirect experiences), is also important as it can help one obtain knowledge of/as virtue or can become a virtuous person. This is because the content of these two types of knowledge is the same; the difference is that one is merely intellectual, while the other is also affective. We can see this more clearly if we keep in mind that, for CHENG Yi, there are many ways to get moral knowledge, as we shall discuss in chapter 7. Among these many ways, both knowledge from reading classics and studying history as indirect experience, on the one hand, and knowledge from investigating external things and handling human affairs as direct experience, on the other hand, belong to knowledge from hearing and seeing. They are both different from knowledge from one's inner reflection (*cha zhu shen* 察諸身), which alone can result in knowledge of/as virtue: "to investigate the principle of things is not as intimate as to reflect upon oneself" (*Yishu* 17; 175). CHENG Yi believes that both types of knowledge from hearing and seeing have something to do with knowledge of/as virtue. The first type of knowledge from hearing and seeing (from one's indirect experiences in reading classics and history) can be transformed into knowledge of/as virtue if, when reading classics, one tries to experience, in one's own heart/mind, what sages experience. For example, CHENG Yi says that "one should go deep into the *Analects*, regarding the questions of Confucius' students as one's own questions and applying sage's answers to these questions as addressed to one's own situation. This way, one will necessarily get it" (*Yishu* 22a; 279). While Cheng does not think that the second type of knowledge from hearing and seeing (from one's direct experience in investigating external things and handling human affairs) can be identified with knowledge of/as virtue, he argues against those who think we should abandon it: "Some people propose that we should abandon knowledge from hearing and seeing as well as mental calculations. If so, one is to 'abandon sagehood and reject wisdom' (*jue sheng qi zhi* 絕聖棄智)" (*Yishu* 25; 168). So it is clear that CHENG Yi does not think that knowledge from hearing and seeing is entirely negative, something that has to be rejected in order to obtain knowledge of/as virtue.[20] For him, the purpose in investigating external things and handling human affairs is not simply to learn about natural and social phenomena but to understand the principle embodied in them. While one cannot grasp the principle of things without using eyes to see and ears to hear, it cannot be grasped by seeing and hearing, as the principle is without shape, sound, or smell. It is in this sense that Cheng states that "without eyes, the heart/mind cannot grasp; without the heart/mind, eyes cannot see" (*Yishu* 6; 90).

From our above discussion, we have a better understanding of the relationship between knowledge from hearing and seeing and knowledge of/as virtue. Knowledge from hearing and seeing, whether indirectly from reading books and listening to others or directly from sensible perceptions of external things, is indeed one source for knowledge of/as virtue. WEN Weiyao 溫偉耀 even goes so far as to claim that "the starting point of all efforts to obtain knowledge is 'knowledge from seeing and hearing,' including reading classics of sages, examining historical figures, communicating and encountering with others in daily life, as well as observing ten thousand things in the universe. However, all these different approaches end with knowledge of/as virtue, which is elevation of moral life" (Wen 1996, 158).[21] In this sense, we can correctly say that knowledge of/as virtue is not knowledge from hearing and seeing, although the former may come from the latter. However, in what sense can CHENG Yi say that the former does not rely upon the latter? First, although knowledge of/as virtue can come from knowledge from hearing and seeing, what knowledge of/as virtue grasps, the principle (*li*), cannot be seen or heard.

Second, while knowledge of/as virtue may come from knowledge from hearing and seeing, one may also obtain it independently of any knowledge from hearing and seeing. WEN Weiyao only sees that knowledge from hearing and seeing can be transformed into knowledge of/as virtue, but he does not see that, for Cheng, knowledge of/as virtue does not have to come from knowledge from hearing and seeing; it can also come directly from inner experience, mentioned by Cheng as one of the many ways to grasp the principle. Since knowledge from hearing and seeing can lead to knowledge of/as virtue but is not always necessary for one to get knowledge of/as virtue (if one can get it from one's inner experience), I think Wen is wrong to claim that "knowledge from hearing and seeing is the beginning of all efforts of learning" (Wen 1996, 158), a view echoed by TU Weiming, who says that "knowledge from hearing and seeing is empirical knowledge, while knowledge of/as virtue is an inner experience, or knowledge from inner experience. The latter cannot be independent of empirical knowledge but cannot be identified as empirical knowledge either" (Tu 2002, vol. 5, 344).[22] So there are really two ways to get knowledge of/as virtue: (1) through direct inner experience; and (2) through knowledge from hearing and seeing, which in turn comes from two sources: (2a) direct external experience in investigating things and handling human affairs; and (2b) indirect experience in reading classics and history. However, merely from knowledge from hearing and seeing (2), knowledge of/as virtue cannot be developed; it has to make use of the inner experience (1). Thus we can explain this somewhat complicated relationship in this way:

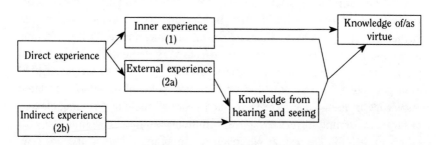

To return to the main point of the Cheng brothers' third unique contribution to the issue of weakness of the will, we now see that they can better explain the difference between the so-called weak-willed persons and ignorant persons than Socrates and Aristotle: although "weak-willed" persons do not have knowledge of/as virtue, they do have knowledge from hearing and seeing, which can become one's starting point to gain knowledge of/as virtue. While it is true that one can get knowledge of/as virtue without knowledge from hearing and seeing, most people get their knowledge of/as virtue with the help of knowledge from hearing and seeing, as it is more difficult to get it entirely from one's inner experience. The Cheng brothers' fourth unique contribution to the solution of the problem of weakness of the will is related to the idea of moral responsibility, to which I now turn.

6. Absence of Weakness of the Will and the Presence of Moral Responsibility

The problem of weakness of the will has interested both ancient and contemporary philosophers, not simply because it is intellectually challenging, as it indeed is (how a person can believe something is better and have the power to do this better thing and yet decide to do something worse). It is more because it involves the issue of moral responsibility. We think that one ought to be responsible for what one does only if (*a*) it is done by free action. In other words, the person can choose either to perform or refrain from performing this action. If the person cannot *not* perform the action, it immediately becomes questionable to ask this person to take responsibility for the action; (*b*) this person should have knowledge of the action. For that reason, we usually do not ask children or mentally deficient persons to take responsibility for actions they perform.[23] Although moral responsibility is different from legal responsibility, two fundamental ideas related to legal responsibility will help us better understand moral responsibility, which is our main concern here. The first is the idea of *mens rea*, according to which we can hold a person legally responsible for a criminal action only if the person has a guilty mind when performing the action. Although this is a controversial issue, as it is generally believed that ignorance of law is no excuse, still it is generally considered as an appropriate criterion.[24] Even those who reject this idea do so mainly for practical reasons: we are unable to determine a person's *mens rea*. If this is the case, then even if this idea cannot be appropriately used in law, it is certainly fruitful when used in morality.[25] The second is the idea of criminal insanity. The famous M'Naghten Rules by the House of Lords of England in 1843 states that a person ought not to take legal responsibility for an action only if, "at the time of committing the act, the accused was laboring under such a defect of reason, from disease of the mind, as not to know the nature and quality of the act he was doing, or, if he did know it, that he did not know he was doing what was wrong" (House of Lords 2000,

668).[26] I believe that these two ideas in legal practices basically correspond to the two criteria in moral discourse.

Now, if we accept such an idea of moral responsibility, philosophers who insist that weakness of the will is not only possible but also actual would maintain that weak-willed persons are responsible for their actions, as they know, at the time when they perform their actions, what they are doing and are able to decide not to perform the actions. On the contrary, if we follow Socrates to think that all people who do bad things do so simply because they lack knowledge, then we cannot hold anyone responsible for any wrongdoings; if we follow Aristotle to think that the so-called *akrates*, when they perform the wrong actions, are no different from people who are asleep, drunk, and mad, then again they should be excused from any moral responsibility for their wrongdoing as their actions are not free.[27] That is why today the skeptic view regarding weakness of will is often not taken seriously, as it seems to be a common phenomenon that one knows something is good and yet acts against such knowledge, and it seems to be our common intuition that we should hold such persons responsible for their actions.

Here again I think the Cheng brothers can provide a better answer to this question. As we have seen, the so-called weak-willed person in Western philosophical discourse is, from the Chengs' neo-Confucian perspective, a person who does have knowledge from hearing and seeing but lacks knowledge of/as virtue. A person who knows (in the sense of knowledge from hearing and seeing) that it is bad to steal may still steal, as he or she does not know it from his or her own heart/mind and therefore does not have genuine knowledge. The question is whether we should hold a person who has knowledge from hearing and seeing but not knowledge of/as virtue responsible for wrongdoings. If asked this question, the Chengs' answer would be positive. This is not because knowledge from hearing and seeing that the person does have satisfies one of the two conditions for moral responsibility, because the Chengs make it clear that such knowledge is not genuine knowledge. In order to understand their view, we need to keep in mind that moral responsibility for the Chengs is not an end-state concept but a historical one. In other words, when we decide whether people should take responsibility for their actions, we cannot just look at the very moment when a person performs an action to see whether the person knows (in the sense of knowledge of/as virtue) that the action is wrong; we know that they do not have such knowledge. We need to see further why this person does not have such knowledge. In the Chengs' view, in the sense that the person who does a wrong thing does not genuinely know it is wrong, the person is not responsible for this action. However, the person should be held responsible, directly, for the lack of the necessary knowledge and therefore, indirectly, for the wrongdoing due to such ignorance.

The issue is in what sense the Chengs can say that one should be responsible for one's ignorance. Am I responsible for my lack of the knowledge that Einstein has? We need to keep in mind that the knowledge that is necessary for moral action is different from scientific, historical, and mathematical knowledge. First, the object of our knowledge, *dao* or principle, as we have already seen, is for CHENG Yi inherent in every one of us (*Yishu* 25; 316). It is in this sense that CHENG Hao claims that one "learns both to know what one possesses and to take care of what one possesses" (*Waishu* 1, 351). Second, the ability needed to gain it, which is different from the ability to perform scientific research or philosophical meditation or poetry writing, is also inherent in every one of us, which is *xin*, our distinguishing mark of being human. Thus CHENG Yi states that

> everyone has this *dao*. Only a superior person can apprehend and practice it. People don't apprehend it in their own heart/mind only because they give themselves up. Thus Mencius says that "when the four beginnings [of humanity, righteousness, propriety, and wisdom] are fully developed, one can take under his protection the whole realm within the four seas, but if he fails to develop them, he will not be able even to serve his parents." Whether to develop them or not is entirely dependent upon myself. (*Yishu* 25; 321)

Here, on the one hand, CHENG Yi points out that the difference between superior persons and inferior persons is that the former make an effort to get to know *dao* within them through their heart/mind, while the latter do not; on the other hand, he makes it clear that there is such a difference between superior persons and inferior persons, not because superior persons are smart or are endowed with exceptional abilities that inferior persons do not have. There is no difference between superior persons and inferior persons, between sages and common people, at birth in this respect (though the Chengs do not deny the mere theoretical possibility of inborn sages). Superior persons and sages become such because they diligently develop what they are born with, while inferior persons become such because they do not make their effort to develop them. That is why, in the above passage, he adds, after quoting from the *Mencius* (where Mencius argues that the distinction between genuine humans and "nonhuman humans" is whether they develop their inborn four beginnings), that whether to develop them or not is entirely up to individual.

This is certainly consistent with Mencius, who says in the same paragraph that "for a man possessing these four beginnings to deny his own potentialities is for him to cripple himself" (*Mencius* 2a6).[28] In this sense, as I mentioned in the previous chapter, on one hand, it is easier to gain moral knowledge of/as virtue than to obtain scientific knowledge (for example), as everyone is born with the ability to gain the former, but not everyone is born with the ability to gain the latter; on the other hand, it is more difficult to gain moral knowledge of/as virtue than to obtain scientific knowledge, as it requires both the mind and the heart part of our *xin*. However, Cheng points out that "sages do not say it is easy [to gain knowledge of/as virtue], so that people will not be conceited; nor do they say it is difficult, so that people will not be discouraged from learning" (*Yishu* 18; 209–210). Thus the Cheng brothers always emphasize the importance of learning.

It is in this context that we can see the significance of CHENG Yi's interpretation of *Analects* 17.3, which is commonly translated as "only the wise above and stupid below cannot be changed," to be discussed in full detail in the appendix. Since Cheng puts such an emphasis on learning, he certainly would not agree that there are people born to be stupid, to say nothing of such people being unchangeable. Thus, in CHENG Yi's view, in the above passage, Confucius "does not mean that people cannot be changed. It means that there is a principle that cannot be changed. Only two kinds of people cannot be changed: those who gave themselves up and those who are unwilling to learn. If one is willing to learn and does not give oneself up, how cannot the person be changed?" (*Yishu* 19; 252). So in CHENG Yi's interpretation, what Confucius means by "unchangeable" is this principle: if one gives up, then the person cannot become wise; if one keeps learning, then the person will necessarily become wise. In another place, discussing the same passage from the *Analects*, Cheng states that "while time is something that sages cannot go against, sages can certainly show us the way to change from ignorance to wisdom and from disorder to order" (*Yishu* 11; 122). Whether this is the original meaning of the statement in the *Analects* is not important here. What is important is that, for CHENG Yi, people do not have the necessary knowledge not because they are stupid but because they do not want to learn. Thus he claims that "for superior persons, nothing is more important than to learn, nothing is more harmful than to stop, nothing is more sickening than to be self-content, and nothing is more sinful than to give oneself up. To learn without stopping, this is how Tang and Wu become sages" (*Yishu* 25; 325). So the real obstacle to our gaining wisdom lies on our own side: self-giving up. Thus, CHENG Yi says that "no failure in action is greater than evil, but it can be changed; no failure in administration is worse than disorder, but it can be rectified; only those who give themselves up cannot become superior persons" (*Yishu* 4; 69).

From our discussion above, it becomes clear why CHENG Yi claims that, on the one hand, all those who do commit wrongdoings act out of ignorance, and, on the other hand, they are to be responsible for their wrongdoings. We have mentioned that his conception of moral responsibility is a historical one and not an end-state one. The person is ignorant not because of a lack of the ability to know, since everyone has the inborn ability. It is rather due to this person's negligence to develop an inborn potential.[29] So the so-called weakness of the will really belongs to phenomenon (*e*) mentioned at the very beginning of this chapter: negligence. It is true that this person does not have the needed knowledge to perform the desired actions but the person is still responsible because he could and should have the required knowledge if he is not negligent. Ultimately, the issue we have here is not whether we can be moral, as we certainly can, but rather whether we are willing to be moral. This is the distinction the *Mencius* makes between *buneng* 不能 (unable) and *buwei* 不為 (unwilling). The reason one is not moral is not that the person is unable to be moral but that the person is unwilling to be moral. While there are things that humans are unable to do, such as "striding over the North Sea with Mount Tai under one's arm" (*Mencius* 1a7), to be moral is not one of them. To say that one cannot do moral things is like saying that one cannot lift a feather or one cannot see a cartload of firewood, as Mencius explains to King Xuan of Qi (*Mencius* 1a7). The reason is that, for Mencius, everyone is born with the four sprouts of morality, as everyone is born with the four limbs: the heart/mind of commiseration, the heart/mind of shame, the heart/mind of courtesy and modesty, the heart/mind of right and wrong. With these four sprouts, Mencius states,

> all you need to do is to make the effort. The problem is not that people do not have sufficient strength, but that they refuse to make the effort. To walk slowly behind one's elders is considered as brotherly love, while to walk quickly ahead of one's elders is considered as the lack of such love. Now is it beyond one's ability to walk slowly? One simply refuses to make the effort. The *dao* of Yao and Shun is simply that of filial piety and brotherly love. . . . The *dao* is like a wide road and is not difficult to find. The trouble is that people do not look for it. (*Mencius* 6b2)

CHENG Yi accepts this Mencian distinction between *buwei* and *buneng*. Sometimes learning is compared to mountain climbing: one makes big strides when it is easy but quits when it is difficult. However, CHENG Yi thinks that this is not an appropriate analogy: "It is indeed difficult to climb the high mountains, though with shapes. However, the *dao* of sages, though without fixed shapes, is really not difficult. The problem is that people do not make effort (*fu wei* 弗為) [to learn it]" (*Yishu* 18; 193).

With this, our final concern is how to avoid negligence or how to take our responsibility to gain the needed moral knowledge. Since the required knowledge is knowledge of/as virtue, what is needed is not only our intellectual effort performed by the "mind" part of *xin* but also moral cultivation performed by its "heart" part. It is here that we come across CHENG Yi's famous two-prong teaching: "Moral cultivation relies upon being reverent, while progress in learning depends on increasing knowledge" (*Yishu* 18; 188).

In appearance, this two-prong teaching seems to imply that moral cultivation and progress in learning are two separate things: the increase of knowledge improves our intellectual learning but not our moral cultivation, just as being reverent helps our moral cultivation but not our intellectual learning.[30] This, however, is a misunderstanding. We may look at the relationship between them from two different aspects. On the one hand, as we have already seen in our discussion in the third section of this chapter, it is obviously false to claim that, for Cheng, the increase of knowledge has nothing to do with our moral cultivation, as he makes it clear that the person who knows what is right will necessarily act according to this knowledge. To see it more clearly, we can take a look at what Cheng means by "being reverent" (*jing* 敬), upon which moral cultivation is said to depend. The first is being vacuous and tranquil: "One who is reverent is naturally vacuous (absolutely pure and peaceful, not being disturbed by incoming impression) and tranquil" (*Yishu* 15; 157). What he means here is to empty one's mind of its artificial desires. That is why he also regards being reverent as having no self to overcome and as having returned to propriety, since the self to be overcome is precisely the private desires (*Yishu* 15; 157). Such a conception of being reverent as being vacuous and tranquil may sound like a Daoist and Buddhist notion, so CHENG Yi adds a second element: one master or being mastered by one (*zhuyi* 主一). How can one be vacuous and tranquil? Interestingly enough, CHENG Yi does not claim that we should keep our mind as an empty bottle. Rather, we should let our mind be fully occupied by only one master (*zhuyi*) which is *dao* or principle.[31] In Cheng's view,

As soon as it [the heart/mind] has its own master, it is emptifying (*xu* 虛). To emptify means not to allow evil things to enter.

If it does not have its own master, it is absorbing (*shi* 實). To be absorbing means to be invaded. For example, if you have a bottle with water in it, then no matter what, no water from river and sea can enter. Is it emptifying? If it does not have water in it, then all water will come in. Is it absorbing? So one's heart/mind can never be used for two purposes. Once it is used for one thing, then nothing else can enter, because it has its master. When one's heart/mind is mastered by its master, one is not to worry about its being disturbed by mental calculations. Now if one is concentrated in reverence, what worry does one have? (*Yishu* 15; 168–69)

In other words, private desires can come into one's heart/mind only because the heart/mind does not have its own master, just as water can come into a bottle only because it is not already filled. Clearly, if one does not understand *dao*, one's heart/mind will not have a master; if it does not have its own master, private desires will come in to disturb the heart/mind; if the heart/mind is disturbed, one's moral quality will decline. It is in this sense that moral cultivation also relies upon one's knowledge of *dao*, because such knowledge is an essential part of being reverent. About this, CHENG Yi states that "there has never been a person who can have sincere intention, rectified heart, and cultivated body without first correctly grasping the principle" (*Yishu* 25; 316). CHENG Hao agrees and says the same thing from a different perspective: "When knowledge is thorough, one's will becomes sincere. If there is knowledge that does not lead to a sincere will, the knowledge is not thorough" (*Yishu* 11; 133).

On the other hand, however, having seen that it is impossible to have moral cultivation without an understanding of *dao*, CHENG Yi does not think it possible to have moral knowledge without moral cultivation. When CHENG Yi contrasts learning (which relies upon increasing knowledge) and moral cultivation (which relies upon being reverent), he does not mean that our knowledge can be increased without moral cultivation. If one's heart/mind is full of artificial desires, it is difficult for the person to have a clear understanding of *dao*, just as it is difficult for a person to empty one's mind of artificial desires if the person does not have a clear understanding of *dao*. Above, we saw that for CHENG Yi, to have moral cultivation in the sense of having sincere will, rectified heart/mind, and cultivated body, one must investigate things in order to extend knowledge. He even claims that "to have sincere will before obtaining the knowledge is to skip the step. A learner of course needs some forced effort, but without obtaining knowledge, how can one act?" (*Yishu* 18; 187). How can we investigate things and extend knowledge? Cheng says that "the investigation of things [to increase knowledge] also needs the accumulation of moral cultivation" (*Yishu* 15; 164); he asks us "to establish sincere will before we investigate things" (*Yishu* 22a; 277). We have seen that, for CHENG Yi, moral cultivation relies upon being reverent, to be reverent relies upon being mastered by one, and to be mastered by one relies upon knowledge of principle. How can we have the knowledge of principle? CHENG Yi tells us, "to obtain *dao*, nothing is more important than being reverent (*jing*). There has never been a person who knows without first being reverent" (*Yishu* 3; 66); and "if you keep and follow your moral cultivation, the heavenly principle will automatically become transparent" (*Yishu* 15; 169). So there is a reflective equilibrium between the increase of our knowledge (of *dao*) and the moral cultivation: the more knowledge we have, the easier it is to have moral cultivation; and the greater moral cultivation we have, the easier it is to increase our knowledge.

7. Conclusion

In the Chengs' view, everyone who has moral knowledge can be moral, and everyone has the ability to acquire the necessary moral knowledge. In other words, one cannot be moral only because one lacks the necessary moral knowledge; and one lacks the necessary moral knowledge only because one is negligent and fails to make the effort to acquire the moral knowledge one could and ought to have. This shows that, for the Chengs, intellect and will, knowledge and moral cultivation, and goodness and truth are never to be separated. Moral cultivation is always based on moral knowledge, yet moral knowledge is never possible without moral effort. Such a realization reveals an even greater significance of the Chengs' solution to the problem of weakness of the will. As we have seen, in the Chengs' view, weakness of the will is nothing but one's negligence in making an effort to exercise one's great body, *xin*, the heart/mind. However, to make conscientious effort to acquire moral knowledge can not only help us avoid the problem of negligence, mentioned as item (*e*) at the beginning of this chapter, but many other problems mentioned there as well. If we are diligent and make the effort to use our great body, the heart/mind, to gain knowledge of/as virtue by ourselves, we will be able to avoid acting (*a*) intemperately or recklessly; we will also be able to resist the "irresistible" desires, which will be channeled in the direction of our nature (*xing qi qing* 性其情), so we will not act (*b*) compulsively; of course, we will then not be (*c*) hypocrites; since such knowledge of/as virtue, unlike scientific knowledge or technological skills, is something obtainable as long as we are not negligent, none of us can legitimately claim to be (*d*) ignorant due to our inborn (in)ability. The only one that the Chengs' discussion seems to have nothing to do with is perhaps phenomenon (*f*) rational choice, but this may show that this is not problematic in the first place, as different people may have different preferences. This last issue, plurality of rational preferences, will be the central concern of the next chapter.

Chapter 4

Love (*ai* 愛)

Ethics between Theory and Antitheory

1. Introduction

In chapter 2, we treated the Cheng brothers' ethics as a virtue ethics. One of the important features of virtue ethics not yet paid attention to, however, is its emphasis on particularity. In virtue ethics, as stated by Rosalind Hursthouse, "an action is right iff it is what a virtuous agent would characteristically (i.e. acting in character) do in the *circumstances*" (Hursthouse 1999, 28; emphasis added). Here I emphasize the last word, "circumstances." What it means is that a virtuous person does not simply apply universal moral principles to all circumstances. Instead, as Michael Slote claims when he comments on Aristotle, a virtuous person is "someone who *sees* or *perceives* what is good or fine or right to do in any given situation" (Slote 2001, 5). A right thing to do in one circumstance or situation may not be so in a different circumstance or situation. In this chapter, I shall focus on this aspect of virtue ethics. I start with a brief examination of the ethical generalism, or what I call ethics of commonality, as characteristic of both the commonsense Golden Rule and Kant's philosophical deontology and its failure to deal adequately with the uniqueness of individual moral patients (section 2). As its alternative, I shall examine the well-known Confucian idea of love with distinction (*ai you chadeng* 愛有差等), interpreted by the Cheng brothers as an ethics of difference through their idea of one principle in diverse appearances (*li yi fen shu* 理一分殊): instead of loving one's family members more than others as commonly understood,

131

this Confucian idea is understood to mean primarily to love different people differently, in ways that take into consideration the differences among objects of love (section 3). Such an ethics of difference thus has an obvious affinity with moral particularism or antitheory in contemporary ethics, as most enthusiastically advocated by Jonathan Dancy. However, I shall argue that in an important aspect the two are also significantly different: while Dancy emphasizes that there is nothing that can be transported from one situation to another, the Cheng brothers maintain that moral agents can learn, not merely formally but also materially, from their past love experiences, as they believe that morality is an attempt to gradually expand (*tui* 推) one's natural love for family members to other people, living beings, and even nonliving beings (section 4). I shall then argue that this is how the Cheng brothers explain the Confucian idea of family love as the root of practicing *ren* 仁, humanity, the most fundamental Confucian virtue, as the love that is to be expanded is a genuine feeling that one first naturally experiences within family (section 5). I shall conclude with a brief summary (section 6).

2. The Ethics of Commonality and Its Problem

Most ethical theories that we are familiar with can be regarded as ethics of commonality, as they assume that moral agents and moral patients are similar in morally relevant aspects. For example, the moral imperative, "Do unto others what you would have them do unto you," commonly known as the "Golden Rule," and its negative formulation, "Don't do unto others what you would not have them do unto you," sometimes also called the "Silver Rule," are based on the idea that what I as a moral agent like or dislike is precisely what others as the recipients of my actions like or dislike. This idea, on which the Golden Rule (in both positive and negative formulations) is grounded, is problematic. As Alan Gewirth points out, "the agent's wishes for himself *qua* recipient may not be in accord with his recipient's own wishes as to how he is to be treated. . . . Thus . . . this may inflict gratuitous suffering on [the recipient]. . . . For example, a person who likes others to quarrel with him or intrigue with him would be authorized by the golden rule to quarrel with others or involve them in a network of intrigue regardless of their own wishes in the matter" (Gewirth 1980, 133).

As the problem with the Golden Rule is obvious, many contemporary philosophers have attempted to rectify it. For example, Marcus Singer proposes an interpretation of the rule in light of his "general principle": What is right for one person must be right for anyone in the same or similar circumstance. The criterion of moral appropriateness of my action toward others is thus not determined by my having the desire to have others acting upon me in the same way. Rather, it requires a person to "judge everyone's conduct, including one's own, from the point of view of an 'impartial rational spectator'" (Singer 1963, 302). The Golden Rule, thus interpreted, reads: "Do unto others as an impartial rational spectator would ask you to do." Alan Gewirth's proposal to avoid the problem he identifies in the Golden Rule is to "rationalize" it in light of what he calls the principle of generic consistency: "*Act in accord with the generic rights of your recipients as well as of yourself*" (Gewirth 1978, 135). To avoid the same problem, R. M. Hare proposes his imaginative role reversal: to put oneself in the shoes of one's patient. However, Hare's role reversal does not aim to understand what the patient actually feels but to know what both the agent and the patient "should feel" from the perspective of a sympathetic impartial observer. This is the requirement of universalizability that he thinks is necessary in any moral reasoning: our action must be one "which we are . . . prepared to accept as exemplifying a principle of action to be prescribed for others in like circumstance" (Hare 1963, 88–89).[1]

It is interesting to note that Singer, Gewirth, and Hare are all Kantian philosophers, so it is not surprising that their various strategies to reformulate the Golden Rule are all guided by Kantian ethics, which is perhaps most representative of ethics of commonality. In Kant's view, ethics must be based on the moral principle that does not consider any particular situations of actual and potential moral agents and patients. He argues that "the ground of obligations must be looked for, not in the nature of man nor in the circumstances of the world in which he is placed, but solely *a priori* in the concepts of pure reason. . . . When applied to man it does not borrow in the slightest from acquaintance with him (in anthropology), but gives him laws *a priori* as a rational being" (Kant 1956a, 57). As we have seen, the fundamental problem with the Golden Rule is that a moral agent may regard her particular interests as also the interests of her moral patients. By deriving moral obligation from the rational will alone, which is supposed to be the same for every rational being (and all human beings are rational beings), and not from "the special predisposition of humanity" or "from certain feelings and propensities" (Kant 1956a, 93), which are different in different people, the danger of the Golden Rule can be avoided. It is understandable why so many contemporary philosophers who come to the rescue of the Golden Rule appeal to Kant.

However, an obvious problem arises with Kant's proposal: If the moral principle is derived entirely from the universal rational will and is completely uninformed of any particularities of moral patients as well as moral agents, how can it be of any practical application? After all, an action is considered moral or immoral because it does something right or wrong to a patient, not merely as a rational being but also as an empirical being. Since the moral agent follows the moral principle, which is derived from the "veil of ignorance" (to use the term of John Rawls, a Kantian philosopher himself), the agent's action lacks the abilities to address the particularities of the moral patient.[2] It is in this sense that I think Hegel's criticism of Kant is still valid and has not been adequately responded to by contemporary defenders of Kant: in Kant's self determination of the rational will, "all that is left for duty itself, in so far as it is the essential or universal element in the moral self-consciousness as it is related within itself to itself alone, is abstract universality, whose determination is *identity without content* or the abstractly *positive*, i.e., the indeterminate" (Hegel 1991, §135). The heart of Hegel's criticism of Kant is that his moral principle is empty of contents, formalistic, and therefore indeterminate in determining the moral value of our actions affecting other people's interest.

While Kant's ethics remains influential, it has been under attack by many contemporary philosophers, particularly the so-called postmodernists, of whom Richard Rorty is arguably the most prominent. Rorty goes so far in his anti-Kantian stance that, for him, the proper response to reading Kant's *The Fundamental Principles of the Metaphysics of Morals* is "either revulsion or a fit of the giggles" (Rorty 2004, 197). However, ironically, even the alternative ethics Rorty proposes is still an ethics of commonality. According to him, moral progress is possible only by increasing "our ability to see more and more differences among people as morally irrelevant . . . to see the differences between people's religions, genders, races, economic status, and so on as irrelevant to the possibility of cooperating with them for mutual benefit and as irrelevant to the need to alleviate their suffering" (Rorty 1998, 11). For Rorty, moral progress is to expand the scope of "us," the scope of those we can identify as "us" instead of "them." This can be realized, in Rorty's view, by the progress of sentiments, which "consists in an increasing ability to see the similarities between ourselves and people very unlike us as outweighing the differences" (Rorty 1998, 181). It is true that, to distinguish his ethics from that of Kant, Rorty is careful to point out that "the relevant similarities are not a matter of sharing a deep true self that instantiates true humanity, but are such little, superficial similarities as cherishing our parents and children—similarities that do not distinguish us in any interesting way from many nonhuman animals" (Rorty 1998, 181). For example, other people "have the same tendency to bleed when pricked[;] . . . they too worry about their children and parents; they are possessed by the same self-doubts, and lose self-confidence when humiliated" (Rorty 2000, 11).

The point that Rorty tries to make is that if we lose sight of commonalities and focus exclusively on differences, we are not able to identify "them" as "us," a possible danger of which is separationism. However, unless Rorty holds a strict conception of negative freedom, thinking that, to be a moral person, all one needs to do is not cause any harm to others, such an emphasis on commonality, it appears to me, must be accompanied by an equal emphasis on difference. One of the banal commonalities that Rorty often talks about is that nobody would like to suffer pain. However, as William I. Buscemi has pointed out, pain itself is not a naked fact. Certain pains may be discernible only to people who have particular religious and philosophical worldviews (see Buscemi 1993, 144 note 6). For example, all starving people like to be fed. However if we ignore the potential differences among different people, we may do something inappropriate: we might provide meat to a vegetarian and may feel offended when the starving vegetarian rejects the meat we offer him. Here Rorty regards such a demand to recognize the difference as a new demand, in contrast to his demand to recognize the commonalities as an old one, and claims that "the new demand is harder to meet than the older, and I am not sure that there is any good reason for the change from the easier to the more stringent demand" (Rorty 2000, 13).[3]

Interestingly enough, what Rorty regards as the new, hard to meet, and unnecessary demand, the demand for "attention to, and respect for, one's distinctive features" is not new at all. We find it in the Confucian idea of love with distinction, particularly as it is interpreted by the neo-Confucian Cheng brothers with their idea of one principle with diverse appearances. In the next section, I shall argue that, in contrast to ethics of commonality, an ethics of difference can be developed from this Confucian idea. The ethics of difference pays attention to the differences among human beings in terms of their ideas and ideals, desires and preferences, habits and customs, and so on, recognizes their equal worth, and requires us to take into full consideration such uniqueness of our moral patients. When we perform actions that affect others, it requires us, instead of acting in whatever way we like, including the way we would like to be acted upon if we were in their positions, to consider what the actual persons who will receive our actions would or would not like. In other words, when we make decisions about the appropriateness of our actions that affect others, what really matters morally is not our desires as agents or subjects, but those of others as patients or recipients of our actions.

3. Love with Distinction

In Confucianism, humanity (*ren* 仁) is the most fundamental virtue. Sometimes
it is regarded as the leading virtue qualifying all other virtues, and it is in this
sense that the Cheng brothers see it as the head and the other four cardinal
virtues—rightness, propriety, wisdom, and faithfulness—as the four limbs;
sometimes it is seen as the complete virtue including all other virtues, and it
is in this sense that the Cheng brothers regard it as the whole body and the
other four virtues as the four limbs of the body. The fundamental meaning of
ren is to love people. Thus, when one of his students asks what *ren* is, Confucius responds that it is "to love people" (*Analects* 12.22). Mencius also states
that a person of *ren* loves people (*Mencius* 4b28). However, what is unique
about love in Confucianism is its conception of family love as paradigmatic. In
the *Analects*, it is said that "filial piety and brotherly love are the root of *ren*"
(*Analects* 1.2).[4] In the *Doctrine of the Mean*, there is a similar claim that "*ren*
is the characteristic element of human beings, and its most important aspect
is to love your family members" (*Zhongyong* 20.5). Mencius held exactly the
same view: "What is the most important duty? It is one's duty toward one's
parents" (*Mencius* 4a19). It is in this sense that Mencius directly links *ren* to
family love: "loving one's parents is *ren*" (*Mencius* 7a15).

Now what causes a problem here is not the Confucian view of family
love as the beginning of *ren*, since such a view does not necessarily contradict
universal love. Confucius himself teaches that "a youth, when at home, should
be filial, and abroad, respectful to his elders. He should be earnest and truthful.
He should love all. Then he is close to *ren*" (*Analects* 1.6). Mencius argues
in the same vein, saying, "Treat the aged of your own family in a manner
befitting their venerable age and extend this treatment to the aged of other
families; treat your own young in a manner befitting their tender age and
extend this to the young of other families" (*Mencius* 1a7). So it is clear that
Confucians do not merely advocate family love. Instead, they ask us to start
from family and then gradually expand this family love to all others. In this
sense, Confucian love is also a universal love, with family love as its starting
point. This conception of love is agreeable to both Moists, who argued against
Confucians, and Hans Küng, who is critical of Confucian love. For example,
the Moist Yuzi 夷子 once tried to interpret Confucian love as meaning that
"there should be no distinction in love, though the practice of it begins with
one's parents" (see *Mencius* 3a5). In Küng's view, Christian love is also "a love,
not of man in general, of someone remote, with whom we are not personally
involved, but quite concretely of one's immediate neighbors" (Küng 1978, 257).

The real problem here is related to the Confucian idea of love with distinction, which is commonly understood to mean that there should be different degrees of love for different kinds of people: stronger love for one's family members and weaker love for others; stronger love for one's immediate neighbors and weaker love for strangers; stronger love for virtuous people and weaker love for evil people; and stronger love for humanity and weaker love for other living beings. For example, even Tu Wei-ming, the most prominent Confucian today, claims that "the responsibility to care for one's own family, clan, kin, neighborhood, village, county, society, nation, world, cosmos is differentiated into varying degrees of intensity" (Tu 1999, 29). This interpretation seems to have some textual evidence in Mencius's debate with the Moists. In Mencius's view, "the Moist idea of universal love amounts to a denial of one's father" (*Mencius* 3b9). Thus, in response to Yizi's 夷子 Moist conception of "love without distinction," Mencius asked, "[D]oes Yizi truly believe that a man loves his brother's son in the same way as he loves his neighbor's new-born babe?" (*Mencius* 3b9). It is here that we have the classical expression of the Confucian conception of love with distinction. While Confucius himself did not live to see this debate, he would certainly agree with Mencius that one's love for parents, for example, is and should be different from one's love for others. In addition, Confucius believed that one's love for virtuous people should be different from one's love for vicious people. Thus when asked whether we should return good to evil, as Christians would advocate, Confucius asked, if so, "with what would you return to good?" In his view, "we should return uprightness to evil and return good to good" (*Analects* 14.34; see Huang 2013a, chapter 2).

Such a conception of love with distinction is problematic from a Christian point of view.[5] Hans Küng, for example, claims that Confucian love in this sense is inferior to Christian universal love: "with Jesus, by contrast, *every* human being—as in the parable of the Good Samaritan—can become the neighbor, can become *my* neighbor. Jesus wants to overcome flesh-and-blood distinctions between family and strangers, adherents to one's own religion and those of another, comrades and noncomrades" (Küng 1989, 118–9).[6] Such a radical love has been vividly expressed in teachings of Jesus such as "[L]love your enemies, do good to those who hate you, bless those who curse you, pray for those who abuse you. To him who strikes you on the cheek, offer the other also; and from him who takes away your coat do not withhold even your shirt" (Luke 6.26). Thus, in appearance, Confucian love with distinction seems to be partial, biased, and therefore inferior to Christian universal love. There have been two responses to this criticism, which seem to me equally inappropriate.

The first emphasizes that the love Confucians advocate is essentially no different from universal love without distinction. For example, Robert Allinson, in order to argue, correctly, that Confucian love is not a gradually weakened love when it expands from family to others, claims, incorrectly, that there is no distinction between Confucian love and universal love. In his view, Confucian family love, put forth as a means to achieve a higher value, "cannot be taken as the highest value that is being espoused: it is therefore a hypothetical value (in strict terms it would be a hypothetical imperative). It does not follow that it possesses no value; it only follows that its value is secondary" (Allinson 1990, 160). In the *Analects*, when it is mentioned that filial piety is the root of *ren*, "the root is certainly the origin, but it is not the end-product. If the end-product or goal is something other than filial piety, then what is really being said here is that filial piety is a way in which one learns how to achieve that something else" (Allinson 1990, 161). Here Allinson correctly argues that filial piety is only a beginning point and not an ending point in Confucius. However, he has confused two meanings of the term "ending point": a ceasing point and a goal. In Confucianism, filial piety is the beginning point, and love for other people and things is the ceasing point but not the goal. Otherwise, we would have to think that family love is only a means to reach the goal, as if we could cease to love parents as soon as we reach the goal of love for all other people and beings.

The second justifies Confucian love with distinction understood as love for different people and things with different degrees. For example, David Wong proposes three reasons to argue for the moral priority of family love over other kinds of love (see Wong 1989, 251–72): (1) love has to start from family love (this is not controversial, but from this it seems that we cannot conclude that family love has to be the strongest); (2) it is human nature to love one's parents more than to love others (this is perhaps true as a matter of fact. However, it is one thing to say that family love is strongest, and it is another to say that family love should be strongest); (3) people should be grateful to their parents for what they have done for them (*gan'en* 感恩)[7] (however, if *gan'en* is the basis of children's love for parents, what will be the basis of parents' love for children? Merely to expect children will return parental love when they grow up? If so, the Confucian idea of love would be indistinguishable from the Moist idea of mutual love [*jianai* 兼愛] that Mencius radically criticizes).

I shall argue that a better defense and more creative interpretation of this apparently problematic Confucian idea of love with distinction is made by the Cheng brothers, particularly CHENG Yi's idea of *li yi fen shu* 理一分殊, normally but not entirely appropriately translated as "one principle with different appearances." CHENG Yi develops this idea in his response to a concern raised by one of his students, YANG Shi 楊時, regarding *Western Inscription* (*Xi Ming* 西銘), a text by ZHANG Zai 張載, whom both Chengs regard very highly.[8] At the beginning of this text, ZHANG Zai claims:

> Heaven is my father and Earth is my mother, and even such a small creature as I finds an intimate place in their midst. Therefore that which fills the universe I regard as my body and that which directs the universe I consider as my nature. All people are my brothers and sisters, and all things are my companions. . . . Respect the aged—this is the way to treat them as elders should be treated. Show deep love toward the orphaned and the weak—this is the way to treat them as the young should be treated. . . . When the time comes, to keep himself from harm—this is the care of a son. To rejoice in Heaven and to have no anxiety—this is the filial piety at its purest. (Zhang 1978, *Zhengmeng* 17: 62; English translation in Chan 1963, 497)

Apparently struck by the first a few sentences that emphasize the unity with ten thousand things, YANG Shi worries that ZHANG Zai here may have fallen into the Moist universal love without distinction.[9] In response, CHENG Yi first states that "the *Western Inscription* performs the same function as Mencius' view of human nature as good and his notion of nourishing one's vital force. This is nothing that Moists can match"; and then he immediately points out, "The *Western Inscription* explains *li yi fen shu* (the one principle with different appearances), while Mozi insists on two roots without distinction. The problem with different appearances (*fen shu* 分殊) [without one principle] is that the private desire would prevail and *ren* would be lost, while the problem with [the one principle] without different appearances is the universal love without rightness" (*Wenji* 9; 609).[10]

In this passage, CHENG Yi makes it clear that, on the one hand, Confucian love is universal love, love for all people and things, and this is what "one principle" means; on the other hand, love for different people and things, to be appropriate, must be different, and this is what "different appearances" means.[11] In his view, those sentences in the *Western Inscription* that emphasize one's unity with the ten thousand things show why love should be universal, while such examples as respecting the aged, deep love for the orphaned and the weak, care of the son, and filial piety for parents show that love for different people should be different. In other words, the Confucian idea of love with distinction, according to CHENG Yi, is not love of different degrees but love of different kinds. It does not mean that one should love some people more than others. Rather it means that one should love different people in different ways, each appropriate to its distinct object. In CHENG Yi's view, on the one hand, if we only pay attention to the one principle (*li yi* 理一) and ignore its diverse appearances, we will commit the Moist mistake of universal love without distinction: loving all in the same way without taking into consideration the uniqueness of each of the objects of our love. On the other hand, if we pay attention to only a particular appearance of love and ignore the one principle of which it is an appearance, we will commit the Yangist mistake of self-love.

With such an understanding of love with distinction in light of one principle with various appearances, we can better understand Mencius's distinction among three kinds of love: "A superior person loves things but is not humane (*ren*) to them. He is humane (*ren*) to people in general but is not affectionate (*qin* 親) to them. He is affectionate to his parents, humane to people, and loves all things" (*Mencius* 7a45). Here, love, being humane, and affection should not be understood as three different degrees of the same love, but as three different kinds of love, appropriate to three different kinds of moral patients: things, humans, and parents. In this connection, the two different attitudes Confucius recommended toward two different kinds of people, "virtue" to virtuous people and "uprightness" to evil people, should also be understood as two different kinds of love appropriate to these two different kinds of moral patients. It is also in this sense that we can understand why Confucius claimed that "only a person of *ren* knows how to love people and hate people" (*Analects* 4.3). In other words, from the Confucian point of view, "hate," just as "love," is a kind of love in a more general sense. On the one hand, the most fundamental meaning of *ren* is to love, so the person of *ren* who knows how to love and hate must be a loving person; on the other hand, as Wing-tsit Chan already pointed out, "hate" here does not have any connotation of ill will (see Chan 1963, 25 note 53). It is rather one's profound feeling of regret that one's beloved moral patient lacks what it should have. So the reason that Confucianism wants to make a distinction is not to decide whom or what we should love or love more and whom or what we should not love or love less; it is rather to decide how to love everyone and everything in ways most appropriate to the person or thing.

Obviously, true love cannot be a transcendent love. It has to be based on one's empirical knowledge of the particular object of love. Otherwise, one would not be able to know the uniqueness of the object of love and therefore would not be able to love the object in an appropriate way. To love different people and things in ways appropriate to these objects of love, one must learn about the uniqueness of the object of one's love. It is for this reason that the Cheng brothers emphasize the importance of knowing people (*zhi ren* 知人). There is a related passage in the *Zhongyong* that says that "superior persons may not neglect self-cultivation; to cultivate themselves, they may not neglect to serve their parents; to serve their parents, they may not neglect to know them; and to know them, they may not neglect to know heaven" (*Zhongyong* 19). Commenting on the sentence about knowing people, one of the Chengs states that "without knowing people, one may be affectionate to their parents not as they are. . . . As a result, the person may humiliate himself or herself and cause harm to their parents" (*Yishu* 4; 72). Similarly, commenting on *Analects* 2.10, where Confucius asks us "to see what people do, to observe what they intend, and to examine on what they rest," CHENG Hao claims that "only this way can one know people as sages do" (*Waishu* 6; 379). Of course, the Chengs acknowledge that it is not easy to know people (*Yishu* 4; 72). However, what is important is to have a sincere heart. For example, "an infant child cannot talk, and so his or her will, intention, preference, and desire are not known to his or her mother as well as to others. However, the mother does not make mistake about these. How is it possible? It is due to nothing but her sincere heart with love and respect. If one loves people as if they were one's own infant children, how can one make any mistake? Therefore, if one is sincere in heart when seeking knowledge of people, one may not be able to get exactly right, but it will not be far off" (*Yishu* 2a; 16).[12]

In this sense, while the Cheng brothers would agree with Mencius that *ren*, of which various kinds of love are appearances, is internal to the person who loves, the actual shape the love takes is determined externally by the object of one's love. Thus, commenting on the famous statement of Confucius that "to overcome oneself and return to the propriety is *ren*" (*Analects* 12.1), CHENG Yi claims that to overcome oneself is "to treat things according to things themselves and not according to ourselves, so that one can become selfless (*wuwo* 無我)" (*Yishu* 11; 125). In this context, he compares the heart/mind of the sage with the "bright mirror" and "still water": "when things that should be loved appear, the sage loves them, and when things that should be hated, the sage hates them" (*Yishu* 18; 210–11). In other words, the sage's hate and love are determined by things and not by themselves. On this point, CHENG Hao entirely agrees. In his view, "when selfless one becomes a sage" (*Yishu* 11; 126); and he claims that "a sage is happy with something because it is the thing that one should be happy with; a sage is angry at something because it is the thing that one should be angry at. Therefore the heart and mind of a sage is not determined by itself but by external things" (*Wenji* 2; 460). In CHENG Yi's view, this is the main distinction between superior persons and inferior persons: "the anger of inferior persons comes from themselves, while the anger of the superior persons comes from things [they are angry at]" (*Yishu* 23; 306).[13]

Of course, this idea, that the actual shape of love is determined by the uniqueness of the given object of love, is not alien to Mencius, although he emphasizes the internality of *ren* and rightness. Mencius himself asks us to pay attention to the uniqueness of different things: "That things are different is part of their nature. . . . If you reduce them to the same, it will only bring confusion to the Empire" (*Mencius* 3a4). In another place, where he emphasizes the importance for a ruler of a kingdom to have the support of its people from the bottom of their heart, Mencius states that, to do so, the ruler "should gather for them what they need and not impose on them what they do not like" (*Mencius* 4a9). Indeed, this is the passage from which the Cheng brothers get their inspiration (see, for example, *Jingshuo* 8; 1157). When CHENG Yi says that "one should respect people's desire but must not impose one's desire upon people" (*Yishu* 25; 319), when CHENG Hao asks rulers to "serve people with what suits them, give people what they need, and not to impose upon them what they hate" (*Waishu* 6; 382; see also *Waishu* 6; 391), and when both brothers underline the passage in the *Great Learning* explaining the idea of a ruler as the parent of its people—"love what people love and hate what people hate: This is how to be the parent of one's people" (*Jingshuo* 5; 1128, 1132)—they are essentially saying the same thing.

From the above, we can see that what is essential to the true love, love with distinction, for the Cheng brothers, is one's becoming selfless. It is this idea of selflessness that can help us understand how the Cheng brothers deal with several clear expressions of the Golden Rule, treated as one form of the ethics of commonality that we contrast with the Cheng brothers' ethics of difference, in Confucian classics. In its negative form, Confucius says, "Do not do unto others what we do not want to be done to us" (*Analects* 15.24); in its positive form, Confucius tells us that "a person of *ren*, desiring to establish one's own character, also establishes the character of others and, wishing to be prominent himself, also helps other to be prominent" (*Analects* 6.30). In the *Doctrine of Mean*, after a similar statement—"what you do not wish others do to you, do not do to them,"—Confucius says, "[T]here are four things in the Way of the superior person, none of which I have been able to do. To serve my father as I would expect my son to serve me: that I have not been able to do. To serve my ruler as I would like my ministers to serve me: that

I have not been able to do. To serve my elder brothers as I would expect my younger brothers to serve me: that I have not been able to do. To be the first to treat friends as I would expect them to treat me: that I have not been able to do" (*Zhongyong* 23; translation in Chan 1963, 101). Finally, in the *Great Learning*, there is the following passage, "what a man dislike in his superiors, let him not show it in dealing with his inferiors; what he dislikes in those in front of him, let him not show it in preceding those who are behind; what he dislikes in those behind him, let him not show it in following those in front of him; what he dislikes in those on his right, let him not apply it to those on the left; and what he dislikes in those on the left, let him not apply it to those on the right" (*Daxue* 10; translation in Chan 1963, 92).

For the Cheng brothers, however, the idea of the Golden Rule expressed in these various classical passages is not central to Confucianism. Confucius says that "there is one thing that goes through my teaching," and Zengzi says, in the same chapter of *Analects*, that this one thing is nothing but the Golden Rule (*Analects* 4.15). What Zengzi says has since been commonly accepted as the correct interpretation of what Confucius means. However, CHENG Yi claims that this one thing that goes through Confucius's teaching is *ren* (*Yishu* 23; 306). In the Chengs' view, the relationship between the Golden Rule and *ren* is similar to that between filial piety and brotherly love, on the one hand, and *ren*, on the other. When asked about the *Analects* passage that is commonly translated as "filial piety and brotherly love is the beginning of the *ren*," the Chengs claim that "it really means that filial piety and brotherly love is the beginning of the practice of *ren*, just as the Golden Rule is the beginning of the practice of *dao*" (*Waishu* 7; 395). It is in this sense that the Chengs can agree that the Golden Rule is indeed "not far from *dao* (*li dao bu yuan* 違道 不遠) [*Zhongyong* 12]," is "close to *ren* (*jin ren* 近於仁)," is "the door to *ren* (*ru ren zhi men* 入仁之門)," is "a way to practice *ren* (*ren zhi fang* 仁之方) [*Analects* 6.30]" (*Yishu* 7; 97), but they insist that "it has not reached *ren* yet," because it is [based on my] desire" (*Waishu* 7; 395): "because it takes one's own likes and dislikes as the criteria in one's interactions with others, and so it has not reached the level of selflessness (*wuwo* 無我)" (*Yishu* 22b; 275), although to become selfless is the most difficult thing to do (*Yishu* 9; 108). As we have seen, for both Chengs, a person of *ren* is selfless; and when one is selfless, one can take care of others according to them and not according to oneself. The Golden Rule can be a way to practice *ren*, is not far from *ren*, and is the doorway to *ren*, because, on the one hand, while there are differences between moral agents and moral patients, there are also similarities. When they are similar, the Golden Rule may be practiced. On the other hand, as we have also seen, it is more difficult to love others according to their likes and dislikes than to do so according to our own likes and dislikes, as it is difficult to have accurate knowledge of others, so when not enough is known about the object of love, one may practice the Golden Rule as the second best and as a way to acquire such knowledge.

4. Extension of Love

One of the central features of Confucian love with distinction, interpreted as an ethics of difference by the Cheng brothers through the idea of one principle with many appearances, is that, while a superior person should love all, the actual shape of the love should be determined by the uniqueness of each particular patient. Thus an action that is morally appropriate toward one person in one circumstance may not be so toward a different person, or the same person, for that matter, in a different circumstance. This is an idea that is also emphasized by moral particularism and antitheory in contemporary ethics. One of the most influential representatives of this school is Jonathan Dancy. Dancy argues against ethical generalism, a view that "the very possibility of moral thought and judgment depends on the provision of a suitable supply of moral principles" (Dancy 2004, 7). There is an absolute (Kantian) conception of moral principle, which "takes a moral principle to be a universal claim to the effect that all actions of a certain type are overall wrong (or right)" (Dancy 2009, §1). The problem with such a conception, in Dancy's view, is that unless there is only one such moral principle or, when more than one, there is no conflict between different moral principles when applied to one and the same situation, moral principles in such an absolute conception cannot help us determine whether a given action is morally right or wrong.

So Dancy's main target of attack is what he regards as the (Rossian) "contributory" conception of moral principles, since the absolute conception cannot be right if the contributory conception is wrong (but not the other way around). The contributory conception "allows that more than one principle can apply to the case before us," and each principle contributes to counting for or against a particular action; but since an action has many relevant features, some moral principles count for it while some others count against it; so "whether the action is overall right or wrong can only be determined by the overall balance of right and wrong in it" (Dancy 2009, §1). Thus, for example, if there is a moral principle against promise breaking, there may still be cases in which the action of promise breaking is considered as right, not because promise breaking itself becomes a moral action, but because the action of promise breaking has some other features which are consistent with some other moral principles that count for the action. This is an atomist view of moral reasons: "a feature that is a reason in one case must remain a reason, and retain the same polarity, in any other" (Dancy 2004, 74). In other words, moral reason is transportable from one situation to another.

Dancy argues against such an atomist view. In his view, there is no guarantee for such transportability. In a nonmoral case, Dancy uses the example of perception of red. In normal situations, the fact that it currently seems to me that something before me is red is a reason for me to believe that there is something red before me. However, in a situation where I also believe that I have recently taken a drug that makes blue things look red and red things look blue, the same fact becomes a reason for me to believe that there is a blue instead of a red thing before me (Dancy 2004, 74; 2009, §3). Dancy claims that the same is true in moral cases. For example, normally the fact that I made a promise is a reason for me to keep it, but in some other situations it may become a reason for me not to keep it (for example, if the promise I make is to not keep the next three promises I will make) (Dancy 2009, §5); normally the fact that an action is prohibited by law is a reason for me not to do it, but in some other situations it may become a reason for me to do it (if it governs an aspect of private life with which the law should not interfere in the first place, for example) (Dancy 2004, 62; 2009, §3); normally the fact that I borrow a book from you is a reason for me to return it to you, but in some situations it may become a reason for me not to (if you stole it from the library) (Dancy 2004, 60).

So, in contrast to moral generalism, Dancy argues for moral particularism, a view that "the possibility of moral thought and judgement does not depend on the provision of a suitable supply of moral principles" (Dancy 2004, 7). Just as generalism is based on an atomist conception of reason, Dancy's particularlism is based on a holist conception of moral reason, according to which "a reason in one case may be no reason at all, or an opposite reason, in another" (Dancy 2004, 7). According to such a moral particularism based on a holist conception of moral reasons, "everything appears to be . . . context-dependent. If one wants to know whether some feature is of value here, one cannot get one's answer by looking to see how it behaves elsewhere" (Dancy 2004, 184). Dancy does acknowledge the existence of what he calls default values or disvalue. Default values or disvalues are the features that bring values or disvalues with them to any particular situation, though once they are brought to a particular situation, they may be wiped out or even reversed by other features of the situation (Dancy 2004, 184–87). The difference between features with default values or disvalues and features that get their values or disvalues only after they are brought into a particular context is important. In the latter, we always need an explanation of why a particular feature has a value or disvalue in a particular context. A feature acquires a value in a given situation through the presence of some other features, which Dancy calls enablers, features that enable the feature in question to have the value or disvalue. If such enablers are not present in a different situation, the same feature in question will not have the value acquired in the previous situation. In the former, however, such an explanation is needed only if these features do not contribute their default values or disvalues in a particular context. A feature loses its default value or disvalue in a given context only because of the presence of some other features in the context that disable it, the presence of the disablers. A default value or disvalue may also be increased by the presence of intensifiers (features that increase the default value or disvalue) or diminished by the presence of attenuators (features that decrease the default value or disvalue) (Dancy 2004, chapter 3).

In appearance, there is a conflict between Dancy's moral particularism and the Cheng brothers' idea of *li yi fen shu* 理一分殊, particularly as we have followed the convention to translate *li* as "principle" so that it becomes "one principle with diverse appearances," since the moral particularists' main target of attack is precisely the conception of moral principle, and the title of Dancy's main work in moral particularism is indeed *Ethics without Principle*. Therefore, it is important to have a clearer understanding of this idea of *li yi fen shu*. As we have seen, although this idea has become central to neo-Confucian metaphysics, CHENG Yi develops it largely to explain the Mencian idea of love with distinctions as expressed in ZHANG Zai's *Western Inscription*. For Cheng, this "one" principle does not mean a universal and abstract love, which has many appearances. Any love is particular and concrete: love for one's parents, for one's spouse, for one's children, for a neighbor, for a friend, for a stranger, for an enemy, and so on. There is no one true, genuine, abstract, and universal love above all these particular forms of love, which is to be applied to any particular situation. In this respect, it is illuminating to point out an important historical fact. It is now commonly accepted that CHENG Yi's idea of one principle with diverse appearances has a Buddhist origin. For example, Huayan 華嚴 Buddhism has a conception of one *li* 理 and many *shi* 事 (events) and claims that the one *li* is complete (instead of partial) in each of the many *shi*. Chan (Zen) Buddhism holds a similar view. As a matter of fact, Chan Master Xuanjue's 玄覺 (665–713) famous analogy of one moon reflected in ten thousand rivers (*yue yin wan chuan* 月印萬川) is used later by Zhu Xi to explain Cheng Yi's idea of *li yi fen shu*. It is interesting that Cheng Yi himself, obviously aware of this famous analogy, does not use it to explain his idea. In the analogy of "one moon reflected in ten thousand rivers," the moon exists in the sky independently of its reflection in the ten thousand rivers. However, as we have seen, for Cheng Yi, there is not a "real" love, like the moon in the sky, that is manifested in different kinds of concrete love. Different kinds of concrete love are all that exist.

It is in this sense that we can claim that Cheng Yi's *li yi fen shu* is compatible with Dancy's moral particularism. However, there is a significant difference in another sense. As we have seen, for Dancy, "the behavior of a reason . . . in a new case cannot be predicted from its behaviour elsewhere. The way in which the consideration functions *here* either will or at least may be affected by other considerations here present. So there is no ground for the hope that we can find out here how that consideration functions *in general*, somehow, nor for the hope that we can move in any smooth way to how it will function in a different way" (Dancy 1993, 60). Here, while emphasizing the importance of the uniqueness of each new situation in moral reasoning, Dancy does not pay enough attention to the importance of moral experience. Dancy does acknowledge that "experience of similar cases can tell us what sort of thing to look out for, and the sort of relevance that a certain feature can have; in this way our judgement in a new case can be informed, though it is not forced or constrained, by our experience of similar cases in the past" (Dancy 2009, §8). However, following another moral particularist, John McDowell, who claims that from moral experience we can get nothing but "the capacity to get things right occasion by occasion" (McDowell 1998a, 94), Dancy maintains that "there is nothing that one brings to the new situation other than a *contentless* ability to discern what matters where it matters, an ability whose presence in us is explained by our having undergone a successful moral education" (Dancy 1993, 50; emphasis added).

In contrast, for the Chengs, although all concrete loves are different (*fenshu* 分殊) they can all be regarded as the same (*li yi* 理一). The reason is that, however different from each other they are, they all look alike and can be regarded as the same love in a sense similar to Wittgenstein's family resemblance. Because they are similar to each other, while one's love experience in one situation cannot be simply "transported" or "switched" to a different situation,[14] it will help one to find the appropriate love in a different situation. Moreover, what we can learn from past moral practices is not merely the *contentless* ability or capacity to get things right in future situations. This is closely related to the Cheng brothers' idea of *tui* 推, expanding one's natural love gradually from one's own family to all sentient beings in the world, the inborn ability that, for the Chengs, distinguishes human beings from animals. Clearly, this ability is not merely the contentless one to get things right, since the ability of expanding must be related to the thing, one's love in past experiences, that is to be expanded.

In previous chapters, we emphasized the Confucian distinction the Cheng brothers make between human beings and animals in terms of morality: only human beings can be moral and those who are immoral are to be regarded as no different from beasts. In other words, the distinctive mark of being human, what makes human beings different from animals, for the Cheng brothers, is to be moral. So to be moral is the distinctive mark of being human. This conception appears to be irreconcilable to the discovery of contemporary evolutionary biology and evolutionary psychology, which have shown that animals and human beings form a continuum in terms of concern for the interest of others. For example, it is found that prairie dogs send out alarm calls to warn other members of their group of perceived dangers, female lions suckle cubs of other lionesses, primates engage in grooming behavior to rid members of their troop of parasites, and soldier aphids forego their own reproduction for the sake of the cline mates (see Betram 1976; Ridley and Dawkins 1981, 42–43; and Silk, Samuels, and Rodman 1981). It is based on such a recognition that Mary Midgley even goes so far as to claim that "we are not just like animals; we *are* animals (Midley 1995, xiii). This idea, however, is not unknown to the Cheng brothers, as we can see from the following passage:

> Mencius regards the four beginnings [of humanity, rightness, propriety, and wisdom] as the four limbs of one's body. . . . This is not something humanly arranged. They are also complete in animals such as cows and horses. Only because they have different material constitutions are they obscured by the constitution of vital force (*qi*). For example, in children's love for their mother and the mother's love for her children, there is also atmosphere of wood [representing the first beginning, *ren*]. Also, how can the heart of shame and dislike [the second beginning] be absent [in animals]? Things such as avoiding harm and seeking benefit and distinguishing between things to love and things to hate are all complete in them. Monkeys, being the most intelligent among animals, particularly resemble human beings. Children and muddled people who are less intelligent than such animals are not few. (*Yishu* 2b; 54)[15]

In this and related passages, the Chengs make several important points. First, we can see that almost one thousand years ago the Cheng brothers were already aware of what contemporary evolutionary biology and psychology tell us today: certain sorts of altruistic love also exist in some animals. In the above passage, it is mentioned that in cows and horses there is a mutual love between children and their mothers (*Yishu* 2b; 54). In two other places, CHENG Yi discusses other cases: "There are [nonhuman] things that also obtain the heaven-principle. For example, bees and ants know how to protect their kings, and jackals and otters know how to perform sacrifice" (*Yishu* 17; 180); and "dogs, cows, and human beings, in terms of knowing what to like and what to dislike, all have the same nature. However, constrained by their respective constitutions, they cannot be changed into each other" (*Yishu* 24; 312).

Second, the reason that such altruistic love exists not only in human beings but also in animals, according to the Cheng brothers, is that the four beginnings that Mencius talks about are present not only in humans but also in animals. We have seen that for the Cheng brothers, human nature is virtuous. Yet they also argue that humans and animals and plants (and sometimes even nonliving things) share the same nature: "all ten thousand things have the same nature, i.e. the five constants [*ren*, rightness, propriety, wisdom, and faithfulness]" (*Yishu* 9; 105). Since in the Cheng brothers, nature is identical to principle (*li* 理), they also claim that human beings share the same principle with all other beings. For example, CHENG Hao makes the famous claim that all ten thousand things, including human beings, form one body: "By 'all ten thousand things form one body,' we mean that they have the same principle. . . . [The difference is that] human beings can extend it, while things, muddled by their *qi*, cannot. However, we cannot therefore say that things do not have it" (*Yishu* 2a; 33).

This last quote leads to the third point: the difference between human beings and animals. If human beings share the same nature and principle with animals, and if animals also have altruistic love as humans do, how are humans different from animals, and in what sense can the Chengs claim that being moral is the distinguishing mark of being human? The Chengs' response is that the difference between humans and animals really lies in the ability of expanding (*tui* 推) the inborn love for those in the small circle to those beyond, which exists in humans but not in animals. This idea of *tui* originates from Mencius and, to some extent, Confucius. According to Mencius, "treat the aged in my own family in a manner befitting their venerable age and then expand (*ji* 及) this treatment to the aged of other families; treat the young in my own family in a manner befitting their tender age and expand this treatment to the young of other families, and you can roll the whole world on your palm" (*Mencius* 1a7). Here Mencius uses the word *ji,* which means the same as *tui,* and the examples he uses to explain the idea of *ji* are the same as those the Cheng brothers use in the above passage: to expand one's feeling of love for family members to others. Moreover, continuing from the same place, immediately after citing a poem in the *Book of Poetry,* Mencius uses the word *tui* itself to explain the meaning of the poem: "What the poem says is that all you have to do is to take your loving heart/mind here to apply it to what is over there. Hence one who expands (*tui*) one's bounty can bring peace to the whole world, while one who does not cannot bring peace even to one's own family. The reason that ancient people are superior to others is that they are good at expanding what they do [in their family]" (*Mencius* 1a7). Although Confucius does not use the world *tui* itself, expansion of one's natural family love is also essential to his teaching. For example, he says that "a youth, when at home, should be filial, and abroad, respectful to his elders. He should be earnest and truthful. He should overflow in love to all" (*Analects* 1.6).

So the idea of *tui* has been important for Confucianism from the very beginning. To highlight it, the Cheng brothers regard it as the criterion to distinguish between human beings and animals. In other words, while animals love those they are naturally disposed to love, they cannot expand this love to those they are not naturally disposed to love. Human beings, however, have the ability to expand their natural love from those they are naturally disposed to love to those they are not naturally disposed to. This is an important point that the Chengs repeat in several other places. For example, commenting on Mencius's statement that "all ten thousand things are complete in me," after claiming that "this is true of both human beings and animals, and animals resemble human beings very much," they also point out that "the only thing they [animals] cannot do is to expand [that in which they resemble human beings]. However, everything that animals are disposed to do, such as building homes and raising children, is natural, and there is no need to learn or teach" (*Yishu* 2b; 56).

Fourth, for the Chengs, while humans and animals have the same nature, they are constituted by different *qi.* In the above mentioned passage, CHENG Hao states that, while the four beginnings also exist in cows and horses, they are clouded by their *qi.* This indicates that the *qi* that animals are endowed with is not clear. In contrast, CHENG Hao points out that "the human *qi* is most clear and therefore can become partner [with heaven and earth]" (*Yishu* 2b; 54). In another place, CHENG Hao claims that the human *qi* is balanced (*zheng qi* 正氣), while the animal *qi* is one-sided (*pian qi* 偏氣):

Between heaven and earth, humans are not the only thing intelligent. One's own heart/mind is also the heart/mind of plants and
animals. However, humans are born with the balanced [*qi*] of
heaven and earth. The difference between humans and animals lies
in the *qi* they are respectively endowed with: while the latter is
one-sided (*pian* 偏), the former is balanced (*zheng* 正). *Yin* alone
cannot bring anything into completion, and *yang* alone cannot
give birth to anything either. Those that got one-sided *qi* of *yin*
and *yang* are plants and animals, and those that get the balanced
qi are human beings. (*Yishu* 1; 4; see also *Yishu* 11; 123)

CHENG Yi agrees with his brother, saying that "humans are born with the balanced *qi* of heaven and earth and this is how humans are different from the
ten thousand things" (*Yishu* 18; 211). In addition, CHENG Yi also makes the
distinction between humans and other beings in terms of the purity (*chun*
純) and impurity (*fan* 繁) of the *qi* endowed. When asked, "Is it true that
humans are born with pure *qi*, while insects are born with impure *qi*?" CHENG
Yi replies affirmatively: "Yes. Humans are from the fine *qi* (*xiuqi* 秀氣) of the
five elements [gold, wood, water, fire, and earth], which originates from the
clear, bright, and pure *qi* of heaven and earth" (*Yishu* 18; 198–99). Sometimes,
CHENG Yi regards this fine *qi* as the *qi* of true origin (*zhen yuan zhi qi* 真元
之氣) (*Yishu* 15; 148).[16]

While I suspect that we can find its counterpart in contemporary explanation of the human-animal distinction (see Dorter 2009, 261), there is no need
to go into details of the Cheng brothers' idea of *qi*.[17] Whatever its cause, the
Chengs' observation that human beings can, while animals cannot, expand their
inborn natural love is still significant. So I would like to conclude this section
by underlining in what sense it is significant. To say that one should expand
one's family love to those outside one's immediate kin is not controversial
at all. Both Moists, who argue against Confucians,[18] and Hans Küng, who is
critical of Confucian love, agree. In Küng's view, Christian love is also "a love,
not of man in general, of someone remote, with whom we are not personally
involved, but quite concretely of one's immediate neighbors" (Küng 1978, 257).
An important issue here is how to expand this family love. This is made clear
in the following passage: "The way the Duke of Zhou treats his elder brothers
and the way Shun treats his younger brother are the same. We need to figure
out what is their intention. Nothing is needed but to expand this intention in
interaction with other people. Of course, there must be distinctions" (*Yishu*
22b; 298). Here, using the example of Shun and the Duke of Zhou, CHENG Yi

continues to show that to become a sage one only need expand one's inborn love. However, what I want to emphasize is the last sentence—"Of course, there must be distinctions"—which shows that, when one expands one's love for one's family members to others, one does not simply transport this love to some other objects. As we have emphasized in the previous section, love, to be appropriate, must take into consideration the uniqueness of each object of love. A kind of love appropriate to one person may be inappropriate to a different person, and a kind of love appropriate to a person on one occasion may become inappropriate on another occasion. So the Cheng brothers' idea of *tui* in connection with their idea of one principle with many appearances stands between the ethics of commonality, for which moral action is nothing but to apply the universal moral principle to each particular situation, and Dancy's radical moral particularism, according to which we must start entirely from scratch in every new situation. According to this via media, what happens in moral practice is to expand one's love learned in previous situations to a new situation, with necessary modifications called for by what is unique in this new situation.[19] In other words, what we can learn from our past moral experiences is not merely the formal ability to get things right in future practices but also the "content" of what is to be considered moral and what is to be considered immoral.

5. Training of Emotions

It is in this context of morality as expansion of love that we can better understand why Confucianism emphasizes so much the importance of family love. In the *Analects*, it is said that "superior persons devote their effort to the root. When the root is established, the way will grow therefrom. Filial piety and brotherly love are *wei ren zhi ben* 為仁之本" (*Analects* 1.2). As we have seen, the last sentence has customarily been interpreted as "filial piety and brotherly love are the root of *ren*." This interpretation reads the character "*wei* 為" as a copula, linking "filial piety and brotherly love" (the subject) and "the root of *ren*" (the predicate). In the Chengs' view, however, the character should be understood as a verb meaning "practice," with *ren*, the word immediately after it, as its direct object. Thus they argue that "'filial piety and brotherly love' are the root of practicing *ren* and not the root of *ren*" (*Yishu* 11, 125). When asked whether a person who practices filial piety and brotherly love is a person of *ren*, CHENG Yi answers with a resounding "no": "Filial piety and brotherly love are only one aspect of *ren*. It may be regarded as the beginning of practicing *ren*, but it may not be regarded as the root of *ren*" (*Yishu* 18; 183).

So while family love is important in its own light, it is also important because it is the necessary starting point of morality, which is precisely to expand the family love. The question is whether morality can have a different starting point. In other words, can morality be an expansion of something other than family love? Mencius mentions three main stages of morality as expansion of love: from affection for parents (*qinqin* 親親) to humanity for people (*renmin* 仁民) and finally to love for things (*aiwu* 愛物). When one of his students asks whether it is possible to reverse the order and start from love for things, CHENG Yi replies: "It is against propriety to be reverent to others without being reverent to one's parents, and it is against virtue to love others without loving one's parents. . . . If one has affection to parents, how can one be not humane to people? And if one has humanity to people, how can one not love things? It is the Moist idea to start from love for things to affection for parents" (*Yishu* 23, 310). The reason is that, for the Chengs, love is a natural feeling or emotion, which one acquires first within the family. Asked by CHENG Yi to understand the true meaning of the famous *Analects* passage on family love as the root of [practicing] *ren*, one of his students made the following report: "When one is just born, a person is endowed with what is central of heaven and earth as well as with what is fine of the five elements. Thus, *ren* is already present in one's endowment at the very beginning. As soon as one is born, no one fails to know to love his or her parents, and, when growing up, no one fails to know to respect his or her elder brother, which is how *ren* functions externally" (*Yishu* 23; 309). Upon hearing that, CHENG Yi states approvingly that this is very nicely said. This is because it reflects CHENG Yi's own view of the relationship between *ren* and love: "The feeling of commiseration is love. Love is a feeling, while *ren* is human nature" (*Yishu* 18; 182). Here *ren* as human nature can be compared to a seed, while love as a human emotion can be compared to the sprout: "As long as there is [human] nature, there will be feeling. How can there be feelings if they are not based on human nature?" (*Yishu* 18; 204). For this reason, the Cheng brothers argue against the Buddhist view that one can perfect one's human nature only by extinguishing one's feeling: "Human feelings of joy, anger, sorrow, and pleasure are all natural expressions of human nature. Now [Buddhists] insist that we should extinguish them in order to return to the original human nature. It amounts to abandoning our human nature" (*Yishu* 2a; 24). The argument here is clear enough: every human being has its nature which is good; human nature must manifest itself as a feeling; such a feeling normally starts with one's love for family members; so morality as the expansion of the local love must start from family love.

In appearance, it is insignificant to maintain that love is an emotion or feeling: of course it is an emotion. However, this is precisely the place where Christian and Confucian conceptions disagree. From the Christian perspective, the Confucian conception of love as a natural feeling is problematic as a moral ideal: it lacks the dimension of universality and normativity: feeling can occur only in a particular situation.[20] In this sense, Confucian love, based on one's natural feeling, cannot function as a moral command like Christian love. As pointed out by Paul Tillich, "If love is emotion, how can it be commanded: emotion cannot be commanded. We cannot demand them of themselves. If we try, something artificial is produced which shows the traits of what had to be suppressed in its production. . . . Love, intentionally produced, shows indifference or hostility in perversion. This means: love as an emotion cannot be commanded" (Tillich 1960, 4). For this reason, love as the highest moral command in Christianity is a love not based on feeling or the emotion of love. Fletcher makes this point most clear: Christian love "is a 'love' of command- ment. And it is an attitude, a will-disposition, and a matter of conative—not the emotive. Only a pervert and stubborn sentimentalism will persist in treating it as feeling. . . . The result is that we are to love the unlikable. Only in this way can we grasp the meaning of 'love your enemies'" (Fletcher 1966, 49).

The Christian love Tillich and Fletcher have in mind is agape, which for Nygren and Grant is the distinctively *Christian* love (see Nygren 1969; Grant 1996). However, there are scholars who disagree on this (see Vacek 1996, 29) and focus on *eros* (see Heyward 1989) and *philia* (see D'arcy 1945) instead. According to them, what make *eros* and *philia* different from agape is precisely that the former are based on one's feeling, while the latter is not. Still, the feeling associated with these two ideas is a self-concerned feeling, since these two ideas are usually emphasized precisely to counter the extreme altruistic tendency of agape. In this sense, it is still different from the feeling associ- ated with Confucian love, which is not self-concerned but is truly altruistic. A closer counterpart in Christianity of Confucian emphasis on love as a feeling is perhaps expressed in the phrase "with whole heart" in the first command- ment, at least according to Origen's interpretation. In this commandment, Christians are asked to love God not only with their whole mind, whole soul, and whole strength, but also with their whole *heart*. The addition of "whole heart" means precisely that one should love God not only resolutely, but also willingly, joyfully, and passionately, which is also precisely what Confucians mean by love as a feeling. Confucians often use these two terms, "feeling" and "heart," interchangeably. When they emphasize the importance of love as a feeling, they are asking us to love everyone and everything (just as Jesus asks Christians to love God) with our whole mind, whole soul, whole strength, and whole *heart*.

The problem with Christian love understood as a feeling in the above sense is two-fold. First, if Origen was correct that there is an order of love, we may ask why Christians are only asked to love God with their whole heart and not to love their neighbors (including enemies) in the same way? Second, if love for God must be wholehearted, how can such a love be commanded? While one may be commanded to change one's mind and to do something one does not like to do, one cannot be commanded to *like* to do something wholeheartedly. In this context, we can see the same problem with Robert Neville's attempt to reconcile Christian and Confucian conceptions of love. In his view, Confucian love is mainly for normal families, while Christian love is applicable to dysfunctional families. For this reason, while Confucian love emphasizes filial piety, Christian love focuses on divine love. Yet, if we see God as the parent of all human beings, Christian love is really not different from Confucian love (see Neville 1999, 207–08).[21] However, family love in Confucianism is an untaught natural feeling one experiences. Thus, when Confucius asks people to expand this family love to others, people know what this means and how to do it. In contrast, if Neville is correct that Christian love is for widows and orphans who lack the experience of family love, then they will be at a loss if asked to love God as they love their fathers and more so if further asked to love their neighbors as they love God.

Thus one of the advantages of the Confucian conception of love as a feeling is its recognition of the genuineness of love: a loving action that is not based on a feeling is not an expression of genuine love. In this sense, love is indeed not something that can be commanded. When a couple no longer love each other, we may be able to command them not to harm each other, to share the necessary care of their children, and even to help each other, but certainly we cannot command them to love each other. At the same time, however, we have to realize that love as a natural feeling is partial. One does have this natural feeling for family members, and one is indeed born with the natural ability to expand this feeling beyond the family, but this does not mean that one will naturally exercise this natural ability to expand the natural feeling of love to all. Thus, while emphasizing that love must be a true feeling or emotion, Confucianism also maintains that we should make every effort to love those "unlovable," those toward whom we have not yet had the feeling of love. Between commanding people to love the unlovable and maintain a moral indifference to them, Confucianism adopts a third alternative: to cultivate a true feeling or emotion of love toward those "unlovable" so that one can truly love them. The so-called "unlovable" are those toward whom we have not cultivated the feeling or emotion of love yet, between whom and our loved ones (particularly our family members) we have not found clear analogies yet, and to whom, to use Richard Rorty's terms, we have been used to referring as "they" rather than "we" (Rorty 1989, 190). Thus the moral education Confucianism advocates is precisely to help us find the analogy between those we love and those we do not so that we can expand our true feeling of love to those "unlovable."

The story between Mencius and King Xuan of Qi mentioned earlier is a good example of such moral education. The king loved the ox and not the lamb because he had the heart of commiseration for the ox that he saw and not the lamb that he did not see. In Mencius's view, we cannot coerce the king to love the lamb before he has the feeling of love for the lamb, but at the same time, we should not approve the king's indifference toward the lamb just because he does not have the true feeling of love for it. The appropriate way is to help the king to imagine that the lamb is just in front of him and is about to be killed. This way the king would be able to expand his heart of commiseration to the lamb.[22] Here the way to help people love the unlovable is not to artificially, coercively, and externally impose the feeling of love upon them. It is rather to help them discover their lost or unaroused feeling of love, since, as Mencius claims, "the heart of commiseration is inborn with everyone" (*Mencius* 6a6). It is precisely in this sense that, for Mencius, "whoever is devoid of the heart of commiseration is not a human" (*Mencius* 2a6). Only because of artificial, external, and coercive forces have people lost their inborn natural feeling of love. Thus to try one's best to restore such a feeling, ironically, becomes a natural activity. For Mencius, when one's inborn heart of commiseration and other gems are fully developed, "he can take under his protection the whole realm within the four seas, but if he fails to develop them, he will not be able even to serve his parents" (*Mencius* 2a6).

This process of moral education, on the way of the gradual expansion of love, is called "naturalizing the human feeling" (*xing qi qing* 性其情) by CHENG Yi. As we have seen, for Cheng, family love as a feeling is the first external appearance of *ren*, which is constitutive of human nature. However, one the one hand, *ren* goes beyond family love and requires one to love the ten thousand things; on the other hand, while human nature is originally good, its external appearance as a feeling is not always good. To explain this, the Chengs appeal to the well-known sentence in the Confucian classic *Zhongyong*: "Before joy, anger, sorrow, and pleasure are emitted, they are in equilibrium; when they are all emitted in due order, they are in harmony" (*Zhongyong* 1; in Chan 1963, 98). The immoral feelings are nothing but the feelings that are not emitted in due order and therefore do not reach harmony (*he* 和), the harmony that corresponds with the equilibrium (*zhong* 中) when feeling is not emitted yet. Since human feelings "are resulted from human nature when it is stimulated by the external things" (*Yishu* 18; 204), the way to deal with our immoral feelings is not to extinguish them but to redirect them from excess and deficiency to the mean, from the wrong place and time to the right place and time, from the wrong object to the right object, and from the wrong way to the right way. In short, it is to "naturalize the feelings 性其情," which is opposite to "letting the human nature accommodate the feelings" (*qing qi xing* 情其性): "Thus enlightened people take care of their feelings so that they accord to the equilibrium [when they are not emitted], straighten their mind, cultivate their nature" (*Wenji* 8; 577). Here "naturalizing" has a double meaning. The first is that one's feeling is based on human nature which is originally good; the second is that immoral feelings result from one's artificial efforts, so to rectify them is to naturalize them, to get rid of its artificiality.[23]

Thus, morality in the narrow sense as an effort to expand one's natural feeling of love can be seen as a transitional stage between two natural stages. As we have seen, for the Cheng brothers, the inborn altruistic love is natural. For example, a mother and her child love each other naturally, where no artificial effort is made and no learning and teaching are needed. Such a natural love, even from our contemporary perspective, while good, important, and indispensable, is not regarded as moral, although it is not regarded as immoral either. It is rather premoral. This is not only true of animals but also of human beings. When human beings are acting out of their natural feelings, even though such natural feelings are good, we may not regard it as moral, as "moral" in its narrow sense is in contrast to "natural." As Richard Rorty points out, on the one hand, when a mother takes care of her sick son, we rarely describe this mother as moral, because she acts naturally. Only when she deprives her son and herself of a portion of food and gives it to a starving stranger do we regard her action as moral, because she acts less naturally (other things being equal). On the other hand, "the term 'moral obligation' becomes increasingly less appropriate to the degree to which we identify with those whom we help: the degree to which we mention them when telling ourselves stories about who we are, the degree to which their story is also our story" (Rorty 1999, 79). This process goes all the way until we reach the stage when we, as we described in the first chapter, feel it natural, effortless, spontaneous, and joyful to love not only our immediate family members, but also, to follow Rorty again, the family in the next cave, the tribe across the river, the tribal confederation beyond the mountains, the unbelievers beyond seas, the menials who have been doing our dirty work (Rorty 1989, 198), and, the Chengs would add, animals, plants, and even nonliving things. By then, one reaches the postmoral stage and becomes a sage. It is in this sense that CHENG Yi makes the point of making an effort to expand one's inborn love, as it is necessary for one to become a sage: "Everyone can become a sage, and the learning of a superior person must culminate in being a sage. People stop short of being sages all because they give up on themselves. Be filial to whom one ought to be filial and show brotherly love to whom one ought to show such brotherly love. Expand them to others and one will become a sage" (*Yishu* 25; 318). At the same time, however, when a student asks him about Mencius's view that one should be "good at expanding what one is doing," CHENG Yi replies that "sages do not need to make such an expansion" (*Yishu* 22b; 302), obviously because sages are persons who love everything naturally, spontaneously, and effortlessly, and therefore have reached the postmoral stage.

This postmoral stage, on the one hand, is similar to the premoral stage, in the sense that one performs altruistic actions naturally, at ease, and without any forced effort, and therefore is neither moral nor immoral but is beyond morality. It is in this sense that the Cheng brothers often compare the heart/mind of a newborn baby (*chi zi zhi xin* 赤子之心), the heart/mind in the premoral stage, and the heart/mind of a sage, the heart/mind in the postmoral stage, as both are pure and identical to *dao* (*Yishu* 18; 202; see also *Wenji* 9; 607–08). On the other hand, the postmoral stage is also different from the premoral stage in the sense that the altruistic love in the postmoral stage, thanks to the exercise of one's inborn ability of expanding the natural love beyond family, is no longer limited to the small circle but covers all human beings, animals, living beings, and even nonliving things. Referring to this love at the postmoral stage, CHENG Yi states that "its content is so subtle that we do not have a name for such a good. We may just call it the ultimate good (*zhishan* 至善)" (*Yishu* 15; 170). Since this ultimate good is beyond morality, strictly speaking, it is not (morally) good. It is in this sense that the later neo-Confucian WANG Yangming, who was deeply influenced by the Cheng brothers, makes the further claim that "the ultimate good is beyond good and evil."

So morality is a stage that exists between the premoral stage and the postmoral stage beyond morality. The premoral stage is the starting point of morality, while the stage beyond morality is the goal of morality. In both stages, one does altruistic things naturally, spontaneously, at ease, and without hesitance, but in the stage of morality necessary to go beyond the premoral stage and to reach the postmoral stage, one has to make an effort to deliberate and act altruistically with some difficulty. In this sense, morality is only a transitional stage. The difference between humans and animals, according to the Cheng brothers, lies precisely in the fact that humans can go through this transitional stage from the premoral to the postmoral stage, while animals can only remain on the premoral stage, because humans can expand this inborn natural love for their parents to others, while animals cannot. Morality is necessary for one to go from the premoral stage to the postmoral stage. What is essential to morality is to make the effort to expand one's inborn altruistic love for one's family member to the ten thousand things, and this ability to expand only exists in humans. Thus we can say that being moral is a distinctive mark of being human. Consequently, if humans do not exercise their inborn ability to expand their natural love, which is the only thing that distinguishes them from animals, they are no longer different from animals. However, "human" beings become indistinguishable from animals not because they lack the ability to extend their inborn natural love but because they do not make the effort. To use CHENG Yi's terms in one of the above quotes, it is because they "give up on themselves," or to use Mencius's term, it is because "they are not willing to expand it instead of being unable to expand it" (*Mencius* 1A7; see also *Yishu* 18; 193). In this sense, they are still different from animals, as they can become humans and even sages, as long as they are willing to make the effort. In contrast, animals do not expand their natural love beyond their small circles not because they are unwilling to expand it but because they are unable to do so. They can never become moral, to say nothing of becoming sages in the postmoral stage. That is why the Cheng brothers claim that humans and animals cannot be changed into each other (*Yishu* 24; 312). Animals cannot become human because they do not have the inborn ability to expand their natural love, and humans cannot become animals because their inborn ability to expand their natural love from within the small circle will never disappear even if they do not exercise it and therefore become virtually indistinguishable from animals.

6. Conclusion

In this chapter, I have discussed the Cheng brothers' ethics as an ethics of difference between ethical generalism and ethical particularism.[24] The central idea of ethics of difference is that moral patients are not all the same.

It underlines the importance for moral agents to learn about their patients' unique ideas and ideals, beliefs and customs, interests and desires before they can determine the appropriate ways to love them. Such an ethics is particularly important in the contemporary world. There is an increasing awareness among us today that we live in a global village. What used to be members of remote clans have now become our immediate neighbors, in both actual and virtual reality. With the emergence of such a global village, there is also an increasing need for a global ethics. Traditional ethical systems were developed primarily to deal with human relationships within a particular ethnic, religious, or cultural group. In this global village, however, we interact with people with ideals, ideas, cultures, religions, and customs very different from ours and from each other. An appropriate global ethics should thus enable us to deal with such entirely new interpersonal relationships in an appropriate way. The lesson we can learn from the Cheng brothers' neo-Confucian ethics is that, when we encounter people with different cultural and religious traditions, we cannot just go ahead and love them but must first learn about their unique ideas, ideals, customs, and ways of behaving. Such a consideration, in addition to helping us find appropriate ways to love them, is itself a way to respect them. To respect people is not merely to refrain from imposing our ideas upon others; it is also to take their unique ways of life seriously.[25]

Chapter 5

Propriety (*li* 禮)

Why the Political Is Also Personal

1. Introduction

The Cheng brothers' neo-Confucian ethics we have examined thus far is centered around personal self-cultivation: Why should I be moral? Can I be moral? How can and should I be moral? In this context, it is important to bring about a common observation, which often is also meant to be a criticism: Confucianism is strong as a personal ethics but weak as a social ethics. Obviously, the validity of this observation depends on the appropriate distinction between personal ethics and social ethics. Of course, this distinction is legitimate to a certain degree. Personal ethics is concerned with individuals: what an individual person should be or do. On the contrary, social ethics is concerned with society or, more particularly, government: how a society should be structured and run. However, to say that personal ethics and social ethics are different does not mean that they are separate: how a society is structured and run will certainly affect what kind of people can and will live in the society. Liberalism in its broad senses—including both classical and welfare liberalism, the dominant political philosophy (in this chapter I use "political philosophy" and "social ethics" interchangeably) in the West today—exploits this distinction between personal ethics and social ethics. It thus makes a parallel distinction between the political and the personal: the political is not personal, and the personal is not political. It claims that political philosophy is concerned only with setting up the rules of games that people play in the public square; it is not concerned with what kinds of people—good or bad, virtuous or vicious, altruistic or egoistic—are

161

playing the games. Its only job is to ensure that the rules are fair and that all play the games according to the rules.

If political philosophy has to be defined in terms of contemporary liberalism predicated on this political/personal division, then we must acknowledge that Confucianism does not have a political philosophy. However, in this chapter, I will try to show that liberalism is wrong in insisting on this division. Not only is the personal political, but the political is also personal. As contemporary feminist thinkers have already made a strong case for the former, I shall focus on the latter in this chapter. Political liberalism is wrong, I shall argue, not because the political principles, laws, and social policies it sponsors are, as it claims, not personal (as any political principles, laws, and social policies are personal), but precisely because they are personal in a bad way: they are detrimental to the cultivation of personal virtues and conducive to the development of personal vices. It is in this context that I shall argue that Confucianism not only has a political philosophy, but its political philosophy also has its advantages over contemporary political liberalism, at least in some central aspects. The main part of this chapter is devoted to a detailed discussion of the Cheng brothers' conception of propriety (*li* 禮) as central to their political philosophy. In their view, rules of propriety, which, instead of laws, should be the primary rules of society, have their origin in humans' natural feelings, which in turn are based on human nature. These rules of propriety aim not only to prevent potential conflicts from arising and adjudicate actual conflicts among individuals but also to cultivate their personal virtues. Thus the Cheng brothers' political philosophy is deeply rooted in the idea that the political is also personal. In this chapter, after revealing the problem with the liberal dichotomy between the political and personal (section 2), I shall argue in what sense Confucianism has a political philosophy (section 3). Central to the Cheng brothers' neo-Confucian political philosophy is the idea of *li* (propriety) in three senses: as external rules, as inner feelings, and as something constitutive of human nature. I discuss each of these three senses (sections 4–6) and show what advantage such a Confucian political philosophy has over political liberalism (sections 7) before I conclude this chapter (section 8).

2. The Political/Personal Division in the Liberal Tradition and Its Problems

Liberalism in contemporary political philosophy is unique, at least partly because it emphasizes a strict division between the political and the personal.

This division has two sides. The first is that "the personal is not political": the function of government is limited to people's lives in the public sphere, while their lives in the private sphere, particularly within the family, are "protected" from governmental interventions. This idea has a legitimate purpose, as it helps in preventing a police state. However, it also has a blind spot, which has been detected by many feminist thinkers. They have insightfully pointed out that the society designed by liberal political philosophy is largely for men who have wives at home doing unpaid work (nowadays many after their regular jobs outside the home and thus with double burdens) for men, and sometimes even abused by men. So at least one of the things "protected" by the liberal political/personal division is injustice within family. In the 1960s, some radical feminists in the so-called second wave of feminism rallied under the slogan "The personal is political," to protest against such a "protection" of the "private" affairs within family from the governmental interference. Some of them proposed very radical measures, such as abolishing family and adopting artificial reproduction, as indispensable means to realize gender equality. Although hardly any feminists today advocate such radical proposals, they have all taken over the slogan. As Susan Moller Okin points out, the "personal sphere of sexuality, of housework, of child care and family life," instead of being abolished, should be brought over to the political domain so that it can be subject to governmental intervention (Okin 1989, 125). Thus, instead of the earlier radical proposals, today's feminists have made some alternative proposals to deal with the injustices within the personal sphere of family. For example, Okin argues that two types of public policies are necessary to alleviate such gender injustices:

> The first would encourage men and women to share the public and the domestic, the paid and the unpaid roles and responsibilities of family life, equally, so that both might participate on an equal footing both in their families and in their various roles (at work, in civil society, and in politics) in the non-domestic spheres of life. Such policies . . . would need to include subsidized early child care and after-school care for children, flexible working hours for parents and other caregivers, gender-neutral parental and other family-related leave, and firmly enforced anti-discrimination laws in all necessary areas. The second type of policies would protect those (perhaps mostly, but not exclusively, women) who choose to undertake the bulk of unpaid work from the vulnerabilities they now incur. Such policies would include equal division of the earner's paycheck between the earning and the non-earning spouse,

such that the latter would not be economically dependent on the former. They would also include reforms of family law ensuring that, in the event of divorce, both post-divorce households would have the same standard of living. (Okin 2005, 240–41)

I think feminists are right in insisting that the personal is political, which, of course, does not mean that the government can be omnipresently intrusive. First, what counts as personal itself is a political and not a personal issue. Second, personal relations within family are clearly not to be entirely "protected" from governmental interventions. Third, some central proposals by feminists today, such as those mentioned by Okin, are indeed not only creative but also reasonable, feasible, important, and perhaps effective in ultimately removing injustices from the personal sphere. However, the liberal division between the political and the personal has a second implication, which is not grasped by such feminists under the slogan "The personal is political," and therefore its related problem is not only unidentified by them but is (or will be) further perpetrated by the very procedures they propose to alleviate the injustice within the personal sphere. What I mean is that, in this liberal tradition, not only is the personal claimed to be not political, but the political is also claimed to be not personal: the function of government is limited to establishing social institutions regulated by just laws and public policies but has nothing to do with the types of persons living within these institutions. In other words, its job is to improve the social institutions so that they are fair to every individual living within the institutions but not to cultivate the virtues of these individuals. This liberal idea has an advantage: it helps to prevent state paternalism and protect individual freedom. However, it also has at least two serious problems.

First, this liberal theory is predicated on a problematic assumption that humans are fundamentally selfish, self-interested, or at least not interested in the welfare of others. Regarding the liberal assumption of self-interestedness of individuals, we do not have to trace back to Thomas Hobbes, who views human nature as evidently evil. John Rawls, the most important contemporary political philosopher, describes the parties responsible for choosing principles of justice in his hypothetical original position as mutually disinterested. These people are the same people in the actual position to be regulated by the principles of justice they choose, except that, in this hypothetical position, they do not know anything particular about themselves. He says that "this does not mean that the parties are egoists, that is, individuals with only certain kinds of interests, say in wealth, prestige, and domination. But they are conceived as not taking an interest in one another's interest" (Rawls 1999, 12). Rawls's idea is that, since the parties in the original position are supposed to choose the principles of justice that will regulate the actual society in which they will live as soon as they finish their job, and since they are only interested in their own welfare, they would want to make sure that the principles of justice they choose will be favorable to them; since they are ignorant of who they are, they cannot reach this goal except by putting themselves in everyone else's shoes.

The reason that the liberal tradition is based on this problematic assumption is perhaps that it takes too seriously a time-honored insight: even a robber band needs just rules to be effective. For example, in his *Republic*, Plato says that "utter rascals completely unjust are completely incapable of effective action" (Plato 1963b, 352e). Later, Saint Augustine makes a similar point: "Justice being taken away, then, what are kingdoms but great robberies? For what are robberies themselves, but little kingdoms? The band itself is made up of men; it is ruled by the authority of a prince, it is knit together by the pact of confederacy; the booty is divided by the law agreed upon" (Augustine, IV.4). At the center of the liberal tradition, Immanuel Kant also claims that "however harsh it must sound, the problem of establishing a state is soluble even for a nation of devils (as long as they are rationals)" (cited in Höffe 1992, 142). Even the neo-Confucian CHENG Yi agrees on that. In his view, a society is governed by propriety (*li*) and music, which is true not only of a good society but also of a bad one:

> When seeing propriety fractured and music deteriorated, people often think that they no longer exist when actually they still do. As long as a state exists for a day, there must be propriety and music for a day, because there must still be distinctions between the above and the below, between the noble and the mean. Only after the propriety and music are completely gone does the state cease to exist. Although robber bands are doing unrighteous things, there are still rules of propriety and music. For only if there is distinction between the above that orders and the below that obeys can they rob. Otherwise the band would be in chaos without leaders and cannot gather for one day to rob. (*Yishu* 18; 225)

I think what all these philosophers say is a simple truth, but this does not mean that when we design laws and public policies for a society, we have to assume that this is a kingdom of robbers. The mainstream of the Confucian tradition goes against this assumption: it believes that human nature is good. However, even if we assume that humans are selfish, self-interested, or at least mutually disinterested, why should it not be the job of government to cultivate their virtue? After all, Xunzi, representing a different branch of Confucian tradition, does believe that human nature is bad. However, precisely because of that, he argues that the central function of the government is to make people good.

Second, more importantly, the society designed by liberals based on the above problematic assumption of human selfishness is detrimental to the moral development of individuals. In appearance, since the liberal tradition insists that the political is not personal, if it does not help cultivate virtues of individuals, we may think that at least it does not induce vices. It just leaves persons as they are. What it does is simply make rules fair to all. This, however, is not true. On the one hand, political principles, laws, and social policies designed on the assumption that the people they regulate are not good are not conducive to the development of moral sentiments. This is one of the main criticisms of the liberal tradition coming from contemporary communitarian philosophers. Michael Sandel, for example, argues that "if an increase in justice does not necessarily imply an unqualified moral improvement, it can also be shown that in some cases, justice is not a virtue but a vice" (Sandel 1982, 34). To show this, Sandel gives an example of the association in which the spirits of benevolence and fraternity are engaged. According to Sandel, the exercise of justice in Rawls's sense in such an association will have brought an overall decline in the moral character of the association.[1]

On the other hand, such political principles, laws, and public policies may induce vices. G. A. Cohen, a contemporary Marxist, believes that "there exists . . . no underlying human nature which could be qualified *as straightforwardly* unselfish or selfish, or selfish in some fixed degree" (Cohen 2002, 119). In his criticism of liberalism in general and Rawls's theory of justice in particular, he claims that "social structures extensively shape the structure of motivation," because human nature is quite "plastic with respect to motivation" (Cohen 2002, 119). In his view, the liberal society not only does nothing to reshape human nature to make it good, but it actually encourages people to be selfish. He particularly has in mind Rawls's difference principle, part of his second principle of justice, which provides a justification of social and economical inequality: the most talented, if not given more, will not make full use of their talents, and, as a result, everyone else will become worse off. So, Rawls argues, it is fair to let the most talented have the right amount of the extra that is enough and no more than enough to motivate them to make full use of their talents so that everyone else in the society can benefit from it. In Cohen's view, this principle not only encourages the selfishness of the most talented: we (the most talented) will not make the greatest contribution we can to the society if we are not allowed to receive a greater share of goods than the rest; it also encourages the selfishness of the least advantaged: we will not allow the most talented to have a greater share if we cannot benefit more from their exercising their talents (see Cohen 2002, chapter 8).

Jeffrie G. Murphy, another Marxist philosopher, makes a much broader criticism of the liberal tradition in this regard. He claims that motives of greed and selfishness are not human nature. They are rather encouraged, generated, and reinforced in the competitive capitalist society, which "alienates men from themselves by creating motives and needs that are not 'truly human.' It alienates men from their fellows by encouraging a kind of competitiveness that forms an obstacle to the development of genuine communities to replace moral social aggregates" (Murphy 1999, 878). However, at the same time, Murphy claims, the competitive capitalist society establishes laws to punish people for doing things out of greed and selfishness that the society itself induces. It is in this sense that he claims that the capitalist society in the liberal tradition is essentially self-contradictory. This is a criticism very similar to the one made by Mencius, according to whom laws not used in conjunction with moral cultivation are equivalent to traps set for people: induce them to be selfish and then punish them for being selfish (see *Mencius* 1a7; 3a3).

All this has shown to us is that liberals are simply wrong to think that the political is not personal. The political is personal: the rules that govern a society will not only determine what kind of a society it is but also determine, to a great extent, what kind of people live in such a society. Although the claim that "The political is personal" is made here as a supplement to the feminist slogan, "The personal is political," to counter the liberal separation between the political and the personal, as I alluded above, it is also a claim to avoid the potential problem of the feminist slogan itself. What feminists propose to do under this slogan merely extends the political domain so that the family, or at least certain aspects of family, can be moved to the public square, and injustices within the family will not be immune to governmental interventions. Thus, many laws and public policies proposed by feminists, such as those by Okin quoted above, aim only to regulate the social institutions, particularly the family, in which husbands and wives live. They can do nothing to make them virtuous husbands and wives. In contrast, just as liberal political philosophy, as we have shown, tends to make individuals generally more selfish, these feminist proposals tend to make husbands and wives less virtuous. It is in this context that a political philosophy that claims that the political is personal is badly needed. It is unfortunate that, while strong in their criticisms of liberalism, both contemporary Marxists and communitarians are weak in providing alternatives. For this reason, I shall turn to the Cheng brothers' neo-Confucianism for a political philosophy that is deeply anchored in the idea that the political is personal.

3. The Possibility of a Confucian Political Philosophy

In a narrow sense, "Confucian political philosophy" is an oxymoron. The word "political" in Chinese is *zheng zhi* 政治, rule (*zhi* 治) by political measures (*zheng* 政). However, although Confucius does not entirely reject *zheng zhi* as Daoists do, his main idea of government is *de zhi* 德治, rule (*zhi* 治) by virtue (*de* 德), and *li zhi* 禮治, rule (*zhi* 治) by propriety (*li* 禮). This is made particularly clear in his famous saying: "If you lead people with political measures (*zheng*) and keep them in order with punitive laws, the common people will stay out of trouble but will have no sense of shame; if you lead them with virtue (*de*), and keep them in order with propriety (*li*), they will have a sense of shame and not make trouble" (*Analects* 2.3). In this chapter, therefore, I shall discuss Confucian political philosophy in a broader sense as a theory of governing or government (*zhi*), keeping in mind that the ideal government for Confucianism is not government by political measures (*zheng zhi*), but by virtue (*de zhi*) and propriety (*li zhi*), both of which imply that the political is also personal.

Moreover, this chapter will focus on government by propriety, for two reasons. First, in one sense, government by propriety includes government by virtue. In appearance, these two are very different. To use contemporary Confucian Xu Fuguan's 徐復觀 terms, we may say that government by virtue is how rulers regulate themselves (self-cultivation, *xiu ji* 修己), while government by propriety is how rulers regulate people (governing others, *zh iren* 治人) (see Xu 2004b, 270–281). To govern by virtue means basically two things. The first is to be an exemplary person for people to follow. It is in this sense that Confucius says that "to govern (*zheng* 政) is to be correct (*zheng* 正). If you set an example by being correct, who dare to remain incorrect?" (*Analects* 12.17). So this idea of government is close to the Daoist idea of government without action (*wu wei er zhi* 無為而治), and Confucius himself says that "to govern with virtue is like the north polar star, which keeps its place and all the stars turn toward it" (*Analects* 2.1). The second is to do good things for people, which is related to the Confucian idea of humane government (*ren zheng* 仁政). Still, Confucius is not as optimistic as Daoists, as he believes

that there are always some people who do not want to make the effort to
learn even after being vexed by difficulties (*Analects* 16.9). For such people, it
is important for sages to establish rules of propriety to guide their lives, and
this is government by propriety (*li zhi*). In this sense, government by virtue
and government by propriety are indeed different: the one is related to rulers'
action or, rather, lack thereof, toward themselves, while the other is related
to their actions toward their people. However, if we see the requirement of
rulers to govern with virtue as rules of propriety set by sages for rulers, we
can see government by virtue is part of government by propriety, the part that
is relevant to rulers, working together with the other part of government by
propriety that is relevant to people.

Second, government by propriety can be seen as including government
or rule by politics or law (*fa zhi* 法治), which Confucius thinks is necessary
as a supplement. Again, in appearance, they are very different. Hu Shi 胡適
perhaps described this most clearly:

> First, *rules of propriety* are more positive recommendations,
> while laws are more negative prohibitions; rules of propriety tell
> people what should be done and what should not be done, while
> laws tell people what may not be done and you will be punished
> if you do them. Second, those who violate laws will be punished
> by punitive laws, while those who violate rules of propriety will
> only be ridiculed by "superior persons" and society but will not be
> punished by punitive laws. Third, rules of propriety and law have
> their respective social groups to apply to. (Hu 1991, 96)

What Hu means by the third distinction refers to a claim made in the Confucian classic *Liji* 禮記 (the *Book of Propriety*): "While rules of propriety do
not go down to inferior persons (*shuren* 庶人), the punitive laws do not apply
up to superior persons (*dafu* 大夫)" (*Liji* 1.50, 27). This is a controversial
distinction from the contemporary egalitarian point of view and therefore has
been repeatedly criticized in several anti-Confucius campaigns since the May
4 movement in China. However, if we understand the relationship between
government by propriety and government by laws within the Confucian tradition, it is actually not as problematic as it may appear. In the Confucian
view, there are three types of people: sages who do things as they wish and
yet never go beyond rules of propriety, superior persons (*junzi* 君子 or *dafu*)
who have a sense of shame and are willing to follow rules of propriety, and
inferior persons (*xiaoren*, *shuren*, or *shumin* 庶民) who have lost their inborn

sense of shame. It is in this sense that Mencius says that "what distinguishes humans from animals is very little, which is abandoned by the *shumin* but preserved by *junzi*" (*Mencius* 4b19; for a similar contrast between *shumin* and *junzi*, see also *Mencius* 7b37). Thus, clearly, these three types of people are not distinguished from each other by hereditary classes but by their different moral qualities: some have perfected their inborn four beginnings of moral virtues (sages), some are in the process of perfecting these beginnings (superior persons), and some have abandoned these beginnings (inferior persons).[2] Of these three types of people, rules of propriety (to say nothing of laws) are not applicable to sages (so we may say that "rules of propriety do not apply up to sages," to parallel the *Liji* statement that "punitive laws do not apply up to *dafu*"), not because sages have the privilege of being free to act against rules of propriety, but because they, just like Confucius at 70, can always act according to their will without going out of bounds. In other words, sages have no need for rules of propriety. Rules of propriety are applicable to *junzi* or *dafu*. On the one hand, they are not yet able to do things always at their will without going out of the bounds of propriety as sages can, so they need rules of propriety to guide their actions; on the other hand, they have a sense of shame, so rules of propriety are effective for them. Since rules of propriety are effective for them, there is no need to apply punitive law to them (so the *Liji* states that "punitive laws do not apply up to *dafu*). However, rules of propriety are not applicable to inferior people (*shuren* or *xiaoren*), because these people, as pointed out by Mencius, have abandoned the only thing that would have made them different from animals, understandably the four beginnings, one of which is a sense of shame, the necessary condition for the rules of propriety to function (so the *Liji* states that "rules of propriety do not apply down to *shuren*"). To such people, punitive laws are necessary to deter them from doing things against rules of propriety. However, within the Confucian tradition, even to such shameless people, punitive laws are merely temporary means, which must be simultaneously supplemented by moral education to restore their lost heart. It is in this sense that I claim that government by law in the Confucian tradition, unlike that in Legalism, of both the West and ancient China, can be considered as part of government by propriety: it is a necessary condition in order for the government of propriety to be effective for shameless people.

This chapter will focus on the neo-Confucian brothers CHENG Hao and CHENG Yi's conception of propriety (*li*). The importance of *li* in the Confucian tradition is too obvious to ignore, and much scholarship has been devoted to it. However, scholarly discussions of Confucian *li* have so far largely been shaped by Xunzi's formulation. This is certainly understandable. It has been a consensus among scholars that, of Confucius's two most important ideas, *ren* 仁 (humanity) is most profoundly developed by Mencius, while *li* is most systematically expounded by Xunzi. What I shall emphasize is that, while Mencius indeed does not have as comprehensive a theory of *li* as Xunzi does, he has a quite different understanding of *li*, which later becomes fully developed by Song-Ming neo-Confucianism, of which the Cheng brothers are acknowledged founders.[3] Particularly striking in this different understanding of *li* is the following: (1) The goal of government by propriety is to ensure that people willingly follow rules of propriety instead of regarding them as external restrictions; (2) external rules of propriety, while aiming to regulate people's feelings, actually have their origin in people's natural feelings; and (3) such natural feelings have their metaphysical foundation in principle (*li* 理), the ultimate reality of the world. In the following, I shall discuss these three main features. Since Confucianism has often been regarded primarily as an ethics governing individual actions rather than a political philosophy, I shall also compare the Cheng brothers' neo-Confucian political philosophy with political liberalism, the dominant political philosophy in the West today.

4. Propriety as External Rules

Propriety is usually understood as rules to regulate people's life. One way to understand the function of propriety, *li*, in this sense is to relate it to music (*yue* 樂), as they are often discussed together by both classical Confucians and the Cheng brothers. First, *li* is order, while *yue* is harmony. CHENG Yi states that "fundamentally, *li* is nothing but order, while *yue* is nothing but harmony"; after affirmatively replying to a student's question about whether "*li* is nothing but the order of the heaven and earth and *yue* is nothing but the harmony of the heaven and earth," CHENG Yi further illustrates the relationship between *li* and *yue*: "There is nothing without *li* and *yue*. Take the two chairs for an example. When they are not put in line to each other, there is no order; when there is no order, it is strange; and when it is strange, there is no harmony" (*Yishu* 18; 225). So order and harmony, and *li* and *yue*, are not entirely separate. CHENG Yi is paraphrasing a passage from the Confucian classic *Liji* 禮記 (the *Book of Propriety*): "*Yue* is the harmony of the heaven and earth, and *li* is the order of heaven and earth. Because of the harmony, everything is transformed (*hua* 化), and because of the order, all things are differentiated (*bie* 別) from each other" (*Liji* 19.13; 476). In this passage, *li* is also related to differentiation, while *yue* is related to transformation. This is the second function of *li* that the Chengs emphasize. In this sense, *li* brings order, which in turn results in harmony, not by making everything homogeneous, but by distinguishing one from another. Thus, explaining propriety in relation to other Confucian virtues, Cheng states that "*ren* is to be impartial; this is what a person is supposed to be. *Yi* is to be appropriate, measuring precisely what is important and what is not important. *Li* is to differentiate, determining one's particular role" (*Yishu* 9; 105; see also *Yishu* 2a; 14). The main social roles in Confucianism are kings and ministers, parents and children, husbands and wives, older and younger brothers, and friends, the so-called five constants (see *Yishu* 4; 73–74).[4] The function of *li* is to make sure that people perform their duties according to these five constants.[5] Third, *li* is related to *jing* 敬, reverence or respect, because of its function of differentiation: "*Yue* is unifying and *li* is differentiating. When unified, people are kind to each other, and when differentiated, people are respectful to each other" (*Liji* 19.9; 473). It is in this sense that CHENG Yi claims that "*jing* is what we mean by propriety" (*Yishu* 15; 143), so "kings and ministers, as well as friend and friend, should all take it as the main duty to respect each other" (*Yishu* 18; 184).

In the sense that *li* are rules of propriety rulers use to regulate people's actions, they perform their function in a way similar to the way that laws perform their function. Of course, the purpose of punitive law, unless used as a provisional supplement to rules of propriety, is to deter people from doing what is wrong. Thus, while people do not act against rules of propriety because they will feel ashamed, people do not act against laws because they are afraid of punishment.[6] This is the main distinction that Confucius tries to make between the two in the passage quoted at the beginning of this chapter. Even with this distinction between rules of propriety and laws, however, most people still need to make some effort to follow rules of propriety. Explaining *Analects* 8.8, in which it is claimed that moral actions "start from the poetry [the *Book of Poetry*], are established by propriety [the *Book of Propriety*], and are completed in music (the *Book of Music*),"[7] Cheng states that efforts still must be made with regard to stages in relation to poetry and propriety, while no such efforts are needed with music (*Yishu* 1; 5). Again, explaining the passage in *Analects* 6.27, "The superior person is versed in learning and is restrained with rules of propriety and thus will not overstep what is right," Cheng points out that "this is not what one gets by oneself (*zide* 自得), and so one cannot but feel some reluctance in compliance with it" (*Yishu* 6; 95).

However, what makes Confucian rules of propriety and, for that matter, laws in Confucianism different from laws in the legalism of ancient China and contemporary Western democracies is that the former do not simply compel people to do good and avoid evil. They are rather tools aiming to cultivate the good human nature inherent in everyone so that they will eventually be able to follow rules of propriety without making any extraordinary effort. If one realizes the inner value of such rules as the external expression of one's own nature, then such reluctance will be gone. Thus, Cheng states: "If one has cultivated a habit of not looking, listening, talking, and acting against propriety, how can one feel *li* as external rules?" (*Yishu* 6; 82). This is the stage that the Chengs relate to joy. In the above-mentioned *Analects* passage (8.8), in addition to poetry and propriety, Confucius also mentions music (*yue*), in which what is established by rules of propriety is completed. The Chengs interpret music (*yue*) here in terms of joy (*le* 樂).[8] Thus, commenting on "completed with music," CHENG Yi says that music makes one joyful in following rules of propriety: One "will be spontaneous with hands waving and feet dancing. Music leads one to calmness, calmness leads one to the long-lasting, the long-lasting leads one to heaven, and heaven leads one to divinity (*shen* 神). Heaven is trustful without speaking, and divinity is awesome without being angry. This even goes beyond the spontaneous hands waving and feet dancing" (*Yishu* 11; 128). By then, rules of propriety are no longer felt as something coming from outside to restrict one's inner feelings but have become something internal to motivate a person's action. Just like a person who dances to music with naturalness and joy, so a person performs moral actions without any awareness of external rules requiring the performance of such actions. In contrast, one feels inner pleasure in performing such actions. Thus CHENG Yi points out that "the complete transformation means one's realization of the oneness between the principle and one's self. Before the transformation, one acts as if using a ruler to measure things and so cannot but have some errors. After the transformation, one's self is the ruler and the ruler is oneself" (*Yishu* 15; 156). In another place, he uses the analogy of scale to explain rules of propriety: "Without a scale, one has no way to know how much a thing weighs. However, sages know how much a thing weighs without using [external] scales: Sages themselves are scales" (*Waishu* 6; 384).

In the Chengs' view, not only can one find joy in following rules of propriety, but one will also feel pain in not following them. In *Analects* 15.35, Confucius says that "humanity (*ren*) is more vital to common people than fire and hot water. I have seen people die by stepping on fire and water, but I have never seen anyone die by stepping on *ren*." Commenting on this passage, one of the Chengs illustrates the kind of people who love to practice *ren*: "To ask them not to practice *ren* is just like asking them to step on fire and hot water" (*Yishu* 8; 102). Commenting on a different passage in the *Analects*, the one about broad learning and regulation by propriety (*Analects* 6.27 & 9.11), CHENG Hao states:

> Versed in broad learning and yet not restrained by propriety, one will necessarily be undisciplined. When restrained by propriety, one is able to follow propriety by some external force but has not known its reason. So what one can do is but to remain within the bounds of propriety. . . . YAN Yuan 顏淵 states . . . , "Let me be versed in learning and restrained with propriety. Otherwise I will not be satisfied." This shows that he has gained knowledge and so can progress without end. (*Waishu* 6; 382)

In Cheng's view, YAN Yuan is an example of someone who has reached the level at which one will feel pain in not being able to follow rules of propriety.

This joyful following of rules of propriety is described by Herbert Fingarette as the magic power of propriety or ritual:

> By "magic" I mean the power of a specific person to accomplish his will directly and effortlessly through ritual, gesture and incantation. The user of magic does not work by strategies and devices as a means toward an end; he does not use coercion or physical forces. There are no pragmatically developed and tested strategies or tactics. He simply wills the end in the proper ritual setting and with the proper ritual gesture and word; without further effort on his part, the deed is accomplished. (Fingarette 1972, 3)

While I think Fingarette's "magic" does catch some interesting aspects of the spontaneous actions of following propriety the Chengs characterize, it is deficient in describing such actions for two reasons. First, it does not disclose the joy one can take in performing such action that the Chengs emphasize so much. Second, magic often goes hand in hand with a sense of something mysterious, but for the Chengs, everyone with genuine knowledge can perform such actions; there is nothing mysterious about it. In the Chengs' view, as we have seen in chapter 3, the reason that people feel reluctant to follow rules of propriety is that they don't have the needed moral knowledge:

> Common people know that one ought not to act against *propriety* (*li* 禮), but they need to make some reluctant effort [in refraining from acting against propriety]. However, they also know that one

ought not to steal, and yet need not make such effort [in refraining from stealing]. From this, it can be seen that knowledge can
be deep and shallow. In the ancient, it was said that those who
find joy in following the *principle* (*li* 理) are superior persons. If
some reluctant effort has to be made, one only knows to follow
the principle and yet cannot find joy in it. When one can reach
the level of joy, then one is joyful when following the principle
and is not joyful when not following the principle. In this case,
why should people suffer from not following the principle? (*Yishu*
18; 186; see also *Cuiyan* 1; 1192)[9]

When asked whether one can seek the great origin of *dao* by looking for joy
by acting according to the rules governing the relationship between king and
minister, father and son, husband and wife, older and younger brother, and
friend and friend, CHENG Yi replies:

Of course one should act according to these rules, but how can one
find joy? Reluctant action cannot bring one joy. One can find joy
only after one knows. So one needs to know before acting. . . . From
the ancient time, people who make reluctant efforts to act have not
been lacking, but few have understood *dao*. . . . After all, one needs
to know first before one can act. Without knowledge, one can only
imitate Yao in action, but lacking Yao's wisdom, how can one act
in line with propriety at ease? When one has something inner, it
will necessarily be manifested outer. . . . The learners indeed need
to make some efforts, even reluctantly, but without knowledge, how
can one act? How can a reluctant act be long-lasting? When one
fully grasps the principle, one will naturally be happy in following
it. . . . Learners need to obtain genuine knowledge. Once obtaining
it, one will naturally act at ease. (*Yishu* 18; 187–88)

Here, as I have shown in chapter 3, the knowledge that the Chengs
are concerned with is not intellectual knowledge, "knowledge of hearing and
seeing" (*wenjian zhi zhi* 聞見之知), but moral knowledge, "knowledge of/as
virtue" (*dexing zhi zhi* 德性之知), something that one has to comprehend not
merely by one's mind but also by one's heart. Thus, CHENG Yi points out that

the real principle, when gotten from one's heart/mind, is naturally
different. What is known merely by hearing what others say is
not actually grasped by the heart/mind. If one grasps it in heart/

mind, one would not be at ease with what one ought not to be
at ease. . . . Everyone naturally avoids stepping on hot water and
fire, because they all actually understand it. If one has the heart/
mind of "regarding evil as hot water," then one will be really different. . . . What one gets from one's heart/mind is called virtue.
Then naturally [quoting *Mencius* 7a21], "it will be manifested
in one's face, with a sleek appearance. It will also show in one's
back and extend to one's limbs, rendering the message intelligible
without words." Where is there any need for reluctant efforts?
(*Yishu* 15; 147)

In the Chengs' view, such knowledge of/as virtue, while requiring not only the
intellectual power (mind) of one's *xin* 心 but also its affective power (heart),
unlike scientific knowledge which requires the ability that not everyone has,
is available to everyone who is willing to make the effort to acquire it.

5. Propriety as Inner Feelings

In the above, we have seen *li* as external rules for action and moral cultivation as internalization of these external rules. However, such internalization
of external values, as pointed out by Tu Weiming, should not be regarded as
submission of the individual to a well-established authority. To explain this, Tu
states that, on the one hand, "sociality is a constituent aspect of the authentic
self," and, on the other hand, society itself "is an extended self" (Tu 1979, 25).
The Chengs, however, provide what seems to me a better explanation by looking at the origin of these external rules of propriety. Xunzi starts his chapter
on propriety by asking, "Where do rules of propriety originate?" His answer
is, "Humans are born with desires. If such desires are not satisfied for them,
they cannot not seek to satisfy them. If their seeking is without any boundar-
ies, they cannot not wrangle with each other. When there is wrangling, there
is chaos, and when there is chaos, there is poverty. The ancient kings hated
chaos and so established rules of propriety to curb them, cultivate their desires,
and provide them with satisfaction" (*Xunzi* 19.1). What Xunzi tells us about
the origin of the rules of propriety is that they were established by sages.
The question is according to what sages established these rules of propriety.
Although he emphasizes that such rules do not merely suppress human desires
but also cultivate and then satisfy them, Xunzi sees such rules of propriety as
something external to human desires.

Like Xunzi, CHENG Yi also affirms that rules of propriety "are absolutely not to extinguish people's desires and force them to do what is impossible. They are rather to prevent people's selfish desires, warn them not to be indulgent, and lead them to get to the right path" (*Yishu* 25; 323). However, following the Mencian line, the Chengs take a step further in this direction. In their view, "sages establish rules of proprieties *according to* human feelings (*yuan ren qing* 緣人情)" (*Yishu* 6; 87; my emphasis). In other words, rules of propriety are not merely to cultivate human feelings; they also originate from human feelings.[10] In this context, CHENG Hao argues that "although propriety and music are what the above [rulers] use to teach people, their origin is from people themselves (*qi yuan ben yu min* 其源本于民)" (*Weniji* 3; 471). In CHENG Yi's view, "everything has its own rule. That of fathers culminates in kindness, that of sons in filial piety, that of kings in humanness (*ren*), and that of ministers in reverence. . . . Sages can have a well-ordered society, not because they create rules for things, but because they let everything follow its own rule" (*Zhouyi Chengshi Zhuan* 4; 968). It is thus made clear that sages did not create rules of propriety out of nothing. They simply formulate the rules people naturally follow. Here, it is important to see the difference between this claim of the Chengs and a similar claim in the Confucian classic *Liji*. According to *Liji*, "due to human feelings (*yin ren zhi qing* 因人之情), rules of propriety are established to regulate them in case people are not restrained" (30.2; 675). Here the *Liji* only says that rules of propriety are made *due to* (*yin* 因), but not *according to*, human feelings, so it does not regard rules of propriety as rooted in human feelings as the Chengs do.

This can be seen more clearly in their respective views of the relationship between human feeling and the virtue of rightness (*yi* 義). While the Chengs often talk about feeling and rightness in concert, the *Liji* sees feeling as something to be governed by rightness:

What are human feelings? They are happiness, anger, sadness, fear, love, hate, and desire. These seven are what one has without learning. What is human rightness? It is the kindness of father and the piety of son, the kindness of older brother and the brotherly love of younger brother, the rightness of husband and the compliance of wife, the benevolence of the elders and the submissiveness of the young, the benevolence of kings and the loyalty of ministers. . . . Therefore sages govern the seven feelings and cultivate the ten kinds of rightness, making people trustworthy and friendly, modest and courteous, and strifeless.

However, without rules of propriety, what can be used to do all those things? (*Liji* 9.13; 275)

So according to the *Liji*, rules of propriety are created to govern human feelings. Although it does mention that these rules preserve the main human desires for drinking, eating, and sex and the main human aversion to death, poverty, and pain (see *Liji* 9.13; 275), it is not mentioned that these rules are made according to human feelings.

In the Chengs' view, however, the rightness mentioned in the *Liji* is actually manifested right in humans' natural feelings. For example, CHENG Yi states: "Confucius said, 'the *dao* between father and son is one's natural endowment.' This refers to filial piety and so the *dao* of father and son is natural. However, is not the *dao* between kings and ministers, older brothers and younger brothers, guest and host, and friend and friend also natural?" (*Yishu* 18; 234). This shows that the rightness in these human relations is not externally imposed upon people but is inherent in their inborn natural feelings. CHENG Hao holds the same view. According to him, rules of propriety must be consistent not only with the greatest rightness (*dayi* 大義), but also with the ultimate human feeling or sentiment (*zhiqing* 至情): "To have the ultimate sincerity in one's whole heart/mind and perfectly perform the *dao* of father and son is great rightness. To remember one's ancestors and fully return their kindness is the ultimate feeling. The ancient kings appeal to human feelings when establishing rules of propriety. Thus they can both illuminate the great rightness to rectify the society and preserve the ultimate feeling to fully realize their heart/mind" (*Wenjin* 5; 516). In other words, although rules of propriety seem external when applied by sages to regulate people's actions, from their origin, they are internal. About this, CHENG Yi states: "There are things that come from the heavenly principle. For example, bees and ants know how to protect their kings, and jackals and otters know how to offer sacrifice. In the same way, the propriety comes from human feeling" (*Yishu* 17; 180).[11] In this sense, propriety becomes one of the distinguishing marks of being human. Thus, Cheng states that "one becomes a barbarian upon the first loss of propriety and becomes a beast upon the second loss of the propriety. Sages were afraid that humans may become beasts and so they established the strict rules in the Spring and Autumn period" (*Yishu* 2a; 43).[12]

It is in this sense that the Chengs make a distinction between the tools of propriety (*li zhi qi* 禮之器) and the root of propriety (*li zhi ben* 禮之本): "The root of propriety lies in the feeling of people, according to which sages guide people. The tools of propriety originate from the custom of people, which the sages use to regulate people" (*Yishu* 25; 327).[13] In the Chengs' view, the tool of propriety, external rules, must be based on the root of propriety, human feelings. Here arises a question: If natural human feeling is to do things as required by the rules of propriety, why is there a need for propriety as external rules to regulate human feelings? Moreover, if rules of propriety themselves come from the human feelings that they intend to regulate, what is the point of such regulation? In the Chengs' view, human feelings, when they are natural, when they are in the mean, will indeed be inclined to do the same things as required by rules of propriety, as rules of propriety themselves are established precisely according to the very same natural human feelings and for the purpose of guiding people to act according to such feelings. However, human feelings may go astray and become excessive or deficient. Excessive or deficient human feelings are caused by one's selfish desires and in this sense are not natural but artificial. External rules of propriety are created according to harmonious human feelings in their mean to regulate violent human feelings at their excess or deficiency. Thus CHENG Hao points out that "propriety is in accordance with human feelings. Human feelings when appropriate are right (*yi* 義)" (*Yishu* 11; 127; see also *Cuiyan* 1; 1177). CHENG Yi, in his famous essay "What Yanzi 顏子 Loved to Learn" explains in more detail:

> From the essence of life accumulated in heaven and earth, those who receive the finest of the five agents are humans. Humans originally are pure and tranquil. Before being aroused, the five moral principles, humanity, righteousness, propriety, wisdom, and faithfulness, are all complete in human nature. With physical body, humans come into contact with external things and thus are aroused from within. When they are aroused from within, the seven feelings, namely, happiness, anger, sorrow, joy, love, hate, and desire, appear. When human feelings become strong and increasingly reckless, human nature becomes damaged. Therefore the enlightened persons control their feelings so that they will be in the mean. They rectify their mind and cultivate their nature. This is to direct human feelings in accordance with human nature [*xing qi qing* 性其情]. The unenlightened persons don't know the need to direct their feelings. They let their feelings loose until they are depraved, fetter their nature, and destroy it. This is to let feelings control nature (*qing qi xing* 情其性). (*Wenji* 8; 577; see Chan 1963, 547–48)

In this passage, CHENG Yi touches upon an important issue that we will discuss in the next section: the distinction and relation between human nature and human feelings. Here it is important to see the obvious relation between this passage and the following *Zhongyong* passage that he certainly has in mind: "Before the feelings of happiness, anger, sorrow, and joy are aroused, it is called equilibrium. When these feelings are aroused and each and all attain due measure and degree, it is called harmony. Equilibrium is the great foundation of the world, and harmony its universal path. When equilibrium and harmony are realized to the highest degree, heaven and earth will attain their proper order and all things will flourish" (*Zhongyong* 1). In light of this *Zhongyong* passage, we can see that for the Chengs, propriety as external rules is needed precisely to direct human feelings to their original proper degrees and measures and avoid their excesses and deficiency. Thus one of the Chengs states that "one has to be in compliance with rules of propriety in looking, listening, talking, and acting. This is to control the outer to calm the inner. In due time, one becomes sincere (*cheng* 誠)" (*Cuiyan* 2; 1254). In another place, CHENG Yi approves one of his students' understanding of *ren*:

> At the time when one is born, *ren* is already present. Once born, no children fail to love their parents, and no grown-ups fail to respect their older brothers. This is how the function of *ren* becomes visible. At that time, they just know how to love and respect, and so are not burdened with external things. When the selfish desires arise from within and things lure from without, then their concern with external things grows daily, while their heart of love and respect decreases daily. Gradually the original heart/mind is lost together with *ren*. (*Yishu* 23, 309–10)

Thus, although rules of propriety are established by sages according to our natural feelings, such natural feeling may go astray and may become unnatural. These rules of propriety are thus indispensable to our moral cultivation. The function of propriety as external rules is basically to ensure that our feelings will not go astray and bring them back to the mean if they have already gone astray. In this sense, to use Nussbaum's term, we can say that rules of propriety perform a therapeutic function (see Nussbaum 1994, chapters 1, 13).[14] They are useful only when human feelings become pathological, whether potentially or actually, diverting from their natural courses. It is in this sense that sages have no use for rules of propriety for themselves, as they will supposedly never become morally pathological.

It is in this sense that the Chengs try to interpret Confucius's view of overcoming oneself (*ke ji* 克己) and returning to propriety (*fu li* 復禮). In their view, the self (*ji* 己) that has to be overcome is not one's true self. One's true self is identical to *dao*: "*Dao* is one and the same thing as one's self; it is not something outside the self that one has to jump into" (*Yishu* 1; 3). The self that has to be overcome is rather the self that has gone astray, away from the true and natural self; it is one's selfish desires, the human feelings that are in excess or deficiency. Thus, CHENG Hao points out that "to overcome oneself (*ke ji*) is to get rid of selfish desires and so it will necessarily restore propriety" (*Yishu* 2a; 18). Since sages do not have any selfish desires, they have no "self" (*ji*) to overcome (see *Yishu* 2a; 28). What is interesting here is that, while Confucius means by *fu li* primarily to return to or restore the rules of propriety of the Zhou 周 dynasty, the Chengs mean by it primarily to return to one's internal natural feeling of propriety from which one has gone astray. In appearance, the Chengs' interpretation does not conform to Confucius's original meaning. However, if we understand that the Zhou rules of propriety that Confucius admires are the rules sages established on the basis of natural human feeling for the purpose of helping people to return to their natural feeling of propriety, then the Chengs' interpretation is not only perfectly consistent with what Confucius means, but further explains the nature of both the Zhou rules of propriety and the nature of following such rules.

6. Propriety as Human Nature

We have seen in the last section that the Chengs make an important distinction between the root of propriety (*li zhi ben*) and the tools of propriety (*li zhi qi*), emphasizing that the external rules are merely tools of propriety based on human feelings, which are its root. In this section, I shall examine a more fundamental distinction the Chengs make, the one between the metaphysical (*xing er shang* 形而上) and the phenomenal (*xing er xia* 形而下) aspects of *li*. About this distinction, CHENG Yi claims that sages establish rules of propriety so that people

> can appropriately handle the relationship between ruler and minister, father and son, old brother and younger brother, husband and wife, and friend and friend. Their phenomenal dimension (*xing er xia*) is their function in ways to eat, drink, wear clothes, and use utensils. Their metaphysical (*xing er shang*) dimension

is subtle, without sound and smell. Common people follow them
with great efforts, the worthy practice them, and sages act from
them. (*Wenji Yiwen*; 668)

According to the Chengs, external rules (*li zhi qi*) are established on the
basis of original human feelings (*li zhi ben*) that are harmonious and in the
mean to regulate the violent human feelings that have gone astray. However,
where do such human feelings as *li zhi ben* come from? In the Chengs' view,
they come from human nature. In the passage we quoted in the previous section
on Yanzi's love for learning, CHENG Yi claims that human nature is what one
is born with that distinguishes human beings from other beings, where the
distinguishing marks of being human are the five cardinal virtues: humanity,
rightness, propriety, wisdom, and faithfulness. When human nature is aroused
by the external things that come into contact with the human body, human
feelings come to the stage. On the one hand, when such human feelings are
natural, not distorted by one's selfish desires, and therefore in the mean, their
original human nature is nourished. On the other hand, when such human
feelings have gone astray, they damage human nature. The distinction between
enlightened people and unenlightened people is that the former direct human
feelings in accordance with human nature (*xing qi qing* 性其情), while the
latter do the opposite (*qing qi xing* 情其性). So in the Chengs' view, while
external rules of propriety are based on human feelings, human feelings themselves are based on human nature. CHENG Yi states that "if there is human
nature, there will be human feelings. How can there be human feelings without human nature. . . . Human feelings do not come from outside. They are
rather inner responses to the outside affections" (*Yishu* 18; 204). So for the
Chengs, while human feelings are indeed aroused by the contact of the human
body with external things, they do not come from these external things but
from their internal human nature. More importantly, for the Chengs, human
nature is no different from the principle, *li* 理, the neo-Confucian conception
of the ultimate reality of the ten thousand things including human beings.
For example, CHENG Yi claims that "human nature is the principle, and principle is human nature" (*Yishu* 22a; 292); and "human nature is the principle,
which is the same whether you are Yao and Shun or a common person"
(*Yishu* 18; 204). Since propriety is inherent in and part of human nature, the
Chengs also identify propriety and principle, both pronounced as *li*. CHENG Yi
points out that "*li* 禮 (propriety) is nothing but not to look, listen, talk, and
act against *li* 理 (principle). *Li* (propriety) is *li* (principle). Everything that is
not heavenly principle is the private desire" (*Yishu* 15; 144), and "whatever

is against *li* (propriety) is against *li* (principle)" (*Zhouyi Chengshi Zhuan* 1; 699).[15] CHENG Hao holds the same view on this, saying that "*li* (propriety) is *li* (principle)" (*Yishu* 11; 125).[16]

With this understanding, we can gain insight into a few related issues. The first is the relation between government by virtue (*de zhi*) and government by propriety (*li zhi*) mentioned at the very beginning of this chapter. It is interesting and important to point out that what the Chengs mean by human nature, from which human feelings arise, which in turn become the basis of propriety as external rules, is humanity, rightness, propriety, wisdom, and faithfulness, the five cardinal Confucian virtues: "These five are constant human natures, and things like commiseration are all human feelings" (*Yishu* 9; 105).[17] For this reason, the Chengs regard human nature as "virtuous nature" (*de xing* 德性) and human virtues as "virtues of nature" (*xing zhi de* 性之德): "'Virtuous nature' is to indicate that human nature is noble. This is same as saying that human nature is good. 'Virtues of nature' is to indicate what human nature possesses" (*Yishu* 11; 125). It is thus clear that, from the Chengs' point of view, ultimately, propriety is not merely external rules, nor is it merely the human feeling to respect others; it is a human virtue inherent in and as part of human nature.[18] While to see propriety as one of the human virtues is quite common in the Confucian tradition, the idea is interesting and important because it helps us better understand the close relationship between Confucian ideas of government by virtue (*de zhi*) and government by propriety (*li zhi*). On the one hand, since government by virtue means that rulers govern their societies from their inherent virtues, one of which is propriety, we can say that government by virtue is also government by propriety: the rulers act according to propriety relevant to their positions as rulers. On the other hand, government by propriety means that rulers use the external rules of propriety to regulate their people. However, since these external rules they use are created by sages according to human feelings, which are aroused from the virtuous human nature, we can say that government by propriety is also government by virtue: the rulers are directing people's feelings according to their (people's) own virtuous nature.

The second is the much discussed relationship between *li* (propriety) and *ren* (humanity) in the *Analects*. It has to be pointed out that most interpretations of this issue have been developed in light of Xunzi's view of propriety as external rules. For example, Tu Weiming argues that "*li* can be conceived as an externalization of *jen* [*ren*] 仁 in a specific social context. No matter how abstract it appears, *jen* almost by definition requires concrete manifestation" (Tu 1979, 10); and he uses a remark by MOU Zongsan 牟宗三, one of the most important contemporary Confucians, to further explain this view of *ren* as internal and *li* as its externalization: "*Jen* needs 'windows' to expose itself to the outside world, otherwise it will become suffocated. . . . Similarly, *li* becomes empty formalism if *jen* is absent. Furthermore, *li* without *jen* easily degenerates into social coercion incapable of conscious improvement and liable to destroy any true human feelings" (Tu 1979, 13).[19] This interpretation is perhaps not that problematic in terms of Confucius, as Confucius does not say much about the internality and externality of either *ren* or *li*. However, in a subsequent essay, Tu tries to show that this interpretation is also consistent with Mencius, who sees humanity, rightness, propriety, and wisdom all as internal. Tu asks, "Is our insistence on the point that otherness, which is thought to be outside the self, is inherent in the structure of *li*, necessarily in conflict with the Mencian idea that *li* is rooted in the mind (*hsin* [*xin*] 心) and not infused into us from without?" (Tu 1979, 21). His answer is:

> Mencius does not say that *li* is inherent in the mind, in the sense that the actualization of *li* involves nothing other than introspective self-discipline. The issue of *li* is "like that of fire which has begun to burn, or that of a spring which has begun to find vent." Its source is grounded in the natural feeling of the mind. But if the feeling in which the rationale of *li* rests is denied development, it may eventually die. Like a fire or a spring, *li* is a movement, a continuous process of extension. (Tu 1979, 23–24)

Here Tu emphasizes that Mencius regards the beginning (*duan* 端) of *li*, not *li* itself, as in the mind. However, an apparent problem with such an interpretation is that, if this is true, we have to say that neither *ren* nor *li* is in the mind, but only its beginnings. Yet, even if this is true, we still cannot say that *li* is the externalization of *ren*. More importantly, although Mencius does think that humans are born only with the beginnings of *ren* and *li* among other Confucian virtues, he thinks that these beginnings can develop from within into Confucian virtues of *ren* and *li*.

As we have seen, following the Mencian line, the Chengs believe that there is indeed a difference between the inner (human nature) and outer (human feelings), in each of the four cardinal virtues. For example, *ren* is the inner human nature, and commiseration or love is its external manifestation. For this reason, CHENG Yi argues against those who confuse *ren* with love or commiseration: "Commiseration is love, but love is feeling, while *ren* is nature. How can love be regarded as *ren*. . . . A person of *ren* of course loves universally, but it is wrong to see universal love as *ren*" (*Yishu* 18; 182; see also 183). This shows that the corresponding externalization of *ren* is not propriety (*li*) but love, which starts from filial piety and fraternity. At the same time, propriety (*li*) is the inner human nature, and the human feelings for doing the same things as required by rules of propriety made by sages according to this tendency are its external manifestation. In other words, for both *ren* and *li* (and, for that matter, for *yi* 義 and *zhi* 智), there is something external (human feeling) and something internal (human nature), but neither of them is the externalization of the other. In other words, *ren* is not merely something internal whose externalization is *li*; nor is *li* something merely external whose inner basis is *ren*. This, however, does not mean that *ren* and *li* are not related. CHENG Hao points out that "*ren* is to be one body with all things. Rightness, propriety, wisdom, and faithfulness are all *ren*" (*Yishu* 2a; 16). Here no distinction is made among the five components of human nature, because in his view, they are all identical to the principle (*li*), the ultimate reality of the universe: "There is only one *li* (principle) under heaven. . . . So reverence is nothing but reverence for *li* (principle), *ren* is nothing but *ren* for *li*, and *xin* 信 (trustfulness) is nothing but *xin* in *li*" (*Yishu* 2a; 38). If CHENG Hao only makes such an implicit claim about the identity of *ren* and *li*, CHENG Yi makes this point more explicitly: "To look, listen, talk, and act according to *li* (propriety) is *ren*. There is no distinction between *ren* and *li* (propriety)" (*Yishu* 25; 322).[20] Of course, *ren* and *li* (and for that matter, *yi*, *zhi*, and *xin* as well) are identical only in terms of their identical relations to the same principle, *li*, the fundamental reality of the universe. When we look at them individually, however, their actual functions are not exactly the same: "*Ren*, *yi*, *li*, *zhi*, and *xin* are all human natures. *Ren* is the whole, while the others are four limbs" (*Yishu* 2a; 14). Here, *ren* is considered as the complete virtue, while the other four are individual virtues included in *ren*. In another place, CHENG Yi explains *ren* as an individual virtue leading other virtues: "Take the analogy with a body: *Ren* is head and the other four are hands and feet" (*Yishu* 15; 154).[21]

I believe that the Chengs' view can help us better understand the relationship between propriety and humanity in the *Analects*, which is much discussed in recent scholarship.[22] The common problem of all such interpretations, it seems to me, is that they each try to provide one single model to interpret all related passages in the *Analects*. However, as we all know, the term *ren*, as well as the term *li*, is used in many different senses, so it is understandable that none of these single models can do full justice to all related passages in the *Analects*, as revealed by these proponents' own criticisms of each other's interpretations.

Now, admittedly, the Chengs' discussions are not directly intended to interpret the same *Analects* passages, but since they allow multiple meanings of both *ren* and *li*, I believe they can better interpret these passages than any of the proposed models. While it will go beyond the scope of this chapter to provide a detailed examination of all relevant passages in the *Analects* in light of the Chengs' perspective, it suffices to make clear the three different relationships that the Chengs' interpretation allows between *ren* and propriety. First, in the sense that they are both identical to *li* (principle), the ultimate reality of the ten thousand things, *ren* and *li* (propriety) are identical. So to follow propriety is to be *ren*.[23] Second, in the sense that *ren* is the complete virtue, which includes propriety as one of the four particular virtues, propriety is part of *ren* (as a hand is part of the body) so that to follow propriety is to partially become *ren*; third, in the sense that *ren* is a particular but leading virtue (as the movement of the hand is directed by one's head), to follow propriety assumes guidance from *ren*.

The third is change and constancy of *li*. It is well known that, in the *Analects*, Confucius sometimes advocates adherence to propriety and sometimes agrees on its change. What is the rationale behind this? In the Chengs' view, the phenomenal aspect of *li*, the tool of *li* (*li zhi qi*), *li* as external rules, is subject to change. Thus one of the Chengs advises: "One should not stick to the ancient in following propriety. One should realize that the atmospheres of different times are different and so one's situation cannot but be different from the ancient. . . . One can still make some modifications of the ancient practices, even though they were created by the sages" (*Yishu* 2a; 22). Here the crucial point is the idea of time or timeliness (*shi* 時) according to CHENG Yi: "What is most important about rules of propriety? Time. It has to follow the time. One should follow [the previous rules of propriety] when they should be followed; one should revise them when they should be revised" (*Yishu* 15; 171).[24] CHENG Yi further uses the following analogy: "Different things are grown in spring, summer, fall, and winter. So the way of cultivation and irrigation should also be different in different seasons. . . . Similarly, *li* should also vary according to time" (*Yishu* 15; 156). For the Chengs, external rules of propriety serve to restore humans' original natural feelings, so whether they should be kept or changed depends upon the effectiveness with which they serve their designed purpose. It is in terms of this idea of timeliness (*shi*) that the Chengs try to explain Confucius's and Mencius's different attitudes toward Zhou: "At the time of Confucius, the only thing to do is to respect Zhou, and at the time of Mencius, revolution may be undertaken. This is because time is different. It cannot be done a day before or after" (*Waishu* 9; 401).[25] In the Chengs' view, during Confucius's time, the Zhou rules of propriety are still like a tree that can be cultivated, while during Menicus's time, the tree is rotten. Thus, although Confucius had the external rules of propriety of the Zhou in mind when he advocated "overcoming oneself and restoring the propriety," in the Chengs' view, this is consistent with their interpretation of *fu li* as "returning to propriety," one of the five internal components of human nature, because at Confucius's time the external rules of propriety of Zhou were still coherent with this part of human nature. On the other hand, Mencius does not follow Zhou because the circumstances of Mencius's time were very different from those of Zhou. So, in order to return to propriety, one of the five components of human nature, one should not try to restore Zhou's external rules of propriety.

However, as pointed out by CHENG Yi, "Why should people make changes according to time? It is to follow *dao*" (*Waishu* 11; 411). CHENG Hao makes the same point: "The rules created by sages are based on human feelings and the principle of things. Even the two emperors and the three kings often change these rules according to the changed situation. However, the great origin, the fundamental way of governing people, has always been the same for both earlier and later sages. . . . If one merely wants to stick to the ancient when it cannot be applied to the present, it is really just to keep the name and abandon the substance" (*Wenji* 1; 452). In the Chengs' view, in contrast to the political aspects of *li* as external rules, the metaphysical aspect of *li* as *dao* is constant. Moreover, to make appropriate changes of such external rules is precisely to make sure the metaphysical *li* 禮 or *dao* does not get lost. It is in this sense that the Chengs regard propriety, humanity, rightness, wisdom, and faithfulness as "five constant human natures" (*Yishu* 9; 105) and claim that "the constant principles for kings and ministers, fathers and sons, do not change" (*Yishu* 2a; 43, see also *Yishu* 5; 77). In the Chengs' view, it is important to keep in mind both the changeability of *li* as external rules and the constancy of *li* as part of human nature. It is wrong to try to change the constant *li* (such as kindness of father to son and filial piety of son to father), as it is wrong not to make changes of external rules according to time.[26]

7. Defending the Neo-Confucian Conception of Propriety as a Political Philosophy

We have presented the Cheng brothers' neo-Confucian conception of *propriety* as a political philosophy, which is more concerned with how to cultivate the virtues of members of a political community than how those members should be ruled. From the above discussion, we can easily notice a significant difference between the Chengs' political philosophy and political liberalism, the dominant political philosophy in the West today. As we have seen, according to the Chengs, while it is necessary to have some external rules to guide people's lives and direct their feelings to follow their natural path, these rules themselves come from people and are based on their natural feelings. In contrast, one of the central ideas of contemporary political liberalism is the so-called neutrality. According to this idea, in order to be fair, rules to govern people and guide their feelings cannot be based on people and their feelings but should be neutral with respect to them. The best known of such neutral procedures is John Rawls's original position with the veil of ignorance. In Rawls's view, political principles, to be fair, are to be established without any consideration of particular facts of the people these political principles are supposed to affect. Thus, he argues that the fairness of his two principles of justice is vindicated by the fact that they are chosen over alternative principles of justice by parties in the original position, none of whom

> knows his place in society, his class position or social status; nor does he know his fortune in the distribution of natural assets and abilities, his intelligence and strength, and the like. Nor, again, does anyone know his conception of the good, the particulars of his rational plan of life, or even the special features of his psychology such as his aversion to risk or liability to optimism or pessimism. . . . The persons in the original position have no information as to which generation they belong. (Rawls 1999, 118)

Such a liberal conception of neutrality may sound attractive, but it is also problematic. In addition to the serious doubt about whether such a neutral procedure is indeed fair and whether his two principles of justice can indeed be derived from this procedure, as raised by many critics, Rawls himself recognizes what he deems to be the stability problem. Since political principles established in this supposedly neutral procedure are blind to actual people living in a society whose basic structure these principles are going to regulate, there is a great likelihood that people are unwilling to follow such principles, as it is highly likely that these principles do not appeal to their feelings; the greater such likelihood is, the greater need there is for penal devices to coerce people to follow such principles; and the greater need there is for such penal devices, the less stable a society is (see Rawls 1999, 505). The reason is that, although the liberal political principles of justice are claimed to be neutral, they are neutral only in terms of the aim or intention: they do not intend to discriminate against any particular persons or group of persons; but they cannot be neutral in terms of the consequence. Inevitably such political principles, just like any other principles, cannot be equally good to all people whose particular situations are unknown to the party choosing these principles in the original position.[27]

In the Chengs' view, the reason contemporary liberals have to face this problem is that they want to take a shortcut by making laws to govern people with complete ignorance of the people to be governed. In contrast, CHENG Hao points out that "in order to maintain a stable society, sages know that one cannot rush to take shortcuts. When making laws, one has to find their root in human sentiments. Only so can they prohibit evil and spread good" (*Wenji* 2; 461–62). Thus the stability problem never arises in the Chengs' neo-Confucian political philosophy. Since rules of propriety are established in accordance with people's natural feelings, people will have an inner desire to follow them. Even when used to restrain feelings that have gone violent, since these rules are based on people's inherent natural feelings, they will still be able to follow these rules, perhaps with some reluctance initially, but willingly and even joyfully eventually. For this reason, there is little likelihood of using the penal devices to compel people to follow such rules, and therefore there is a great likelihood of having a stable society.

From this Confucian perspective, the problem with the liberal idea of neutrality is related to the distinction Thomas Hobbes makes between makers and matters of government, between its agents and its objects, and between its producers and its consumers (see Hobbes 1962, 19). As Charles Beitz contends, most traditional political theories are wrong in that they all look at citizens merely as matters, objects, or consumers of the government and not at the same time as its makers, agents, and producers (see Beitz 1989, 97–100). In other words, these political theories are primarily concerned with how the government can use laws to govern people and not how these laws should be established in relation to people. This is also the problem with the liberal political theory with neutrality as its central idea. Of course, Confucianism, whether of Confucius or of the Cheng brothers, has yet to develop fully a theory of democracy, as rules of propriety governing people's actions are indeed not created by people themselves but by sages. However, in my view, these sages certainly did a much better job than the parties in Rawls's original position, as they appealed to people's natural feelings and used them as the standard when they established rules of propriety. So although rules of propriety *for the people* are not made *by the people*, they are based on people's natural feelings, so it can be said that they are *of the people*.[28]

In relation to this, one of the distinguishing marks of modern society is often regarded as rule of law (fa zhi). For this reason, Confucianism, at least its political philosophy, is often regarded as outdated, as rule of law is certainly not the highlighted aspect in Confucianism. For the same reason, some contemporary Confucians have tried to reform Confucianism to meet this demand of modern society. However, it seems to me that Confucius's observation, cited at the beginning of this chapter, is still valid in contemporary society: "If you lead people with politics (zheng) and keep them in order with punitive laws, the common people will stay out of trouble but will have no sense of shame; if you lead them with virtue (de), and keep them in order with propriety (li), they will have a sense of shame and not make trouble" (Analects 2.3). In a legalist society, people follow laws often not because they think this is what they ought to do or love to do but simply because they are afraid of legal punishment. So in many cases, if they can be sure that their actions in violation of laws will not be detected and therefore can avoid legal punishment, in other words, if they can have something like Gyge's ring in Plato's Republic as discussed in chapter 1, they will perform such illegal actions without any hesitation. In contrast, in the Chengs' neo-Confucian conception of government by propriety, people will feel ashamed and even unpleasant if they do not follow rules of propriety. In this case, they will not only act morally as required by appropriate rules of propriety but will also act morally in the areas where no rules of propriety exist or rules of propriety have become inappropriate.

One might object that such a neo-Confucian political philosophy focusing on government by propriety is too idealistic. After all, there are shameless people, while the success of government by propriety is based on the assumption that people have a sense of shame. The Chengs in particular and Confucians in general are indeed more optimistic about human conditions than most of the prevailing Western political philosophers. They trust that everyone has a sense of shame and the ability to act from their inner sense of propriety. Of course, the Chengs are fully aware that there are some shameless people, people who have lost their original inner heart. In their view, such people even existed in the times of Yao and Shun, presumably the most ideal societies in Chinese history. For CHENG Yi, it is impossible to have a society made entirely of superior persons (junzi 君子) without any inferior persons (xiaoren 小人):

> If sixty percent of people are superior, then there will be order
> in the society; if sixty percent of people are inferior, there will be
> disorder in the society. If seventy percent of people are superior, the
> society will be well-ordered; if seventy percent people are inferior,

the society will be in great chaos. Thus, even in the times of Yao 堯 and Shun 舜, there were still inferior persons, but Yao and Shun used propriety, music, and laws to guide them to be good and to fulfill *dao* 道. The reason that there were noble people in every household is that there were moral teachings, so that even if someone has the intention to do evil, he or she could not do it. (*Yishu* 15; 162)

For this reason, just like Confucius, the Chengs do not entirely reject coercive laws. As discussed in the third section of this chapter, what makes Confucianism, including the Chengs' neo-Confucianism, unique is that (1) such laws are primarily cautionary: "Although punitive laws are established, they are not expected to be violated" (*Wenji* 9; 593); (2) such laws are only supplementary in that they are necessary only to deter shameless people, the number of which must be relatively small due to the goodness of human nature; and (3) such laws are only provisional in that they should be immediately followed by moral teachings with the aim to restore their inherent but lost sense of shame.[29] CHENG Yi makes this point particularly clear in the following passage, with such shameless people in mind:

> To enlighten the inferior people (*xia min* 下民), prohibitive laws should be made public, so that these people will not dare to violate them; then to teach those who follow them. Since ancient time, sagely kings govern by establishing punitive laws to have uniformity among people, illuminating them with their teaching to better people's custom. First punitive laws are established, and then there will be moral cultivation. Although sages advocate virtues instead of punitive laws, they are not one-sided. So at the beginning of government they establish laws; and at the beginning of enlightening [people], they make sure that people do not dare to violate these laws. This is to break their chain of ignorance. . . . With such chain of ignorance not first broken, good teaching cannot enter. When such punitive laws are carried out, it is true that they do not understand them from their heart/mind, but at least they are deterred from disobeying; later they can gradually understand the teaching of goodness and change their distorted mind, and the prevailing habits and customs can then be transformed. If only the punitive laws are used, the inferior people may be threatened [not to do evil things] but will not be enlightened, and so will only not

cause trouble but do not have a sense of shame. (*Zhouyi Chengshi Zhuan* 1; 720; see also *Wenji* 9; 591)

This last point, that laws have to be accompanied by moral education, is particularly important. The reason that Confucian political philosophy, particularly from the perspective of contemporary liberals, seems to be overly optimistic or utterly unrealistic is that liberal political theory, as discussed at the beginning of this chapter, assumes that human beings are selfish and self-interested, or at least disinterested in the welfare of others. For this reason, the important task of government is to make laws, which contain such selfish desires within certain limits. However, from the Cheng brothers' neo-Confucian perspective, contemporary liberals are wrong to think that human beings are naturally selfish; they fail to realize that the basic structure of society their political principles are supposed to regulate is at least partially responsible for the existence of selfish people. For the Cheng brothers, there are indeed selfish people. However, the task of government is not simply to make laws to resolve the conflict among selfish people but to transform these people into moral people by restructuring the society so that it can be more congenial to the development of people's natural goodness. Without the cultivation of good people, justice of laws that liberals emphasize so much, as pointed out by many communitarian critics such as Alasdair MacIntyre and Michael Sandel, will become vice instead of virtue, as they can be perfectly used within a robber band. Given this consideration, the Cheng brothers' neo-Confucian political philosophy based on the goodness of human nature is not utopian or unrealistic.

We are living in a so-called postmetaphysical culture, in which there is a natural aversion to anything metaphysical, which is why Rawls emphasizes that his theory of justice is political and not metaphyscal. The rationale behind such an aversion is that metaphysics is presupposed to discuss something that by definition is beyond our human access. Richard Rorty is particularly blatant about this. In his view, in metaphysics, "unknowability and unconditionality go hand in hand. Both expressions name a goal which we can never know ourselves to have reached, and which we can never know we are closing in on rather than veering off from" (Rorty 1996, 75). Whether such an aversion is indeed natural or not, it is important to see that the metaphysics that the Chengs present to us is not the same one to which there is such a natural aversion.[30] While I shall devote the whole next chapter to an discussion of their moral metaphysics, it suffices here to mention some of its salient features. First of all, the Chengs do not start with a metaphysical conception of human nature, from which to infer corresponding human feelings, on bases of which the rules of propriety are established. On the contrary, the Chengs start from the empirical human feelings and then infer the corresponding human nature. For example, CHENG Yi argues: "Human nature is all good. The reason we say it is good is because this is what we see from the feelings of the four beginnings" (*Yishu* 22a; 291). Here he does not say that these feelings are good because human nature is good, but that human nature must be good because these feelings are good. We know that for the Chengs, *ren* is human nature, while commiseration is feeling. However, CHENG Yi tells us that "we know that there is *ren* because there is commiseration" (*Yishu* 15; 168). Similarly, we have mentioned that propriety is related to reverence (*jing*). Now, CHENG Yi argues, "there is reverence in one's seriousness in ways of clothing and looking. Thus, while without shape, we can easily see reverence" (*Yisu* 18; 185).[31]

The question, however, is then: What is the point to make this metaphysical assumption of human nature as good, when we already know that the human feelings, from which such an assumption is made, are good? After all, only human feelings are needed for sages to establish rules of propriety. Indeed, in Rorty's view, to explain why human feelings are naturally good by talk of their expressing human nature, which is identical to human virtue, "is like explaining why opium makes you sleepy by talking about its dormitive power" (Rorty 1989, 8). The issue here hinges upon whether such a metaphysical conception of human nature is intended to be descriptive or normative. If it is descriptive, it means to tell us what human nature objectively is. If it is normative, it means to suggest what all human beings should become. In my view, the Chengs' metaphysical conception of propriety as part of human nature is also normative and not merely descriptive. The reason they make such an assumption from the observed human feelings is their conviction or hope that all human beings can be moral. Even Rorty does not have any aversion to such a normative metaphysics. As a matter of fact, he argues that such a hope is indispensable for the moral progress; indeed, he even acknowledges that he himself also has "a faith in the future possibilities of moral humans, a faith which is hard to distinguish from love for, and hope for, the human community. I shall call this fuzzy overlap of faith, hope and love 'romance'" (Rorty 1999, 160). It is important to point out that the Chengs' metaphysical hope of human nature as good, just as Rorty's faith in the future possibilities of moral humans, is not wishful thinking. This is not merely because such a hope is based on empirical fact that there are human feelings that are naturally good. More importantly, this is because such hope can in turn help realize what is hoped for. In other words, the object or truth of this faith, hope, or belief is not something independent of the faith, hope, or belief and, particularly, not independent of actions issuing from such a faith, hope, or belief. To determine its truth, as Kant points out, is "only to discern the possibility or impossibility of willing the action by which a certain object would be made Real, provided we had the ability to bring it about" (Kant 1956b, 59).[32]

8. Conclusion

In this chapter, as an alternative to contemporary political liberalism, which is based on the idea that the political is not personal, I have examined the Cheng brothers' political philosophy centered around their unique understanding of the important Confucian idea of propriety (*li*). *Li* is normally understood, largely in terms of Xunzi's definition, as external rules to govern personal behavior. The Cheng brothers also emphasize the important role *li* as such external rules play in a society. However, they stress that such external rules are created by sages according to people's natural feelings. They are not externally imposed upon individuals. Rather, they aim to guide people's feelings to follow their natural course and bring them to the natural course when they go astray and therefore become unnatural. Thus, rules of propriety, which are primary rules of actions in a society for the Cheng brothers, have it as their fundamental job to cultivate the personal virtues of members of a society. Even punitive laws, which the Cheng brothers think are also indispensable even in the time of Yao and Shun, the ideal sage kings, not only play a secondary role in governing a society, but also must be used only as provisional and supplementary means to the cultivation of individuals' personal virtue. So the Cheng brothers' neo-Confucian political philosophy is concerned not only with the political but also with the personal, because the political is personal. It is natural that liberal-minded philosophers will be critical of such a political philosophy, regarding it as unrealistic and ineffective. In the last section, I have discussed how such criticisms can be met.

Chapter 6

Creativity (*li* 理)

The Metaphysic of Morals or Moral Metaphysics?

1. Introduction

Although a Western neologism, Chinese scholars have now basically accepted the term "neo-Confucianism" to label Song-Ming Confucian learning, perhaps partially because they disagree among themselves about how to characterize it: learning of mind/heart (*xin xue* 心學), learning of principle (*li xue* 理學), learning of mind and (human) nature (*xin xing zhi xue* 心性之學), learning of human nature and principle (*xing li zhi xue* 性理之學), learning of *dao* (*dao xue* 道學), or simply, the Song learning (*song xue* 宋學). However, if we call it "*neo*-Confucianism," we immediately face a question that we would not face if we use any of the other terms: In what sense is this Confucianism new in comparison to classical Confucianism? There have been numerous attempts to explain this newness (see, for example, Mou 1990, 1.11–18; Chang 1963, 43–55). In my view, what is most unique about neo-Confucianism is its development of moral metaphysics as an ontological articulation of moral values advocated by classical Confucians. Of course, classical Confucians do not reject metaphysics. As a matter of fact, all the terms and ideas neo-Confucians use in their project of ontological articulation can be found in the writings of classical Confucianism. It is only that, in classical Confucianism, such terms and ideas either lack a clearly metaphysical meaning, or if they do have such a metaphysical meaning, they do not occupy a central place in their system. The main concern of classical Confucians was how to live a moral life, not

195

to provide an ontotheological foundation for such a moral life. It is in this sense that we can see the neo-Confucian ontotheological articulation not as an external transformation of classical Confucianism, but as the fulfillment of an inner requirement of the latter, as its self-transformation.[1]

In the previous chapters, particularly in chapter 5, I touched upon the Cheng brothers' moral metaphysics and argued that this is a benign metaphysics, likely immune to the criticisms of metaphysics raised by contemporary philosophy, for two reasons: (1) this is not a metaphysics that the Cheng brothers establish first, from which they deduce moral principles; rather it is a metaphysics they construct from human moral experiences; and (2) it is a metaphysics more of a normative nature, telling us what we ought to do, than of a descriptive nature, showing us what is the case. In this chapter, I shall provide a more focused discussion of the actual content of the Cheng brothers' moral metaphysics with its central idea of *li* 理 as the ultimate reality. In the process, I hope to show another reason why this is a benign metaphysics, which can be properly regarded as a postmetaphysical metaphysics: *li* as the ultimate reality of this neo-Confucian moral metaphysics is not some fixed, reified entity, thing, or being, but is the dereified creative activity manifest in the ten thousand things in the world. It is similar to Heidegger's Being (act of to be) of beings and not the being, even the most fundamental being, that has Being. Of course, since the Cheng brothers' metaphysics is a *moral* metaphysics, *li* as the ultimate reality is not merely the act of to be, Being, but the life-giving activity (*sheng* 生) of beings. Before I proceed, however, I shall first explain the idea of moral metaphysics and its difference from Kant's metaphysic of morals and moral theology, largely in light of Mou Zongsan's discussion, even though my own interpretation of the Cheng brothers' metaphysics is quite different from Mou's.

2. Metaphysic of Morals, Moral Theology, and Moral Metaphysics

The distinction between the metaphysic of morals and moral metaphysics is made famous by Mou Zongsan 牟宗三, one of the most influential contemporary Confucians and a Kantian scholar, when he compares and contrasts the Kantian ethics and Confucian ethics. According to Mou,

> the former is a metaphysical study of morals, primarily discussing the fundamental principles of morality from the metaphysical

perspective; its subject matter is morality, not metaphysics itself. Metaphysics is only a tool used to study morality. The latter is a moral approach to metaphysics itself, including ontology and cosmology. It extends the heart/mind and human nature seen from the moral nature itself to the origin of the universe. So it goes from morality to metaphysics. (Mou 1990, 1.140)

To understand this distinction, it is good to see how Kant himself conceives his moral metaphysic. In his preface to the *Groundwork of the Metaphysic of Morals*, Kant first makes a distinction between *empirical* philosophy and *pure* philosophy: the former "sets forth its doctrines on the basis of experience," while the latter "sets forth its doctrine as depending entirely on *a priori* principles" (Kant 1956a, 55). Then within pure philosophy, he further distinguishes between logic and metaphysics: the former is "wholly formal," while the latter is "confined to determinant objects of the understanding" (Kant 1956a, 55–56). Finally, within metaphysics, he distinguishes between metaphysic of nature and metaphysic of morals: the former is in contrast to physics just as the latter is in contrast to practical anthropology, as physics and practical anthropology are empirical, while the two-fold metaphysics are rational. In Kant's view, "each metaphysic [has] to be scrupulously cleansed of everything empirical if we are to know how much pure reason can accomplish in both cases and from what sources it can by itself draw its own *a priori* teaching" (Kant 1956a, 56). So in the metaphysic of morals, the ground of obligation is looked for "not in the nature of man nor in the circumstances of the world in which he is placed, but solely a priori in the concepts of pure reason" (Kant 1956a, 57). In the metaphysic of morals, "we are not concerned with accepting reasons for what *happens*, but with accepting laws of what *ought to happen*, even if it never does happen" (Kant 1956a, 94).

Kant holds largely the same view in his *Metaphysics of Morals*: "If . . . a system of knowledge *a priori* from mere concept is called *metaphysics*, then practical philosophy . . . will presuppose and require a metaphysic of morals" (Kant 1964b, 14). Here Kant still emphasizes that a metaphysic of morals, as a metaphysic, is a system of knowledge a priori from mere concept, and not from experience. About the latter, Kant states most clearly that "it is not from observation of ourselves and our animal nature that morality derives the teaching set forth in its laws—not from observation of the ways of the world, of what is done and how people behave. On the contrary, reason commands what ought to be done even though no example of this could be found, and it takes no notice of the advantage we can gain by following its commands" (1964b, 13). It is true that Kant allows the empirical to play some role in his moral metaphysics in this book. Immediately after the above-quoted passage regarding the need for a metaphysic of morals, Kant states that "just as a metaphysic of nature must also contain principles for applying those universal first principles of nature as such to objects of experience, so a metaphysic of morals cannot dispense with principles of application; and we shall often have to take as our object the particular *nature* of man, which is known only by experience, to show in it the implications of the universal moral principles" (Kant 1964b, 14). However, right after this, Kant states very clearly: "[B]y this we in no way detract from the purity of these principles or cast doubt on their *a priori* source. That is to say, in effect, that a metaphysic of morals cannot be based on anthropology but can be applied to it" (Kant 1964b, 14). So the empirical has nothing to do with moral principles; it is only related to the application of moral principles.

Thus, according to Mou, Kant's metaphysic of morals is merely metaphysical exposition of morals or metaphysical deduction of morals. The exposition or deduction is metaphysical, in Kant, because it is pure and independent of experience (Mou 1990, 1.136). The problem with such a metaphysic of morals, in Mou's view, lies in its inability to bridge the gap between the moral "ought" and the natural "is": the former belongs to the rational world, while the latter belongs to the phenomenal world. His metaphysic of morals only tells us what we ought to do but does not explain how it is possible for us to be moral. To answer the latter question, Mou notices that Kant does have a moral theology, which is Kant's attempt to establish the objective reality of God from the approach of practical reason (Mou 1990, vol. 1, 140). As briefly mentioned in chapter 1, for Kant, morality is the supreme good but is not a complete good. Complete good has to also include happiness, which is required even in the judgment of impartial reason, in addition to morality. While moral law commands "wholly independent of nature and of its harmony with our faculty of desire (as incentives)," Kant points out, "happiness is the condition of a rational being in the world, in whose whole existence everything goes according to wish and will" (Kant 1956b, 125). So in order to explain the possibility of morality, Kant appeals to the idea of the highest good, which includes both morality worthy of happiness and happiness proportional to morality. Since for Kant morality itself does not necessarily bring one happiness, and happiness does not necessarily lead to morality, Kant has to "postulate the existence of God as necessarily belonging to the possibility of the highest good" (Kant 1956a, 129). This is Kant's moral theology.

Mou claims that there are some similarities between Kant's moral theology and Confucian moral metaphysics. On the one hand, both are related to the problem of the possibility of morality, which Kant's metaphysic of morals left unanswered. However, Kant's solution to the possibility of morality through moral theology is at least potentially problematic. As Lewis White Beck points out in his *A Commentary on Kant's Critique of Practical Reason*, for Kant, the highest good, which includes happiness, is necessary to the moral disposition. In other words, one is unlikely to act morally if no happiness proportional to it results. This, in Beck's view, cannot "leave the purity of will undefiled" (Beck 1960, 243). The Confucian view of morality and happiness, as we examined in the first chapter, can avoid the problem. On the other hand, Kant's moral theology and Confucian moral metaphysics are both normative, the reality of whose objects depend upon our willing action. However, while God in Kant's moral theology is merely a postulate of practical reason, the ultimate reality, *li*, in neo-Confucianism is not merely a postulate of human reason. While it is not something that we can perceive by our senses, it is based on our empirical knowledge.

In this sense, the Confucian moral metaphysics is more similar to what Charles Taylor calls "ontological articulation" in his argument against contemporary political liberals. Unlike many of his fellow communitarians, Charles Taylor does not see modern values advocated by these liberals, such as individuality, autonomy, tolerance, neutrality, and procedure, as problematic. In Taylor's view, these are all life goods, things a good life cannot go without. However, he argues that it is important to see why they are life goods or what constitutes their goodness, what "makes certain of our actions or aspirations good . . . [and] constitutes the goodness of these actions or motives" (Taylor 1989, 92). His primary task in *Sources of the Self* is to search for such a constitutive good, a task he characterizes as providing an ontological articulation of the liberal values or intuitions. Such an ontological articulation, Taylor argues, "does not offer us a consideration we have to acknowledge quite independently of our ethical intuitions; rather it is an attempt to articulate these intuitions, to make them more perspicuous and palpable" (Taylor 1995, 138). Similarly, as indicated in the previous chapter, for the Cheng brothers, we assume human nature, which is identical to *li*, the ultimate reality of the world, is good, because we can observe that humans' natural feelings are good.

Here, as Mou particularly notes, human nature in Confucianism is not what Kant means by "special predisposition of humanity" or "some special bent peculiar to human reason and not holding necessarily for the will of every rational being," nor is the natural human feeling in Confucianism what Kant means by "certain feelings and propensities" (Kant 1956a, 93; see Mou 1990, 1.122). In Mou's view,

> it is a great mistake to regard Mencius' conception of human
> nature as good and *Zhongyong*'s conception of human nature as
> destiny of heaven as what Kant means by human nature in such
> phrases as "particular attributes of human nature," "humans"
> particular natural features,' "propensities, inclination, and natural
> dispositions." . . . Mencius' human nature is humans' inner moral
> nature, and the *Zhongyong*'s human nature as destined by heaven
> further relates humans' inner moral nature to heavenly *dao*, destiny
> of heaven, and so it is not only immediately moral, but is also
> onto-cosmological. (Mou 1990, 1.122)

In Mou's view, human nature in Kant is what neo-Confucians refer to as *qizhi zhi xing* 氣質之性, human nature of special endowment of *qi*, which is contingent and relative, while the human nature in Confucian moral metaphysics is what neo-Confucians regard as *tian ming zhi xing* 天命之性, human nature as destined by heaven, which is necessary and universal. So, in contrast to Kant's metaphysic of morals, which is merely a study of a priori moral principles, and Kant's moral theology, which is about the existence of God as the postulate of practical reason, Confucian moral metaphysics, as Mou points out, has metaphysics, not morality, as its subject matter. It is not a moral theory with a metaphysical approach but a metaphysical theory with a moral approach. Its goal is not to show that morality needs to have a metaphysical methodology but to show that the metaphysical reality itself has its moral tendency. In Mou's view, once such a moral metaphysics is established, there will be no need for an additional moral theology, because "such a moral metaphysics is already a theology. The two have become one" (Mou 1990, 1.10).

3. *Li*: Ontological Articulation of Confucian Morality

While Charles Taylor, in his ontological articulation of modern liberal values, found three constitutive goods that constitute the goodness of modern liberal values (nature, reason, and God), the Cheng brothers, in their ontological articulation of Confucian values, disclosed only one source of good that constitutes the goodness of Confucian values: *li* 理. The term *li* has been translated into English in many different ways. Le Gall and Zenker translated it as "form," since *li* is to *qi* 氣 (vital force) as form is to matter. However, as pointed out by Forke, this translation reads too much Aristotelianism into neo-Confucianism (see Needham 1956, 472); Bruce translated it as "law" (Bruce 1922, 2), perhaps because neo-Confucians, including the Chengs, sometimes used *li* and *ze* 則 (rule) interchangeably; Carsun Chang translated it as "reason" to indicate the double meaning of *li*: as a reason a thing is such a thing instead of a different thing, and as something that is the object of not sensation but reason (see Chang 1963, 185).[2] This translation captures the explanatory dimension of *li* but fails to express its normative meaning. As it originally means the grain or vein of wood or jade, Wing-tsit Chan and many others have translated it as "pattern" or "principle," which has become most popular. (In previous chapters, therefore, I have followed this use for convenience.) One of the problems with this translation, as pointed out by Antonio Cua, is that, since *li* is also a fundamental concept of Confucian moral philosophy, which according to Cua is fundamentally a virtue ethics, to translate *li* into principle will obscure the unique feature of Confucian ethics (see Cua 2003b, 631). Joseph Needham prefers to translate it as "organism," as for him "it is not pattern thought of as something dead, like a mosaic. It is dynamic pattern as embodied in all living things, and in human relationships, and in the highest human values" (Needham 1956, 558). Along this line, in the due course of this chapter, I shall suggest that *li* is best translated as "creativity." However, before the reason for this translation is given later, I shall simply use *li*, leaving it untranslated.

Of course, as pointed out by many scholars, the term *li* is not a creation of the Cheng brothers.[3] However, it is in the Chengs that *li* not only obtains, for the first time, the central place in a philosophical system; it is also regarded as the ultimate reality of the universe. Thus, CHENG Hao claims that "the ten thousand things all have *li* and it is easy to follow it but difficult to go against it" (*Yishu* 11; 123). CHENG Yi states more clearly the ontological importance of *li*: "Only because there actually is *li* can there actually be a thing; only because there actually is a thing can there actually be a function" (*Chengshi Jingshuo* 8; 1160); and "the ten thousand things under heaven can all be explained by *li*. If there is a thing, there must be a rule" (*Yishu* 18; 193). So it is clear that for the Chengs, *li* is ontologically prior to things. It explains not only how a thing exists but also why a thing is such a particular thing instead of something else. If there is no *li*, there can be no things; things exist because of *li*.

It is in this sense that the Chengs use *li* interchangeably with many other terms that have been traditionally used to refer to the ultimate reality. For example, CHENG Hao claims that the ultimate reality, which does not have any sensible quality, "is called change (*yi* 易) with respect to its reality; is called *dao* with respect to its *li*; is called divinity (*shen* 神) with respect to its function; and is called nature (*xing* 性) with respect to its being the destiny in a person" (*Yishu* 1; 4). CHENG Yi makes the same claim: "When in heaven, it is destiny (*ming* 命); when in rightness, it is *li*; when in human beings, it is nature (*xing*); when controlling the body, it is heart/mind (*xin* 心). As a matter of fact they are all the same *dao*" (*Yishu* 18; 204); again, "with respect to *li* it is called heaven (*tian* 天); with respect to endowment, it is called nature, and with respect to being in a person, it is called heart/mind" (*Yishu* 22a; 296–297). In these passages the Chengs regard *li* as identical to *dao*, nature, heart/mind, divinity, change, and heaven, among others. While these terms traditionally had somewhat different meanings, by identifying them all with *li* and with each other, the Chengs stress that the ultimate reality that is referred to by each of those terms has all the qualities implied by the terms.[4] While I will discuss in some detail the meaning of change in the next section and the meaning of divinity in the fifth section, I shall briefly explain in what sense the Chengs argued that *li* means the same thing as other terms do.

First, they identify *li* with *dao*. In the Chengs' view, *dao* is metaphysical (*xing er shang* 形而上), in contrast to *qi*, which is physical (*xing er xia* 形而下), and therefore it is without form. While metaphysical, *dao* also governs the human relationship, and thus CHENG Yi claims that "everyone knows that the five relationships are nothing but one *dao*" (*Yishu* 18; 223). Now in the Chengs' view, *li* is nothing but this *dao*. Thus, when asked what is heaven-*dao*, CHENG Yi answers that "it is *li*. *Li* is nothing but the heaven-*dao*" (*Yishu* 22a; 290). Although sometimes the Chengs make some distinction between them and claim that *li* refers to *dao* of a particular thing, while *dao* refers to the single *li* of the ten thousand things, generally speaking, they use the two interchangeably.

Second, they identify *li* with *xing*. *Xing* is often translated in English as "*human* nature." However, in the Cheng brothers, it is an ontological rather than an anthropological idea and so can be simply translated as "nature," as what they have in mind is not only the nature of human beings but also the nature of all other beings. As a matter of fact, the nature of ten thousand things is the same nature for the Chengs. Thus, CHENG Yi points out that "what the heaven endows is destiny and what things receive is *xing*" (*Zhouyi Chengshi Zhuan* 1; 698). CHENG Hao made it clearer that this nature applies to both humans and other beings (see *Yishu* 2a; 30). In the Chengs' view, all ten thousand things exist because of *xing* and so there is not a single thing without *xing*. Moreover, in their view, *li* is precisely this *xing*. As CHENG Yi points out, "nature is nothing but *li*, and what is so-called *li* is nothing but nature" (*Yishu* 22a; 292). For this reason, he argues that "all the three, to fully grasp *li*, completely realize one's nature, and entirely reach the destiny, are but one thing. As soon as one fully grasps *li*, one completely realizes one's nature;

and as soon as one completely realizes one's nature, one entirely reaches the destiny" (*Yishu* 18; 193).

Third, they identify *li* with heart/mind (*xin*). Here again, the heart/mind is not merely the heart/mind of humans, but also that of heaven and earth. In this sense, it is also an ontological/metaphysical concept, as it does not have shape (*Cuiyan* 2; 1258) and is not limited (*Yishu* 18; 204). In the Chengs' view, the heart/mind of one person is also the heart/mind of heaven and earth. Thus, if one can fully understand one's heart/mind, one can also fully understand the whole of humanity and other beings and thus form the trinity with heaven and earth. Now, for CHENG Hao, "heart/mind is *li*, and *li* is heart/mind" (*Yishu* 13; 139), and in this sense "heart/mind is also *tian*" (*Yishu* 2a; 15). For this reason, "heart/mind, nature, and *tian* are not different from each other" (*Yishu* 2a; 15). In the Chengs' view, "heart/mind and *li* are one. It is just that people cannot understand their oneness" (*Yishu* 5; 76).

Fourth, they also identify *li* with *tian* (heaven). In pre-Confucian time, *tian* was once used to refer to a personal God as dominator, creator, sustainer, revealer, and judge (see Fu 2003, 227), so it is the term most frequently used to refer to the ultimate reality. Along this line, CHENG Yi also claims that "*tian* is the source of the ten thousand things" (*Zhouyi Chengshi Zhuan* 1; 698). Now in the Chengs' view, "*tian* is nothing but *li*" (20, 132). Because of this equation between *tian* and *li*, the Chengs often use the two words together to form a new phrase, *tian li* 天理, and CHENG Hao even claims that, "although I have learned much from others, the two words '*tian li*' are what I grasped myself" (*Waishu* 12; 424). Since, however, not only the two words separately, *tian* and *li*, but even the two words combined into one phrase, *tian li*, were used before CHENG Hao (see Tang 1985, 156–57), scholars have been interested in learning in what sense CHENG Hao claimed that it was something he grasped by himself. On the one hand, DENG Keming 鄧克銘 argues that *tian* in *tianli* is a noun, naming a subject that has the *li* so that it is *li* that is possessed by *tian* in contrast to *li* possessed by other things (Deng 1993, 49–50). Such an interpretation is not plausible for two reasons. The first is that the Chengs, particularly CHENG Hao, repeatedly claim that the *li* of the ten thousand things are all the same, so there is no reason to emphasize the *li* possessed by heaven; second, such an understanding of *tian* and *li* as a subject-property relationship is obviously inconsistent with the Chengs' claim that *tian* is nothing but *li*. Thus, particularly having CHENG Yi in mind, HSU Fu-kuan (XU Fuguan) believes that *tian* here serves as an adjective to mean "natural," so *tianli* means the "natural *li*" (see Hsu 1986, 50). This has some ground, as CHENG Yi does claim that "*tianli* is naturally so" (*Yishu* 2a; 30), and "the reason it is called *tian*, [is] because it is the natural *li*" (*Cuiyan* 2; 1228). Such an interpretation focuses on CHENG Yi's understanding of *tianli*, while for CHENG Hao, the particular meaning of *tian* is its omnipresence, as he said that "when meaning comprehensive and all penetrating, we use the word *tian*" (*Yishu* 2a; 30). Moreover, this interpretation also goes against the Chengs' identification of *tian* with *li*. So in my view, *tian* is used here, just like *dao, nature, heart/mind, destiny*, and so on, as a different term to refer to the same reality called *li*. *Tianli* here, as pointed out by MOU Zongsan, is used to express CHENG Hao's unique understanding of the true meaning of classical Confucianism (see Mou 1990, vol. 2, 54). In the next section, I shall discuss more precisely what this true meaning is.

As the ultimate reality of the ten thousand things, *li* is the same in all the ten thousand things. CHENG Hao underscores the importance of humans' forming one body with ten thousand things. He argues that "the reason that ten thousand things can be in one body is that they all have *li*. It is all because of this" (*Yishu* 2a; 33). On this CHENG Yi concurs: "There is only one *li* under heaven, and so it is everywhere. It is changeless from heaven to earth and tracing back to the eras of three kings" (*Yishu* 2a; 38). He further argues that "the *li* of ten thousand things between heaven and earth is not different from each other" (*Jingshuo* 1; 1029), so "the heart/mind of one person is also the heart/mind of the heaven and earth; the *li* of one thing is also the *li* of the ten thousand things" (*Yishu* 2a; 13).[5] This means that for the Chengs *li* is universal and at least in a qualified sense eternal.

However, at the same time, the Chengs write of different *li*. For them, there are not only *wu li* 物理 (the *li* of things), but also *ren li* 人理 (the *li* of human affairs). CHENG Yi makes it clear that "whatever I can see is a thing, and everything has its *li*. For example, fire producing warmth and water giving out the coldness, and one's being king or minister and father and son, all these are *li*" (*Yishu* 19; 247). Here CHENG Yi talks about both *wu li* (the *li of* being fire and water) and *ren li* (the *li* of being king and minister, father and son). CHENG Hao even uses the phrase *ren li* explicitly: "Learners do not need to seek far. One may get it [*li*] at hand by understanding the *li* of human affairs (*ren li*)" (*Yishu* 2a; 20).[6] More concretely, CHENG Yi claims that "everything in the world can be understood in light of *li*. Wherever there is a thing, there is a standard; and everything has its *li*" (*Yishu* 18; 193). Thus, when asked whether one can understand ten thousand *li* by investigating one thing, CHENG Yi's answer is categorically negative (see *Yishu* 18; 188). In other words, there are not only *li* of things and *li* of human affairs or relations, but there are even different *li* for different things and for different human affairs and relations.

So what is the relationship between one *li* and many different *li*? Are the Chengs contradicting themselves when they claim both that there is one *li* that is the same among all ten thousand things and that all ten thousand things have their different *li*? In his discussion of CHENG Hao's *li*, MOU Zongshan makes a distinction between two different kinds of *li*, *li* as the ontological/metaphysical foundation of the universe (as expressed in claims such as "the reason the ten thousand things form one body is that they all have this *li*") and *li* as the natural tendencies of particular things (as expressed in such claim as "the ten thousand things all have their own *li*"). As the former, there is only one *li* under heaven; but as the latter, each thing has its own unique *li* (Mou 1990, vol. 2, 81).[7] However, in my view, a better understanding of this relationship is the Chengs' idea of "one principle with many appearances (*li yi fen shu* 理一分殊)" that I mentioned in chapter 4 in the discussion of their view of love. This is an idea first developed by CHENG Yi, perhaps inspired by the Huayan 華嚴 Buddhist view of the relationship between *li* and event (*shi* 事). In Cheng's view, this complicated Buddhist idea really says nothing but "the ten thousand *li* share one *li*" (*Yishu* 18; 195), or "ten thousand things share one *li*" (*Cuiyan* 1; 1180).[8] In appearance, by "one principle with many different appearances," he meant two different things: in one case, these different appearances are the ten thousand things, while in another case, they are different *li* of the ten thousand things. However, in Cheng's view, these two meanings are consistent. Since, according to Cheng, everything has its *li*, and *li* is ontologically prior to things, appearances of one *li* in ten thousand things are no different from manifestations of one *li* in many different *li*. As to the precise meaning of one *li* with many manifestations, Cheng makes it clear in his comments on ZHANG Zai's *Western Inscription* (*Xi Ming* 西銘): "*The Western Inscription* explains one *li* with different appearances, while Mozi emphasized two roots without distinction" (*Wenji* 9; 609). In Cheng's view, if we only emphasize one *li* and ignore its many appearances, we will be led to Mozi's love without distinctions. However, in Cheng's view, as argued in chapter 4, it is important for us to love different objects differently. The appropriate love for one's parents should be different from the appropriate love for one's spouse and children; the appropriate love for a person of virtue should be different from the appropriate love for an evil person; the appropriate love for a human being should be different from the appropriate love for other living beings. On the other hand, if one only knows some particular appearances and fails to see the one principle of which they are appearances, then one cannot go beyond the small circle in which one knows how to love. For example, if one only knows how to love one's parents but does not realize that this love of parents is merely a particular appearance of one *li*, *ren* (to be humane), then one will find it difficult to love other human beings, to say nothing about other living beings.[9] Here it is important to see that, when CHENG Yi says that the ten thousand *li* lead to one *li*, he does not mean that there is one *li* over and above the ten thousand *li*, as if over and above all different particular kinds of love, there were a general love. Whenever one loves, one loves in a particular way. One can never love in a general way. The one *li* that all different kinds of love embody, *ren*, does not exist except in these different kinds of love. Thus, as also pointed out in chapter 4, when explaining the idea of one principle with many appearances, CHENG Yi does not use the metaphor of one moon reflected in the ten thousand rivers as it was used in Buddhism before him and in ZHU Xi after him. The reason is that this metaphor suggests that there is one real or true *li* (moon) that is over and above the ten thousand *li* (its reflections in the thousand rivers). The moon can exist without its reflections in ten thousand rivers, but the one *li* in the Chengs cannot be separate from the ten thousand *li*.[10]

In relation to the Chengs' one *li* with many different manifestations, it is sometimes claimed that their *li* has some similarity with Plato's form.[11] It is true that in the sense that both form and *li* are ontologically prior to things, they are indeed similar. However, it is important not to ignore a fundamental difference between the two. In Plato, while everything must partake in a form, a form does not have to exist in a thing. This is made most clear in his analogy of image or reflection. A shadow of a tree cannot exist without a tree of which it is a shadow. However, a tree can exist without any shadows. It is sometimes claimed that the Chengs' *li* is similar in this respect, particularly in CHENG Yi. For example, according to HOU Wailu 侯外蘆 and his group, the Chengs' view is that "outside the material world, there is an eternal *tian-li* that exists independent of this material world as its root and foundation" (Hou 1997, 150).[12] However, I shall argue that this is a misunderstanding. In the Chengs, while *li* is indeed ontologically prior to things, it does not exist outside things.

To better understand this, it is important to have an overview of the Chengs' view about the relationship between *li* and vital force (*qi*). Cheng makes the distinction between the two in this way: "Everything that has shape is vital force; while *dao* does not have shape" (*Yishu* 6; 83).[13] Thus, the vital force and actual things made of vital forces are ontologically identical, as they both have shape, in contrast to *li*, which does not have shape or other sensible qualities. Then can *li* or *dao* be outside *qi*? The Chengs' answer is a resounding "No!" Interpreting the statement in the *Book of Changes* that "the unceasing transition between *yin* and *yang* is *dao*," CHENG Yi claims that "*dao* is not *yin* and *yang*. *Dao* is the unceasing transition between *yin* and *yang*" (*Yishu* 3; 67). Here, although he says that *li* or *dao* is not the *qi* of *yin* and *yang*, he also says that *li* is the unceasing transition between *yin* and *yang*. If so, it is clear that *li* cannot be outside these vital forces. CHENG Yi states this more clearly: "There is no *dao* if there are no *yin* and *yang*. The *becoming so* of *qi* is *dao*. *Yin* and *yang* are *qi* and so are physical, while *dao* is metaphysical" (*Yishu* 15; 162). Such an interpretation can be confirmed by the Chengs' view on the relationship of a related pair of concepts: *dao* and *qi* 器 (instrument or concrete thing). Regarding the distinction between the two, CHENG Hao quotes the *Book of Change*: "[W]hat is metaphysical or above the form (*xing er shang*) is called *dao*, while what is physical or below the form (*xing er xia*) is called concrete thing" (*Yishu* 11; 118). Now although it is important, for the Chengs, to make the distinction between the *dao* as the metaphysical and *qi* as physical and emphasize the ontological priority of the former over the latter,[14] they also emphasize their inseparability. Thus, CHENG Hao claims that "outside *dao* there are no things and outside things there is no *dao*" (*Yishu* 4; 73).[15]

Here it is important also to mention a related misconception that for the Chengs, *li* gives birth to *qi* or the ten thousand things. It is true that the Chengs do argue for the ontological priority of *li* over *qi* and the ten thousand things, but they never claim that it is also a temporal priority. As a matter of fact, for the Chengs, it is *qi* that "gives birth to the ten thousand things" (*Cuiyan* 2; 1226), so "at the beginning, the ten thousand things were nothing but transformations of *qi*" (*Yishu* 5; 79). Does this mean that for the Chengs, while *qi* gives birth to the ten thousand things, it is *li* that gives birth to *qi*? This cannot be the case, since it assumes that *li* can exist before *qi*, which the Chengs categorically deny. I quoted above a passage from CHENG Hao: "The reason that the ten thousand things form one body is that they all have *li*. This is only because [it] comes from that (*zhi wei cong na li lai* 只為從那 裏來)" (*Yishu* 2a; 33). Scholars often interpret the last sentence as meaning that the ten thousand things come from *li*, but from the context it is clear that CHENG Hao means that the fact that the ten thousand things can form one body comes from the fact that they have *li*. If *li* is not what produces *qi* and things, then what is *li* in relation to *qi* and things? It is nothing, I shall argue, but the *qi*'s giving birth to the ten thousand things, which is no different from what I discussed above regarding *dao* as the unceasing transition between *yin* and *yang*.[16] This is an important idea, which I shall discuss in more detail in the next section.

The reason that it is sometimes believed that for the Chengs, particularly for CHENG Yi, *li* exists before *qi* 氣 (vital force) and *qi* 器 (instruments or concrete thing) is that some of their claims can be and have been easily misunderstood. The Chengs do claim that "only because there is a *li* can there be an object" (*Jingshuo* 8; 1160); "there is *li* and so there is *qi*, and there is *qi* and so there is number" (*Jingshuo* 1; 1030); and "because there is *li* there is image; and because there is image, there is number" (*Wenji* 9; 615). Many scholars have thus interpreted such statements as saying that *li* exists before, and can exist independently of, *qi* and things.[17] From our discussion above, however, it is clear that this is not what the Chengs mean. This can be further confirmed by what CHENG Yi says immediately after the above passage in which he talks about the relationship between *li* and image: "Therefore, the *Book of Changes* illustrates *li* with images and knows *dao* from the image" (*Wenji* 9, 615). This shows that *li* and *dao* can only be known from images or things. If *li* can exist independently of images, just as the moon can exist independently of its reflections in rivers, then we can know *li* without the help of the images, just as we can know the moon without the help of its reflection in rivers. We can relate this passage to another of CHENG Yi's, also on *li* and image: "The most hidden is *li*, while the most manifest is the image. Substance and function are from the same source, between which there is no slight gap" (*Yizhuang*, Introduction, 689). Here he used the substance/function relationship to describe the *li*/image relationship and made it unmistakably clear that *li* cannot be separated from things.[18]

4. *Sheng* 生 (Life-Giving Activity): Dereification of the Ultimate Reality

What precisely then is *li* that ontologically determines *qi* and things and yet is temporally inseparable from them? As we have seen, CHENG Yi says that "it does not have shape" (*Wenji* 9; 615), and CHENG Hao adds that it "does not have sound or smell" (*Yishu* 1; 4). For this reason, it is sometimes claimed that *li* must be some spiritual entity (Cai 1996, 71). However, this is obviously wrong, for CHENG Yi further points out that, because *li* does not have shape, sound, or smell, "we have to understand it through images" (*Cuiyan* 1; 1205). If it is a spiritual entity, how can we understand it through material images? How do we understand such a *li* that is not material image and yet has to be understood through material images, something that is not what we can use sense organs to perceive but has to be grasped through what we can perceive? Although many scholars have realized that it is wrong to regard the Chengs' *li* as something similar to Plato's Idea as far as the latter can be considered as

independent of concrete things, still it is quite common to see it as the common essence of things or common law that governs these things or principle
these things follow or patterns these things exhibit, so far as this essence or
law or principle or pattern is not considered as separable from these actual
things. Many English translations of *li* mentioned in the last section, although
very different from each other, are indeed all based on such an understanding.

In this section, I attempt to show that such a reified understanding of
the Chengs' *li* (understood as some *thing*, even if something invisible) is wrong;
instead, I shall argue that *li* in the Cheng brothers is primarily not some *thing*,
but the *activity* of things. As a matter of fact, according to Xu Heng's 許衡
Explanation of Script and Elucidation of Characters (*Shuo Wen Jie Zi* 說文解
字), *li* originally was a verb, meaning to work on jade. Since jade is a gemstone
with veins and clouds of varying colors, the carver has to be adept at following
the veining. Chen Rongjie (Wing-tsit Chan) does notice that. However, he argues
that the meaning of *li* has undergone a transition from the physical (*xing er
xia*) meaning of "governing" in the ancient classics to its metaphysical meaning of "pattern" in neo-Confucianism, a transition from its use as verb to its
use as a noun (Chen 1991, 57). However, the transition of its use from a verb
to a noun, if there is indeed such a transition, really indicates the reification
of *li* as some *thing*, as it is originally not a thing but an activity. From the
Heideggerian point of view, nothing reified can be regarded as metaphysical
in its true sense. Even God conceived as the absolute being, however different it is from any and all other things, is still some *thing*, and in this sense
is still *xing er xia* (below the form), whose ontological or metaphysical Being
still needs to be explained. It is my contention that the unique contribution
of the Cheng brothers is to dereify the Confucian idea of the ultimate reality
by their unique interpretation of the term *li*. In other words, *li* used in the
Cheng brothers is still a verb meaning some *activity*, not a noun referring to
some *thing*. For example, when using examples to illustrate what he means
by "nowhere between heaven and earth there is no *dao*" (*Yishu* 4; 73), Cheng
points out that "in the relation of father and son, to be father and son lies in
affection; in the relation of king and minister, to be king and minister lies in
seriousness (reverence). From these to being husband and wife, being elder
and younger, being friends, there is no activity that is not *dao*. That is why we
cannot be separated from *dao* even for a second" (*Yishu* 4; 73–74).[19] It is in
this sense that in his commentary on the *Book of Changes*, Cheng Yi claims
that "Confucians in the past have all seen the heart/mind of the heaven and
earth as something quiet. Only I myself argue that we should see it as activity"
(*Yishu* 18; 201). Only in this sense can we understand why the Chengs claim

that *li* is not perceivable but can only be understood through what is perceivable. *Li* as activity indeed does not have shape, sound, or smell, as only things that act have shape, sound, and smell. For this reason we can never perceive things' activities, as we can only perceive things that act. For example we can perceive a running car, but we cannot perceive the car's running.[20]

Yet what exactly do the Chengs mean by activity? It is not any kind of activity. For them it is the life-giving activity (*sheng* 生).[21] Thus, CHENG Hao claims that "the reason why it is said that the ten thousand things form one body is that they all have this *li*. It all comes from this fact. 'The unceasing life-giving activity is called change.' It is right in this life-giving activity that *li* is complete" (*Yishu* 2a; 33). As pointed out earlier, the first two sentences may give the impression that *li* is some thing from which the ten thousand things come, but the remaining sentences immediately correct such an impression, as he uses the statement from the *Book of Changes* to make it clear that *li* is the life-giving activity. CHENG Yi concurs: "*Li* as life-giving activity is natural and ceaseless" (*Yishu* 15; 167). The Chengs believe that the existence of the ten thousand things is due to *li* not because *li* is considered as something independent from *li*. It is rather because the life-giving activity of the ten thousand things has the ontological priority over the ten thousand things that have the life-giving activity. Without the life-giving activity, the ten thousand things cannot exist, as they would lack the act of "to be." Of course, for the Chengs, the life-giving activity is always the life-giving activity of the ten thousand things, and the ten thousand things are always things that have the life-giving activity.[22]

In the last section, we saw that the Cheng brothers identify *li* with many other terms that have been traditionally used to refer to the ultimate reality. It is interesting to see how they also use the life-giving activity to interpret these terms. What do *dao* and *tian* mean? In interpreting the statement from the *Book of Changes* that "the unceasing life-giving activity is called change,"[23] CHENG Hao makes it clear that this unceasing life-giving activity "is how *tian* can be *dao*. Tian is *dao* only because it is the life-giving activity" (*Yishu* 2a; 29). CHENG Yi completely agrees on this: "*[D]ao* is the natural life-giving activity of the ten thousand things. A thing's coming into being in the spring and its growing in the summer are both *dao* as the life-giving activity. . . . *Dao* is the unceasing natural life-giving activity" (*Yishu* 15; 149). We have also seen the Chengs relating *li* to heart/mind, both that of humans and that of heaven and earth. Now they also interpret it in terms of life-giving activity: "The heart/mind is nothing but the *dao* of life-giving activity. Because of this heart/mind, one's body is born. The heart/mind of commiseration is *dao* of humans as the life-giving activity" (*Yishu* 21b; 274). Again, "the heart/mind resembles the seed of grain. Its *li* as life-giving activity is *ren*" (*Yishu* 18; 184).

Similarly, we have seen the Chengs identifying *li* with *xing* (nature). CHENG Hao also explains *xing* in terms of life-giving activity, particularly in his interpretation of Gaozi's *sheng zhi wei xing* 生之為性 in the *Mencius*, a creative interpretation, according to MOU Zongshan (see Mou 1990, vol. 2, 146). This phrase of four Chinese characters is normally understood to mean "what one is born with is nature." However, CHENG Hao quotes it together with the statement from the *Book of Changes* that "the greatest virtue of heaven and earth is the life-giving activity" and then explains this statement in his own words: "The most spectacular aspect of things is their atmosphere of life-giving activity" (*Yishu* 11; 120).[24] It is thus clear that this phrase, to CHENG Hao, no longer means "what one is born with is nature" but "one's life-giving activity (*sheng*) is nature."[25] CHENG Yi does not agree on such an interpretation and believes that what Gaozi means is indeed "what one is born with is nature." However, he claims that nature here is nature as material endowment (*qi zhi zhi xing* 氣質之性) and so is physical or below the form (*xing er xia*),[26] to be clearly distinguished from nature as the destiny of *tian* (*tian ming zhi xing* 天命之性), which is metaphysical or above the form (*xing er shang*). In CHENG Yi's view, only nature in the latter sense is identical to *li*, which means the life-giving activity. Thus he states: "We cannot talk about nature without any distinction. In 'what one is born with is nature,' the nature refers to one's endowment; while in 'what one is ordained by heaven is nature,' the nature refers to *li*" (*Yishu* 24; 313). In his view, what Gaozi means is nature as endowment, while what he means is nature as the destiny of *tian*, which is identical to *li*. So fundamentally, he agrees with his brother that *xing* is a life-giving activity.

Here it is perhaps necessary to say a few words about my radical interpretation. The best way to see it is to contrast it with the one provided by MOU Zongsan. Mou makes a distinction between the two Chengs. According to Mou, *li* in CHENG Hao, "as an ontological being, is not a static being, but a dynamic being that always acts" (Mou 1990, 2:78), while in CHENG Yi it is a substance that only exists but does not act, so it is static (Mou 1990, 1:44; 2: 287).[27] Here, Mou's view has actually raised two issues. First, he claims that there is a difference between CHENG Hao and CHENG Yi. From our discussion above, it is clear that the claim that the two brothers disagree with each other about whether *li* is activity or not is obviously untenable. As we have seen, CHENG Yi makes no fewer or less straightforward claims that *li* is the life-giving activity.[28] So here I shall try to explain why Mou and many others think that *li* for

CHENG Yi is a static being without activity. This, in my view, must be at least partially due to the fact that CHENG Yi often talks about "the constant *dao*" and "the constant *li*" (see *Zhouyi Chengshi Zhuan* 3; 862). In his interpretation of *Zhongyong*, CHENG Yi gives us the same impression: "Not being partial is *zhong*, and not change is *yong*. *Zhong* is the straight *dao* under heaven, and *yong* is the constant *li* under heaven" (*Yishu* 7; 100). We might think that, since *li* for CHENG Yi is constant, it must be static. However, it is important to see in what sense CHENG Yi claims that *dao* or *li* is unchanging. For CHENG Yi, *dao* or *li* is nothing but life-giving activity, and this life-giving activity is an ongoing universal process. If a thing exhibits life-giving activity at one time and lacks it at another time, then we may claim that the life-giving activity is not constant. In other words, for CHENG Yi, what is constant is precisely the change, the activity, of the ten thousand things. The only fact that does not change is that things have the life-giving activity; or to put it more radically, the only thing that does not change is the change itself. This sense of constant *li* is made unmistakably clear in the following passage of CHENG Yi: "No *li* under heaven can be constant without activity. When there is activity, there will be a beginning after the ending, and so it can last forever without end. Nothing born between heaven and earth, including the solid and sturdy mountains, is without changing activities. So to be eternal is not to be fixed; to be fixed is not to be constant. The constant *dao* is nothing but the unceasing activity of change" (*Zhouyi Chengshi Zhuang* 3; 862).[29] So CHENG Yi actually says exactly the same thing as his brother CHENG Hao, although in a different way: the life-giving activity is ceaseless. As a matter of fact, in this sense, CHENG Hao agrees with CHENG Yi that "there is a constant and unchanging *li* for one to be a king or minister, father or son" (*Yishu* 2a; 43).

Second, even when Mou distinguishes CHENG Hao from CHENG Yi and claims that *li* in CHENG Hao is active, he still believes that *li* is some *thing*, some *entity*, some *substance*, whose fundamental feature is to act (Mou 1990, 2:136). Thus *li* remains a *being*, although a being that always acts. This is what Mou means by CHENG Hao's *li* as "something with both being and activity" in contrast to CHENG Yi's *li* as "something with being only without activity." *Li* is thus considered as some transcendental being that has the life-giving activity, which is different from the life-giving activity of material things or vital force (Mou 1990, 2:56). In other words, the fundamental reality of the ten thousand things is still a reified thing, even if it is an active thing. Such an understanding is quite in line with the traditional Christian conception of God, as the Christian God is also conceived as both being and activity: a being that acts or an active being. This interpretation of *li* as an active being has now become very popular. As both CHENG Yi and CHENG Hao put so much emphasis on the idea of life-giving activity in their discussion of *li*, almost no scholars of the Chengs' philosophy would fail to see it. However, it has always been claimed that, in the Chengs, *li* (*tian, xing, xin, shen, dao*) is principle (heaven, nature, heart/mind, divinity, and *dao*) that is dynamic. *Li* has thus become the substance that gives life to *qi* or the ten thousand things. For example, LI Rizhang argues that, in the Chengs, "the relationship between *li* and *qi* is one between one that can give life to others and one that is given birth to" (Li 1986, 65). However, such an understanding has two inherent difficulties, both of which were well recognized by Li himself. First,

> *li* as the root of the universe is above image and shape, while *qi* represents the ten thousand things and so has image and shape. . . . [H]ow can the "metaphysical" noumenon give life to the physical phenomenon? After all, "giving life" means that something material giving birth to one or more other material things, as mother giving birth to children, or plants and tree giving birth to fruits, or body giving birth to (growing) hair. Now since "noumenon" has no shape and image, how can it give birth to anything? (Li 1986, 66; see also Lü 1996, 78–79)

Second, according to Cheng, *li* gives life to the ten thousand things, yet each of the ten thousand things given birth to by *li* also has *li*. "This," claims Li, "is incomprehensible" (Li 1986, 77). I think Li is exactly right in pointing out these two serious problems of such an understanding of *li*. However, instead of regarding them as inherent in the Chengs' conception of *li*, I shall argue that this is due to our misunderstanding of the Chengs' conception.

A. C. Graham provides us with a good analogy to understand the Chengs' idea of *sheng*, the life-giving activity in neo-Confucianism: "the analogy behind their thinking is not a man making a pot, but rather a tree growing from its hidden root and branching out" (Graham 1992, 108). The distinction here is one between a Christian conception of creation and the neo-Confucian conception of life-giving activity. Central to this distinction is that in the Christian picture, there is an external and transcendent being (potter) that creates the ten thousand things (pots); while in the neo-Confucian picture, it is the ten thousand things that give life to themselves: the ten thousand things are simply growing.[30] In the Chengs, *li* is not a transcendent being that has the life-giving activity; it is nothing but the transcending life-giving activity. It might be asked, if *li* is the creative life-giving activity, whose activity is it then?

Of course, the Chengs are not making a quasi-Buddhist claim that this is an action without agent or a doing without a doer. The life-giving activity is the life-giving activity of the ten thousand things in the world.[31] CHENG Hao states it most clearly: "There are no things outside *dao*, and there is no *dao* outside things" (*Yishu* 4; 73). *Dao* is not something that acts; it is the activity itself. *Dao* is activity, and activity cannot be outside things, which are made of *qi*. This understanding can actually better explain the difference between the Christian God and the Chengs' *li*, a difference that Mou himself is interested in. Mou points out that "although in Christianity, we can also say that everything comes from God's creative activity, we cannot say every individual thing also has the same creative activity as that of God. However, in Confucianism, it is necessary to say that every individual thing also has this absolute creative activity" (Mou 1990, 2:59). However, if we understand *li* as the life-giving activity of a transcendent being and not of these individual things made of the vital force (*qi*), then we will inevitably face the second question LI Rizhang detects, and the life-giving activity of the transcendent being, *li*, becomes separated from the life-giving activity of the ten thousand things. That would indeed be a very odd and quite unintelligible picture. CHENG Yi, however, argues that it is the life-giving activity of the material *qi* that gives life to the ten thousand things, saying that "*qi* naturally has the life-giving activity. The life-giving activity of human *qi* is that of the true origin (*zhen yuan* 真元). The *qi* of nature (*tian*) also has the unceasing life-giving activity" (*Yishu* 15; 148). Thus understood, we can easily see why each of the ten thousand things possesses the *li* completely: everything has its life-giving activity, and there is indeed no life-giving activity over and above the life-giving activities of the ten thousand things, as there is no thing over and above the ten thousand things in this universe. In this relation, since *li* does not give birth to the ten thousand things, but is the life-giving activity of these ten thousand things, the question about how something metaphysical can produce something physical is also dissolved.

5. *Shen* 神 (Divinity or God): Toward a Confucian Theology

Earlier in this chapter, we mentioned MOU Zongsan's view that the Confucian moral metaphysics is at the same time a moral theology. However, he does not tell us in what sense the Confucian moral metaphysic can be regarded as theological. I shall explore that dimension of Confucian moral metaphysics in this section.

In the pre-Confucian era and even among some earlier Confucians, *tian* was sometimes used to refer to a personal god. However, since *tian* is now understood as *li* by the Chengs, it loses such a meaning of divinity. CHENG Yi claims that the heaven-*dao* "is simply *li*; *li* is the heaven-*dao*. Thus to say that 'high heaven shook with anger' by no means implies that there is a man up above who shakes with anger; it is simply that the *li* is like this" (*Yishu* 22a; 290). *Li* thus receives a naturalistic rather than a supernatural interpretation in the Chengs. For example, CHENG Yi claims that "*li* as life-giving activity is natural and ceaseless" (*Yishu* 15; 167). In this sense, heaven, conceived as *li*, is obviously very different from the traditional Christian idea of God. In other words, *li* as the ultimate reality in neo-Confucianism lacks the religious dimension. QIAN Mu therefore argues that since *tian* and *li* are entirely knowable, we cannot have a religious feeling toward *tian* or *li* (Qian 2001, 230).[32] In other words, we can at most have a Confucian metaphysics but not a Confucian theology.

In this context, however, it is important to examine the role of another important idea in the Chengs' philosophy: *shen* 神 (divinity or God). It is true that sometimes *shen*, particularly in CHENG Yi, means spirit and so often goes together with ghost as in the phrase *gui shen* 鬼神. In this sense, following ZHANG Zai, CHENG Yi argues that *shen* is made of *qi*, the vital force, and is something physical and not metaphysical. For example, CHENG Yi claims that "ghost and spirit are creatures" (*Jingshuo* 1; 1028), and they are merely transformations of the vital force (*Yishu* 2a; 288).[33] It is in this sense that CHENG Yi argues that ghost and spirit (*gui shen*), believed by common people and in superstition to be something completely spiritual, does not exist: "I once asked those who love to talk about ghost and spirit, but none of them ever saw ghost or spirit. They all heard people talk about them. Because they do not understand, they start to believe. Even if there are those who claim to have seen or heard ghost and spirit, we should not believe them, as they are all sick, either with their mind or with their eyes" (*Yishu* 2a, 52). It is along this line that CHENG Yi uses the transformation of *qi* (*qi hua* 氣化) to explain many natural phenomena that have often been explained by ghost and spirit. For example, he claims that "the wind is the flow of *qi* between heaven and earth and is not something that can be produced by a man-made figure" as believed in superstition (*Yishu* 2a, 52.); CHENG Yi states that rain "is caused by the evaporated water," so it cannot be sought by any superstitious activities (*Yishu* 22a; 288); CHENG Hao claims that an eclipse, which superstition believes can cause disaster to humans, happens "because the moon does not receive the sun light" (*Yishu* 11; 130).

Yet, as discussed earlier, the Chengs do use *shen* in a different sense, as referring to the same reality referred to by such terms as heaven, *li*, *dao*, and nature. For example, talking about heaven, CHENG Hao claims that "its reality (*ti* 體) is change, its *li* is *dao*, and its appearance (*yong* 用) is *shen*; its being in humanity as destiny is called nature; to follow the nature is called *dao*; and to cultivate *dao* is called teaching" (*Yishu* 1; 4).[34] CHENG Yi relates *shen* to nature and argues that "*shen* and nature are always together" (*Yishu* 3; 64). In this sense, *shen* is obviously not the physical vital force but is the metaphysical reality that is also referred to as *dao*, *li*, heaven, and nature: the life-giving activity. For the Chengs, "the reason that it is cold in the winter and it is hot in the summer is *yin* and *yang*; the reason of change and move-ment is *shen*. So *shen* does not have a location and change does not have a body" (*Yishu* 11; 121). Here *shen* is clearly distinguished from *qi*. *Shen* does not have a location, as change does not have a body, because both refer to the life-giving activity, while only things that act have location and body. However, if *shen* is indeed a metaphysical and ontological idea, in what sense can we regard it also as theological if we intend to translate it as divinity? According to Graham, here "*shen* is not a personal spirit but a daemonic power or intel-ligence which is active within the operations of heaven and earth and which emanates from the person of the sage" (Graham 1992, 111–12); and Graham emphasizes that, in the *Book of Changes*, it is more frequently used not as a noun but as an adjective, to mean "psychic," applied to *dao*, change, and sages (Graham 1992, 112). Graham's interpretation does make some sense. However, in this way, *shen* becomes a secondary concept to describe one aspect of *dao*, change, or *li*. Yet, as we have seen above, for the Chengs, just as *dao*, change, *li*, nature, and heaven, *shen* is used to refer to the same ultimate reality, the life-giving activity.

The reason that the Chengs use *shen* to refer to this ultimate reality is to illustrate its two related aspects: the mysterious wonderfulness (*miao* 妙) and the unpredictability (*buce* 不測) of the life-giving activity.[35] For example, CHENG Hao states that "*tian* is nothing but *li*. We call it *shen* to refer to the wonderful mystery of *li* 理 in the ten thousand things, just as we call it lord (*di* 帝) to emphasize its being the ruler of events" (*Yishu* 11; 132); and "the mysterious wonderfulness of transformation is what is meant by *shen*" (*Yishu* 11; 121). CHENG Hao indicates in these quotations that *tian*, *shen*, and *di*, among other terms, refer to the same ultimate reality. Since these terms have traditionally had their unique connotations, they can refer to different aspects of the same reality. Here, *shen* can express the mysterious wonderfulness of *li* as the life-giving activity better than *tian*, *di*, and any other words. CHENG Yi concurs:

"When the *qi* is complete, the *li* is straight; and when the *li* is straight, there will be impartiality, and when the impartiality is complete, it is *shen*" (*Wenji* 9; 597), as "*shen* means the extreme mysterious wonderfulness" (*Yishu* 3; 64). The life-giving activity appears mysterious and wonderful to us, because it is beyond our comprehension and anticipation. Thus, CHENG Hao claims, "The unceasing life-giving activity is called change, and the unpredictability of the change is called *shen*" (*Yishu* 11; 133). In what sense is the life-giving activity mysteriously wonderful? Cheng provides us with some examples: "[I]t is swiftness without hurrying and reaches destiny without moving. This is something one has to ponder deeply in order to understand and for this reason it is called *shen*" (*Yishu* 11; 121). Here, it is natural for us to think that we have to hurry in order to be fast, and we have to travel in order to arrive somewhere. When the life-giving activity is fast without hurrying and reaches destiny without moving, it is beyond our understanding, and it becomes something mysterious and wonderful at the same time. As a matter of fact, as CHENG Hao points out, "*shen* does not have swiftness nor will arrive anywhere, but we have to use these terms to describe it."[36] Similarly, CHENG Yi says that "the *heaven-li* is to have things done without action and to reach a goal without walking" (*Yishu* 18; 215). From our human point of view, we need to do something in order to get something done, so when we see things get done without seeing any effort, we regard it as mysteriously wonderful.

In order to avoid misunderstanding, it is important to keep in mind that *shen* is not some *thing* that is wonderful and mysterious but is the wonderful mystery of the life-giving activity of the ten thousand things that are made of the vital force *qi*. It is in this sense that CHENG Hao claims that "there is no *shen* outside vital force (*qi*), and there is no vital force outside *shen*" (*Yishu* 11; 121). Apparently, there may seem to be some inconsistency in our interpretation above. On the one hand, in order to emphasize the mysterious wonderfulness and unpredictability, we make a distinction between the life-giving activity as the ultimate reality and human activity; but on the other hand, we mention that the life-giving activity is nothing but the life-giving activity of the ten thousand things, including human beings. In order to show that there is no such inconsistency, it is important to point out that, while the life-giving activity among human beings is indeed no different from the activity of human beings, it is not the same as every individual human being's conscious activity. This point can perhaps be better appreciated if we compare it with the idea of "serendipitous creativity" by Gordon Kaufman, an influential and creative contemporary Christian theologian, in his reconstruction of Christian theology. What he calls serendipitous creativity is the tendency in cosmic, evolutionary, and human history to outrun human expectations and purposes. Talking about such serendipitous creativity in human history, he points out that "although the movements of history are shaped in many ways by human decisions and actions, much more is going on in them than simply the realization of deliberate human intentions" (Kaufman 1993, 273). To illustrate this serendipitous creativity in human history, Kaufman uses such examples as these: Columbus intended to find an easier way to India but unexpectedly discovered America; a group of Dutch settlers intended to found New Amsterdam which, beyond their expectation, developed into the modern New York City; King John signed the Magna Charta to guarantee certain feudal rights, but without his anticipation, it became the foundation of constitutional liberties and modern democracy.[37] Understood as such a serendipitous creativity, we can see why the life-giving activity in the Chengs is nothing but the life-giving activity of the ten thousand things including human beings and yet appears to us mysteriously wonderful and unanticipated. It is of course the activity of the ten thousand things (including human beings) and yet is not simply the sum of all individual activities of the ten thousand things.

Of course, the life-giving activity appears to be mysteriously wonderful and incomprehensible only to common people but not to sages, because sages, or rather the activities of sages, are identical to the life-giving activity itself. CHENG Hao thus states that "sages are no different from heaven and earth" (*Yishu* 2a, 17); CHENG Yi also says that "the *shen* of sages is the same as *tian*. How can they be different? That is why they can hit the mean without trying hard and obtain understanding without thinking. Their heart/mind is no different from heaven and earth" (*Yishu* 2a; 22). In other words, when one becomes a sage, one can understand the life-giving activity of the ten thousand things, or what Kaufman calls serendipitous creativity, and so can act naturally in light of this cosmic life-giving activity. It is for this reason that CHENG Hao claims that "sage is selfless" (*Yishu* 11; 126), and CHENG Yi states that "sages are faultless" (*Waishu* 2; 364). Thus, although Confucius says that to be *ren* is to overcome one's selfish desires (and return to propriety), CHENG Hao claims that "in sages, there is nothing to be overcome" (*Yishu* 2a; 28). Sages do have emotions as common people do, but "they are happy with things that one should be happy with, and are angry at things that one should be angry at. Sages' being happy or angry does not depend upon their own mind but upon the things they are happy with or angry at" (*Wenji* 2; 461). Because of this, not only the life-giving activity as the ultimate reality does not seem to be mysterious to sages, but activities of sages will appear mysteriously wonderful and unpredictable to common people. For example, common people cannot understand how "sages never try to memorize anything, and yet they can remember everything" (*Yishu* 3; 64). So when explaining Mencius's statement that "when beyond one's understanding, sages are *shen*," CHENG Yi points out that "this does not mean that *shen* is above sages. *Shen* is merely sages beyond one's understanding. This means that sages' behaviors are so mysteriously wonderful that we cannot anticipate them" (*Yishu* 17; 177).

Here we may wonder whether this feature can legitimately be called *shen*, and if so, whether *shen* can legitimately be translated into divinity or God in Western languages. In terms of the former, we have to realize that *shen* (divinity) is used in contrast to *ren* 人 (human beings). In this sense, from the above, it is clear that the life-giving activity can be legitimately regarded as *shen*. For humans, we need to hurry in order to be fast, to move in order to arrive somewhere, and, in general, to exert some effort in order to have something done. So when we see someone is hurrying, we can anticipate that person is fast; when we see someone is moving, we can anticipate that person will arrive somewhere; when we see someone is exerting some effort, we can anticipate that person will have something done. However, the life-giving activity of the ten thousand things (including human beings) is different: fast without hurrying, arriving somewhere without moving, and accomplishing things without trying to do them. It is precisely in this sense that the Chengs regard the life-giving activity as *shen*. This sense of *shen*, however, is not an arbitrary use the Chengs make of the term. Before them, ZHOU Dunyi 周敦頤 and ZHANG Zai used *shen* in the same sense. For example, according to Zhou, "When the heaven-*dao* prevails, the ten thousand things are in harmony; when the highest virtue is cultivated, the ten thousand people are transformed. The greatest harmony and transformation, because we cannot see any of its artificial effort and we do not understand its reason, is called *shen*" (Zhou 2000, 36). He further makes a contrast between things and *shen*: "Not being quiet when moving and not moving when being quiet, this is a thing; moving without movement and being quiet without being quiet, this is *shen*" (Zhou 2000, 37). ZHANG Zai makes a similar claim: "The ten thousand things appearing mysteriously wonderful is called *shen*" (Zhang 2000, 237), and "with regard to its unpredictability, it [the ultimate reality] is called *shen*" (Zhang 2000, 241). As a matter of fact, even in modern Chinese, *shen* still has this meaning of mysterious wonderfulness and unpredictability.

Now if *shen* does have this meaning of mysterious wonderfulness and unpredictability, can we appropriately regard it as divinity or even God? It is true that this conception of *shen* is very different from the traditional Western conception of God as some *thing* that is beyond, beneath, or behind the ten thousand things in this world. However, many contemporary Christian theologians have questioned the plausibility of such a deified conception of God and the resultant two-story world picture. For example, Gordon Kaufman points out that "there do not seem to be any compelling reasons any longer which can be cited in its favor . . . Indeed, it is not clear just what counts as a reason for speaking of the existence and nature of some being—a cosmic agent—who exists on the other side of a metaphysical divide as absolute as that supposed to obtain between the creator and creation" (Kaufman 1993, 272).[38] Thus, instead of conceiving God as creator, Kaufman suggests that we should conceive God as creativity, "the evolutionary and historical processes which produce us" (Kaufman 1993, 330).[39] By such a reconception, Kaufman aims to underscore this important fact: "Change is more fundamental than structure: all structures come into being in the course of time and eventually pass away again in time" (Kaufman 1993, 252). It is interesting to see that Kaufman also focuses on the idea of change that the Cheng brothers borrowed from the *Book of Changes* in their discussion of *li*. Since these evolutionary and historical processes or the creativity exhibited in them cannot be completely understood by us, Kaufman regards them as serendipitous creativity. It is in this sense that Kaufman claims that God is a mystery (see Kaufman 1993, 312).[40]

While *li* as the life-giving activity is *mysterious* and *unpredictable*, it is mysteriously and unpredictably wonderful, because it is closely related to the central Confucian moral value, *ren* (humanity). As we have seen, the most important Confucian values are *ren*, righteousness, propriety, wisdom, and faithfulness. In the Chengs' view, among these five virtues, *ren* is important as in one sense it includes all other virtues (see *Yishu* 2a; 14). Thus, in their ontotheological articulation of Confucian values, the Chengs' primary focus is on *ren*. What is *ren*? After he said that "the atmosphere of life-giving activity (*sheng yi* 生意) is most spectacular," CHENG Hao continued that " 'what is great and originating becomes (in humans) the first and chief (quality of goodness).' This quality is known as *ren*. *Ren* is something that makes for oneness with heaven and earth" (*Yishu* 11; 120). In other words, *ren* is good not only because it is a human value; it is actually no different from the ultimate reality, the life-giving activity. *Ren* thus has not only to be understood in relation to the idea of *tian* as *li*, which is life-giving activity, but can also be seen as nothing but this life-giving activity. For CHENG Hao, to be alive is *ren*, and to be dead is the lack thereof. It is in this sense that the two Chengs play puns on the meaning of *ren*. CHENG Yi understands *ren* from its meaning of the power of a seed to grow into a tree (*Yishu* 18; 184), while CHENG Hao understands it from its meaning as ability to feel life (as lack of *ren* means "numb") (*Yishu*

2a; 15). In other words, the ultimate reality itself is moral. Thus, having said that "'the ongoing life-giving activity is called change.' This is how *tian* can be *dao*. Tian is *dao* only because it is the life-giving activity," CHENG Hao claims that "what follows this life-giving activity is good. Goodness has a meaning of origin (*yuan*) and so it was said that '*yuan*' is the growth of the goodness. The ten thousand things all have the atmosphere of spring [life], and this is what is meant by 'what continues it [life-giving activity] is good'" (*Yishu* 2a; 29).[41] Here Cheng makes an explicit connection between *li* as life-giving activity and moral goodness.[42]

6. Conclusion

In this chapter, I have examined *li*, the central idea of the Cheng brothers' neo-Confucian moral metaphysics, a metaphysics concerned with the ultimate reality which itself is moral. While the term *li* has often been translated as law, pattern, and, more commonly, principle, I argue in this chapter that, as the ultimate reality of the ten thousand things in the universe, it is not something behind, beneath, or beyond the ten thousand things. It is immanent in the ten thousand things. Moreover, it is immanent in the ten thousand things not as their essence or substance but as their life-giving activity. In the sense that *li* for the Chengs is not some reified entity but dereified activity, it is similar to Heidegger's Being of beings. While Being is always Being of beings, beings cannot "be" and therefore will be nothing without Being. Similarly, while as life-giving activity *li* is always the life-giving activity of the ten thousand things, the ten thousand things cannot exist and will be nothing without the life-giving activity. It is in this sense that the Cheng brothers regard *li* as the most fundamental reality of the universe. It is also in this sense that the Cheng brothers' metaphysics of *li* is a moral metaphysics, because *li* as the life-giving activity is closely related to moral goodness, and the most important Confucian moral value, *ren*, in the Cheng brothers' view, should also be regarded as a life-giving activity.

Chapter 7

Classics (*Jing* 經)

Hermeneutics as a Practical Learning

1. Introduction

Hermeneutic practice, as an interpretation of the classics or texts in general, is perhaps as old as human civilization. Yet as a self-conscious reflection upon this process of interpretation, hermeneutics in its strict sense did not emerge in Western philosophy until Schleiermacher, who is considered to be the father of modern hermeneutics (see Schleiermacher 1986; Huang 1996). It remained a marginal field in philosophy for long time, until Hans-Georg Gadamer's *Truth and Method* (Gadamer 1993) brought it into the heart of philosophy. Many contemporary philosophical debates cannot be fully understood without an adequate understanding of some central hermeneutic issues. Hermeneutics now not only considers how to correctly interpret a text grammatically or how to correctly understand an author psychologically, but also how to correctly explain the very activity of the understanding of the reader existentially. In this context, we might wonder what contribution CHENG Yi could possibly make to the fully developed conversation in contemporary Western hermeneutics.

It is the purpose of this chapter to show that contemporary hermeneutics indeed has much to learn from the ontological turn CHENG Yi initiated in Confucian hermeneutics. I make this claim for basically three reasons. First, the central debate in contemporary Western hermeneutics revolves around the question of whether a correct interpretation should aim at the objective meaning of the classics independent of both their authors and readers, at the

223

original intention of authors beyond both the classics and readers, or at the preunderstanding of readers independent of both authors and texts. Cheng Yi, however, unified the three by means of *dao*, since for him (Confucian) classics are carriers of *dao*, the sages wrote classics with an intention to illuminate *dao*, and readers project upon these classics a preunderstanding of *dao*. Second, Western hermeneutics basically focuses on the interpretation of classical texts, religious or secular. Even the so-called ontological turn of hermeneutics initiated by Heidegger simply means a hermeneutics of human existence. Although in Heidegger's view human existence is the very existence toward understanding Being, the properly ontological question, hermeneutics in his case can at most be regarded as a prolegomena to ontology (what he calls fundamental ontology) but not ontology per se.[1] Hermeneutics in Cheng Yi, however, is nothing but ontology, since for him hermeneutics is essentially the hermeneutics of *dao*, the ultimate reality of the universe. Third, Western hermeneutics basically aims at understanding. In this respect, even Gadamer's hermeneutics, which claims to be a practical philosophy, is not an exception, since it is still only interested in understanding, even though this involves not merely readers' understanding of the text or of the author, but also of themselves, that is, their self-understanding.[2] Cheng Yi's hermeneutics, however, unifies understanding *dao* and practicing *dao*. In his view, it is a self-contradiction to say that one understands *dao* and yet is unable to practice it. In this sense, his hermeneutics is a more genuine practical philosophy. In the following, I shall try to make these three points by discussing the various aspects of Cheng Yi's hermeneutics of *dao*.

2. Classics as Carriers of *Dao* (*Jing Yi Zai Dao* 經以載道)

Hermeneutics has always played an important role in the Confucian tradition, as all major developments in this tradition have been in the form of new interpretations of the Confucian classics.[3] It can be fairly claimed that without Confucian hermeneutics, there is no Confucian tradition, just as without Confucian tradition, there is no Confucian hermeneutics.[4] The ontological turn Cheng Yi initiated in Confucian hermeneutics is therefore not about whether these classics are important but why. In the pre-Song period, many Confucians in the hermeneutic tradition had an almost blind faith in what they considered infallible classics; all they could do was provide literary commentaries and exegeses upon these classics or their earlier commentaries and exegeses.

Of course CHENG Yi, taking the transmission of the Confucian tradition as his highest mission, did not doubt the importance of these classics, but for him they were important because they "are carriers of *dao*, just as the tools are servants of their purpose" (*Yishu* 6; 95). In other words, the classics are important only because they are tools serving the purpose of carrying *dao*. From this perspective, CHENG Yi argues, although the six Confucian classics are all different in terms of their concrete contents, they are the same in the sense that they all carry the same *dao* (*Yishu* 18; 193).

Whether CHENG Yi's claim, that classics are carriers of *dao*, represents the ontological turn as I state here, however, depends upon how we understand the *dao* that is carried by Confucian classics. Of course, the word "dao" could simply mean "teaching," and therefore the *dao* carried by Confucian classics would obviously be Confucian teaching. More specifically, it could mean the Confucian teaching about how to become a sage, since it is the Confucian idea that everyone has the potential to become a sage, and it is the goal of Confucianism to help people realize this potential. I believe that CHENG Yi does not intend to deny such a generally accepted understanding at all in his claim that classics are carriers of *dao*. As a matter of fact, in his famous essay on Yanzi, CHENG Yi points out that what makes Yanzi unique is not his potentiality to become a sage but "his resolve to learn *dao* to become a sage" (*Wenji* 8; 577). The question then is what precisely the *dao* of Confucius or the Confucian teaching about how to become a sage is. Although Confucius said many things about how to become a sage, and different Confucians have emphasized different aspects, if only one word is to be used to summarize his whole teaching, again there seems to be hardly any controversy: the *dao* of Confucius is *ren* 仁. CHENG Yi has no intention of denying such a commonsense understanding, for he makes it clear that a sage is one who fully fulfills *ren* (*Yishu* 18; 182).

The way CHENG Yi completes his ontological turn in his claim that classics are carriers of *dao* is found in his unique understanding of the Confucian idea of *ren*. Granted, there have been many different interpretations of the Confucian idea of *ren*, and even Confucius himself talked about *ren* variously. However, before CHENG Yi it was basically understood as a social and moral idea, best summarized by HAN Yu 韓愈. HAN Yu declared that, although *dao* is common to Confucianism, Daoism, and Buddhism, it takes different meanings for them. In Confucianism, it means "*ren* and *yi* 義," where "universal love is *ren* and appropriate action is *yi*" (Han 1963, 454). CHENG Yi fundamentally disagrees on this. In his view, while *ren* certainly has its moral dimension, it also has its ontological foundation. Consequently, he relates *ren* to human nature (*xing* 性): "Love is feeling whereas *ren* is the [human] nature. How can love be taken exclusively as *ren*? . . . It is wrong for HAN Yu to say that universal love is *ren*. A man of *ren* of course loves universally. But one may not therefore regard universal love as *ren*" (*Yishu* 18; 182).

In other words, *ren* is not a feeling a human being may or may not have; it is the very nature of human beings. What is *ren* as human nature in contrast to love as human feeling then? To answer this question, CHENG Yi further relates *ren* to the human mind (*xin* 心), which for him is a life-giving activity. To explain this, he uses an analogy: "The mind is comparable to a seed of grain, and the nature of growth is *ren*" (*Yishu* 18; 184).[5] Here, using a pun based on the word *ren*, which also means "seed," particularly the stone of a fruit such as a peach or an apricot, CHENG Yi indicates that growth is the nature of the human mind and *ren* is nothing but this very nature of the human mind. Now, to explain exactly what this human mind is, CHENG Yi further relates mind to principle (*li* 理), the central idea of his philosophy and the philosophy of neo-Confucianism as a whole, and claims that mind and principle are identical. Since principle for CHENG Yi is the underlying reality of things, he argues that sages see the minds of billions of people as one mind because they are all connected with one principle (*Zhouyi Chengshi Zhuan* 1; 764). Other people cannot see this unity, because they have selfish and artificial desires, which of course vary greatly from one person to another and can hardly be unified. Finally, to have a clear understanding of the principle, CHENG Yi returns to the idea of *dao* and claims that "principle is nothing but *dao*" (*Yishu* 22a; 290). This time, however, *dao* has clearly obtained a more fundamental dimension than simply a moral teaching, for it is nothing but the activity "to give life to ten thousand things spontaneously . . . without end" (*Yishu* 15; 149).

By relating *ren* to nature, mind, principle, and ultimately *dao* in this manner, CHENG Yi has certainly provided a much broader picture of *ren*. Yet, if CHENG Yi here is merely talking about human mind, human nature, human principle, and human *dao*, then *ren* is still not an ontological idea, but perhaps only an ontical or, at most, a fundamental-ontological idea, to use Heidegger's expressions.[6] Yet, CHENG Yi's claim is much more radical. In his explanation of *ren*, he collapses the distinctions among mind, nature, principle, and *dao*, all containing the root meaning of "life-giving activity"; at the same time he also collapses the distinction between human and heaven. In other words, human mind, nature, principle, and *dao* are at the same time the mind, nature, principle, and *dao* of heaven, and therefore also the mind, nature, principle, and *dao* of everything in the universe. Consequently he argues that "the mind of one person is also the mind of heaven and earth, the principle of one thing is also the principle of the ten thousand things, and the movement of one day is also the movement of one year" (*Yishu* 2a; 13). For him, there is only one ultimate reality that governs heaven, earth, and humans: "In Heaven it is called the *dao* of heaven; on earth it is called the *dao* of earth, and in humans it is called the *dao* of humans," but in reality they are one and the same *dao* (*Yishu* 22a; 282). Therefore, *dao* as the life-giving activity is not only the fundamental reality of human beings, or all living beings, but is also the ultimate reality of everything, including what we might regard as nonliving beings.[7]

Seen from this broad picture, we can conclude with some justification that CHENG Yi's statement that classics are carriers of *dao* represents an ontological turn in Confucian hermeneutics. The *dao* carried by Confucian classics can still be understood as the Confucian teaching about how to become a sage, and this Confucian teaching can still be understood as *ren*. However, in CHENG Yi's view, *ren* can no longer be understood merely as a human feeling of love, but has to be related to the nature, mind, principle, and *dao*, the ultimate reality of the whole universe. Consequently, *ren*, as Confucian *dao* ("teaching") about how to become a sage, is no longer merely a moral virtue but becomes an ontological principle of the life-giving activity.[8] To understand *ren* as life-giving activity does not deny that a person of *ren* still loves universally, but it provides this universal love with an ontological articulation: love itself is a life-giving activity. It is in this sense that CHENG Yi claims that "there is no difference between sages and *dao*" (*Yishu* 18; 209), because a sage is but the person of *dao,* and whoever follows *dao* thoroughly is a sage. So ultimately, the *dao* carried by classics is *the dao,* the ultimate reality of the universe. It is in this sense that CHENG Yi's claim that classics are carriers of *dao* is not merely a hermeneutic claim but also an ontological claim; more appropriately, it is an ontological-hermeneutic claim.

3. To Grasp *Dao* through Classics
(*You Jing Qiong Li* 由經窮理)

When claiming that classics are carriers of *dao* and further that the *dao* carried by classics is not merely the *dao* ("teachings") of sages but also the *dao* (the ultimate reality) of heaven, earth, and the ten thousand things, including human beings, CHENG Yi seems to regard classics as secondary to *dao.* While this might be true, CHENG Yi has no intention to downplay the importance of classics: since classics are carriers of *dao,* it becomes extremely important for seekers of *dao* to study these classics. First, as carriers of *dao,* these classics must have *dao* carried within them. So, CHENG Yi claims, "the *dao* of everything, whether big or small, far away or near, above or below, fine or crude, is all in classics" (*Yishu* 1; 2).[9] Second, while it is true that *dao* as the ultimate reality of the universe does not appear only in classics or only after these classics were written by sages, it is nevertheless the case that these Confucian classics first taught *dao* as the unifying principle of both humans and heaven. It is in this sense that CHENG Yi claims that, to seek *dao*, "nothing is better than to study classics" (*Yishu* 1; 2), and "we should turn to classics to investigate the principle" (*Yishu* 15; 158), keeping in mind that *dao* and principle are identical for Cheng.[10] Therefore, in his claim that classics are carriers of *dao*, CHENG Yi's emphasis is not that we should look for *dao* without reference to classics (although he does think that *dao* also exists outside classics) but that the proper way to study these classics is to understand the *dao* they transmit. This is why, immediately after his analogy between classics carrying *dao* and tools serving their purposes, CHENG Yi points out that "to study classics without knowing *dao* is as useless as to work on tools without knowing their purposes" (*Yishu* 6; 95). The question then is how to grasp the *dao* carried by classics.

On the one hand, CHENG Yi makes a distinction between the classics' literal meaning (*wenyi* 文意) and their underlying principle (*yili* 義理). The latter is obviously more important than the former, for the underlying principle is nothing but the *dao* carried by classics, while the literary meaning only serves to carry the underlying principle. Of course, our understanding of the literary meaning will help us understand the underlying principle, and vice versa. Yet, CHENG Yi insists that, on the one hand, "since classics are carriers of *dao*, to recite their words and make exegeses of their meaning without paying attention to *dao* is *useless*" (*Wenji-Yiwen*; 671; emphasis added); and on the other hand, "one who is good at learning should not be constrained by words. If you can make sense of *dao*, it is *harmless* even if you are wrong in interpreting the literal meaning of some words" (*Waishu* 6; 378; emphasis added). It is indeed on this basis that CHENG Yi launches his most radical criticism of the Han dynasty Confucian hermeneutics, the predominant one up to his time. The Han hermeneutics was primarily interested in providing detailed (word by word, sentence by sentence, and chapter by chapter) commentaries and exegesis of classics or even of the previous commentaries and exegeses of classics. In other words, they were interested in the literal meaning of classics, not the fundamental principle (*dao*) they carry. Here CHENG Yi asks, "What use is there for the Han hermeneutics? It is only concerned with the sentence-chapter exegesis. For example, it takes them 20,000–30,000 words just to explain the two title words *Yao Dian*. This is really because they do not know what is essential" (*Yishu* 18; 232). From CHENG Yi's point of view, when we need to search for the inner meaning, the Han hermeneutics looks for the outer (literal) meaning; and when we need to aim at the root, the Han hermeneutics is only interested in the branch (exegesis) (*Yishu* 25; 319); the result is that they got what is said but lost what is meant (*Yishu* 15; 163).

It is also on this basis that CHENG Yi carries out his own hermeneutic practice. In his view, it is not only harmless to be wrong in interpreting the literal meaning when the fundamental principle has been grasped; it is also beneficial to cast doubts, introduce changes, make deletions within classics, and even rearrange the whole Confucian canon in order to make their literary meaning consistent with fundamental principles. For example, to indicate the great importance he found in them, CHENG Yi separated the *Great Learning* (*Daxue* 大學) and the *Doctrine of Mean* (*Zhongyong* 中庸), two chapters of *The Book of Rites* (*Liji* 禮記), from the book itself and made them into two independent books. At the same time he elevated the *Mencius* to the status of a classic. These three books, together with the *Analects*, eventually formed the "Four Books" (*Sishu* 四書) that from then on exerted extremely important influences within Chinese intellectual history. CHENG Yi also claimed that there were many errors in the *Book of Zhou Rites* (*Zhouli* 周禮) and the *Book of Rites* (*Liji*) and that some chapters of the latter were not really authored by the sages. For the same reason, he was able to adjust several sentences and delete some words in the *Great Learning* (*Yishu* 19; 254; *Cuiyan* 1; 1201; *Jingshuo* 2; 1040).

On the other hand, CHENG Yi makes a distinction between authors' literary products and their original intentions. Classics are works of sages, and "sages wrote classics only to illuminate *dao*" (*Yishu* 2a; 13). In CHENG Yi's view, to understand classics, you must know the sages who wrote them in the very process of reading them. Therefore, he points out that "one who learns should be able to know the person by reading the person's books. If you have not known the person, that means you have not understood what is said" (*Yishu* 22a; 280). In consistency with his view of looking for the fundamental principle (the objective meaning) of classics as carriers of *dao*, CHENG Yi also emphasizes the understanding of the original intention of sages as authors of classics. He urges, "When you read classics, it is not enough just to understand the language. You have to know the character and personality (*qixiang* 氣象) of sages and worthies" (*Yishu* 22a; 284). As I will point out later, studying classics and seeking *dao* for CHENG Yi are not merely to gain intellectual knowledge but are the very process of learning from sages in order to become a sage. CHENG Yi tells us that "either you do not plan to learn from sages at all, or if you want, you should carefully appreciate their characters and personalities, which can not be done simply through words" (*Yishu* 15; 158).

The issue then is how to get to know sages, appreciate their characters and personalities, and learn from them by reading classics. CHENG Yi provides us with some practical instructions. For example,

> We readers should try to understand why sages wrote classics. We should try to understand how sages become sages, why we are not sages yet, and so to search for the mind of sages and the reason why we have not reached it yet. Read and appreciate classics during the day and meditate on them in the night, calm our mind, get rid of our passions, and overcome our doubts. Then we will be able to have the enlightenment [into the intention of sages].
> (*Cuiyan* 1; 1207)

In other words, we should try to make ourselves contemporary with sages and put ourselves in the situations they discuss. For example, when we read the *Analects*, "we should take the pupils' questions as our own questions, and see sages' answers to them as what we can hear today" (*Yishu* 22a; 279). This, however, cannot be obtained if our mind is disturbed, our passions are out of control, and our doubts are present.

Yet, we have to notice that CHENG Yi's hermeneutics, with its focus on the objective meaning of classics and the original intention of their authors, is not against the spirit of contemporary Western hermeneutics with its focus on readers' preunderstanding. When he asks us to calm our mind, get rid of passions, and overcome our doubts, CHENG Yi only asks us to get rid of our private or artificial desires. He does not mean that we should empty our mind so that it becomes a blank slate in order to receive the external *dao* that is carried by classics. There are two reasons, both of which will become clearer in our discussion in the next section, but I would like to briefly mention them here. The first is that our mind is already *dao*, so the *dao* carried by classics is not alien to our mind. To understand the *dao* carried by classics in this sense is also our mind's self-understanding. The second is that, when we read classics, our mind is not a blank slate, but is one with preunderstanding of *dao*. This is not harmful, but actually beneficial to our understanding of the *dao* carried by classics. Therefore it should not be discarded but projected upon our understanding. As a matter of fact, CHENG Yi goes so far as to claim, immediately after he states that "sages wrote classics only to illuminate *dao*," that "people today cannot start to study classics if they do not already have some understanding of their underlying principle" (*Yishu* 2a; 13).[11] Therefore, while he claims that we cannot have a full understanding of *dao* without classics, he also believes that we cannot secure such an understanding if we merely rely upon books (see *Cuiyan* 1; 1185; *Yishu* 15; 165). In short, the objective meaning of classics, the original intention of sages, and the preunderstanding of readers for CHENG Yi are all united, because classics are carriers of *dao*, sages wrote classics only to illuminate *dao*, and we read classics always with a mind that is nothing but *dao*.

4. Multiple Ways to *Dao* (*Qiong Li Duo Duan* 窮理多端)

If we cannot understand *dao* carried by classics without some preunderstanding, there must be other ways to understand *dao*. While it is certainly true that *dao* is carried by classics, it does not mean that *dao* exists only in classics. In this case, we must be able to approach *dao* from other perspectives. This is exactly what CHENG Yi believes: "There are many ways to grasp the principle: to read books to illustrate the principle; to examine people and events in history to make the distinction between the right and the wrong; to handle human affairs and settle them appropriately. These are all ways to fully grasp the principle" (*Yishu* 18; 188). These and some other ways of seeking *dao* are also mentioned in another place, where he answers the question of how to understand the principle: "Read *The Book of Poetry* (*Shijing* 詩經) and *The Book of Documents* (*Shujing* 書經), study history, examine external objects and events, and handle human affairs. One should be persistent in searching and thinking until one becomes fully good. It is not the case that there is only one way" (*Cuiyan* 1; 1191). In these two passages, in addition to studying Confucian classics, CHENG Yi has mentioned four other important ways to approach *dao*, each of which we shall examine in some detail.

1. Study History (*Kao Gujin* 考古今)

In CHENG Yi's view, in order to understand the *dao* carried by classics, it is important to study history, for there is a close relationship between Confucian classics and history. He describes such a relation as one between the substance of *dao* (classics) and its function (history), between medical prescriptions (classics) and descriptions of using medicines to cure people of disease (history), and between laws (classics) and legal cases (history) (see *Yishu* 2a; 19; *Waishu* 9; 401).[12] It is in this sense that we cannot understand history as the function

of *dao* without an understanding of classics as its substance, just as we cannot understand classics as the substance of *dao* without an understanding of
history as its function, since in his view "substance and function are from
the same source, and there is not even a slight separation between the two"
(*Yizhu*, Preface, 689). What we should do therefore is use history to examine
events mentioned in classics and use classics to discern the true and the false
in history. In this process, we will have a better understanding of both classics
and history, resulting in a better understanding of *dao*.

Obviously, studying history as a way to understand *dao* for CHENG Yi
is not simply collecting and memorizing various historical facts. Rather, he
encourages us, "Whenever you read history, you should not exhaust all your
energy in memorizing the detailed events. You have to understand the principle
of order and disorder, peace and danger, prosperity and decline, and continuity
and discontinuity" (*Yishu* 18; 232). The idea is that people and events in history
are functions of *dao*, and therefore if one aims at memorizing the data about
these people and events, one will miss the *dao* that is displayed in them. Then
one will be unable to understand these historical figures and events themselves,
even if the facts about them are memorized. In CHENG Yi's view, one can obtain
an understanding of *dao* not only when the *dao* is actually followed, but also
when it is not followed. In his work, we are given several vivid discussions of
how CHENG Yi himself reads history. For example, after reading history for a
while, Cheng would regularly close his book and start deeply thinking, "predict-
ing" the successes or failures of events and "helping" plan out the subsequent
events. Then he would open the book to check whether his predictions matched
the actual historical developments. If there was any conflict, he would start to
think again (see *Yishu* 19; 258; *Yishu* 24; 313).

In these exercises, CHENG Yi uses his understanding of *dao* previously
obtained either in reading history or from other sources he mentioned, to
understand the *dao* functioning in history. Whenever this preunderstanding
of *dao* seems to be in conflict with history, he pauses to consider whether it
is because his preunderstanding of *dao* is wrong or because *dao* was actually violated in these historical events. If it is the former, he would revise
his understanding; if the latter, his understanding of *dao* would be further
strengthened. In CHENG Yi's view, it is indeed more important to take note of
the latter case, for in history, "there are many lucky successes as well as many
unfortunate failures. People today often think that what succeeds must be right
and what fails must be wrong. They do not know there are many wrong things
that succeed and many right things that fail" (*Yishu* 19; 258). In other words,
dao is not always displayed within successful historical events, and people fail

not necessarily because they have violated *dao*. What is important then is not simply to distinguish between successes and failures in history, but to discern *dao*, both when it is followed and when it is violated.

2. Handle Human Affairs (*Kui Renshi* 揆人事)

Both reading classics and studying history are ways of learning about *dao* from books. However, in CHENG Yi's view, "a learner of *dao* should not limit themselves to talking about books. One should also be able to obtain it by conforming oneself to the propriety in one's behavior, composure, and encounters with others" (*Waishu* 10; 404). This is what he means by approaching *dao* through "handling human affairs and settling them in an appropriate way," that is, according to rules of propriety (*li* 禮). Here, by human affairs, CHENG Yi has in mind the five relationships between father and son, ruler and subject, husband and wife, elder and younger brothers, and friend and friend. Regarding the virtues associated with propriety, CHENG Yi refers to the Mencian view: "Love between father and son, duty between ruler and subject, distinction between husband and wife, precedence of the old over the young, and faithfulness between friends" (*Mencius* 3a4). We can understand *dao* by conducting ourselves according to rules of propriety in these five human relationships, because propriety is not merely a set of external rules imposed upon us to constrain our actions. Propriety is not different from principle, which, as we have already shown, is the same as *dao*, nature, mind, and *ren*. Therefore he points out that "propriety is nothing but to not look at, to listen to, to say, or to do anything against principle. So *li* 禮 (propriety) is *li* 理 (principle)" (*Yishu* 15; 144), and whatever is against the propriety is also against the principle.

This being the case, we may be able to understand why we can also understand *dao* in our daily activities of dealing with human affairs if we can settle them in appropriate ways. Nevertheless the question is: If we have not yet understood *dao* and, therefore, the rules of propriety which the sages established to regulate the five relationships do seem external to us, how can we act appropriately in human affairs? The answer is that sometimes we may act in appropriate ways without understanding the appropriateness. As children, we were taught by our parents and teachers to act in an appropriate way without a genuine understanding of its appropriateness. However, the important point is that, if we keep acting this way, it is natural for us gradually to understand it. So, although we do not understand *dao*, we can still perform actions according to rules of propriety that the sages have set for us, even without a self-conscious understanding of these rules of propriety as identical to the *dao* we seek. A person who understands *dao* will certainly do things according to *dao*, but people who do things in accordance to *dao* may not necessarily be persons who already understand *dao*, that is, be persons of *dao*. It is important, however, to conduct ourselves according to propriety even when propriety appears to be external to us, for it is in this very process that we will start to gradually understand it. As soon as we get the understanding, propriety will no longer appear to be external to us, and we can act according to *dao* spontaneously without paying attention to rules of propriety.[13]

3. Reflect upon Oneself (*Qu Zhushen* 取諸身)

In his famous article on Yanzi, Cheng Yi complains that "the way to learn [*dao*] has been lost to us. People do not seek within themselves but outside themselves, and so engage in extensive learning, effortful memorization, clever style, and elegant diction, making their words elaborate and beautiful" (*Wenji* 8; 578). *Dao* is vast and great. Where should a seeker of *dao* start? In Cheng's view, since *dao* is in everything, it is important to investigate all these things, yet "the most appropriate way of doing so is nothing but to reflect upon oneself" (*Yishu* 17; 175). Why? Cheng Yi's answer is that "*dao* is right within oneself. It is not the case that *dao* is one thing and self is another, as if one has to jump out of oneself to look for *dao*" (*Yishu* 1; 3). Since *dao* is right within us, does it seem odd for us to look far to search for it? To do so is just like a person living in Chang'an 長安 (the capital) who tries to look for the capital outside Chang'an.[14] Since *dao* is the measure of everything, Cheng Yi points out, if we do not realize that *dao* and self are the same, then "we are using an external ruler to measure things and some errors in measuring will then be inevitable. However, when their identity is realized, the self becomes the ruler and the ruler becomes one's self" (*Yishu* 15; 156).

Although Cheng Yi occasionally talks about innate knowledge and ability, which is certainly more congenial to his brother, Cheng Hao, and may sound like Plato's theory of recollection, Cheng Yi's main point here is not that our mind has the innate knowledge of *dao*, as if we only need to turn inward so that the mind can recollect this knowledge. Rather, his view is that, just as *dao* is in all external things, it is also in ourselves, and the *dao* in ourselves is nothing but our mind. So he states that "the mind is nothing but [human] nature. What is called destiny in heaven, what is called nature in humans, and what is called mind when regarded as a master, are actually the same *dao*, which unifies all" (*Yishu* 18; 204). In other words, what is within us is not knowledge of *dao* but *dao* itself. Although *dao* is right within us, this does not mean that we necessarily have knowledge of it. If you do not try to know it, you can never get it. Therefore, CHENG Yi points out, "what is to be known is indeed inherent within us; yet you cannot get it if you don't reflect upon it"; and more clearly, Cheng argues, *dao* is in everyone, but only superior people can experience and practice it. Other people do not have the experience of it and cannot practice it, because they have just given up (*Yishu* 25; 316), not because *dao* is not within them (*Yishu* 25; 321). It is important therefore to exert your mind to the utmost; if you do so, you can know its nature, and when you know its nature, you have also known heaven.[15]

4. Investigate External Things and Events (*Cha Wuqing* 察物情)

The Confucian tradition tended to emphasize the inner reflection upon one's mind and human affairs while ignoring the investigation of external things and events. This, however, is something with which CHENG Yi does not agree. When asked whether we should hate external things in this connection, CHENG Yi answers unambiguously: "How should the external things be hated? If we hate the external things, that means we do not know *dao*" (*Yishu* 18; 195). In his view, *dao*, or principle, is in everything, even a tree or a blade of grass. Everything should be investigated in order to seek *dao*. While reflecting upon one's own mind is indeed important, investigating external things is not less important. In our search for *dao*, there is indeed no distinction between the inner and the outer: "Things and the self are governed by the same principle. If you understand one, you understand the other, for the truth within and the truth without are identical. . . . To seek in our own nature and feelings is indeed to be concerned with our own moral life. But every blade of grass and every tree possesses principle and should be examined" (*Yishu* 18; 193).

Here CHENG Yi's view seems to contradict his distinction between the knowledge from seeing and hearing and the knowledge as/of virtue discussed in chapter 3. As CHENG Yi puts it, "when a thing [the body] comes into contact with another thing [external object], knowledge so obtained is not from within. This is what is meant by extensive learning and much ability today. Knowledge of/as virtue does not depend on seeing and hearing" (*Yishu* 25; 317). In CHENG Yi's view, real knowledge cannot be obtained by relying upon seeing and hearing. What is needed is an inner experience (see *Yishu* 17; 178). If this is true, why do we need to investigate external things such as a tree or a blade of grass?

To answer this question, we must realize that, for CHENG Yi, the investigation of external things is not to gain particular knowledge of these things, which is the business of science, but to know them as the manifestations of *dao*. Ten thousand things are all different, but their *dao* is all the same. The reason that we can exhaust all things is that they all have the same *dao* or principle. Hearing and seeing are important for us to obtain some particular knowledge about these external things, but we cannot obtain knowledge of *dao* merely by relying upon hearing and seeing. *Dao*, as we have seen, is the life-giving activity. What you can see and hear are things that have the life-giving activities. If you merely focus on the things that have the life-giving activities, you will be blind to the life-giving activity itself. This is similar to Heidegger's discussion of Being. What can be seen are beings, while the Being of beings (these beings' activity of "to be") is hidden. It is therefore important to understand the hidden. This is ironic: what is hidden is precisely the activity of disclosing—the Being of beings in Heidegger and *dao* of things in CHENG Yi. In order to understand *dao*, the life-giving activity that is hidden, one has to see and hear the living things that are given. However, if one is focusing on the living things seen and heard, one will lose sight of the life-giving activity that brings about these living things and therefore will not be able to understand *dao*. It is in this sense that CHENG Yi claims that "all Confucians from ancient times hold that we can see the mind (*dao*) of heaven and earth in its quietness, and only I say that we should see it in its activity" (*Yishu* 18; 201). In other words, while seeing and hearing (without which external things cannot be approached) cannot directly lead us to the true knowledge of the invisible and inaudible *dao*, they are indispensable for us to obtain such knowledge through external things, even though ultimately we need to use our inner mind to grasp the *dao* in external things, just as we need to use our same mind to reflect upon itself, which itself is also *dao*.

5. Hermeneutics as a Practical Learning
(*Jingxue Shixue Ye* 經學實學也)

We have discussed CHENG Yi's various ways, including human practice, of developing an understanding of *dao*. Yet for CHENG Yi, the hermeneutics of *dao* is not merely an intellectual exercise to satisfy one's curiosity about *dao*. What is more important is to practice *dao*, not merely as a way to understand *dao*, but also as a way to realize the self-transformation into sagehood. If one remains the same person morally and ontologically after one has read classics, studied history, acted according to rules of propriety, reflected upon one's own mind, and investigated external things, then one might as well not have read, studied, acted, reflected, or investigated them at all (*Yishu* 4; 71; *Yishu* 18;

206). For CHENG Yi, "hermeneutics is a practical learning" (*Yishu* 1; 2) one studies classics "only to understand the principle (*dao*), and one understands the principle only to put it into practice" (*Cuiyan* 1; 1187). As we have seen, the Confucian *dao* is essentially the *dao* of how to become a sage; a sage is not merely a person who has intellectual knowledge of *dao*, but also one who has the moral virtue to act in accordance to *dao*. Indeed, for CHENG Yi one cannot claim to have had a full understanding of *dao* without practicing *dao* at the same time, just as one cannot self-consciously practice *dao* without an understanding of *dao* at the same time.

Here, it is important to notice a significant difference between CHENG Yi's view of knowledge and practice and the common Western philosophical conception of them. Largely due to the Aristotelian distinction between intellectual and moral virtues, Western philosophers have become used to thinking that one can perfectly understand a thing (for example, "to lie is evil") and yet may still decide to act against one's understanding (for example, to go ahead and lie anyway). The familiar explanation is that one has two different faculties functioning here: the intellect decides what something is, and the will decides what one is to do. CHENG Yi argues against such a dichotomy. As we have seen in chapter 3, in his view, to say that one understands *dao* and yet does not act accordingly is a self-contradiction. In other words, one who has moral knowledge will necessarily act morally, and one who fails to act morally does so only because of a lack of knowledge. Of course, the knowledge in question is knowledge of/as virtue and not knowledge from hearing and seeing.[16]

If the view that profound knowledge will lead to perfect practice is preferable to the Aristotelian dichotomy between knowledge and practice, as I think it is, there is nevertheless no agreement whether CHENG Yi actually holds this view. The difficulty is largely caused by his famous statement: "Moral cultivation relies upon being reverent, while intellectual learning depends on increasing knowledge" (*Yishu* 18; 188). This does not mean that moral cultivation and intellectual learning are two different things, as if there were two different sources. In this respect, FENG Youlan is wrong in thinking that, unlike ZHU Xi, CHENG Yi sees, correctly in Feng's view, knowledge and practice as two separate things (see Feng 1998, 178).[17] Yet, as I have argued in much detail in chapter 3, CHENG Yi, just like ZHU Xi after him, holds the view that profound knowledge will necessarily lead toward moral practice, just as moral cultivation is conducive to the increase of knowledge.

On the one hand, it is true that for CHENG Yi moral cultivation relies upon being reverent, but this does not mean that reverence has nothing to do with knowledge. What is reverence? In CHENG Yi's philosophy, it has two basic meanings. One is being vacuous and tranquil: "One who is reverent is naturally vacuous (absolutely pure and peaceful, not being disturbed by incoming impression) and tranquil" (*Yishu* 15; 157). What he means here is that one should empty one's mind of its artificial desires. That is why he also regards being reverent as having no self to overcome and as having returned to propriety, since the self to be overcome is precisely one's private desires (*Yishu* 15; 157; *Yishu* 15; 143). Only when these desires are overcome can one discover one's original mind, which is identical to *dao* as the ultimate reality of the world. The other is having one master. How can one be vacuous and tranquil? Interestingly enough, Cheng Yi does not think that our minds should be kept as empty bottles. Rather, they should be occupied by only one master (*zhuyi* 主一), which is *dao*. In Cheng Yi's view, "When the mind has this master it will prohibit all stirrings from occurring. When the mind does not have this master, then all these stirrings will occur. It is like a bottle filled with water. Even when thrown into the ocean, it will not permit any water to come in" (*Yishu* 15; 169). That is to say, private desires can come into one's mind only because the mind does not have its own master, just as water can come into a bottle only because it is not already filled. Clearly, if one does not understand *dao*, one's mind will not have its master; if it does not have its own master, private desires will come in to disturb the mind; if the mind is disturbed, one's moral quality will decline. It is in this sense that moral cultivation also relies upon one's knowledge of *dao*, because such knowledge is an essential part of being reverent.

On the other hand, however, having seen that it is impossible to have moral cultivation without the learning of *dao*, we must be careful to avoid thinking that, for Cheng Yi, it is possible to have knowledge without moral cultivation. Wing-tsit Chan, for example, holds such a view when he contrasts Cheng Yi with Wang Yangming: "Cheng merely says that true knowledge will lead to action, but does not say that action leads to knowledge, as Wang does" (see Chan 1963, 558).[18] This is a misunderstanding, because when Cheng Yi contrasts intellectual learning (which relies upon increasing knowledge) and moral cultivation (which relies upon being reverent), he does not mean that our knowledge can be increased without moral cultivation. If one's mind is full of artificial desires, it is difficult for the person to have a clear understanding of *dao*, just as it is difficult for a person to empty one's mind of the artificial desires if the person does not have a clear understanding of *dao*. Here, Cheng Yi makes it clear that "the investigation of things [to increase knowledge] also needs the accumulation of moral cultivation" (*Yishu* 15; 164), and "if you keep and follow your moral cultivation, the heavenly principle will automatically become transparent" (*Yishu* 15; 169). This is why CHENG Yi thinks that to deal with human affairs in our daily life according to rules of propriety is also an important source of knowledge of *dao*, as discussed in the previous section.

6. Hermeneutic Circles (*Jiao Xiang Yang Ye* 交相養也)

I have argued above that CHENG Yi's hermeneutics is a hermeneutics of *dao*, and there are many ways leading toward *dao*. How are these different ways related to each other? Typically, CHENG Yi provides us with two apparently contradictory answers. On the one hand, he says, "It is not necessary to investigate everything under heaven. One has only to investigate the principle in one thing or event to the utmost and the principle in other things or events can then be inferred. . . . [T]he different ways toward *dao*] are just like thousands of tracks and paths to the same capital. Yet one can enter if one has found just one way. Principle can be investigated in this way because all things share the same principle" (*Yishu* 15; 157). Here, CHENG Yi seems to believe that all these different ways are independently sufficient to approach *dao*. The idea is that the same *dao* is in everything, so if one can exhaust it in one thing, then one does not need to investigate other things but can just apply it to them. At the same time, however, when asked whether it is enough to just investigate one thing, CHENG Yi answers, "How can one understand everything like this? Even Yanzi would not dare say he could readily understand all principles by investigating only one thing! One must investigate one item today and another tomorrow" (*Yishu* 18; 188). In relation to this, CHENG Yi provides us with a couple of practical instructions. On one occasion, he suggests that we start from what is easy for us, although what is easy for one may not be easy for another. For example, CHENG Yi believes that it is easier for ancient people to understand *dao* by studying classics, while it is easier for his contemporaries to use their understanding of *dao* to study classics (*Yishu* 15; 164–65). On another occasion, he suggests that when we experience difficulty in following a certain way, we should try a different way; after we gain some understanding of *dao* through that way, we can come back to the original one, which may no longer seem to be difficult (see *Yishu* 18; 186–87).

So should we just follow one way, or should we, after all, follow all different ways to seek *dao*? It is sometimes claimed that CHENG Yi indeed contradicts himself here.[19] However, if we pay attention to the context in which CHENG Yi makes his point, it is possible to reconcile these two aspects of his thoughts. What is crucial is a distinction between what is ideal (or hypothetical) and what is actual in our search for *dao*.[20] Of course, since *dao* fully exists in every thing, one can get it if one could exhaust one thing. However, we have to realize that there is a hypothetical tone in CHENG Yi's claim here. The fact is that no one could possibly exhaust any single thing, and therefore the only alternative is to examine things one by one so that *dao* gradually becomes clear to us. Therefore, if we are talking about the actual and not the ideal process of our efforts to understand *dao*, all these different ways have to work together to support each other.[21] A better approach to *dao* through one of these different ways can help us approach *dao* even better through other ways. In this process, we will be able to obtain an increasingly clear understanding of *dao*.

Here one might want to say that, however original this view from CHENG Yi's philosophy is, it is nothing but what has now become a platitude regarding the hermeneutic circle, made familiar to us largely by Schleiermacher, Heidegger, and Gadamer. This is perhaps true, but we also must realize that the hermeneutic circle presented by CHENG Yi is a much broader one than the one between part and whole in Schleiermacher or the one between *Dasein*'s preunderstanding and *Sein*'s disclosing in Heidegger and Gadamer. As discussed earlier, it involves interpreting classics, reading history, exerting one's mind upon itself, observing external things, and acting within the five relationships in an appropriate way. Indeed, we can say that CHENG Yi's hermeneutic circle is a circle consisting of many small circles. First, there is a circle between classics and history: our understanding of the principle carried in classics will help us better understand historical events, while our familiarity with historical events will help us better understand the principle carried in the classics. Second, there is a circle between reading books and investigating things: the more books we read (both classics and history), the easier it is for us to investigate things (both external and internal); yet the more things we investigate, the easier it is for us to understand books. Third, there is a circle between investigating external things and reflecting upon one's inner heart/mind: the more knowledge one obtains by examining external things, the easier it is for one to see the true nature of one's own heart/mind; yet the better one sees one's true nature, the easier it is for one to see the underlying principle of external things.[22] Finally, there is a circle between understanding *dao* and practicing *dao*: the better one understands *dao*, the (morally) better a person becomes; the (morally) better a person becomes, the better one understands *dao*.

Through this hermeneutic circle of circles, we can get closer and closer to *dao*. It is in this sense that *dao* cannot be obtained in a sudden enlightenment, but can only be gradually approached in this open-ended process of mutual support among various ways to *dao*. Indeed, to talk about a "*dao* to be gradually approached" is already a misunderstanding, since, properly speaking, *dao* is not something standing over against us to be approached by us but is the very process or the very way of approach. Sages, who are identical to *dao*, are not ones who stop being on the way. They are sages only because they are able to be on the way forever without any artificial effort to stay on the way. In this sense different ways to *dao* are indeed not merely ways to *dao*, as if they are what we can throw away as soon as we obtain *dao*. They are actually nothing short of *dao*; they are already *dao* itself, since *dao*, both literally and philosophically, means nothing but Way.

7. Conclusion

In this chapter, we have presented the hermeneutic theory of the Cheng brothers, particularly CHENG Yi, based on their rich experiences in interpreting Confucian classics. We have outlined the three unique features of their hermeneutics. They unified, around the idea of *dao*, the three elements, which often appear to be in tension with each other in other hermeneutic theories (original intention of the author, objective meaning of the text, and the reader's preunderstanding); they initiated an ontological turn in hermeneutics; and they emphasized the self-transforming nature of hermeneutic practice. These three features are inseparable from their identification of multiple hermeneutic circles: between study classics and reading history, between reading books and examining things, between investigating external things and reflecting upon oneself, and between understanding *dao* and practicing it. Realizing that any discussion of hermeneutic theory is inevitably abstract, I shall conclude this short chapter. To better understand the Chengs' hermeneutics, I shall discuss one example of their (particularly CHENG Yi's) hermeneutic practice (their interpretation of the *Analects* 8.9 and 17.3) in the appendix.

Appendix

Neo-Confucian Hermeneutics at Work

CHENG Yi's Philosophical Interpretation of *Analects* 8.9 and 17.3

1. Introduction

In chapter 7, I discussed CHENG Yi's neo-Confucian moral hermeneutics, with the multiple hermeneutic circles as one of its central features. To show how such a neo-Confucian hermeneutics actually works, in this appendix, I shall discuss CHENG Yi's interpretation of two related controversial passages in the *Analects*: "Common people can (are permitted to) be made to follow it [the way] but cannot (are not permitted to) be made to know it" (*min ke shi you zhi bu ke shi zhi zhi* 民可使由之, 不可使知之) (8.9);[1] and "only the wise above and the stupid below do not change" (*wei shangzhi yu xiayu buyi* 惟上智與下愚不移) (17.3).[2] Critics of Confucius often regard these two passages as evidence that Confucius advocated a policy of keeping people in ignorance (*yumin* 愚民), while his defenders usually propose that the passages are merely his lamentation over the fact that people are ignorant (*minyu* 民愚). So it seems that both critics and defenders of Confucius agree that people are ignorant, with the difference being only over whether people are originally ignorant (*minyu*) or are made ignorant (*yumin*). In CHENG Yi's view, however, neither interpretation catches Confucius's true meaning because both attempt a literal interpretation of the two passages without a general understanding of the sage's normative principles carried in the Confucian classics. In the following, I shall contrast CHENG Yi's philosophical interpretations of these two passages with more conventional interpretations, to show in what sense the former is superior to the latter.

2. Conventional Interpretations of *Analects* 8.9

Earlier in this text, I tentatively translated the passage from *Analects* 8.9, *min ke shi you zhi bu ke shi zhi zhi* 民可使由之, 不可使知之, as "common people can (are permitted to) be made to follow it and cannot (are not permitted to) be made to know it," to reflect the most fundamental point of disagreement in interpreting this passage. The meaning of the word *shi* 使 is clear: "to make; to cause" (since the sentence is in passive voice, it means "to be made; to be caused"). There has not been much serious disagreement about the meaning of the two verbs, *you* 由 (to follow) and *zhi* 知 (to know) (although I shall argue later that the most distinctive feature of Cheng's interpretation is his unique interpretation of *zhi*), and there seems to be a general consensus that *zhi* 之 (it), the object of the two verbs, means the way (*dao*). A little more controversial perhaps is *min* 民, here translated as "common people." Sometimes it is interpreted as broadly as *ren* 人 (human beings) so that the passage means that any human individual can (is permitted to) be made to follow it but cannot (is not permitted to) be made to know it;[3] sometimes it is interpreted as narrowly as referring to Confucius's students other than the seventy-two who are proficient in the six arts;[4] but more frequently, it is interpreted as referring to the people who are to be governed. Despite its various interpretations, it seems that it is not a crucial point. Since the sentence is in the passive voice, it is appropriate to relate *min* to those who can (are permitted to) make *min* follow the way and yet cannot (are not permitted to) make them know it. Although there will certainly be different interpretations about who they are, it suffices to say that they are those who not only follow but also know the way, so *min*, whoever they are, must be those who neither follow nor know it. Thus the question is still why *min* can (are permitted to) be made to follow the way and yet cannot (are not permitted to) be made to know it. The crucial issue here is whether the word *ke* 可 and its negation *bu ke* 不可 should be interpreted as "can (cannot)" or "are (are not) permitted to," as the word itself does have both meanings.

According to one interpretation, *ke* means "be permitted to" so that this *Analects* passage can be read: "Common people are permitted to be made to follow the way but are not permitted to be made to know it." As mentioned above, many critics of Confucius and Confucianism adopt this interpretation (see, for example, Yang 1980, 59). However, this interpretation is also adopted by more sympathetic commentators. For example, Qing dynasty scholar YAN Xizhai 顏習齊 (1635–1704) not only defended this interpretation but also argued against the alternative interpretation of *ke* to mean *neng* 能 (can). In his view, if the way is made known to people,

> then their ears and eyes will be deluded and their heart/mind will be misled. That is why it is not permitted to be made known to people. With this sagely learning getting lost, later Confucians have claimed that what is meant here is that people cannot be made to know and not that they are not permitted to be made to know. For this reason, everyone tries to invent ways to make people know it; the result is that both scholarship and the way of government are destroyed. (Cheng 1990, 533)

In his *Annotations on the Analects* 論語注, Jin 晉 dynasty scholar ZHANG Ping 張憑 related this interpretation to Confucius's distinction between government by virtue and government by punitive laws:

> When governed with virtue, everyone acts according to their nature. Everyone under heaven uses it [the way] in their daily life without knowing it. This is why it is said "[common people] are permitted to be made to follow it." When, however, common people are governed with punitive laws so as to prevent them from doing wicked things, they would know such punitive laws and so would take care to get around them and do the wicked things in clever ways. That is why it is said that "[common people] are not permitted to be made to know it." The point is that government should be run with virtue, so that people will easily follow with virtue. Government may not be run with punitive laws because common people will know the methods used. (Cheng 1990, 532)

Slingerland follows this interpretation in his translation of and comment about this passage, saying that it "accords well with the sentiment of [*Analects*] 2.3, when Confucius declares that ruling by a publicized legal code merely inspires the common people to devise devious ways to get around the law" (see Slingerland 2003).

    This interpretation, however, has at least two problems. First, linguistically, in this interpretation, *zhi* 之 would have two different meanings in its

two appearances in this passage. As the object of the verb *you* 由 (to follow),
it means "the way" or the "virtue," while as the object of the verb *zhi* 知 (to
know), it means "punitive laws." The original text, however, seems to intend to
produce a sharp contrast between what people can (are permitted to) do and
what they cannot (are not permitted to) be made to do: "To follow it" versus
"to know it." So the word *zhi* 之 in its two appearances obviously refers to
the same thing. Second, philosophically, such an interpretation amounts to
saying that Confucius advocated a policy of keeping people in ignorance, which,
as pointed out by CHEN Daqi 陳大齊 (1887–1983), "is contrary to Confucius'
thought. In two different places, [*Analects*] 9.29 and 14.28, Confucius says that
the person who knows will not be deluded. On this principle, unless Confucius
wishes to keep people in delusion forever, he would not be unwilling to transform people from ignorance to knowledge" (Chen 1996, 153).[5] In other words,
if we accept this interpretation, we have to conclude that Confucius or the
Analects is not coherent.[6] In Chen's view, the word *ke* implies ability and *bu
ke* means the lack thereof, so the *Analects* passage really means that common
people "can" be made to follow the way but "cannot" be made to know it.[7] This
is the second conventional interpretation of this passage we need to examine.

So, instead of interpreting the word *ke* as "to be permitted to," most
commentators interpret it to mean "can." The question is why people cannot be
made to know certain things. The typical answer is that common people lack
the intellectual ability to know it (the way). For example, in his *Annotations on
the* Analects 論語注, the Han 漢 dynasty scholar ZHENG Xuan 鄭玄 (127–200)
holds that "the word *min* 民 really means *ming* 冥 [the stupid], who are at a
remove from the way of humanity" (Cheng 1990, 532). Although not regarding people to be at a remove from humanity, in his *Notes from Reading the
Four Books* 四書溫故錄, the Qing Dynasty scholar ZHAO You 趙佑 also noted
that the common people are stupid: "The nature of all common people is good
and so they can be made to follow the way. The nature of common people is
originally stupid and so they cannot be made to know it. So to maintain the
order, rulers should discuss the way among themselves and establish rules for
people to follow. If so, everything will be in order" (Cheng 1990, 532–533).
Most contemporary scholars also hold this view. For example, D. C. Lau argues,

> Confucius did not disguise the fact that, in his view, the common
> people were very limited in their intellectual capacity. He said,
> "The common people can be made to follow a path but not to
> understand it" (8.9). They cannot understand why they are led
> along a particular path because they never take the trouble to

study. . . . It is not surprising that Confucius should have taken
such a view. . . . The common people are greatly handicapped.
They rarely have the capacity and practically never the opportunity. When on the rare occasion they have both the capacity and
the opportunity, they are unlikely to be able to put up with the
hardship. (Lau 1979, 36)[8]

Although this is quite a popular interpretation, it is difficult to think
that this is indeed what Confucius meant. There is a very famous statement
in *Analects* 15.39: "Education should be provided for all without distinction"
(*you jiao wu lei* 有教無類), whether they are rich or poor, noble or lowly, with
high or low intellectual abilities.[9] If Confucius indeed thought that common
people are too stupid to know the way, then he would have instead said that
education should be provided for all who have high intellectual abilities. Not
only did he not say that, but his own career in education proved the opposite.
Although we do not have entirely reliable sources (see Hu 1991, 1:87–88), we
do learn from *Records of the [Grand] Historian* 史記, *Mister Lü's Springs and
Autumns* 呂氏春秋, and other parts of the *Analects* that, among Confucius's
students, Zilu 子路 was originally "uncultivated" (*ye ren* 野人), Zigong 子貢 was
engaged in commerce, Zhonggong's 仲弓 father was a "lowly person" (*jianren*
賤人), Zizhang 子張 was from a family of low status in the state of Lu 魯, and
Yan Zhuju 顏涿聚 was a robber (see Cai 1982, 192). In fact, among Confucius's
students, very few are from rich or noble families. If Confucius knew that these
people cannot be made to know the way, he would be wasting his time with
them. Of course, Confucius did not waste his time. Among those mentioned
here, Zilu, Zigong, and Zhonggong are among Confucius's most accomplished
students. Xu Fuguan 徐復觀 (1904–1982), a prominent contemporary Confucian, thus argues that one of the most important contributions that Confucius
makes to Chinese culture is that he "breaks free of all unreasonable distinctions among human beings and advocates that all humans are of one class
and are equal" (Xu 1999, 64). In addition to *Analects* 15.39, Xu Fuguan also
cites a passage in *Analects* 18.6 to support his claim: "We cannot live together
with birds and beasts. If I do not associate with humans, with whom shall I
associate?" In Xu's view, Confucius here simply separates humans from beasts
without making further distinctions among humans.

In this connection, it is perhaps necessary to take a look at *Analects*
7.7, which is normally understood to mean that Confucius never refused to
teach anyone who came with a small present for tuition. According to Huang
Kan 皇侃 (488–545) and a few others, the phrase *shu xiu* 束脩 in this passage

means a bundle of ten strips of dried meat (with *xiu* referring to dried meat and *shu* meaning ten). In his *Superfluous Comments on the Four Books* 四書賸言, the Qing dynasty scholar MAO Qiling 毛奇齡 (1623–1716) tells us that *shu xiu* is a small present that literati and officials (*shidafu* 士大夫) carried with them when they went abroad (Cheng 1990, 445). If this is the case, then critics of Confucius may be right in claiming that Confucius does not mean to provide education for all, because he has at least set a limit on access to education in terms of property: although ten strips of dried meat might be deemed a small present for *shidafu*, it was certainly not something "small" for poor people of his time (or even for some poor people in remote areas of China today) (see Yang 1980, 58; Cai 1982, 193).[10] If Confucius does, in fact, refuse to teach people who do not come with this present, this would contradict his statement in *Analects* 15.39. There are, however, additional alternative interpretations of *shu xiu* that would enable this *Analects* passage to be read as being consistent with *Analects* 15.39. For example, in his *Occasional Notes on the* Analects 論語偶記, the Qing dynasty scholar FANG Guanxu 方觀旭 quotes ZHENG Xuan's 鄭玄 interpretation of *shu xiu* to mean "the age of 15" and cites uses of the term in this sense in *Discourses on Salt and Iron* 鹽鐵論 (West Han dynasty), LIU Xiang's 劉向 (c.77–6 b.c.e) *Biographies of Notable Women* 烈女傳, and *History of the Later Han* 後漢書 (in Cheng 1990, 447). This interpretation was also accepted by the Qing dynasty scholar HUANG Shisan 黃式三 (1789–1862) in his *Later Notes on the* Analects 論語後案 (Cheng 1990, 446). On this interpretation, in *Analects* 7.7 Confucius is saying that he never refuses to teach anyone who is 15 years old or above. Among contemporary scholars, LI Zehou 李澤厚 is one of the few to adopt this interpretation. Li argues that it is consistent with *Analects* 2.4, in which Confucius says that he sets goal on learning at the age of fifteen (Li 1999, 171).[11]

Since neither of these two conventional interpretations of *Analects* 8.9—which focus on the two different meanings of the word *ke* and its negation—seems consistent with Confucius's overall ideas, other scholars have tried to make this *Analects* passage plausible by punctuating it differently. According to the traditional punctuation, on which the above two conventional interpretations are based, this passage is divided into two parallel and contrasting parts: "*min ke shi you zhi* 民可使由之," and "*bu ke shi zhi zhi* 不可使知之." In his *Examination of the* Analects 論語稽, the Qing dynasty scholar HUAN Maoyong 宦懋庸 punctuates it differently and, accordingly, provides a different interpretation of this passage. In his view, this passage should be read "*min ke* 民可, *shi you zhi* 使由之; *bu ke* 不可, *shi zhi zhi* 使知之," meaning that if people approve it/them (rule or rules proposed by government), then make people follow it/them; if people do not approve it/them, then make them know it/them. This interpretation makes some sense, but as pointed out by YANG Bojun 楊伯峻, punctuating the sentence this way renders it ungrammatical, as the object of the verb *shi* 使, presumably "people," is missing in both parts of the sentence. If Confucius really tries to say what Huan makes him say, it should be written as *"min ke* 民可, *shi zhi you zhi* 使之由之; *bu ke* 不可, *shi zhi zhi zhi* 使之知之"* (Yang 1980, 81). Inventing new punctuation has become a favorite procedure among contemporary Chinese scholars to make sense of this passage. Here are a few more representative examples: (1) *"min ke shi* 民可使, *you zhi* 由之; *bu ke shi* 不可使, *zhi zhi* 知之,"* meaning "If common people follow the virtuous ruler, leave them alone; if common people do not follow the virtuous ruler, let them know" (see Yu and Wu; for criticisms of this reading, see Zhou); (2) *"min* 民, *ke shi you zhi* 可使由之, *bu ke shi zhi zhi* 不可使知之,"* meaning "for common people, [rulers] should use (virtue) to guide them and not use it to force them" (see Peng and Pang; for criticisms of this reading, see Yin and Wu); (3) *"min ke shi* 民可使, *you zhi bu ke* 由之不可, *shi zhi zhi* 使知之,"* meaning "Common people can be forced, but cannot be allowed to do at their will. They should be made to know the way" (see Kong; for criticisms of this reading, see Peng); (4) *"min ke shi you zhi* 民可使由之? *Bu* 不. *Ke shi zhi zhi* 可使知之,"* meaning "can common people be left alone? No. They should be made to know" (see Wang). It should be noted that all these new interpretations are proposed in the context of contemporary China, where many Confucian scholars are trying to recover the true Confucian spirit and promote a positive image of Confucius in the shadow of the anti-Confucius campaign during the Culture Revolution. Thus, they all try to provide favorable readings of this difficult passage. However, the weakness of these interpretations is also clearly revealed by their proponents' criticism of each other, as all these new ways of punctuation are quite forced and implausible. It is in this relation that we can better appreciate the significance of the philosophical interpretation of the same passage by CHENG Yi, who also aims to promote Confucianism in a society profoundly influenced by Buddhism.

3. CHENG Yi's Interpretation of *Analects* 8.9

One of his students asked CHENG Yi about *Analects* 8.9: " 'Common people can (are permitted to) be made to follow it but cannot (are not permitted to) be made to know it.' Is this because sages do not want to make people know it or because people themselves are unable to know it?" Obviously, the student expects CHENG Yi to make a choice between the two alternative conventional interpretations discussed above: either people are not permitted to know it, or people are unable to know it. CHENG Yi replied: "It is not that sages do not want people to know it. The reason that sages establish their teaching is to let everyone know it so that everyone can become worthy. Sages, however, can only make people follow it. How can they make them fully understand it (*jin zhi zhi* 盡知之)? This is because sages cannot do it" (*Yishu* 18; 220). In appearance, CHENG Yi simply sides with those who interpret the word *ke* as "can" and so believes that it is not that sages do not want to make people know it, but that people cannot know it.[12] This is usually what CHENG Yi is thought to believe, because this view was popularized largely through ZHU Xi's 朱熹 (1130–1200) *Collected Annotations of the* Analects 論語集注, in which a similar passage of CHENG Yi is quoted from his annotation of *Analects* 8.9. ZHU Xi prefaces this quotation with his own interpretation: "What people can be made to do is an 'ought' (*dangran* 當然), while what people cannot be made to know is a 'why' (*suoyiran* 所以然)" (Zhu 1985, 1.33). Obviously, ZHU Xi is trying to explain what people cannot be made to know. *Suoyiran* is something much more difficult to know than *dangran*; common people lack the ability to know it.[13]

In his reply to the student's question, however, CHENG Yi does not simply pick one of the two alternatives provided: either that sages do not want to make people know it, or that people cannot know it. Instead, he says that it is because "sages are unable to do it." This is most interesting. We have mentioned that *bu ke* can either mean "not be permitted to" or "cannot." There is no doubt that CHENG Yi adopts the latter sense. So far, however, we have not noticed the fact that when a negative sentence is in the passive voice, such as "*A* cannot be made to do *x* (by *B*)," the reason for the "cannot" can either be that *A* lacks the ability to do *x* or that *B* lacks the ability to make *A* do *x*. So the reason that people cannot be made (presumably by sages) to know the way can either be due to people's lack of the ability to know it or the sages' lack of the ability to make people know it. Perhaps because it seems derogatory to say that sages might lack some ability, almost all commentators who choose to interpret *bu ke* as "cannot" think that it is people who lack the ability. Yet, in the above quoted passage, CHENG Yi makes it unmistakably clear that it is because sages lack the ability that people cannot be made to know the way. If so, can we say, following PANG Pu 龐樸, that, instead of regarding common people as ignorant (*minyu* 民愚), CHENG Yi regards sages as ignorant (*shengren zi yu* 聖人自愚) (Pang 1999)?

In order to answer this question, it is important to understand why CHENG Yi believes that it is sages who lack the ability to make people know the way;

and in order to answer this question it is important to keep in mind Cheng's distinction between knowledge (gained) by hearing and seeing (*wenjian zhi zhi* 聞見之知) and knowledge of/as virtue (*dexing zhi zhi* 德性之知). As we have seen in chapter 3, the significant distinction between these two types of knowledge is that knowledge by hearing and seeing is superficial in the sense that it does not incline us to act accordingly, while knowledge of/as virtue is profound in the sense that it inclines us to act accordingly. Obviously, in CHENG Yi's view, what sages are unable to make people have is not knowledge gained by hearing and seeing—they can be instructed of this type of knowledge—but knowledge of/as virtue, the knowledge that will incline people to act appropriately. Then why cannot sages make people have knowledge of/as virtue? In Cheng's view, while knowledge by seeing and hearing is external knowledge, knowledge of/as virtue is internal knowledge coming from one's inner experience. Thus, Cheng claims that "learning, generally speaking, cannot be obtained through knowledge by hearing. One can obtain it only by silently apprehending it in one's own heart/mind (*mo shi xin tong* 默識心通)" (*Yishu* 17; 178). In his view, *mo shi xin tong* is not easy: "[I]t is easy to learn but difficult to know; it is easy to know, but it is difficult to know by personal experience (*ti er de zhi* 體而得之)" (*Yishu* 25; 321). Here the word *ti* 體, by which one can personally attain knowledge of/as virtue, is extremely important to Cheng. It is both a noun referring to *xin* 心 (one's heart/mind), what Mencius calls *dati* 大體 (the great body), in contrast to our physical body which he calls *xiaoti* 小體 (the small body), and a verb referring to the activity of the heart/mind. So knowledge of/as virtue is something that one can get from one's whole *xin*, not only its mental function (mind) but also its affective function (heart).

Now we are in a better position to understand why sages lack the ability to make people know the way. The knowledge that people need to have is knowledge of the way, which CHENG Yi calls knowledge of/as virtue. Unlike knowledge gained through hearing and seeing, knowledge of/as virtue has to be not only understood by one's mind but also experienced in one's heart, although mind and heart are simply two different functions of the same *xin*. So while sages certainly can teach people about the way, and people may also understand the teaching in their mind, until people can experience it within their own heart so that they are willing to act accordingly, the teachings of the sages will remain merely knowledge of seeing and hearing to ordinary people. As I also emphasized in chapter 3, by its very nature, knowledge of/as virtue cannot be taught but has to be obtained by oneself (*zide* 自得). Thus *zide* has become one of CHENG Yi's most important ideas. In his view, "nothing is more important than getting it by oneself in learning. Getting it by oneself is not to get it from outside" (*Yishu* 25; 316). To say that one has to get it oneself, of course, does not mean that one does not need to be taught by others. The point is that if what is taught by others is not internally experienced by oneself, it remains merely a piece of information which one may fully understand and yet is not ready to act upon; in other words, it remains merely knowledge of hearing and seeing. In order for it to be something of one's own, something that one not only understands but also firmly believes, something one is ready to act upon, one has to get it by oneself. Thus, since the classics contain the sages' teachings, CHENG Yi states, "to study the classics is the best way to learn. If, however, one does not get it [*dao*] oneself, then even if one goes through Five Classics thoroughly, there is nothing but empty words" (*Yishu* 1; 2). When asked how learners can *zide*, CHENG Yi replies: "If learners take time internally in appreciating and experiencing the sage's teaching, then they will get it themselves. Learners should search deeply into the *Analects* regarding the questions of Confucius' students as their own questions and regarding the sage's replies to them as if they were hearing them today. If so, they will naturally get it" (*Yishu* 22a; 279).

So, according to CHENG Yi, *Analects* 8.9 does not mean that people are not permitted to know the way but that people cannot be made to know it; people cannot be made to know the way not because people lack the ability to know it, but because sages lack the ability to make people know it; and sages lack the ability to make people know it not because sages are deficient, lacking in the power or knowledge they should have, but because the type of knowledge in question here is knowledge of/as virtue, which, by its very nature, everyone has to gain by himself or herself. Thus understood, in Cheng's view, to ask sages to make people know the way is to ask sages to do something logically impossible: to provide people with something that, by its very nature, people can only get by themselves. This interpretation certainly makes sense. Before we conclude our discussion of CHENG Yi's interpretation of this *Analects* passage, however, it is perhaps necessary to say something about possible objections to it. A general misgiving with CHENG Yi's interpretations of Confucian classics is that he does not do careful textual analysis but simply imposes some general philosophical ideas upon the texts. In this particular case, for example, it might be argued that the central ideas CHENG Yi uses, such as "knowledge of/ as virtue" and "getting it by oneself," are absent in Confucius's *Analects*. In response, we may acknowledge that Confucius does not make the distinction between knowledge of/as virtue and knowledge from hearing and seeing. I do not, however, believe it is objectionable to claim that Confucius's knowledge of the way is not merely intellectual but also something that inclines one to act.

This can be seen clearly from the close connection between *zhi* 知 (knowledge), on the one hand, and *ren* 仁 (humanity) and *yi* 義 (rightness), on the other. When asked about knowledge, Confucius replied, "A person who does his best to work according to rightness due to people . . . can be regarded as having knowledge" (*Analects* 6.22). Here, in Confucius's view, knowledge has to be related to the moral action of *yi*. On the one hand, he argues that a person who has knowledge must choose *ren*. Thus he argues that we cannot "consider people as having knowledge if they do not choose to settle in *ren* 仁" (*Analects* 4.1) and that "the person who has knowledge seeks *ren*" (*Analects* 4.2).[14] On the other hand, he argues that a person of *ren* must have knowledge: "Without knowledge, how can one be *ren*?" (*Analects* 5.19). When Confucius laments that "there are few people who know virtue" (*Analects* 15.4), obviously what he has in mind is not people who have heard about virtue (knowledge by hearing and seeing) but people who are inclined to act by their knowledge of virtue. In this sense, it can be claimed that CHENG Yi's idea of knowledge of/as virtue (*dexing zhi zhi*) has its origin in the *Analects*.[15]

Now, let us look at CHENG Yi's idea of getting it by oneself. In order to have knowledge of/as virtue, CHENG Yi argues that we cannot rely upon hearing and seeing; we can only rely upon *mo shi xin tong* 默識心通. Here, *mo shi xin tong* originates from Confucius's *mo er shi zhi* 默而識之 in *Analects* 7.2, where Confucius says that to silently gain knowledge from inside (*mo er shi zhi*) is one of the qualities he possesses. In his commentary on this *Analects* passage, CHENG Yi explains that, by *mo shi*, Confucius means to gain knowledge within oneself (*you zhu ji* 有諸己) (*Jingshuo* 6; 1144). This *mo shi xin tong* or *mo er shi zhi* is closely related to CHENG Yi's important idea of getting it by oneself (*zide*), an idea he picks up from Mencius (see *Mencius* 4b14). It is true that we do not find this idea of getting it by oneself in Confucius's *Analects*, but in CHENG Yi's view, the idea is implicit there. When commenting on *Analects* 7.8 in his *Interpretation of the* Analects 論語解, he further points out: "'Do not teach people who are not eager to learn or anxious to explain themselves.' This means to teach only when students are sincere. 'When I have pointed out one corner of a square to someone and he does not come back with the other three, I will not point it out to him a second time.' This means to wait for the students to get it by themselves (*zide*) after they are taught" (*Jingshuo* 6; 1144).[16] In another place where he interprets the same passage, CHENG Yi emphasizes the idea of *si* 思, normally translated as thinking: "When Confucius teaches people, he 'does not teach people who are not eager to learn or not anxious to explain themselves' [*Analects* 7.8], for knowledge will not be solid when taught to people who are not eager to learn and do not express themselves. When they are eager to learn and explain themselves, they will be energetic. Learners need deep *si*" (*Yishu* 18; 208). Learners need deep *si*, because *si* is crucial to getting it by oneself. When asked how people can get knowledge by themselves, CHENG Yi simply replies: "*si*" (*Yishu* 22a; 296). In Cheng's view, it is for this reason that Confucius says that "to learn without *si* will be bewildering, and to *si* without learning will be in peril" (*Analects* 2.15). We have to understand that *si* for CHENG Yi does not merely mean intellectual thinking but also inner reflective experience. Although he sometimes uses them together, he draws a distinction between *si* and *lü* 慮 (mental calculation). In his view, it is through *si* that one can get it by oneself, and "to act after getting it by oneself is different from acting after *lü*. Once one is able to get it by oneself, everything becomes as natural as using one's hand to pick up things. Through *lü*, however, one cannot reach *zide* and one will feel some unnaturalness, just like using a stick to pick up things" (*Yishu* 2a; 22).[17]

4. Conventional Interpretation of *Analects* 17.3

We have argued that *Analects* 8.9 does not mean that people are too stupid to know the way or that sages are too impotent to make people know the way, but that knowledge of the way, by its very nature, has to be obtained by learners themselves. If this is true, the question is whether everyone has the ability to attain knowledge of the way by himself or herself? In appearance, Confucius denies it in *Analects* 17.3: "Only the wise above and the stupid below do not change." So it is important to discuss CHENG Yi's interpretation of this *Analects* passage along with *Analects* 8.9. In order to appreciate the unique-ness of Cheng's interpretation, it is also helpful to start with the conventional interpretation of this passage and its drawbacks.

    One controversial issue in interpreting this passage is what Confucius means by "wise" and "stupid": intellectual ability or moral quality? In his essay, *On Nature* 論性篇, Qing dynasty scholar RUAN Yuan 阮元 (1764–1849) argues that "wise" and "stupid" here do not refer to the goodness and badness of human nature but to intellectual abilities: "The stupid are not evil. The wise are good, but the stupid are also good" (in Cheng 1990, 1185). In connection with *Analects* 16.9, where Confucius talks about people who are born with knowledge, people who know by learning, people who learn after being vexed with difficulties, and people who do not learn even after being vexed with difficulties, CHEN Daqi also argues that Confucius's main purpose is to argue that "there are different levels of inborn intellectual ability. . . . Those who are born with knowledge have the highest intellectual ability, those who know by learning have lower intellectual ability, and those who learn after being vexed with difficulty and those who do not learn even after being vexed with difficulty . . . have very low intellectual ability" (Chen 1970, 86). Tu Weiming holds the same view. Commenting on this *Analects* passage, he claims that

> this does not mean that Confucians pay special attention to the wise above and the stupid below but that they are not concerned with the wise above and the stupid below, because the wise above is a very small percentage among human population, perhaps just people like Yao, Shun, Yu, Tang, Wen, and Wu, while the stupid below are those who are unable to reflect and live their lives at all. In contemporary physiological and psychological terms, they are retarded people or even idiots. The great majority, including Confucius himself, is between the wise above and the stupid below. (Tu 2002b, 1.280)

I do not think such an understanding of the wise and the stupid from the intellectual point of view is correct. Knowledge, *zhi* 知, is an important idea in the *Analects*. Confucius's interest, however, is in moral knowledge. Moral knowledge, of course, also relies upon one's intellectual ability, but everyone possesses the intellectual ability needed to be good.[18] It is more appropriate to understand the wise and the stupid here in their moral rather than intellectual senses. Most commentators hold this view. Han scholars JIA Yi 賈誼 (200–168 BCE) and WANG Chong 王充 (29–97), for example, argue that "the wise" refers to good people, while "the stupid" refers to evil people. In his *Reflections upon the Four Books* 四書反身錄, the Qing dynasty scholar LI Zhongfu 李中孚 (1627–1705) explains this view in some detail:

> The wise above understand the good and live a sincere life and will not change throughout their lives. The stupid below are only concerned with fame and personal benefit to the end of their lives. Is it not that they do not change? Those who are slow intellectually can preserve their good heart, do good things, and be good persons. So, while intellectually slow, they are the wise above. Those who are quick-witted, if harboring evil intentions, doing bad things, and unwilling to be good persons, are the stupid below. (Cheng 1990, 1188)

    With such a moral rather than intellectual understanding of "the wise
above" and "the stupid below," most commentators interpret this *Analects*
passage in connection with two other related passages. One is *Analects* 16.9,
mentioned above: "Those who are born with knowledge are above; next are
those who know by learning; next again are those who learn after being vexed
by difficulties; and those who do not learn even after being vexed by difficulties are common people below." For example, in *Collection of Essays from
the Hall of Inquiry into Characters* 問字堂集, the Qing dynasty scholar Sun
Xingyan 孫星衍 (1753–1818) argues that the wise above and the stupid below
in *Analects* 17.3 refer, respectively, to those who are born with knowledge
and those who do not learn even after being vexed with difficulties. Those
who know by learning and those who learn after being vexed by difficulties
are those between the wise above and the stupid below, people in the middle
(*zhongren* 中人) mentioned in the other related passage: "You can talk about
higher learning with people above the middle but not with people below the
middle" (*Analects* 6.21). With people divided into these three categories, the
wise above, the stupid below, and average people in the middle, commentators
usually interpret *Analects* 17.3 in connection with the immediately preceding
passage: "People are alike by nature but become apart from each other by
practice" (*Analects* 17.2). The connection between these two passages is indeed
obvious, and some commentators even claim that *Analects* 17.2 and 17.3 are
originally one single chapter. The question is how to understand this connection. According to the conventional interpretation, 17.2 refers to the majority
of people in the middle who can become good or bad depending upon their
personal effort, while 17.3 refers to the exceptional people at the two extremes,
the wise above (often interpreted and translated as "the wisest") and the stupid
below (often interpreted and translated as "the stupidest"): the former will not
become bad and the latter will not become good. On this understanding, 17.2
provides a general principle that people can become good or evil depending
upon how they act, and 17.3 qualifies this principle with two exceptional cases
of people whose nature cannot be altered regardless of their actions.
    In order to make sense of such an interpretation, it is natural (even
though surprising) for commentators to portray Confucius as one who advocated a theory of human nature that is neither good (more fully developed
by Mencius) nor evil (more fully developed by Xunzi) nor mixed with good
and evil (more fully developed by Gongsun Ni 公孫尼), but as of three grades
(*xing sanpin shuo* 性三品說): some humans' nature is good, some humans'
nature is evil, and some humans' nature is mixed with good and evil (more

fully developed by DONG Zhongshu 董仲舒 [197–104 BC.E] and HAN Yu 韓愈 [768–825]). For example, HUANG Shisan maintaines that

> according to the three grades theory of human nature, because
> some humans' nature is good, there are [good] sons, Shun 舜
> and Yi 禹, from [bad] fathers, Shou 瞍 and Gun 鯀; because some
> humans' nature is bad, there are [good] fathers, Yao 堯 and Shun,
> with [bad] sons, Zhu 朱 and Jun 均; because some humans' nature
> is mixed with good and bad, there are people in the middle (*zhon-
> gren* 中人). When Confucius talks about people in the middle, he
> is referring to those whose nature is mixed with good and evil.
> They are people "whose nature is alike but who grow apart from
> each other through practice." Those who are above the people in
> the middle are the wise above and those who are below the people
> in the middle are the stupid below. (Cheng 1990, 1185)

Thus, he further claims that, together with *Analects* 17.2, Confucius believes that "there are people above whose nature cannot be changed into evil, people in the middle whose original good nature may be changed into evil, and stupid people below whose nature cannot be changed into good" (ibid). WANG Chong 王充 also argues that

> Confucius says that "humans are alike in nature and become apart
> through practice." Therefore the nature of people in the middle
> depends upon practice. They become good if they practice good
> things and become bad if they practice bad things. Those who are
> extremely good and those who are extremely bad have nothing to
> do with practice. Thus Confucius says that "only the wise above
> and the stupid below do not change." Their nature is either good
> or bad, which cannot be changed by the transformation of sagehood
> or the teachings of the worthies. (Cheng 1990, 1186)

HUANG Kan further explains how these three grades of human nature originated. In his view, humans, at birth, are endowed with *qi* 氣:

> There are both clear and turbid qualities of *qi*. If one is endowed
> with the clearest quality of *qi*, then one will be a sage; if one is
> endowed with the most turbid quality of *qi* then one will be a

benighted person. Because the *qi* of a benighted person is of the most turbid quality, then even if this *qi* were allowed to settle it would not become clear. Because the sage has the clearest quality of *qi*, then even if it were disturbed it would not become turbid. So even if the wise above is in a chaotic society, his integrity will not be disturbed; even if the stupid below is surrounded by Yaos and Shuns, his evil cannot be changed. Thus it is said that the wise above and the stupid below do not change. However, below the wise above and above the stupid below . . . there are those whose clear *qi* is in excess of their turbid *qi*, those whose turbid *qi* is in excess of their clear *qi*, and those who have an equal measure of clear and turbid *qi*. In such people, if their *qi* is allowed to settle, it will become clear, whereas if it is disturbed, it will become turbid. These people change as the world around them changes. If they encounter good then they become clear and rise; if they encounter bad then they become sullied and sink. (Cheng 1990, 1187)[19]

Although this interpretation seems to make some sense, it sends us an immediate alarm as it is based on the assumption that Confucius adopts the three-grades theory of human nature and so it is this particular theory, and not either of the two definitely more influential theories—Mencius's theory of human nature as good and Xunzi's theory of human nature as evil[20]—that should be considered as the orthodox Confucian theory. As is well known, unlike later Confucians, Confucius himself does not say clearly whether human nature is good or evil or mixed with good and evil. There are only two places in the *Analects* where human nature is mentioned, and 17.2 is the only place where something definite is said about human nature, "humans are alike by nature" (the other place is 5.13, where his student Zigong complains that one cannot hear Confucius's view on human nature and the way of heaven).[21] This does not mean, however, that Confucius does not have a theory of human nature. In order to understand his view of human nature, *Analects* 17.2 is indeed important because it says that all humans are alike by nature. Here he does not say "some humans" or "most humans" are alike by nature. It shows at least that the three-grades theory of human nature cannot be correct, as humans of these three different natures cannot be regarded as "alike." It does not, however, say how humans are alike in nature. So in order to understand *Analects* 17.2 correctly, it is more important to relate it to the general ideas of the *Analects*. In this respect, I agree with Xu Fuguan 徐复觀. In his study of the pre-Qing theories of human nature, Xu argues that Confucius actually holds the view of human nature as good, because "Confucius believes that *ren* 仁 is inherent in every human life. It is for this reason that he can say, 'Is *ren* far away? It is here as soon as I desire it' [7.30] and 'to practice *ren* depends upon oneself' [12.1]. . . . Since Confucius believes that *ren* is inherent in every human life, although he does not explicitly say that *ren* is human nature . . . he actually believes that human nature is good" (Xu 1999, 97–98). In addition, Confucius is even reported as saying that "*ren* 仁 is *ren* 人" (*Zhongyong* 16; 700). Here he sees *ren* as a defining feature of human beings. In this sense, at least on the issue of human nature, I agree that Mencius's theory of human nature as good represents Confucius's own view better than any other theories of human nature.[22]

5. CHENG Yi's Interpretation of *Analects* 17.3

CHENG Yi also understands the wise and the stupid in this *Analects* passage in their moral rather than intellectual sense. In other words, the wise are morally good persons, whereas the stupid are morally bad persons. Whether a person is morally good is not related to intellectual ability. On the one hand, the morally wise person is not necessarily one with high intellectual ability: "Even those who are extremely unintelligent can also gradually make moral progress" (*Zhouyi Chengshi Zhuan* 4; 956). On the other hand, the morally stupid person is not necessarily a person of lesser intelligence. Of morally stupid people, CHENG Yi argues, "not all are intellectually deficient; many of them, such as SHANG Xin 商辛 [the last King of Shang Dynasty, named Zhou 紂], have superior intellectual abilities that ordinary people do not have" (*Zhouyi Chengshi Zhuan* 4; 956). While acknowledging that there are morally good persons and morally bad persons, CHENG Yi claims that the difference between them has nothing to do with human nature. So he argues against the three-grades theory of human nature. In his view, "the nature of all humans is the same" (*Yishu* 25; 319). Moreover, he advocates the Mencian view that "the nature of all humans is good" (*Zhouyi Chengshi Zhuan* 4; 956). According to him, "Mencius overshadows all other Confucians because he sheds light on human nature. No human's nature is not good. . . . Human nature is the same as principle (*li* 理) and principle is the same from Yao and Shun to common people" (*Yishu* 18; 204). In his view, the distinction between the wise above and the stupid below in *Analects* 17.3 is not a distinction of human nature, in which they are alike, as Confucius affirms in 17.2. There is no difference between the wise above and the stupid below at birth in this respect: "From childhood, the sagely quality is already complete in everybody" (*Yishu* 25; 323). Since the nature of the stupid below, just as that of the wise above, is originally good, "it is not their nature to be stupid below. They are stupid because they have not made full use of their *cai* 才 (natural endowment)" (*Yishu* 25; 323). Here CHENG Yi is referring to *Mencius* 6a6, where Mencius says that there are people who are not as good as others because they fail to make the best use of their natural endowments. In Cheng's view, Mencius's "four beginnings [humaneness, rightness, propriety, and wisdom] are the natural endowment (*cai*) for one to be good. There are people who are not good, because they do not make full use of the natural endowment of the four beginnings" (*Yishu* 19; 253). So the distinction between the wise above and the stupid below is caused by their effort, or the lack thereof, to exercise their *cai*. The wise above are wise because they exercise their *cai*; the stupid below are stupid because they do not exercise their *cai*. A new understanding of the relationship between *Analects* 17.2 and 17.3 thus emerges. According to the conventional understanding, the distinction between the wise above and the stupid below in *Analects* 17.3 provides some qualification to *Analects* 17.2, where the general principle that humans are alike by nature is stipulated. Thus the nature of the wise and the nature of the stupid are not only unlike each other but also unlike that of the common people mentioned in 17.2. In this new understanding, however, 17.3 does not qualify but further explains how humans, who are alike by nature, grow apart through practice so that there is a distinction between the wise above and the stupid below. In other words, "the wise above" and "the stupid below" in 17.3 are not exceptions to, but part of, the "humans" in 17.2.

Here CHENG Yi interprets Confucius's "the stupid below" as people who lack self-confidence (*zibao* 自暴) and give up on themselves (*ziqi* 自棄). In his commentary on the *Book of Changes*, when asked why there are people who cannot be transformed, CHENG Yi replies:

> The nature of all humans is good, although there are stupid below in terms of *cai* 才. There are two types of people who belong to the stupid below: those who lack self-confidence and those who give up on themselves. If one cultivates oneself to become good, there is no one who cannot be changed. Even those who are extremely unintelligent can also gradually make moral progress. Only those who lack self-confidence and do not trust themselves and those who abandon themselves and do not want to make any effort cannot be transformed to enter the way even if they were surrounded by sages. These are what Confucius refers to as the stupid below. (*Zhouyi Chengshi Zhuan* 4; 956)

So in Cheng's view, *zibao* and *ziqi* are the two greatest enemies in moral cultivation. As long as people think that they cannot become wise and do not try to become wise, then they can never become wise. Thus, in Cheng's view, "no failure in action is greater than evil, but it can be remedied; no failure in administration is worse than disorder, but it can be rectified. Only those who lack self-confidence and give themselves up cannot become superior persons" (*Yishu* 4; 69).[23] Here the people CHENG Yi refers to as being *zibao* and *ziqi* are precisely the same people Confucius refers to as being unwilling to learn even after being vexed by difficulties (*kun er bu xue*). It is important to point out, however, that although in some conventional interpretations the stupid below are also identified as those who do not learn even after being vexed with difficulties, commentators have not noticed that Confucius here does not say that these people are too stupid to learn but simply that they *do* not learn. So he does not say that these people cannot be changed if they start to learn.

In contrast, the wise above, in CHENG Yi's view, are those who have gained knowledge, knowledge of/as virtue in contrast to knowledge of hearing and seeing, whether innate (*sheng er zhi zhi* 生而知之) or learned; and, in the latter case, whether they learned it before they were vexed by difficulties (*xue er zhi zhi* 學而知之) or after it (*kun er zhi zhi* 困而知之). It is important to note that, for CHENG Yi, the wise above are not merely those who are born with knowledge. On the one hand, this is because, in his view, what is important is to acquire the needed knowledge; it is not important how it is acquired. Thus, he repeatedly states that "whether you get the knowledge by learning or through birth, its function is the same" (*Yishu* 18; 213; see also *Yishu* 25; 325). On the other hand, although CHENG Yi does not deny the existence of people with inborn moral knowledge, his emphasis is on the importance of learning. Thus, while acknowledging that Confucius was born with knowledge, he asks, even so "what harm does learning cause to him?" (*Yishu* 15; 152). Sometimes he emphasizes knowledge by learning so much that he virtually ignores innate knowledge. This attitude of CHENG Yi's toward people born with knowledge is quite similar to that of Confucius. CHENG Yi and other later Confucians regarded Confucius as a sage born with knowledge, but Confucius himself denied it. As pointed out by CAI Shangsi: "Confucius himself does not really believe that there are indeed 'people who are born with knowledge,' for he not only laments that he has never seen a 'sage,' not only denies that he himself is a sage by birth, but also clearly denies that he himself is 'one born with knowledge'" (Cai 1982, 99).

With such an understanding of the wise above and the stupid below, we are ready to understand CHENG Yi's interpretation of the *Analects* passage: "Only the wise above and the stupid below do not change." In appearance, CHENG Yi seems to simply deny what Confucius says. For example, when asked whether the stupid can be changed, he replies: "Yes. Confucius says that the wise above and the stupid below do not change, but there are reasons for them to change. . . . It is wrong to say that the stupid below cannot change. They share the same human nature with others and so how can they not be changed?" (*Yishu* 18; 204). When asked whether those who are below the average people have to remain so throughout their life, CHENG Yi replies: "There is also a way for them to make moral progress" (*Yishu* 9; 107). For this reason, in his *On Doubts about the Four Books* 四書辯疑, the Yuan dynasty 元 scholar CHEN Tianxiang 陳天祥 (1230–1316) argues against CHENG Yi: "Confucius says that the stupidest cannot be changed, while Cheng thinks that they can be changed. If CHENG Yi is correct, then Confucius must be wrong" (Cheng 1990, 1188).[24]

   CHENG Yi, of course, does not think that he is arguing against Confucius. In his view, he is rather providing a correct interpretation of this *Analects* passage in light of the general principle that Confucius tries to convey. He argues that, in this passage, Confucius "does not mean that people cannot be changed. It means that there is a principle that cannot be changed. Only two kinds of people cannot be changed: those who lack self-confidence and those who abandon themselves. They are unwilling to learn. If they are willing to learn, have confidence in themselves, and do not give up on themselves, how can they not change themselves?" (*Yishu* 19; 252). So, in CHENG Yi's interpretation, what Confucius means by "unchangeable" is this principle: On the one hand, if people give themselves up and lack self-confidence, then they cannot become wise. On the other hand, if people continue to learn, they will necessarily become wise. So what Confucius means is that this principle governing the moral transformation of human beings will never change, not that the stupid cannot be changed into the wise.[25]

   What is important is that, for CHENG Yi, people do not have the necessary knowledge not because they are stupid by nature but because they do not want to learn. If they start to learn, they will become wise. Superior persons and sages are so because they diligently develop what they are born with, while inferior persons are so because they abandon their efforts to develop their innate moral tendencies. That is why CHENG Yi claims that it is entirely up to oneself. So CHENG Yi emphasizes the importance of learning. He argues that "for superior persons, nothing is more important than to learn, nothing is more harmful than to stop, nothing is more sickening than to be self-content, and nothing is more lamentable than to give up on oneself. To learn without stopping is how Tang and Wu become sages" (*Yishu* 25; 325). For him, "everyone can become a sage. The learning of a superior person must not stop until he becomes a sage. Those who stop before becoming sages are all due to their having given up on themselves" (*Yishu* 25; 318). For this reason, CHENG Yi encourages people to set high goals for themselves. He states that "people in the world often question that they could become sages. This is because they do not have self-confidence (*zixin* 自信)" (*Yishu* 25; 318). In his view, on such matters, it is not necessarily good to be modest. One should not be satisfied with being a second-class person while politely letting others become first-class people. In contrast, "in learning, one ought to aim at the way, and in being a person, one ought to aim at being a sage. To say that one is unable to do so is to cripple oneself, and to say that one's head [heart/mind] is unable to do so is to cripple one's head. . . . It is fine to have such humiliation as long as one still tries; it is not permissible to have such humiliation as an excuse for not trying" (*Yishu* 18; 189).

6. The Role of Sages: Education

We have examined CHENG Yi's interpretation of the two controversial passages in *Analects* 8.9 and 17.3, showing them to be superior to some of the more conventional interpretations. For CHENG Yi, people cannot be made to know the way, because knowledge of the way is knowledge of/as virtue (*dexing zhi zhi*), which has to be obtained by oneself (*zide*). Although people cannot be made to know the way, they can still know the way by themselves as long as they have confidence in themselves and do not abandon themselves. The stupid below who do not become wise are simply those who lack self-confidence and give up on themselves. If they are resolved to learn, they can also become wise. Here it is important to tackle a question likely to arise from our discussion so far: "Does this mean that people have to be entirely self-reliant in seeking the way"? This is indeed what WANG Yanlin 王彦霖, one of CHENG Yi's students, believes to be the case: "People can become good only when they are willing to become good by themselves. So they cannot be made to be good." If so, there would be no role for sages to play in moral cultivation. To this, however, Cheng replies: "What you say is indeed true. People themselves have to try to become good. This does not, however, mean that they should be left alone. This is the reason for education. 'Cultivating the way is called education.' How can there be no education (*jiao*)!" (*Yishu* 1; 2).[26]

So, while emphasizing getting it by oneself, CHENG Yi also stressed the importance of education:

The way to maintain people's lives (*shengmin zhi dao* 生民之道) should be based on education. If everyone under heaven receives education, inferior people cultivate their person, and superior people cultivate their way, then the worthy and the able will be gathered in government and good practices will be carried out in society. Propriety and rightness will prevail and customs will become pure and beautiful. Although there are punitive laws, no one will violate them. The prosperity of the three dynasties resulted from teaching in such a way. (*Wenji* 9; 593)

In Mencius's terms, education means that those who already possess knowledge and awareness (*xianzhi xianjue* 先知先覺) should awaken those who have yet to do so (*houzhi houjue* 後知後覺): "Take an analogy. Suppose everyone is asleep. Others have not awoken, but I awake first. So I shake those who have not awoken so that they can awake" (*Yishu* 2a; 32).[27] Since CHENG Yi believes that human nature is originally all good, education is first of all to cultivate the original goodness to ensure that it will grow and not get lost. For this reason, he develops the idea of "cultivating correctness in childhood (*yang zheng yu meng* 養正于蒙)": "The unaroused state is called childhood (*meng* 蒙). To cultivate correctness (*zheng* 正) in the pure and unaroused state of childhood is the art of sages. It becomes more difficult to prohibit incorrectness in the aroused state. To cultivate correctness in childhood is the utmost goodness of learning" (*Zhouyi Chengshi Zhuan* 1; 720). In other words, if original goodness gets lost, then it is difficult to get it back. So the best thing to do is to take care of the original goodness, so that when it is aroused, it will remain correct. Thus, CHENG Yi argues, "the way to educate people is similar to training a young bull. To control it before it is able to harm people with its horns is the greatest good. . . . If people are not to be educated, then there is a need for instruments of punishment to control them. If, however, their hearts are guided by the way, then no such instruments are needed, as they will be transformed by themselves" (*Yishu* 2a; 14).[28] Even when there is already incorrectness in the aroused state, still "it is easier to stop human evil at its beginning. It is more difficult to control it when it is fully developed" (*Zhouyi Chengshi zhuan* 2; 830–31).

It is best to educate people when they are young. This does not, however, mean that no moral education is needed for grown-ups, especially those who have lost their original goodness. CHENG Yi argues that the best way to get them back on the right track is not through the application of laws and punishments but with moral education. In his commentary on the *Book of Changes*, he states that sages

> know that evil things in the world cannot be constrained by force. So, by observing its roots and grasping its fundamentals, the sages block the origin of evil. Without recourse to strict legal punishments, by itself evil ceases to exist. For example there is robbery because people's selfish desires arise when they see something beneficial. When people do not receive education and are forced into poverty, even if there are capital punishments every day, how can they win over the selfish heart of billions of people? Sages, however, know the way to stop them. They do not advocate awful punishments but establish governance and education, letting people have land to cultivate and making them know the way of shame. This way, even if you reward thieves, nobody will steal. (*Zhouyi Chengshi Zhuan* 2; 831)

In Cheng's view, there are two effective types of moral education. One is education by setting an example (*shen jiao* 身教); and the other is education by teaching about the way (*yanjiao* 言教). In regard to the former, commenting on Mencius's view that "when the ruler is humane (*ren*), everyone will be humane, and when the ruler is dutiful, everyone will be dutiful" (*Mencius* 4b5), CHENG Yi states that "the order or disorder of the world depends upon the humaneness or inhumaneness of the ruler" (*Waishu* 6; 390). For this reason, he develops the idea of "rectification of the incorrect heart/mind of the ruler (*ge jun xin zhi fei* 格君心之非)" as the root of rulership: "There are two ways to rule: through the root or through the branch. From the root, the only thing to do is to rectify the incorrect heart/mind of the ruler in order to rectify higher officials, and to rectify higher officials in order to rectify lower officials" (*Yishu* 15; 165). When the lower officials are rectified, common people will be rectified by themselves. So, CHENG Yi claims that "if you want to govern others, you need to govern yourself first" (*Jingshuo* 8; 1155). This view of CHENG Yi's about example-setting as a way of education is, of course, a typically Confucian view. Confucius himself says that "if the ruler sets an example by being correct, who would dare to remain incorrect?" (*Analects* 12.17); "when the ruler loves propriety, no common people dare not love it; when the ruler loves rightness, no common people dare not love it; and when the ruler loves faithfulness, no common people dare not love it" (*Analects* 2.1). This is what

Confucius calls "governing with virtue," which can be compared with the pole star that does not move while all other stars revolve around it (*Analects* 2.1). For Confucius, the reason is that "the virtue of superior persons is like wind, while the virtue of inferior persons is like grass. When the wind blows over the grass, the grass is sure to bend" (*Analects* 12.19).

CHENG Yi has the Confucian classics in mind when he talks about education by spreading the sages' moral teachings (*yan jiao* 言教). In his view, "the sages had no choice but to write the Six Classics; just as there would be no way to maintain people's daily lives if there are no farm tools and pottery" (*Yishu* 18; 221). In other words, while sages themselves have no use for classics, they know that, just as tools and pottery are necessary for people's daily life, so classics are necessary for people's moral cultivation, because "sages wrote classics solely to illuminate the way" (*Yishu* 2a; 13). Of course, as we have seen, the knowledge that sages can teach people through classics is merely knowledge from hearing and seeing and not knowledge of/as virtue, and it is the latter that really matters in moral education. Does this mean therefore that the sages' teachings are useless? As explained in chapter 3, although it is true that what matters here is knowledge of/as virtue, CHENG Yi argues that knowledge by hearing and seeing is also important as it can be developed into knowledge of/as virtue, if, when reading classics, one tries to experience, in one's own heart/mind, what sages experience so that it becomes one's own. For this reason, Cheng thinks that when those who already know and are aware of the way (*xianzhi xianjue*) teach those who are yet to know and become aware of the way (*houzhi houjue*), the former need to make sure that the latter get it by themselves. In his view, this is indeed how Confucius taught his students. Thus, commenting on *Analects* 7.8, CHENG Yi argues that, when Confucius says, "Do not enlighten those who are not eager to learn and do not bring new horizons to those who are not anxious to give an explanation," he is "asking one not to teach a student until the student is sincere"; and when Confucius says, "Do not repeat if one cannot come back with three other corners after one corner is presented," he means that "after teaching students, one should wait until they get it themselves" (*Chengshi Jingshuo* 6; 1144). CHENG Yi assures us that by studying classics in this way, we will be able to get to know the way: "If we can not get it [*dao*] through learning, then why did the ancient sages teach people so diligently? Did they try to mislead later people?" (*Wenji* 8; 579–80).

So, in CHENG Yi's view, although one has to know the way by oneself, moral education, whether in the form of setting an example or moral teachings, is still extremely important. It might, however, be asked, "Since both ways of education are effective only for those who are willing to learn, then what about those who think that they cannot learn or are unwilling to learn at all?" Cheng argues that there are such people in all ages, including the time of Yao and Shun. Sages, however, do not leave even these people alone. For such people, they establish some more or less coercive measures to stop them doing evil and force them to do good. However, even for such people, coercive measures are used only as something cautionary, provisional, and supplemental. On the one hand, it is CHENG Yi's conviction that such measures will be enough to deter people from doing evil things, while the measures themselves, hopefully, are never used (*Wenji* 9; 593). On the other hand, such measures are not supposed to be used alone. Because these measures cannot make people understand why such rules and laws have to be followed, they must be preceded and immediately followed by moral teachings.[29]

7. Conclusion

In the above, we have examined CHENG Yi's philosophical interpretations of the two controversial *Analects* passages in contrast to conventional interpretations provided by Confucian scholars both before and after him. In his view, by saying that common people *"bu ke"* be made to know the way in *Analects* 8.9, Confucius does not mean that common people *are not permitted to* be made to know the way, but that they *cannot* be made (by sages) to know the way; they cannot be made to know the way, not because they are too stupid to know the way, but because sages lack the ability to make them know the way; and sages lack the ability to make common people know the way, not because sages are deficient, but because the type of knowledge needed here, knowledge of/as virtue, that naturally inclines its possessors to act accordingly, by its very nature, has to be obtained by people themselves through their own inner experiences. In Cheng's view, the moral ability to obtain such knowledge, unlike the intellectual ability to make scientific discoveries or technological inventions, is innate in every common person. For this reason, he does not agree with the common interpretation of the other controversial passage, *Analects* 17.3: "Only the wise above and the stupid below do not change." According to the common interpretation, Confucius here is saying that those born to be wise (moral) will not become stupid (immoral) and those born to be stupid will not become wise; only those born to be mixed can be made to be either moral or immoral. In Cheng's view, however, everyone is born to be good, and as long as one makes diligent efforts, one can become a sage. There are immoral people only because they do not make such effort and give up on themselves. Thus, in Cheng's view, what Confucius regards as unchangeable in *Analects* 17.3 is the principle that one can become wise (a moral person) as long as one makes diligent effort toward that goal, and one cannot become wise as long as one is unwilling to make the needed effort. In his unique interpretations of these two *Analects* passages, Cheng emphasizes the importance of the self-cultivation of moral agents. However, he does not ignore the important role sages can play in such moral cultivation. Sages show those who are willing to make such effort how to become moral by writing classics and by their own exemplary actions; sages create rules of propriety and even penal laws to induce those who are unwilling to make such effort to be moral and deter them from being immoral. As I have pointed out, in comparison to Han learning, the Confucian hermeneutics before and after Song learning, the neo-Confucian hermeneutics that Cheng helps to establish in general and Cheng's neo-Confucian interpretations of these two passages in particular are more philosophical than philological. The emphasis of such a hermeneutic strategy is to use the fundamental Confucian principle, grasped through reading various Confucian classics, as well as many other ways, to guide our interpretation of individual passages. Though such interpretations may fall short of evidential and textual criticisms, they are strong in presenting a coherent Confucian teaching that is philosophically interesting and profound.

Notes

Introduction

1. Liu Xiaogan recently noticed an interesting phenomenon: while it is understandable that comparativists in the West use terms and concepts from their own philosophical traditions to explain and interpret things in Chinese philosophy to their Western audience, which is their *geyi* after all, it is strange that contemporary Chinese scholars also use Western philosophical terms, terms with which they and their Chinese audience are less familiar, to explain and interpret Chinese philosophical ideas. Liu coined the term *fanxiang geyi* 反向格義 (reverse meaning-matching) to describe this phenomenon (Liu 2008a, 108–32). Since comparativists on both sides use Western concepts to explain and interpret Chinese philosophy, the result is what Kwong-loi Shun describes as asymmetry: "[T]here is a trend in comparative studies to approach Chinese thought from a Western philosophical perspective, by reference to frameworks, concepts, or issues found in Western philosophical discussions. This trend is seen not only in works published in the English language, but also in those published in Chinese. Conversely, in the contemporary literature, we rarely find attempts to approach Western philosophical thought by reference to frameworks, concepts, or issues found in Chinese philosophical discussions. Given that Chinese ethical traditions are no less rich in insights and resources compared to Western ethical traditions, or at least many of us would so believe, this asymmetry is deeply puzzling" (Shun 2009, 470).

2. The problem may be avoided only by MacIntyre's "bilinguals": people who are raised in one tradition but become members of another tradition. But even they, for MacIntyre, may be unable to resolve conflicts of beliefs between these two traditions, despite their perfect understanding of both sides' views (see MacIntyre 2010).

3. For this reason, Stalnaker acknowledges that his bridge concept performs a similar function to Robert Neville's "vague categories" (Neville 2001a, 9–16; Stalnaker 2006, 26n61).

4. Bryan van Norden uses "the lexical fallacy" to refer to the same idea, and he cites Henry Rosemont as an example of committing such a fallacy (van Norden 2007, 22).

5. However, perhaps due to what Shun regards as asymmetry and what Liu Xiaogan describes as reverse meaning matching (*fanxiang geyi*) in contemporary study of Chinese philosophy, the situation of Chinese philosophy in China can hardly be compared with that of Western philosophy in the West. In other words, Western philosophy defines what philosophy is not only in the West but also in China, so much so that in recent years there has been a hot debate among Chinese intellectuals in China on the legitimacy of Chinese philosophy: whether there is such a thing called *Chinese* philosophy, with the suspicion that Chinese tradition consists merely of some thought but not philosophy. For this reason, when I tentatively presented some preliminary results of this study at a number of Chinese universities, I surprisingly met with extraordinary enthusiasm among students of Chinese philosophy, relieved that Chinese philosophy after all is not bad as *philosophy*.

6. To say this of course does not mean that we should not study these aspects. As a matter of fact, only after we study the various aspects of a philosopher or a philosophical text can we know which aspects are philosophically appealing or not.

7. When asked about my methodology of comparative philosophy, I once used the following imperfect analogy to explain it. The Cheng brothers' various philosophical ideas are regarded here as tools, each of which fits into its own designated space in the toolbox. Some of these tools are taken out of the toolbox in this study to solve problems in the Western philosophical tradition. When the job is done, if we can still put these tools back into their original slots in the toolbox, we have not twisted them in the process of using them; if we cannot put them back, we have somehow twisted them to accomplish our tasks. So there is still a criterion whether our understanding of Chinese philosophical texts is adequate or not when we use them to answer Western philosophical questions. Thus, in his discussion of the two orientations in interpretation of classics, the objective orientation toward the text and subjective orientation toward the present, Liu Xiaogan points out that these two orientations do not exhaust all possible approaches to philosophical classics, and he particularly mentions my approach to comparative philosophy as a plausible way that does not fit well into either of the two orientations (see Liu 2008b, 87).

8. Hereafter citations of the Cheng brothers will be indicated by title and chapter (*juan* 卷) numbers of the individual works followed by the page numbers in Cheng and Cheng 2004.

Chapter 1: Joy (*le* 樂): "Why Be Moral?"

1. John van Ingen makes a useful distinction among personal egoists, universal egoists, and individual egoists and claims that the question we are discussing here is one raised by a personal egoist: "(a) *Universal* egoist: Everyone ought to seek her own self-interest and disregard the interest of all others in cases of conflict; (b) *Individual* egoist: Everyone ought to seek my (the individual egoist's) self-interest; and (c) *Personal* egoist: I (the personal egoist) ought to seek my own self-interest exclusively, the

interests of others being valued only instrumentally as an aid in the pursuit of my singular value" (Ingen 1994, 39).

2. In addition to the issue of "who" should be moral, Michael D. Bayles has also pointed out a couple of other complexities of the question Why be moral?: what it is to be moral (act morally or be a moral person, for example) and what "moral" means (see Bayles 1973).

3. Davis holds a similar view. He argues that there is no nonmoral reason to answer the question: "In a very important sense moral awareness carries with it its own authority and legitimacy. In answer to the question, 'Why be moral?' we may say simply, 'Because you *know* you ought to.' We simply know we ought to do what seems to us right, and we know this in a way that is subject to no skeptical attack. An awareness of a moral duty contains in itself, as an intrinsic part of what a 'duty' is, the justification, the authority, the reason for its being obeyed" (Davis 1991, 8; see also 19).

4. As a matter of fact, Bradley does find an end, that is, self-realization: " 'Realize yourself as an infinite whole' means, 'Realize yourself as the self-conscious member of an infinite whole, by realizing that whole in yourself.' When that whole is truly infinite, and when your personal will is wholly made one with it, then you also have reached the extreme of homogeneity and specification in one, and have attained a perfect self-realization" (Bradley 1935, 80). However, Bradley does not consider self-realization as the end of morality. In his view, self-realization as the final end is something "with which morality is identified, or under which it is included" (Bradley 1935, 81). About the absurdity of the question "Why be moral?" Thomas Scanlon also argues that "attempts to answer the question, Why be moral? face an acute dilemma. Anything that looks like a moral reason for taking morality seriously will be unsatisfactory, since it seems to presuppose the very concerns whose justification is in question. On the other hand, most answers that are clearly nonmoral are also unsatisfactory. In particular, attempts to show that being moral is in one's self-interest face a double burden. First, they advance a claim that is implausible on its face in view of the evident conflicts between self-interest and the demands of morality. Second, if they were to succeed they would appear to provide the wrong sort of reason for being moral. A person who accepted morality only because of its supposed contributions to his or her self-interest would strike us as more expedient than virtuous" (Scanlon 1996, 197).

5. A. I. Melden concurs: Plato contends "that a man can not get away with injustice—he may escape the punishments usually imposed by his society, but he can not escape the costs which his soul must assume—but unless men are concerned with each other's wants and satisfactions, the alleged torments of the soul do not follow. Why not an amoral Gyges who is wholly indifferent to the welfare of others except when it affects his own, smugly cheerful in the harmony of soul obtained by virtue of a clear imposition of constraints upon his desires and appetites—concerned with *his* future but satisfied in his indifference to the fortunes of others" (Melden 1948, 451).

6. Of course, as Vlastos argues, "what a man does is, for Plato, only an 'image' of what he is; his 'external' conduct is only a manifestation of his 'inner' life which is the life of the 'real' man, the soul. Hence when he asks himself in what it is that a

man's justice 'truly' consists he feels constrained to look to what goes on inside a man, in a man's soul" (Vlastos 1987, 126).

7. I think Gerald J. Postema is correct in saying that Hume here "seems to beg the question. Fitness for society depends on the willingness of others to put trust and confidence in one, and that depends only on the *appearance*, not on the *reality*, of one's commitment to justice. The knave might agree that knavery is not for everyone, since it takes a special cunning and skill" (Postema 1988, 35).

8. David Gauthier follows Hume in this respect: the "truly sensible knave still mistakes his/her true interest. For in being a knave s/he makes him/herself unfit for society—a person to be excluded from, rather than included in, the mutually advantageous arrangements that society affords" (Gauthier 1982, 24).

9. Victoria S. Wike, in her careful study of happiness in Kant's ethics, tries to see the more positive role that Kant allows happiness to play in ethics. First, "Kant clearly identifies happiness as a natural and inevitable end of human beings. He sees that in this role as natural end, happiness is of value. It is not to be renounced. It is not evil" (Wike 1994, 83). Second, Kant considers happiness as a means to one's duty and therefore an indirect duty. Here Wike cites Kant as saying that "to assure one's own happiness is a duty (at least indirectly); for discontent with one's state, in a press of cares and amidst unsatisfied wants, might easily become a great *temptation to the transgression of duty*" (Wike 1994, 91). Third, "the highest good, a moral end, indeed the highest moral end, contains happiness as one of its components. Since happiness is in the highest good, the investigation of the role of happiness in ethics must consider the role of the highest good in ethics" (Wike 1994, 115).

10. Bill Shaw and John Corvino also point out that Kant's idea of the highest good is developed to deal with the issue of moral motivation: "[A]lthough the reason for acting morally is that it is the right thing to do, we nevertheless act morally with the 'aspiration' that we will be rewarded in the afterlife. That reward is not the reason for moral behavior, but in some way it motivates us to attend to the actual reasons, namely, duty and right reason" (Shaw and Corvino 1996, 376).

11. Against Nielsen, Davis tries to defend Kant's idea of the highest good. In his view, Kant's highest good has to be distinguished from wishful thinking, which "is to be condemned, not because it is immoral, but because it does not work and does not promote human welfare. But certainly a good case can be made that belief in the triumph of goodness will do far more to promote human welfare than any alternative 'realistic belief'" (Davis 1991, 15). However, to the person who asks the question "Why should I be moral?" the promotion of human welfare certainly cannot become a motivation to be moral; if it could, the person would not raise the question in the first place.

12. Hospers disagrees on such a view. According to him, even if we could accept what seems to him the problematic claim that morality is necessary for happiness, it is not sufficient for happiness: "[N]o matter how moral the man may be, he is not happy when he is being tortured on the rack, or when he suffers from cancer of the bone, or when his family is being fed to the lions" (Hospers 1961, 179). As we have seen,

Confucians do not think pain and suffering are good things. They should be avoided. They should not be avoided, and one should feel joy in not trying to avoid them, only if to avoid them one has to violate morality. So poverty and even death are something painful, but to avoid poverty and death by being immoral is more painful. Thus one feels joy in poverty or in accepting death because the morality is not violated.

13. I discussed the issue of moral motivation in relation to Confucius and Mencius elsewhere (see Huang 2010d).

14. These three levels, common people, superior persons, and sages, correspond to knowing (zhi 知), loving (hao 好), and finding joy (le 樂) in dao that Confucius mentions: "to know it [dao] is not as good as to like it; and to like it is not as good as to find joy in it" (Analects 6.20). In Cheng's view, of course, "to know" here obviously refers to knowing through hearing and seeing and not through the inner experience of one's heart/mind. Commenting on this passage, Cheng Yi states: "[W]hen I try to know something, it is something over there that I want to learn about; when I love something, although I firmly believe it, I still have not got it. When I find joy in it, it becomes part of me" (Waishu 2; 361).

15. This Confucian argument about the distinction between humans and beasts, in one sense, is quite similar to the argument J. S. Mill develops in his response to the criticism that utilitarianism regards human beings as no different from beasts when it sees pleasure as the highest goal of human life. In Mill's view, there are different pleasures and utilitarians "assign to the pleasures of the intellect, of the feelings and imaginations, and of the moral sentiments, a much higher value as pleasures than to those of mere sensation"; as "few human creatures would consent to be changed into any of the lower animals, for a promise of the fullest allowance of a beast's pleasure; no intelligent human being would consent to be a fool, no instructed person would be selfish and base, even though they should be persuaded that the fool, the dunce, or the rascal is better satisfied with his lot than they are with theirs" (Mill 1972, 8–9).

16. However, in a different place, Aristotle seems to allow the possibility of virtuous actions not being pleasant: "there are many things we should be keen about even if they brought no pleasure, e.g., seeing, remembering, knowing, possessing the virtues. If pleasures do necessarily accompany these, that makes no odds; we should do these even if no pleasure resulted" (Aristotle 1915, 1174a4–8).

17. Aristotle's view on this issue is not entirely consistent. For example, he also claims that "those who say that the victim on the rack or the man who falls into greater misfortunes is happy if he is good, are, whether they mean to or not, talking nonsense" (Aristotle 1915, 1153b17–20). Rosalind Hursthouse, a contemporary neo-Aristotelian, disagrees with McDowell's view we discussed earlier and states, "I do not think that we have conceptions of eudaimonia, benefit, harm, disaster, etc. such that no sacrifice necessitated by virtue counts as a loss, nor do I think that this is because we are all imperfect in virtue" (Hursthouse 1999, 185).

18. In this sense, Hursthouse argues that a nonvirtuous person is a defective human being: "just as 'there is something wrong with a free-riding wolf who eats

but does not take part in hunt (and) with a member of the species of dancing bees who finds a source of nectar but does not let other bees know where it is,' there is something wrong with a human being who lacks, for example, charity and justice. . . . [O]ur defective wolf or bee might, in virtue of their defects, live longer than more perfect specimens of their kind, and, in the case of the wolf, live a life with less injury and pain in it. But they would both still fail to live well as a wolf or a bee. . . . [A]nalogously, an ethically defective human being, one who lacks the virtues, might live a long and very enjoyable life, but he would still fail to live well as a human being, to live a good human life" (Hursthouse 2004, 264).

19. To solve this problem, Yu Jiyuan makes a distinction between contemplative life (C-life) and contemplative activity (C-activity): "Although C-activity is the dominant aspect of a C-life, it cannot be the sole content of a C-life. The difference between them . . . is that various goods are obstacles to C-activity, but are necessary for the C-life" (Yu 2007, 198). In the context of our discussion, while moral actions may be obstacles to contemplative activity, they are necessary for a contemplative life. This is an interesting distinction and perhaps can solve the internal problem of Aristotle. However, our problem still exists: since it regards contemplation as the distinguishing mark of being human, it cannot provide the appropriate answer to the question "Why be moral?"

20. Later, WANG Yangming, a neo-Confucian in Ming dynasty, expressed this idea most vividly using the analogy of gold: "Sages are sages because their heart/minds are in complete accord with the heavenly principle, not mixed with any human desires. This is just as pure gold is pure gold because of its perfection in quality, not mixed with any copper or lead. People who have reached the state of being in complete accord with the heavenly principle are sages, just as gold that has become perfect in quality is pure gold. However, sages are different from each other in terms of ability and strength, just as different pieces of pure gold are also different from each other in terms of the weight. . . . While different in terms of ability and strength, people are all sages as long as the heavenly principle in them is pure, just as different pieces of gold are all pure gold as long as they are all perfect in quality, even though they weigh differently" (Wang 1996, 62).

Chapter 2: Virtue (*de* 德): Is a Virtuous Person Self-Centered?

1. Thus, Gary Watson points out that, in character utilitarianism, "the value of the outcome of possessing and exercising certain traits is the ultimate standard of all other values. It shares with act utilitarianism the idea that the most fundamental notion is that of a good consequence or state of affairs, namely, human happiness" (Watson 1997, 61).

2. For other problems with such a reading of Kant's maxims, see Louden 1997, 290–92. Robert Louden himself also thinks that Kant is a virtue ethicist, at least to some extent. However, instead of maxims, Louden focuses on Kant's good will, which

in his view, is "a state of character which becomes the basis for all of one's actions"; from this, Louden infers that "what is fundamentally important in his [Kant's] ethics is not acts but agents"; and in this sense Kantian ethics is also a virtue ethics, since "Kant defines virtue . . . as 'fortitude in relation to the forces opposing a moral attitude of will in us.' The Kantian virtuous agent is thus one who, because of his 'fortitude,' is able to resist urges and inclinations opposed to the moral law" (Louden 1997, 289). However, Louden himself also acknowledges a problem in reading Kant as a virtue ethicist, for in Kant "both the good will and virtue are defined in terms of obedience to moral law. . . . Since human virtue is defined in terms of conformity to law and the categorical imperative, it appears now that what is primary in Kantian ethics is not virtue for virtue's sake but obedience to rules. Virtue is the heart of the ethical for Kant. . . . But Kantian virtue is itself defined in terms of the supreme principle of morality" (Louden 1997, 290).

3. Vincent Shen argues that this approach to Confucian ethics is very different from the one adopted earlier by some contemporary neo-Confucians "such as Mou Zongsan and his followers [who] use Kant's categorical imperative to interpret Confucian ethics, neglecting the importance of ethical practice" (Shen 2002, 31). This is perhaps true. However, when Mou links Confucian ethics and Kantian ethics, he regards them primarily not as against virtue ethics but as against the heteronomous ethics such as Christian ethics. Mou regards the central idea of Kant's ethics as autonomy or self-legislation of moral agent, as this is a revolt against the Christian idea of God as the law-giver for human actions. It is this idea of autonomy that Mou sees as congenial to Confucian ethics, as he sees Confucian ethics as also autonomous and not heteronomous. In this sense, Mou is not necessarily against the interpretation of Confucian ethics as a virtue ethics, as virtue ethics is obviously also an autonomous and not heteronomous ethics.

4. For a detailed examination of Kant's criticism of such a conception of morality as self-centered, see Irwin 1996.

5. When discussing the Confucian idea of "for the sake of the self," Tu Wei-ming points out that "the Confucian insistence on learning for the sake of the self is predicated on the conviction that self-cultivation is an end in itself rather than a means to an end. Those who are committed to the cultivation of their personal life for its own sake can create inner resources for self-realization unimaginable to those who view self-cultivation merely as a tool for external goals such as social advancement and political success" (Tu 1995, 105). In Tu's view, if Confucians "don't subscribe to the thesis that learning is primarily for self-improvement, the demand for social service will undermine the integrity of self-cultivation as a noble end in itself" (Tu 1995, 106). While I think Tu is right in explaining this Confucian idea of "for the sake of the self," he does not pay enough attention to the close relationship and even identity between "for the sake of oneself" (moral cultivation of self) and "for the sake of others" (virtuous actions toward others).

6. For example, Bill Shaw and John Corvino argue that Hosmer here does not take into serious consideration Gyges's ring in Plato: "[W]e cannot tell whether true

morality will fare better than the mere appearance of morality in generating corporate success. Furthermore, we see no way at all to test whether true morality will fare better . . . [H]ow can we expect them [managers] to behave morally when they believe that they can hedge their bets and achieve as much or more success by vice than by virtue?" (Shaw and Corvino 1996, 378).

7. Thus she states: "Here is an occasion where, say, if I speak out as I should, I am going to be shut in an asylum and subjected to enforced drugging; here is another where doing what is courageous maims me for life; here is another where if I do what is charitable I shall probably die. The answer to the particular question, on these occasions, just cannot be 'if you want to be happy, lead a successful, flourishing life, you should do what is honest or courageous or charitable *here*—you will find that it pays off'" (Hursthouse 1999, 171).

8. David Copp and David Sobel disagree: "Perhaps it is true, despite our objections, that, 'for the most part, by and large,' being honest and generous and kind and caring benefits a person. But for all we have seen, it might also be true that, 'for the most part, by and large,' being selfish, detached, and cautious benefits a person" (Copp and Sobel 2004, 531). They do recognize, however, that "one of the advantages of Hursthouse's proposal . . . is that it does not depend on a moralized conception of flourishing. She admits, for example, that sacrifices required by virtue can count as losses in eudaimonia" (Copp and Sobel 2004, 531).

9. In this respect, Hursthouse also makes the interesting observation that "the fully virtuous character is the one who, typically, knowing what she should do, does it, desiring to do it. Her desires are in 'complete harmony' with her reason; hence, when she does what she should, she does what she desires to do, and reaps the reward of satisfied desire. Hence, 'virtuous conduct gives pleasures to the lover of virtue' (1099a12); the fully virtuous do what they (characteristically do), gladly" (Hursthouse 1999, 92).

10. Of course, not all virtues are other-regarding. Some virtues are self-regarding, and some virtues are both self-regarding and other-regarding. However, even those merely self-regarding virtues, such as temperance (in drinking, eating, playing, etc.) are at least not selfish traits that tend to cause harm to others.

11. Thomas Hurka, for example, asks "the question of how distinctively virtue-ethical a theory is whose central explanatory property is in fact flourishing. . . . This ethics would not be at all distinctive if it took the virtues to contribute causally to flourishing, as productive means to a separately existing state of flourishing" (Hurka 2001, 233).

12. For some serious criticisms of Aristotle's ethics as a virtue ethics, see Santas 1997.

13. In response to this challenge, Yu Jiyuan argues that "a good life for human beings must involve the exercise and manifestation of this characteristically human feature [rationality]. If one's life is dominated by appetite, it 'appears completely slavish' and 'is a life for grazing animals' (*NE*, 1095b19–20)" (Yu 2007, 66). Appetite is a life without reason, but it is not necessarily against reason. It can be guided by reason. A life of appetite regulated by reason is obviously not a life for grazing animals but a properly human life,

a life of practical reason, although for Aristotle a properly human life is not merely a life of appetite regulated by reason; it also includes the intellectual life. If life of appetite, broadly understood as bodily life, even when guided by reason, is still not properly human life, then no morally virtuous life could count as properly human life, as what a virtuous person does to others is, in most cases, to enhance the bodily lives of others.

14. In addition to the function argument, Nussbaum discusses Aristotle's argument for the political nature of human beings (see Nussbaum 1995, 102–110), by which Williams is equally unconvinced: "Glaucon and Adeimantus, agreeing that human beings are essentially or typically rational and they essentially or typically live in societies, could still deny that human reason is displaced at its most effective in living according to the restrictive requirements of society" (Williams 1995, 199).

15. Hursthouse argues that "Bernard Williams . . . has pinpointed basically the same dilemma. If 'good human being,' as it figures in the modern naturalism project is, like 'good wolf,' a biological/ethological/scientific concept, then it is objectively all right, but it won't yield anything much in the way of ethics; it will be largely morally indeterminate. . . . A concept of human nature formed within our ethical outlook may yield us quite a rich hoard—but then, of course, the rich hoard will not be objectively well-founded but the mere re-iteration of the views involved in the ethical outlook" (Hursthouse 2004, 165).

16. Michael Thompson makes essentially the same point when he claims, "What merely 'ought to be' in the individual we may say really 'is' in its form" (Thompson 1998, 295).

17. Toner develops his idea of "natural norm" through his unique conception of the first nature and the second nature. The universal human nature can be regarded as the first nature, while virtue can be considered as the second nature. However, "first and second nature must be related so that the second is a natural outgrowth of the first, and so that that in our given makeup is (first) natural which does tend toward an ethically mature second nature" (Toner 2008, 236).

18. Michael Slote, whose version of virtue ethics emphasizes the symmetry between agent and patient, tries to avoid this Kantian asymmetry, particularly in his earlier writings: "[I]n common-sense terms we admire both what a person is able to do to advance his own or other people's happiness and what a person is able to do to advance the admirability either of himself or others. We commonly admire people for their possession of self-regarding and other-regarding virtues . . . and we also admire people who help others to develop admirable or virtuous traits of character. . . . And so I think it is part of common-sense virtue ethics to assume that people should be concerned with the happiness and virtue . . . *both of others and of themselves*" (Slote 1992, 111). More recently, however, Slote does not insist on the strict symmetry in the sense that a virtuous person does not have to pay equal attention to his or her own happiness and that of others (instead he argues that there should be balance between the two), although he still thinks that a virtuous person should pay equal attention to his or her own virtue and that of others (see Slote 2001, 77–78).

19. McKerlie distinguishes between egoist eudaimonism and altruistic eudaimonism: "One answer says that Aristotle gives to each agent the single fundamental goal of making his or her own life realize *eudaimonia*. I will call this view the 'egoistic eudaimonist' interpretation. The alternative interpretation takes Aristotle to be an altruistic eudaimonist. He thinks that as well as aiming at *eudaimonia* in our own lives we should also have as a fundamental aim that at least some other people realize *eudaimonia*" (McKerlie 1991, 85). As we shall see, McKerlie himself argues for the second way of understanding Aristotle.

20. As Julia Annas points out, "the best or perfect kind of friendship is one in which each person is friend with the other because of that person's goodness, specifically his good character—indeed this kind of friendship is often called friendship of character" (Annas 1993, 249–50).

21. The absurdity of this is also clearly seen by CHENG Yi. When told that those who understand *dao* and those who do not, superior people and inferior people, mutually promote each other, CHENG Yi clearly asks, "[H]ow can it not be the case that everyone be a superior person? . . . Otherwise, it would be thought that the existence of human beings, instead of relying upon sages and worthies, relies upon [morally] stupid people" (*Yishu* 21a; 272).

22. In this context, it is interesting to bring a famous passage in *Analect* 6.30 to our discussion: "one who wishes to establish oneself establishes others, and one who wishes to be noble lets others be noble." This passage is normally understood as the Confucian version of the Golden Rule in its positive expression (in contrast to its negative expression in *Analects* 12.2, "Do not do unto others what one does not wish others do unto oneself"). However, Qing scholar MAO Qiling 毛奇齡, in his *Corrections of the Four Books* 四書改錯, interprets it to mean that one cannot establish oneself without establishing others, and one cannot make oneself noble without letting others be noble. In other words, to establish others is the intrinsic content of establishing oneself, and to let others be noble is the intrinsic content of making oneself noble. For this reason, MAO Qiling relates this passage not only to the idea of "realizing oneself (*cheng ji* 成己)" and "realizing others (*cheng wu* 成物)" in the *Doctrine of the Mean* that we have already discussed, but also to "manifesting one's clear character (*ming mingde* 明明德)" and "loving people (*qin min* 親民)" at the very beginning of the *Great Learning*, to "making oneself alone perfect (*du shan qi shen* 獨善其身)" and "making the whole Empire perfect (*jian shan tian xia* 兼善天下)" in *Mencius* 7a9, and to "cultivating oneself (*xiu ji* 修己)" and "bringing security to people (*an ren* 安人)" in *Analects* 14.42 (see Cheng 1990, 429). In this understanding, the two items in each of these pairs are inseparable: one cannot realize oneself without realizing others, manifest one's clear character without loving people, make oneself perfect without making the world perfect, and cultivate oneself without bringing peace to people, and vice versa.

23. The Chengs also gave some details about superior persons' way of moral education. For example, "in educating people, superior persons sometimes guide them, and sometimes refuse to see them. In each case, superior persons do so because they

know what is missing in a given person. The common purpose of both ways of educating people is to let people fully realize themselves" (*Yishu* 4; 70–71); also, "superior persons have priority in educating others: they first start with things small and near and then proceed to things great and far" (*Yishu* 8; 102).

24. Robert Merrihew Adams also emphasizes the importance of moral moving power: "the forming of ethical beliefs is not an entirely separate process from that of forming ethical feelings and desires, and the former will not go well if the latter goes badly" (Adams 2006, 213).

25. It is important to point out that, in discussing the self-centeredness objection to virtue ethics, we have been primarily focused on the eudaimonistic version of virtue ethics and not other versions of virtue ethics, some of which, the aretaic one advocated by Slote, for example, are claimed to be immune to such an objection, as it focuses on what is admirable. However, Hurka argues that his charge of foundational egoism is also applicable to such a version of virtue ethics, for "an aretaic theory likewise gives a self-regarding explanation, that the action will be something admirable on the agent's part, and this is, again, not the right explanation. Because they focus so centrally on the agent's virtue, virtual-ethical theories find the ultimate source of his reasons in himself, in what virtuous actions will mean for his flourishing or admirability" (Hurka 2001, 248).

26. Christine Swanton, for example, argues that "in defense of eudaimonism, one may claim that reasons for 'type or range X' pertain to the point of X as a virtue, and that in turn is constituted by the aim or target of X. So, for example, if X is the virtue of friendship, X-type reasons have to do with expressing friendship in acts of affection, promoting the good of the friend, and so on. No surreptitious or covert egoism seems lurking here. In short, reasons for type X derive from the target of X and are not themselves reasons for a claim that X is a virtue" (Swanton 2003, 79).

27. In addition to parental love of children, Philippa Foot also uses the example of friendship to make the same point: "What friendship requires a friend to do for a friend may indeed be onerous, involving even life itself. But what is done in friendship is done gladly, *con a more*" (Foot 2001, 102).

28. Elsewhere I have discussed this self-centeredness objection to virtue ethics in relation to ZHU Xi's neo-Confucianism (see Huang 2010a).

Chapter 3: Knowledge (*zhi* 知):
How Is Weakness of the Will (*akrasia*) *Not* Possible?

1. In some of Plato's later dialogues, for example in the *Republic* (Plato 1963b, 430e–431b), Socrates discusses the weakness of the will issue again. There are disagreements among scholars about Socrates's view in these dialogues. Some think that it is consistent with the view in *Protagoras* (see Dorter, 315; Guthrie, 435–436), while others think it is the opposite (see Gerson 1986, 359; Lesses 1987, 148). I shall not enter the debate here.

2. As a matter of fact, Socrates himself also realizes that his view about weakness of the will is against common opinion, and thus he talks to Protagoras: "I expect you know that most men don't believe us. They maintain that there are many who recognize the best but are unwilling to act on it" (Plato 1963a, 352d).

3. Aquinas later considers this as a distinction between potential knowledge and actual knowledge or between passive knowledge and active knowledge. See Aquinas, part 1 of the Second Part, Q.77 A.2.

4. In this passage, Aristotle also indicates that there are two practical syllogisms leading to contradictory actions (conclusions) going on in the mind of the *akratic* person, but he does not mention all the premises in these two syllogisms. Scholars have made numerous attempts to supply these missing premises. I think that the most successful one is provided by Aquinas, which is to be discussed here along with Davidson's view.

5. Helen Steward agrees with this interpretation of Aristotle's view in this chapter of *Ethica Nicomachea*, but she thinks that Aristotle seems to disagree in many passages of his *Ethics Eudemia* and *Magna Moralis* (see Steward 1998, §2). However, in these places, Aristotle is primarily trying to explain the idea of *akrasia* (just as we may try to explain the idea of a unicorn or even a squared circle) without necessarily affirming it as factual or even possible. This is most clear in the passage Steward mentions from *Ethics Eudemia*, where Aristotle says that "no one wishes what he thinks to be bad; but surely the man who acts incontinently does not do what he wishes, for to act incontinently is to act through appetite contrary to what the man thinks best" (Aristotle 1915, 1223b7–9). Here Aristotle obviously is telling us what *akrasia* or incontinence means, for immediately he states that "whence it results that the same man acts at the same time both voluntarily and involuntarily; but this is impossible" (Aristotle 1915, 1223b9–11).

6. Augustine's discussion of weakness of the will is from a very different context. He seems to think that, after the Fall, it is not that some people sometimes, or all people sometimes, or some people all the time have weakness of the will; it is rather that all people all the time have weakness of the will; moreover, such weakness of the will can only be overcome with the grace of God. For a careful discussion of Augustine's view, see Pang-White 2000, 2003. For a general survey of philosophical discussions of *akrasia* from Aristotle to the period of modern philosophy, see Gosling 1990, chapters 5–7; for a general survey of contemporary discussion of this issue before Davidson, see Charlton 1935, chapters 4–6.

7. Even Watson and Pugmire agree with Davidson that there are people who intentionally do things other than what they have the best reasons to do. Their skepticism of weakness of the will largely arises from their view that such actions are more from people's desires than from their reason, so their actions are not free (see Watson 1977, 323–26; Pugmire 1982, 188–189). If so, however, they should have not affirmed the possibility or actuality of weakness of will, but merely phenomenon *b*: compulsion.

8. Arthur Walker provides a good summary of this literature up to 1989 (see Walker 1989).

9. Commenting on this passage, CHENG Yi points out that "one's heart/mind is much more important than one's chickens and dogs. To look for one's lost chickens and dogs without looking for one's lost heart/mind is to love what is unimportant while ignoring what is more important to the greatest extent. This is because one does not think" (*Yishu* 25; 317).

10. In this regard I think Wing-tsit Chan is wrong when he contrasts CHENG Yi with WANG Yangming 王陽明 and claims that "Cheng merely says that true knowledge will lead to action, but does not say that action leads to knowledge, as Wang does" (Chan 1963, 558; see also Cai 1996, 114; and Pang 1992, 170).

11. In a very detailed comment on a previous version of this chapter, A. S. Cua suggested that I should translate *dexing zhi zhi* as "knowledge from virtue," paralleling my translation of *wenjian zhi zhi* as "knowledge from hearing and seeing." While it seems to me an interesting alternative translation, it suggests that you first have virtue and then have knowledge from the virtue, but for CHENG Yi knowledge and virtue are concurrent: you cannot be virtuous without relevant knowledge, and you cannot have knowledge without being virtuous.

12. In their comments on a previous version of this chapter, LI Chenyang and WU Kuangming both raised the issue of the possible problem of circular reasoning here: Profound and genuine knowledge of/as virtue, in contrast to superficial and common knowledge from seeing and hearing, is defined in terms of its ability to lead us to act, while proper action, in contrast to blind and forced action, is in turn defined by its being guided by profound and genuine knowledge of/as virtue. My response is that, from an observer's point of view, there is indeed no other way to determine whether a person's knowledge is genuine or not than observing whether the person acts accordingly. However, the person knows clearly what type of knowledge he or she has even before his or her action (or lack thereof) according to his or her knowledge, as knowledge of/as virtue is obtained not only by one's mind but also by one's heart, while knowledge from hearing and seeing is merely understood by one's mind.

13. For example, PANG Wanli argues that "genuine knowledge is from direct experience and originates from heart/mind, while ordinary knowledge is from indirect experience. Genuine knowledge comes from life experience and practice, while ordinary knowledge comes from hearsay" (Pang 1992, 152).

14. In one of the very few discussions of weakness of the will in the context of Confucianism, Joel Kuppermann emphasizes the distinction between moral knowledge, on the one hand, and mathematical, scientific, and historical knowledge, on the other. In his view, while the latter "is assimilated to being able to state, explain, and justify a correct answer," the former, using Plato's words, "is not something that can be put into words like other sciences; but, after a long-continued intercourse between teacher and pupil . . . it is born in the soul and straightway nourishes itself" (Kuppermann 1981, 1). This is a good description of CHENG Yi's knowledge of/as virtue, although Cheng's distinction between knowledge of/as virtue and knowledge from hearing and seeing is not one between moral knowledge and nonmoral knowledge (in this sense MENG Peiyuan

is wrong to see these two distinctions as the same distinction; see Meng 1998, 374). Although Cheng often uses nonmoral knowledge, as in the story of the farmer and tiger, to explain the distinction between the two types of knowledge, both knowledge of hearing and seeing and knowledge of/as virtue that he is interested in are related to morality.

15. De Bary, in his study of neo-Confucianism, devotes a whole chapter to this idea in his book, *Learning for One's Self*. In his view, *zide*, which he translated as "getting it by or for oneself," has two important senses: "One, relatively low-keyed, is that of learning or experiencing some truth for oneself and deriving inner satisfaction therefrom. Here *zide* has the meaning of 'learned to one's satisfaction,' 'self-contented,' 'self-possessed.' The other sense of the term is freighted with deeper meaning: 'getting it or find the Way in oneself'" (De Bary 1991, 43); and he relates this second sense to its use by Mencius (4b14).

16. It is interesting to note that, while in the Western philosophical tradition, body and mind are usually considered as two separate entities, in this Confucian tradition, they are both regarded as *ti*: one is the small *ti*, and one is the great *ti*.

17. JIANG Xinyan, in her article on the same topic, also recognizes the difference between these two types of knowledge. However, in her view, this is a difference "to different degrees" (Jiang 2000, 246). My view, however, is that they are two different types of knowledge. However much knowledge from hearing and seeing a person may have, and however perfect such knowledge is, such knowledge itself cannot incline the person to act.

18. Thus, after some careful comparisons between Aristotle and the CHENG Yi-ZHU Xi school of neo-Confucianism, JIANG Xinyan concludes that they "both believe that a weak-willed person's practical knowledge, that is, his knowledge about what he ought to do, is defective" (Jiang 2000, 247–48); however, Kenneth Dorter compares WANG Yang-ming and Socrates on their views of weakness of the will and concludes that "Wang's paradoxical doctrine that knowledge and action are inseparable entails Socratic paradox that virtue is knowledge, so Wang's arguments support Socrates' doctrine as well. Like Socrates, Wang claims that to know the good is to do the good" (Dorter 1997, 333).

19. Cheng's knowledge of/as virtue is more similar to Aristotle's practical wisdom. As we have seen, Aristotle thinks that one's practical knowledge will also necessarily lead to action. If this is the case, then knowledge that the "weak-willed" person tends to lose is definitely not practical wisdom; if this is the case, then the solution to the ignorance of the "weak-willed person" that Aristotle wants to provide here should not be to regain the lost knowledge, as he suggests here, since such knowledge, even regained, will get lost again whenever it is needed. The person should rather seek practical wisdom, which will never be lost once obtained. Should Aristotle take this route to solve the problem of weakness of the will, he would be doing exactly the same thing as the Chengs do.

20. However, FENG Richang 馮日昌 is wrong when he goes to another extreme, saying that "knowledge from hearing and seeing is what CHENG Yi values most" (Feng 1991, 175–77).

21. QIAN Mu also points out that "it is not that we don't need knowledge from hearing and seeing; it is rather that we need the effort of thinking over and above hearing and seeing" (Qian 2001, 68).

22. So ultimately we need to obtain knowledge of/as virtue; there is no doubt that, for Cheng, knowledge of/as virtue is superior to knowledge from hearing and seeing. In this sense I think LU Lianzhang 蘆連章 is wrong to claim that "CHENG Yi believes that 'knowledge from hearing and seeing' and 'knowledge of/as virtue' each has its advantages and disadvantages. . . . Knowledge from hearing and seeing is knowledge from one's sense organs and so may be confused by external things; knowledge of/as virtue is what one was born with, coming from inner heart/mind and so is subject to subjective biases. Each has its strengths and weakness. The two should complement each other in order to lead to 'true knowledge'" (Lu 2001, 142). This view was first developed by CHEN Zhongfan 陳鍾凡, who claims that "knowledge of/as virtue may be obscured by subjective prejudices, while knowledge from hearing and seeing may be confused by external things. The two have their respective strengths and weaknesses. Thus only if they can be made complementary to each other can knowledge be deepened" (Chen 1996, 104).

23. This is a view that can be traced back to Aristotle, who argues that only voluntary actions and passions are blameworthy or praiseworthy. In other words, we can only ask people to be responsible for their voluntary actions and passions. Then he explains that "those things, then, are thought involuntary, which take place under compulsion or owing to ignorance" (Aristotle 1915, 1109b35–1110a1).

24. For example, Stephen J. Morse argues that "as long as we maintain the current conception of ourselves as intentional and potentially rational creatures, as people and not simply as machines, the *mens rea* requirement in criminal law is both inevitable and desirable" (Morse 2003, 51).

25. John Locke has made a good point in this relation: "Though punishment be annexed to personality, and personality to consciousness, and the drunkard perhaps be not conscious of what he did, yet human judicatures justly punish him; because the fact is proved against him, but want of consciousness cannot be proved for him. But in the Great Day, where the secrets of all hearts shall be laid open, it may be reasonable to think, no one shall be made to answer for what he knows nothing of" (Locke n.d., book 2. 27.22).

26. Its American counterpart is the "Insanity Defense" by the American Law Institute in 1956, which also states that "a person is not responsible for criminal conduct if at the time of such conduct as a result of mental disease or defect his capacity either to appreciate the criminality of his conduct or to conform his conduct to the requirements of law is so substantially impaired that he cannot justly be held responsible" (The American Law Institute 2000, 669).

27. Therefore, TU Weiming argues that "the Socratic position that 'wrongdoing involves a failure of practical wisdom (phronesis), that is, essentially involves ignorance

of what is good' fails to address the central issue of voluntary wrongdoing for which the moral agent must be held responsible. The Aristotelian attempt to locate the sources of *akrasia* in characterological factors (the identification of a sort of akratic ignorance, for example) seems, in the Mencian perspective, one-sided" (Tu 1983, 222).

28. Tu Weiming, after discussing the same paragraph from the *Mencius*, correctly points out that, "while it is perfectly understandable that a respectable person may not be aware of the unrealizable potential in his nature, such as scientific, and artistic talents, it is inconceivable, in the Mencian sense, that a mature member of our society can be ignorant of his gems and, therefore, not be responsible for his acts as a moral agent" (Tu 1983, 222–23).

29. I discuss this issue of moral responsibility, including both moral praise and moral blame, in more detail in Huang 2013f.

30. Thus Carsun Chang claims that Cheng Yi "was the first of the Sung philosophers to attach importance to the intellectual process as distinct from the valuational" (Chang 1963, 219).

31. Although Cheng Yi does not say it explicitly, it is quite clear that he means *dao* or *li* by "one." Lao Siguang 勞思光 holds the same interpretation: "one master here means the oneness of the heart/mind and *li* and so undisturbability by external things" (Lao 2003, 238). Pang Wanli also agrees on this (see Pang 1992, 246).

Chapter 4: Love (*ai* 愛): Ethics between Theory and Antitheory

1. For a critical examination of these three contemporary efforts to reformulate the Golden Rule, see Huang 2005b, 395–402.

2. Thomas E. Hill Jr. has recently argued that, after "we strip from the core of Kant's ethics certain unnecessary doctrines, no matter how dear to the old man's heart these may have been" and "render some of Kant's abstractions more concrete" (Hill 2000, 62), we can develop what he calls "Kantian pluralism." Hill's Kantian pluralism, as he states, expands on two of Kant's ideas: rational agents and respect for persons. On the one hand, "because Kantian ethics starts from the idea of rational agent abstracting as far as possible from particular cultural commitments and preferences, argument should tend to support a relatively open society with liberties protected and diversity permitted" (Hill 2000, 30); on the other hand, "in so far as we value and respect persons as having the two kinds of indispensable values—(*a*) the necessary means of life and (*b*) self-identifying ground projects—we have presumptive reason both for non-interference and for aid, provided the projects and the means themselves are compatible with due respect for others" (Hill 2000, 78). Here, while one can perform the duty of noninterference with others by remaining a rational agent, to fulfill the duty of aid, the proper aid, that is, to others, one has to be an empirical agent to learn about the patient as an empirical being. While I am somewhat skeptical about the possibility of developing such pluralism from Kant, it is certainly a welcome attempt. Still, such a Kantian pluralism

works only in terms of our actions toward moral patients who are also rational beings and thus leaves us unguided when interacting with moral patients who are not rational beings, such as children and mentally challenged adults, animals, and even plants. In my view, while rationality is a prerequisite for moral agents (we cannot hold a nonrational being responsible for what it does), it is certainly not a prerequisite for moral patients (we can hold a rational being responsible for what it does, even to a nonrational being). For an exchange on Kant's view of human treatment of animals, see Broadie and Pybus 1992, Regan 1999, and Pybus and Broadie 1999.

3. For a detailed critical examination of Rorty's view of difference and a Confucian critique of this view, see Huang 2009, section 4.

4. Although this statement is made by Youzi 有子, a pupil of Confucius, it is a general consensus that this also reflects Confucius's own view. The original Chinese statement, "*xiao di ye zhe qi wei ren zhi ben ye* 孝弟也者其為仁之本也," can be interpreted in two very different ways. My translation here follows the common interpretation. However, as I shall point out later in this chapter, the alternative interpretation suggested by the Cheng brothers makes better sense.

5. According to Origen, however, Christian love is really a love with distinction in this sense:

> our Teacher and Lord . . . gave understanding of the order to those who can hear the Scripture, saying, "Set ye in order charity in me." *Thou shalt love the Lord thy God with thy whole heart and with thy whole soul and with thy whole strength and with thy whole mind. Thou shalt love thy neighbour as thyself.* He does not say that thou shalt love God as thyself, that a neighbour shall be loved with the whole heart, with the whole soul, with the whole strength, with the whole mind. Again, He said: *love your enemies*, and did not add "with the whole heart . . . and He does not say 'Love your enemies as yourself'" . . . It is enough for them that we love them and do not hate them. (Origen 1957, 296)

6. While Hans Küng presents a typical Christian view, some Christian theologians today also perceive problems with such a view. For example, Stephen Pope, drawing on the development of contemporary social biology, argues that human nature determines that human love has a different order of priority: first is the love for oneself and then for others; first for parents and then for neighbors; and first for immediate neighbors and then for remote neighbors. In his view, although Christian ethics of love is not based on human nature but on divine grace, divine grace does not destroy human nature but makes the deficient human nature perfect; moreover, the way divine grace makes human nature perfect is not abolishing the order of priority in love but by making this order appropriate. For example, loving one's family members is appropriate; nepotism is not (see Pope, 1994; see also Browning, 1992).

7. Tu Wei-ming holds the same view: "we are grateful not only to those who are instrumental in making our life possible, livable, and meaningful, but also to those

who, in numerous ways, bring happiness and richness to our daily practical living"
(Tu 1999, 24).

8. CHENG Hao, speaking of this text, states that "only Zihou 子厚 [ZHANG Zai]
has such a power to write it. No one else can do it. No one since Mencius has ever
reached this level" (*Yishu* 2a; 39). CHENG Yi agrees that "no one else can write this
text" (*Yishu* 23; 308).

9. Indeed, the Moist term for universal love, *jian ai* 兼愛, is used by ZHANG Zai
in a different passage: "Nature is the single source of the ten thousand things. It is
not something that only I have privately. Only great persons can fully realize the *dao*.
Therefore, their establishing must be establishing all, their knowing must be knowing
all, and their love must be universal love (*jian ai* 兼愛)" (Zhang 1978, 5).

10. Here CHENG Yi is responding to a question by his student YANG Shi 楊時
regarding ZHANG Zai. Enlightened by CHENG Yi, Yang made a very important point in
this relation: "Things under heaven are particular appearances of one principle. Knowing there is only one principle, one practices *ren*; knowing that its appearances are
different, one becomes just (*yi* 義)" (see CHEN 1996, 143). To be just is to love different
people differently. For more discussion on the relation between love with distinction
and justice, see Huang 2005b, 38–40.

11. It is interesting to note that Origen, in his commentary on the Song of Songs,
states that God's love, in contrast to human love, is a love with distinction in this
sense. While God does love all that are, "He did not for this reason love the Hebrews
and Egyptians in a like way, nor Pharaoh as He did Moses and Aaron. Again He did
not love the other children of Israel as He loved Moses and Aaron and Mary, nor did
He love Aaron and Mary in the same way He loved Moses. . . . He who *has disposed all
things in measure and number and weight* undoubtedly regulates the balance of His
love according to the measure of each. For surely we cannot think, can we, that Paul
was loved by Him in the same way when he was persecuting the church of God, as
he was when he was himself bearing persecutions and torments for her sake" (Origen
1957, 192–93; emphasis original).

12. I have been arguing that love with distinction should be understood as different kinds, rather than different degrees, of love appropriate to different kinds of objects
of love. This however, does not mean that superior people necessarily love everyone to
the same degree. As a matter of fact, normally, superior people also love their family
members more than other people, but this is explained, at least in part, by the fact
that they know their family members better than other people and so can love them
more appropriately. This constitutes a new argument against the Moist idea of universal
love. For Mozi, in appearance, when I love my family members to the same degree as
I love all others, my family members receive less love from me than if I love my family more than others. However, given that all others also love their family members to
the same degree that they love all others (including my family members), my family
members receive more love from everyone else than if they love their parents more

than they love all others. As a result my parents receive the same amount of love if we practice his universal love without distinction as when we practice the Confucian love with distinction (see *Mozi*, chapter 15). Mozi here does not recognize that to love a person requires one to know the person. Obviously I know my family members better than I know other people, just as other people know their family members better than they know my family members, and, due to the limit of human knowledge, no one can have appropriate knowledge of everyone. Thus if we practice Mozi's universal love without distinction, hardly anyone will receive adequate and appropriate love (for a similar argument, although an argument based more on efficiency than on ethics of difference, see Donaldson 2008, 137).

13. This is similar to what Aristotle says: "those who are not angry at the thing they should be angry at are thought to be fools, and so are those who are not angry in the right way, at the right time, or with the right persons" (*Aristotle* 1915, 1126a5–6).

14. Bernard Williams, in his argument about the thickness of the morally relevant descriptions of actions, claims that such descriptions are nontransportable from context to context (Williams 1985); and Dancy states that his particularism does not allow such a switch argument: "an attempt to determine what to say here by appeal to what we say about something else" (Dancy 1993, 64).

15. P. J. Ivanhoe notices this irreconcilability in his discussion of the Confucian view as expressed by Mencius. Still, Ivanhoe points out, "in terms of the form, flexibility, persistence, and range of what we care about, a good case can be made for Mengzi's claim" (Ivanhoe 2002, 185 note 6).

16. LU Lianzhang argues that "CHENG Yi's *qi* of true origin (*zhenyuan zhi qi*) comes from the Daoist religion. In Daoist religion, heaven and earth have *yuan qi*, so do humans. Humans have *yuanqi* when they are born, which gradually declines when one grows up and therefore needs to be supplemented. However, food and drink cannot do the job. It can only be supplemented by the *yuanqi* of heaven and earth" (Lu 2001, 138–139).

17. For a more detailed discussion of CHENG Hao's view of human nature as good and the origin of evil in relation to *qi*, particularly his distinction between guest or alien *qi* (*keqi* 客氣) and host *qi* (*zhuq* 主氣), similar to CHENG Yi's distinction between external *qi* (*waiqi* 外氣) and internal *qi* (*neiqi* 內氣), see Huang 2009.

18. For example, the Moist Yuzi 夷子 once tried to interpret Confucian love as meaning "there should be no distinction in love, though the practice of it begins with one's parents" (see *Mencius* 3a5). Mencius of course disagreed with this interpretation.

19. In this sense, it is to some extent similar to what Gilbert Harman describes as direct inductive inference or transductive inference, which "goes from data about previous cases to a classification of a new case. This classification does not involve first making an inductive generalization from data about previous cases and background assumptions . . . and then deducing a conclusion about the new case from that inductive generalization" (Harman 2005, 48). On the one hand, it is not to classify the new case

within the same category of the previous cases but merely as something neighboring them; on the other hand, "transductive inferences need not set precedents" but will leave other possible nearby cases maximally undecided (Harman 2005, 54).

20. Mencius himself seemed to have recognized that. In his discussion with King Xuan of Qi 齊宣王, he says that the reason the king asked people to exchange a lamb for an ox for sacrifice is not that he was stingy but because he had the heart of commiseration. However, if the king did have the heart of commiseration, why did he want to make a choice between the lamb and the ox? Mencius's response is that the king "saw the ox but not the lamb. The attitude of a superior person toward animals is this: once having seen them alive, he or she cannot bear to see them die; and once having heard them cry, he or she cannot bear to eat their flesh" (*Mencius* 1a7).

21. In this connection, it is interesting to compare Tu Wei-ming's quite creative interpretation of the same statement of Confucius: Confucian ethics does require us to go beyond family, because "we should behave as filial sons of heaven and earth. Such a conception of filial piety is conducive to both society and ecology" (see Tu 1999, 29).

22. In the text, the purpose of Mencius's use of the analogy of ox and lamb is to help the king expand his love for the ox, for which he has the true feeling of love, to his people, for whom he has not had the true feeling of love. On this point, I agree with David Wong's criticism of David Nivison. According to the latter, Mencius tries here to disclose a logical contradiction of the king: he had the heart of commiseration toward the ox about to be killed, and yet he did not have the same heart toward people who were experiencing the same pain and suffering (see Nivison 1980). The difficulty with Nievison's interpretation is that, if one does not have the feeling of love for someone, then one will be unable to love the person even if the feeling is illogical and one tries to overcome the logical contradiction (for Wong's criticism, see Wong 1991, 37–43).

23. A common contrast between Confucianism and Christianity is that, while Confucianism emphasizes the original goodness of human nature, Christianity underscores the sin and fall of humanity. This seems to explain why Christianity *commands* a universal love *without distinction*: it has to be *commanded*, because humanity has already fallen into sin from which it cannot pull itself out; and it has to be *without distinction*, because all humans are sinners and are the same in the eyes of God (I would like to thank the late Harvard professor Gordon Kaufman for pointing this out to me in a private correspondence). This is perhaps true, but I think the difference between Confucian and Christian views of human nature is not as consequential as it may appear. Whether human nature is *originally* good or evil (as a matter of fact, an important Confucian school represented by Xunzi argues that human nature is evil), it is clear from our above discussion that Confucianism may well agree with Christians that humans *currently* are not good or at least not as good as they should be. That is why it emphasizes moral cultivation to either restore (for those who believe human nature is originally good) or build up (for those who believe that human nature is originally evil) human goodness. Now Confucianism is against love without distinction because,

even though humans may not be as good as they should be (or all are sinners in the Christian view), they are nevertheless still different from each other, and our love has to take such difference into consideration in order for it to be appropriate love; Confucianism is against the conception of love as a command because commanded love is no longer from one's inner heart. So really Confucian love represents a higher idea of love: you should not only love everyone and everything (not merely some humans or things) equally; you should also love each person or thing in a way most appropriate to the particular person or thing out of your inner heart.

24. I develop this ethics of difference more fully in relation to the Daoist text *Zhuangzi* (see Huang 2005a, 2006, 2010b, 2010c, 2014, and forthcoming).

25. In this sense I also disagree with John Rawls. In his view, to respect our fellow citizens is an important feature of democratic society, so we should not impose our particular religious and metaphysical views upon others. I think this is correct. However, he goes on to argue, incorrectly, that we should not take into consideration any of our fellow citizens' claims if they are not universally shared. For Rawls's view, see Rawls 1997; for some detailed arguments against Rawls's view, see Huang 2001, chapter 5.

Chapter 5: Propriety (*li* 禮):
Why the Political Is Also Personal

1. Edwin Baker and Robert Audi defend Rawls against Sandel's criticism, saying that Rawls's social justice is not inconsistent with individual benevolence and fraternity (see Baker 1985, 917–20; Audi 1989, 294). I think Baker and Audi are wrong, as will be clear in my discussion of G. A. Cohen's view.

2. Although Xunzi 荀子 still regards *dafu* and *shuren* as different classes, he regards the two classes as defined by morality and not heredity: "If descendants of kings, dukes, literati, and senior officials (*dafu*) cannot adhere to propriety and rightness, they should be ranked as inferiors (*shuren*). If descendants of inferior people (*shuren*) acquire learning and apply it in conduct and adhere to propriety and rightness, then they should be promoted to the post of prime minister and senior officials (*dafu*)" (*Xunzi* 9.1).

3. Xu Fuguan, in an article on propriety and music, also asserts that the Chengs are the most important postclassical Confucians on the issue of propriety (see Xu 2004a, 210).

4. Fred Dallmayr makes an interesting point in this regard, saying that these five relationships should be supplemented by the sixth one: "that between citizen and citizen in a shared public sphere and under a common rule of law" (Dallmayr 2003, 207). In the last part of this chapter, I shall discuss a negative effect of rule of law, especially when it is not accompanied with rule of propriety and rule of virtue, both of which focus on the cultivation of moral persons instead of the resolution of conflict among individuals. In this context, the addition of this sixth relationship may become less significant.

5. It is in this sense that a society governed by propriety is a hierarchical one in which "there is distinction between the great and the small, the above and the below, and the beautiful and the ugly. . . . The distinctions between the above and the below and between the noble and mean are the 'ought' of principle (*li* 理) and the fundamental of propriety (*li* 禮)" (*Zhouyi Chengshi Zhuan* 1; 749). However, as pointed out by XIAO Gongquan 蕭公權, a renowned historian of Chinese political philosophy, "the differentiation and inequality caused by government of propriety are not something arbitrary, but are determined by people's abilities" (Xiao, 91). In other words, those who are above and those who are below are determined by their moral cultivation. Those who are above may fall below, and vice versa. Thus, for CHENG Yi, what is important is that one be qualified for the task assigned, which means that "only the worthy and the able should hold official positions" (*Wenji* 5; 524). Moreover, in the Chengs' view, anyone can become worthy and able as long as one tries. As a matter of fact, "anyone can become a sage" (*Yishu* 25; 318), since "human nature is the same for everyone. Those who doubt that they can become sages just lack the self-confidence" (*Yishu* 25; 318), or "they gave up and abandoned themselves" (*Zhouyi Chengshi Zhuan* 4; 956). Also, those above may be downgraded if they cease to carry out their moral cultivation, and those below may be promoted if they begin and continue their moral cultivation. Xunzi holds the same view on this: "No persons of virtue are to be left unhonored, no persons of ability are to be out of official posts, no one of merits are to be left unrewarded, and no persons of guilt are to be left unpunished" (*Xunzi* 9.15).

6. Leonard Shihlien Hsü thus points out, "Law can only regulate the external behavior of man, but man's mind will not be rectified thereby. If the mind is not rectified, he is liable to commit anti-social acts. The innate force that prevents a man from committing crimes is his sense of shame which can be developed only by means of education and moral discipline" (Hsü 1975, 160–61).

7. The philosophical richness of this *Analects* passage has not received its deserved attention. Although Confucius here refers to the three classics, I believe that he actually describes the process of moral development. By reading poetry (and stories), one cultivates one's moral sentiments, for example, the sentiment of sympathy for people who suffer as described by the emotional language of poetry or stories. Thus, one's moral action starts from poetry; however, one's moral sentiments, as sentiments stimulated by poetry, are not stable, so they need rules of propriety to stabilize them. Thus, one's moral action is established by propriety; yet when one follows rules of propriety, one is not acting from one's desire yet, so one needs to reach the stage of music at which one performs moral actions as naturally as one dances to music. Thus, one's moral action is completed in music. I shall emphasize this last point in this section.

8. As I pointed out in the first chapter, music (*yue*) and joy (*le*) are pronounced differently but written the same: 樂.

9. We can see that CHENG Yi here changes "following propriety (*li* 禮)" to "following principle (*li* 理)" in the course of discussion without any explanation. As I shall point out in section 6 of this chapter, this does not indicate any confusion in his mind or an accidental slip of the tongue; it is rather his view that these two are indeed identical.

10. While rules of propriety are normative, human feelings are natural. By basing the normative on the natural, however, as I have shown in chapter 2, the Cheng brothers do not commit the so-called naturalistic fallacy.

11. Leonard Shihlien Hsü thus observes: *"Li* assumes that there are good natural elements in the human mind, and that if these are only cultivated by systematic exercise, duties will be fulfilled spontaneously. *Li* does not create duties artificially, but assumes that it is natural, for instance, for the father to be kind to his son and the son to be attached to his father. This is called 'following human nature,' which is the foundation of *li*'s moral code. *Li* emphasizes the development of naturally good sentiments and the observance of natural reason so that the greatest social harmony may be obtained" (Hsü 1975, 95).

12. PAN Fuen 潘富恩 and XU Yuqing 徐余慶, in their study of the Cheng brothers, point out that "humanity, rightness, propriety, and wisdom all originate from people's feeling. They are made systematic by rulers above and then applied back to people" (Pan and Xu 1988, 160).

13. Xunzi also talks about *li zhi ben* 禮之本. However, the word *ben* 本 in Xunzi does not mean the origin or root from which rules of propriety are derived but the fundamentals that rules of propriety are made to serve, so it seems to me misleading to translate it as "bases" (Burton Watson) or "roots" (John Knoblock): "There are three fundamentals *(ben)* for *li* to serve: Heaven and earth, which are the fundamentals of life; ancestors, who are fundamentals of species, and rulers and teachers, who are fundamentals of government. . . . Therefore, rules of propriety serve heaven above and earth below, honor the ancestors, and respect rulers and teachers" *(Xunzi* 19.4). It is also somewhat different from what Antonio Cua means by the same term. Cua distinguishes the inner aspect and outer aspect of *li zhi ben.* The inner aspect of *li zhi ben* is "a person's commitment to the practice of *li*," while the outer aspect of *li zhi ben* is *li*'s function in joining humans, heaven, and earth together to form a triad (see Cua 2003a, 274–80).

14. However, there is a significant difference between Nussbaum's and the Chengs' understanding of the "therapy of desire." Still caught in the intellectualistic tradition of the West, Nussbaum believes that desires are intelligent in the sense that desires are based on beliefs, so pathological desires that need therapy are desires based on false beliefs. Consequently, the needed therapy is "to use philosophical argument to modify the passions," and "thus in asking philosophy to deal with anger and fear and love, the medical model is not asking it to use device alien to itself. It can still seek agreement, fit, and truth in the fabric of discourse and belief taken as a whole" (Nussbaum 1994, 39). The Chengs would perhaps agree that desires or feelings are intelligent, not because they are rooted in beliefs, but because beliefs and desires, never separate from each other, mutually determine each other. If desires need argument for cure, then arguments also need desire for power. Thus the standard used to determine whether a particular desire is pathological is not truth based on rational argument but the natural desires from which this desire may or may not have diverted.

15. As pointed out by CHEN Rongjie 陳榮捷 (Wing-tsit Chan), this identification of *li* (propriety) and *li* (principle) has its origin in the *Liji* (19.34; 489) (see Chen 1996,

85). However, it is important to see that the Chengs' unique understanding of *li* (principle) as the ultimate reality of the universe is quite different from the understanding of *li* as governing (*zhi li* 治理) in the *Book of Rites*.

16. So in the Chengs, *li* (propriety) means three different things: external rules, human feelings, and human nature, which is identical to *li* (principle). In this sense, I hold a different view from WONG Wai-ying, according to whom, ultimately, *li* only means external rules and therefore only has an auxiliary function in moral development in the Chengs' philosophy (see Wong 2003).

17. Obviously, here the Chengs have in mind Mencius's discussion of human natures and their beginnings in human feelings: "The heart of commiseration is the beginning of humanity, the heart of shame is the beginning of rightness, the heart of courtesy is the beginning of propriety, and the heart of right and wrong is the beginning of wisdom" (*Mencius* 2a6). In this passage, Mencius regards propriety as one of the four virtues comprising human nature and the heart of courtesy as one's feeling flowing from such a virtue/nature. So in Mencius, propriety (*li*) primarily does not refer to external rules governing human actions. This is a significant distinction between Mencius and Xunzi.

18. XU Fuguan also claims that virtue and propriety are one and not two: propriety comes from virtue but is not, as the Chengs argue more radically, itself a virtue. He says, "Propriety (*li*) is the concrete externalization of the prevalent principle (*li*). The origin from which propriety comes is the heavenly principle, which is also called virtue. When the virtue is externally manifested, it becomes propriety. So virtue and propriety originally are one and not two" (Xu 2004a, 246).

19. NI Peimin also states that "if we say that *ren* is the internal quality or disposition that makes a person an authentic person, then *li* is the body of external behavior patterns that allow *ren* to be applied and manifested publicly. . . . When *li* is properly performed, it is in accord with *yi*" (Ni 2002, 52).

20. It is in this sense that CHENG Yi argues against Laozi: "Laozi says, 'when *dao* is lost, there is *de*, when *de* is lost, there is *ren*, when *ren* is lost, there is *yi*, and when *yi* is lost, there is *li* (propriety).' Here, *dao*, *de*, *ren*, *yi*, and *li* are separated into five" (*Yishu* 25; 324). In his view, since they are all identical to the principle, one cannot be lost without the others being lost at the same time.

21. In the Chengs' view, there are five items, *ren*, *yi*, *li*, *zhi*, and *xin*, in human nature, but there are only four beginnings in human feelings. This is because *xin* 信 (faithfulness) in human nature does not have its external feeling. However, in the Chengs' view, we know the existence of inner human nature because of the external feeling. Since there is no external feeling of *xin*, how do we know that it is within our human nature? In the Chengs' view, "*xin* is the belief that there are *ren*, *yi*, *li*, and *zhi*. We know there is *xin* because of the presence of the opposite feeling: not-*xin* (not believing). So *xin* does not have its beginning (*duan* 端)" (*Yishu* 9; 105; see also *Yishu* 18; 184). CHENG Yi explains it: "While the other four have their beginnings, only *xin* does not. Because there is no-*xin*, we know there must be *xin*. For example, east and

west, south and north already have their definite places. There is no need to talk about *xin*. If one takes east for west and south for north, there is no-*xin*" (*Yishu* 15; 168).

22. SHUN Kwong-loi summarizes some of the main interpretations and then provides an interpretation of his own on this issue (see Shun). Most recently, building on Shun's interpretation, LI Chenyang provides yet another interesting interpretation (see Li).

23. CHENG Yi also discusses the identity of *ren* and *li* in direct connection with the *Analects*. When asked why overcoming oneself and returning to propriety is *ren*, he replies that "where there is something against propriety, there are selfish desires. If there are selfish desires, how can one be *ren*? Only when these selfish desires are fully overcome and nothing but propriety is left can there be *ren*" (*Yishu* 22a; 286).

24. In another place, he makes the same point: "What is great about rules of propriety is time: It has to allow addition and omission. We know that Xia 夏, Shang 商, and Zhou 周 all did some additions and omissions of rules of propriety. So those who inherit the Zhou rules of propriety should also do some additions and omissions. . . . This is because ancient people and contemporary people and their lives and physical conditions are not the same" (*Yishu* 15; 146).

25. Thus, when talking about the similar view of ZHU Xi 朱熹, de Bery observes ZHU Xi's thought of the ritual order as the embodiment in human society of principles inherent in the universe, principles which had both static and dynamic aspects and claims that "they represented both a basic structure or pattern in the universe (*li*) and a vital process of change and renewal" (de Bery 1986, 127–28).

26. In chapter 6, I shall further explain that constancy itself in the Cheng brothers is not something static. It is rather the unceasing life-giving activity (*sheng* 生).

27. Rawls thinks that his later idea of overlapping consensus developed in his *Political Liberalism* (see Rawls 1996, 133–72), together with his earlier idea of congruence developed in his *A Theory of Justice* (Rawls 1999 [1971], 496–505), can help solve this stability problem. I disagree (see Huang 2001, 202–29).

28. I have discussed the Confucian view of the contemporary debate between liberal neutrality and state perfectionism in some details in Huang 2013c.

29. P. J. Ivanhoe's idea of a "fallback" option in his discussion of rights is equally appropriate to our discussion of the function of laws. In Ivanhoe's view, "we can regard enjoying our rights in the way that we enjoy having a fire department or ambulance service in our community. . . . As valuable as these services are, they are things we hope *we don't ever* have to call upon" (Ivanhoe 2008, 33–34).

30. The type of metaphysics that Rorty criticizes is the one that would like to obtain "premises capable of being known to be true independently of the truth of the moral intuitions that have been summarized. Such premises *are* supposed to justify our intuitions, by providing premises from which the content of those intuitions can be deduced" (Rorty 1998, 171–72).

31. This view that we know the metaphysical human nature through our experience of human emotions is more fully developed by Zhu Xi, which is discussed in some detail in Huang 2011a, 269–73.

32. I have some more detailed discussion about the difference between reality as precondition of a belief and reality brought into existence by a belief (and its resultant action); see Huang 1995.

Chapter 6: Creativity (*li* 理):
The Metaphysic of Morals or Moral Metaphysics?

1. I here borrow the terms "inner requirement" and "self-transformation" from some contemporary Confucians, who claim that the development of democracy and science are the inner requirements of Confucianism, so it is a Confucian self-transformation (see Li 2001). For this reason, I think Carsun Chang is wrong to argue that "without the introduction of Buddhism into China there would have been no Neo-Confucianism" (Chang 1963, 43). In my view, the introduction of Buddhism perhaps colored the particular ontological articulation developed by neo-Confucians and even triggered this project but would not determine whether there would be such an ontological articulation. Chen Rongjie (Wing-tsit Chan) also claims that neo-Confucianism is the inner development of classical Confucianism, as neo-Confucians are primarily to get rid of some superstitious elements in the *Book of Changes* and then use that classic to provide a metaphysical foundation for Confucian morality in other Confucian classics (Chen 1991, 71).

2. CHENG Chung-ying provides a similar interpretation: *Li* "is both principles of being and intimate knowledge of such" (Cheng 1991, 479).

3. As CHEN Rongjie 陳榮捷 (Wing-Tsit Chan) points out, "the word *li* is not mentioned in the *Analects*. It appears several times in the commentaries on the *Book of Changes*. Mencius did speak of *li* in the sense of moral principles, but not in the sense of the law of being, and not as a major concept. It was instead the Neo-Daoists in the third and fourth centuries who conceived of *li* as governing all existence. The Buddhists in the next several centuries followed suit by formulating their famous thesis of the harmony of principle and facts. Challenged by the Buddhists, the Neo-Confucians seized upon the sayings in the *Book of Changes* and the book of *Mencius* and made principle a basic concept in their philosophy. For the first time in Chinese history an entire system was built on it" (Chen 1991, xvii–xviii. See also Chan 1967; Tang 1985, 21–69; Mou 1990, 1:1–4).

4. I think therefore LU Lianzhang 蘆連章 is wrong to think that for the Chengs, while *li* is primary, other categories such as *tian, xing* (nature), *xin* (heart-mind), and *ming* (destinity) are secondary (see Lu 2001, 116). In contrast, I believe Mou is fundamentally right in pointing out that "the substance, the principle, and the function refer to the heavenly creativity . . . and so change, *dao*, and divinity are all different names for the *tian dao* 天道 (heavenly dao) itself" (Mou 1990, 2:23).

5. There are many other passages making a similar point: CHENG Yi claims that "there is only one *li* under heaven. While there are different roads, the destination is the same; while there are different ways of thinking, their goal is the same. While

things are all different and change constantly, none of them can be against the one [*li*]" (*Zhouyi Chengshi Zhuan* 3; 858); "nature is *li* and *li* is the same from Yao and Shun to common people" (*Yishu* 18; 204); and again, "although things are different, their *li* is the same. Thus, while the world is great, and beings are diverse, spread with many distinctions, the sages can unify them" (*Zhouyi Chengshi Zhuan* 3; 889).

6. Thus I believe QIAN Mu 錢穆 was wrong to claim that there is only *wu li* 物 理 (*li* of things), but no *ren li* 人理 (*li* of humans) in neo-Confucianism (Qian 2001, 228). In Qian's distinction between classical Confucianism of Confucius and Mencius and neo-Confucianism of CHENG Yi and ZHU Xi, classical Confucians talked about the *dao* of heaven and of human, but not *dao* of things; while neo-Confucians talked about the *li* of heaven and of things, but not specific *li* of humans.

7. I think Mou's interpretation is wrong. Cheng states that "a human being's being given birth to (*sheng* 生) by man and woman is no different from the ten thousand things' being given birth to by heaven and earth. There is no difference between the two" (*Yishu* 18; 223). This shows that humans and the ten thousand things are the same in terms of their *sheng*. Is *sheng*, then, to be regarded as ontological or natural? We will see the problem with Mou's interpretation more clearly when we discuss the Chengs' characterization of *li* as life-giving activity (*sheng*) in the next section.

8. Although it is primarily CHENG Yi who develops the idea of one *li* with different manifestations, CHENG Hao also agrees: "In the beginning, the *Doctrine of Mean* talks about one *li*; then it spreads into the ten thousand different appearances; at the end they all unified into one *li* again" (*Yishu* 14; 140).

9. ZHU Xi provides an interesting answer to our question using the concept of application: "The ten thousand things all have their own *li*, and all *li* come from one source. However, because of its different locations, its applications are also different. For example, one ought to be *ren* in being a king, to be reverent in being a minister, to be filial in being a son, and to be affectionate in being a father. Everything is the same in its *li* but is different in the applications of *li*" (Zhu 1997, 356).

10. HON Tze-ki points out that "CHENG Hao saw no ontological difference between the 'one' and the 'many.' As a general principle of transformation, the *li* of the one remains empty until it is particularized in unique instances of self-transformation, the *li* of many. Conversely, the *li* of the many would, in essence, be particular manifestations of the *li* of the one" (Hon 2003, 40). Hon's use of "*li* of the one" and "*li* of the many" is misleading, as it still suggests the universal *li* belongs to one which is over and above the ten thousand things that have the *li* of many. If he uses "one *li*" and "many *li*," the above passage will make much better sense. Thus, HUANG Siu-Chi's view on this issue seems to be more acceptable: "This one-in-many ontological view held by CHENG Hao may be referred to as a monistic-pluralistic position, since the one universal Principle is inherent in all principles of actual things, which in turn may be understood through the Principle of Heaven" (Huang 1999, 88–89).

11. Carsun Chang, for example, claims that *dao* in neo-Confucianism is "what Plato calls the region of purity and eternity and immortality and unchangeableness"

(Chang 1963, 47). Fung also argues that *li*, particularly as pronounced by CHENG Yi, is "somewhat similar to the 'idea' or 'form' of the ancient Greeks," in the sense that *li* was considered "independently subsisting apart from actual things" (Fung 1953, 507).

12. LI Rizhang 李日章 also thinks that the Chengs should have argued that *li* as noumenon can manifest itself in things. However, "noumenon is something eternal. It may and may not manifest itself in things. When it does manifest itself, there will be the ten thousand things; but when it does not, although there are no things, it itself still exists" (Li 1986, 66).

13. As the Chengs have identified *li* with nature, it is also claimed that "it is incomplete to talk about nature without talking about the vital force; and it is not clear to talk about the vital force without talking about nature" (*Yishu* 6; 81). This also shows the inseparability between the vital force and nature, which is equivalent to *li*.

14. Because CHENG Hao once says that "*qi* is *dao*, and *dao* is *qi*" (*Yishu* 1; 4), FENG Youlan argues that CHENG Hao does not make any distinction between the two (Feng 1988, 107). This is a misunderstanding. From the context it is clear that CHENG Hao uses "is" not in the sense of "identity" but "inseparability": immediately before this statement, he also quotes from the *Book of Changes* that "The metaphysical is *dao* and the physical is *qi*" and adds that "it is important to say it so clearly" (*Yishu* 1; 4). If he really thinks that there is no distinction between *dao* and *qi*, he would have no objection to ZHANG Zai, who sees *qi* (vital force) as the heaven-*dao*. In his view, ZHANG Zai is wrong in "talking about *qi* (instrument) and not *dao* as the metaphysical" (118). So I agree with Carsun Chang that "CHENG Hao is as strict as CHENG Yi in maintaining a distinction between *dao* and *qi*" (Chang 1963, 193).

15. Later, ZHU Xi does develop a view similar to Plato's: "Before there are heaven and earth, there is already *li*. Only because there is *li* are there heaven and earth; if there is no *li*, there will be no heaven and earth, and there will be no humans and things" (Zhu 1997, 1).

16. Here it is also necessary to mention the usual distinction between the Chengs and ZHANG Zai. It has often been claimed that for Zhang, it is *qi* that produces *li*, while in the Chengs it is *li* that produces *qi*. As a matter of fact, neither Zhang nor the Chengs believe that the two, *li* and *qi*, can be separated for even a moment. The difference is only that, for Zhang, *qi* is ontologically prior to *li*, while the Chengs held the opposite view. In this sense, I do not agree with Hon's following distinction between *li* and *qi*: "While *li* is structured and orderly, *qi* is dynamic and creative. While *li* provides the universe with a system of operation, *qi* sets the universe in motion, propelled by the duality of *yin* and *yang*. To move unceasingly, the universe requires both the structure of *li* and the dynamism of *qi*" (Hon 2003, 44). The real distinction between the *qi* and *li*, as I shall argue, is that, while *qi* acts, *li* is this action of *qi*. The real distinction between Zhang and the Chengs is that for Zhang *qi* is primary because *li* as action belongs to the substance *qi*, while for the Chengs, *li* is primary, because *li* is precisely the existence of *qi*, so without *li*, *qi* will lack its existence and become nothing.

17. For example, LU Lianzhang 蘆連章 argues that this shows that for Cheng

qi is given birth to by *li* (Lu 2001, 137); CAI Fanglu 蔡方鹿 also argues that "on the relationship between *li* and things, Cheng believes that there first exists *li* and then there exist things" (Cai 1996, 69–79).

18. PANG Wanli 龐萬里 has also made this point: CHENG Yi believes that *li* and *qi* "cannot exist independent from each other. When there is one there must be the other. Therefore, the order of *li*, *qi*, and image is made in terms of their importance, and it is not a temporal order" (Pang 1992, 95).

19. This point is made even clearer when *li* as activity is put in contrast with *qi* as object or instrument in ZHU Xi: "[T]his chair is an object, and that it can be sat in is its *li*; the human body is an object, and that it speaks and moves is its *li*" (Zhu 1997, 1768).

20. This almost anticipated what Heidegger has to say many hundreds years later: Beings have Being and yet Being of beings does not have Being. For this reason, he argues that there is an ontological difference between Being and beings: Being is ontological (metaphysical), while beings are ontic (physical). It is for the same reason that, for the Chengs, *li* as activity is metaphysical, while *qi* as things is physical.

21. CHENG Chung-ying also takes "the notion of *sheng* as the most unique concept, deeply ingrained in Chinese philosophy—one may even suggest that the whole history of Chinese philosophy is a development of the philosophy of *sheng*. The notion of *sheng* comes from observations such as how plants grow from seeds to full forms, how animals produce their young, how human parents give birth to offspring. By extending the experience of *sheng*, one also sees how the universe, or heaven and earth, could rise from a state of seed to a universe teeming with multitudes of things. It is a process of germination, nurturing, and expansion, and then regeneration in terms of cycles of life or circulation of energy" (Cheng 2002, 106). Cheng even argues that the idea of *sheng* is a central idea in Confucius's *Analects*. Among sixteen appearances of the word *sheng* in the *Analects*, Cheng provides some detailed analysis of seven that he believes have ontological meaning of creativity or life-giving activity. Cheng's discussion is interesting, although I am not convinced that the word *sheng* is indeed used in its ontological sense in the *Analects* (see Cheng 1992, 856–62).

22. Chengs also use life-giving activity to explain death: "The event of death is nothing but *sheng*, as there is no other *li*" (*Yishu* 2a; 17); and "end (*xi* 息) should be interpreted as *sheng*, as end is nothing but *sheng*. A thing is given birth to as soon as another comes to end. There is no gap between the two" (*Yishu* 11; 133).

23. CHENG Chung-ying translates these double Chinese characters *sheng sheng* as "creative creativity" (see Cheng 1997, §7), but the meaning of such a translation is not clear. Is there any creativity that is not creative? In my understanding, the double use of the same Chinese character means that it is not a once and for all activity but an ongoing and unceasing one. So I translate it as "unceasing life-giving activity."

24. TANG Junyi 唐君毅 also clearly perceives this difference. In his view, unlike Gaozi, *xing* in the Chengs refers to the life-giving activity. For example, "the *xing* of an egg is not its being round and white but its giving birth to chick; the *xing* of an infant is not its being short, little, and ignorant, but its being able to grow up into a

child and adult; the *xing* of fire is not its red color but its being able to make other things warm" (Tang 1966, 722).

25. While this is indeed a creative interpretation, it is perhaps not an entirely arbitrary one, especially in light of CHENG Chung-ying's view. Cheng perceptively notes "the morphological formation of the term *xing*—which semantically combines life-production and heart" (Cheng 2000, 46). However, Cheng holds a popular view that *xing* is something that has the life-giving activity, and thus he states that "*xing* gives rise to life" (Cheng 1997, §7). However, in my view, *xing* does not give rise to life; *xing* is the life-giving activity.

26. It is thus wrong for LU Lianzhang to claim that the *xing* in CHENG Hao's interpretation of the claim by Gaozi is also nature as embodiment (Lu 2001, 116).

27. Mou's view has not only been generally accepted by scholars in Taiwan, many of whom are Mou's students; it has also become popular among scholars in mainland China. For example, PANG Wanli also argues that the two brothers have different understandings of *li*: while CHENG Hao understands it from the perspective of change and movement, CHENG Yi understands it from the perspective of the static structure of things. Pang also cites ZHANG Dainian, among others, to support this interpretation (Pang 1992, 59).

28. It is also important to note that, for this reason, CHENG Yi emphasizes that "things (*wu*) are events (*shi*). If one grasps the *li* from events, then there will be nothing not understandable" (*Yishu* 15; 143). The fact that he regards things as events indicates clearly that he regards things as dynamic, and the fact that he understands *li* from the dynamic aspect of things indicates clearly that *li* for him is the dynamism of things. It is for this reason that he says, as we have seen, that "Confucians since ancient time have all seen the heart/mind of heaven and earth as still (*jing*); only I myself see it as moving."

29. Commenting on this passage, PANG Wanli perceptively states that what CHENG Yi means here "is not that *li* itself can change. As constant *dao*, *li* is changeless. What is meant is that it is a constant law that things given birth to by heaven and earth always change" (Pang 1992, 75).

30. Here I only use Graham's analogy and use it in my own way. The conclusion I draw from the analogy is very different from Graham's. Graham actually arrives at an interpretation of the neo-Confucian idea of life-giving activity (*sheng*) that is not very far from the Christian idea of creation, despite his own claim otherwise. For example, he argues that "the Song philosophers do not conceive the origin of things as 'creation' by Someone standing outside the universe, but as 'breeding' 'growth' (*sheng*) from Something at the root of the universe. . . . It is precisely because the production and growth of things is not explained by preceding physical causes that it is necessary for them to postulate an unseen source out of which things are continually manifesting themselves" (Graham 1992, 108–09). Here, Graham assumes that for the Chengs, the ten thousand things are originating from "Something at the root of the universe," an "unseen source." This "something unseen," as I shall argue, simply does not exist for

the Chengs. For them everything can be seen, and what cannot be seen is the life-giving activity, which is *li*, an activity that is not a thing.

31. In this sense, it is obviously wrong for PANG Wanli to claim that CHENG Hao's *li* is a spiritual substance, resembling Hegel's absolute spirit (Pang 1992, 67).

32. CHENG Chung-ying concurs: "Because of the development of systematic metaphysics in Neo-Confucianism, there is clearly little personalism in the Neo-Confucian consciousness of the ultimate and the total. . . . The introduction of *li* is clearly premised on the reflection that anything in the nature of things can be fitted into a rationally explicit system of understanding; nature is to be understood rather than merely experienced, or, in other words, what is to be experienced must be understood as a matter of the intelligent and perceptive mind" (Cheng 1991, 460–61).

33. ZHU Xi later further develops such an interpretation: "[I]n relation to *qi, shen* is nothing but *qi*, but it is the finest *qi*" (Zhu 1997, 27). Again, "the reason I regard *shen* as physical (*xing er xia*) is that it is after all nothing but *qi* that is particularly glorious" (Zhu 1997, 2176).

34. Here, CHENG Hao refers to change as *ti* 體 (normally translated as substance) of heaven, while he refers to *shen* as *yong* 用 (usually translated as function) of heaven. However, from the context it is clear that he does not see the relationship between change and *shen* as one between substance and function. Both, together with other terms mentioned in this passage, are simply different ways to refer to the ultimate reality. This is the reason I translate these two terms in a different way here.

35. Here it is important to realize that *shen* is nothing but this mysterious wonderfulness and unpredictability. MENG Peiyuan argues that the mysterious wonderfulness and unpredictability are attributes of *shen*. Such an understanding again reifies the ultimate reality (Meng 1989, 106), as it sees *shen* as some *thing* that is mysterious.

36. In this sense, I think ZHANG Delin is wrong to think that CHENG Hao here is using sophistry (*guibian* 詭辯) to describe the metaphysical divinity (see Zhang 2000a, 65).

37. Kaufman also explains this serendipitous creativity with the example of conversation: "A conversation . . . is not simply an interchange of discrete 'acts,' in which each agent is attempting to realize a particular goal. Though in each remark the speaker is attempting to say something that is fitting at that moment, what happens in conversation cannot be understood simply as the summing up of all these individual actions. Often the interchange comes to have a 'life of its own' (as we say), and it may well go in directions no one had anticipated and lead to new insights and ideas which none of the participants had thought of before" (Kaufman 1993, 275).

38. Moreover, Kaufman believes that such a reified conception of God is politically dangerous, as it "can easily become, for example, a notion of an essentially authoritarian tyrant, one who is arbitrary and unjust in the exercise of omnipotence" (Kaufman 1993, 270); it is metaphysically unintelligible, as "the world-picture generated in connection with it is fundamentally dualistic and is thus difficult to reconcile with major strands of contemporary thinking" (Kaufman 1993, 271); and it is theologically naïve, as "this model

presupposes that selfhood or agency can be conceived as freestanding, as metaphysically self-subsistent and self-explanatory; but everything we know today about persons suggests that they could neither come into being, nor continue to exist, independently of long and complex cosmic, biological, and historical processes" (Kaufman 1993, 271).

39. Robert Neville, an influential Christian theologian who is seasoned in the Confucian tradition, also calls Christians to abandon the view that "God is a being apart from the world"; instead of a creator, the Christian God should be understood as the act of creativity. In his view, "the act depends on nothing and the world depends on the act. The world has no separate being from the act, although the ontologically creative act is not itself another thing within the world. Its nature is part of the created world, but its creativity is not. In the West, the ontological creative act is called God" (Neville 2007, 127).

40. Tu Weiming, one of the most distinguished contemporary Confucians, in a dialogue with Kaufman and Neville, also asserts that their reconstruction of Christian theology is consistent with Confucian theology. Tu dereifies heaven and regards it as creativity itself: "Heaven as a life-generating creativity may have been present all along" (Tu 2007, 116); "Heaven is creativity in itself and human beings learn to be creative through self-effort" (Tu 2007, 118); and "there is an explicit way that the Confucians understand Heaven as creativity in itself" (Tu 2007., 123).

41. The moral nature of the ultimate reality also echoes in Kaufman's theology. In his view, God as serendipitous creativity is indeed a mystery for us, but we can still recognize its directionality: "[T]here is the fact that the movement in and through time, as we trace it through the long history of the universe and particularly through the evolution of life on earth, seems to be irreversible and in this respect unidirectional. That is, although many whirls and eddies and detours appear in the cosmic and evolutionary development, and many cycles of night and day, of seasonal changes, and of birth, growth, and decay are to be found here on earth, there seems to be through all of this an essentially continuous movement onward toward new forms, toward unprecedented developments," which "involve the appearance of new evolutionary lines" (Kaufman 1993, 282).

42. In Huang 2007a, I compared and contrasted the Chengs' neo-Confucian theology with both classical Confucian theology and contemporary Confucian theology.

Chapter 7: Classics (*Jing* 經):
Hermeneutics as a Practical Learning

1. Heidegger explains the relationship in this way: "[W]ith regard to its subject-matter, phenomenology is the science of the Being of entities—ontology. In explaining the tasks of ontology we found it necessary that there should be a fundamental ontology taking as its theme that entity which is ontologico-ontically distinctive, Dasein, in order to confront the cardinal problem—the question of Being in general. . . . The

phenomenology of Dasein is a *hermeneutic* in the primordial significance of the word, where it designates this business of interpretation" (Heidegger 1962, 61–62).

2. Thus, concluding his essay entitled "Hermeneutics as a Practical Philosophy," Gadamer points out that, "when I speak about hermeneutics here, it is theory. There are no practical situations of understanding that I am trying to resolve by so speaking. Hermeneutics has to do with a theoretical attitude toward the practice of interpretation, the interpretation of texts, but also in relation to the experiences interpreted in them and in our communicatively unfolded orientations in the world" (Gadamer 1981, 112). So what he means by "hermeneutics as a practical philosophy" is that hermeneutics is similar to ethics. It tells us what the right thing to do is, but our knowledge of it is not a guarantee that we will do it.

3. According to ZHOU Yutong 周予同, an authority on the history of Chinese hermeneutics, the word *jing*, translated here as "classics," has nothing to do with classics etymologically. It was used to refer to classics only from the late period of Warring States, with its first appearance in *Xunzi*. As to what and how many are considered to be Confucian classics, there have been variations throughout history, with six in the period of Warring States, five during Emperor Wu Han, seven in *Hou Hanshu* 后漢書, nine in *Jiu Tangshu* 旧唐書, twelve in the reign of Tang Wenzong, thirteen in the Song dynasty, and twenty two in the Qing period (see Zhou 1996, 842–53).

4. In the view of FENG Youlan, "in the history of Chinese philosophy, from Confucius to King Huainan 淮南 is the period of doctrine of the masters (*zixue* 子 學), and from DONG Zhongshu to KANG Youwei is the period of hermeneutics of classics (*jingxue* 經學)" (Feng 1981, 195).

5. As shown in the previous chapter, CHENG Hao used another pun on the word *ren*, the lack of which also means to feel numb (*Yishu* 2a; 15). Why? In CHENG Hao's View, just as the limbs' inability to feel sensation is called lack of *ren*, so a human's inability to feel the principle is also the lack of *ren* (see *Yishu* 2a; 33). In the sense that to be numb is lack of life, CHENG Hao actually is making the same point as his brother.

6. The main distinction here, according to Heidegger, is that while "ontical" refers to a particular being, "ontological" refers to the Being (the activity of "to be") of beings. A particular being has Being, but the Being is not a particular being. Given that human being is one of many particular beings, any conception specific to human beings can also be considered as an ontical conception. Of course, Heidegger realizes that human being is a very unique being (*sein*), and he calls it *Dasein*, in the sense that human being, while also a particular being, is the very being toward Being in the sense that only humans can ask the question of the meaning of Being. In this case, an understanding of human being is fundamental to ontology, but it itself is still not the ontology proper, which is about Being itself (see Heidegger 1962, 33–35).

7. A question might arise here: In what sense can we say the life-giving activity is also the mind, nature, principle, and *dao* of nonliving beings? To this, CHENG Yi provides an explanation in his *Commentary on the Book of Change*, "no principles under heaven can last forever without activity. With activity, a thing will begin again when it

ends, and can therefore last forever without limit. Nothing given life to by heaven and earth, even as solid and dense as huge mountains, can remain unchanged. Thus being long lasting does not mean being in a fixed and definite state. Being fixed and definite, a thing cannot last long. The constant *dao* is to change according to circumstances" (*Zhouyi Chengshi Zhuan* 3; 862).

8. Commenting on this aspect of CHENG Yi, Wing-tsit Chan perceptively points out that such an ontological understanding "brought the concept of *ren* to the highest stage up to his time" and represents his unique contribution (Chan 1963, 560).

9. CHENG Hao has the same view: "The great origin of *dao* is in classics. Classics are *dao*. The secret of the heaven and the earth these classics discovered and the mind of sages these classics described are all the same" (*Wenji* 2; 463).

10. As I argue in the previous chapter, CHENG Yi, together with his brother, is instrumental in developing the doctrine of principle as the official Song-Ming Confucianism. But as we can see here, for CHENG Yi, the doctrine of principle is inseparable from the hermeneutics of classics. This is indeed the prefiguring of the claim made by GU Yanwu 顧炎武 during the Qing dynasty that the doctrine of principle is nothing but hermeneutics of classics.

11. CHENG Yi makes a distinction here between ancient learners of *dao* and contemporary learners of *dao*. In his view, while the former can begin with classics to understand the fundamental principle, the latter must start from some understanding of the principle to study classics, as ancient people know more about sages who wrote these classics (*Yishu* 15; 164–65).

12. It should be noted that when he talks about history in these two passages, CHENG Yi primarily refers to the *Spring and Autumn Annals*, which itself is a Confucian classic. However, his view is still applicable to history in general. This is not only because the *Spring and Autumn Annals* is also a history, but because, at the same time he claims that classics are carriers of the *dao* of sages, he makes it clear that the *Spring and Autumn Annals* has its function. This of course does not mean that CHENG Yi is trying to downgrade this text; nor does it imply that this text is the same as any other texts of history.

13. In this sense, CHENG Yi holds a similar view to Aristotle's conception of virtues. A person can become a virtuous person by doing virtuous things, although a person who does virtuous things is not necessarily a virtuous person. In order to become virtuous, "the agent also must be in a certain condition when he does them; in the first place he must have knowledge, secondly he must choose the acts, and choose them for their own sakes, and thirdly his action must proceed from a firm and unchangeable character" (Aristotle 1915, 1105a30–35).

14. This analogy, as almost any analogy, has its limits. While the capital cannot be found outside Chang'an, *dao* can also be found outside oneself. CHENG Yi's point here is only that, since *dao* is also within you, it is more appropriate for us to search for it from within. This line of thinking of course is even more congenial to his brother CHENG Hao. In his treatise on *ren*, CHENG Hao emphasizes Mencius's view "that all things

are already complete in myself. One must examine oneself and be sincere (or absolutely real), and only then will there be great joy" (*Yishu* 11; 129). In his reply to his uncle ZHANG Zai, he also mentions that "the ancients considered it wrong to seek afar when the truth lies nearby" (*Wenji* 2; 461).

15. CAI Fanglu interprets CHENG Yi here as saying that "returning to oneself, one will be able to obtain the inherent knowledge" (Cai 1996, 111). Thus, Cai believes that CHENG Yi holds a theory of innate knowledge. What is crucial here, however, is that CHENG Yi is talking about what is to be known, the object of knowledge, *dao*, not our knowledge of it. This distinction between the object of knowledge and the knowledge of the object perhaps can also answer the question A. C. Graham has with CHENG Yi's statement that the mind is principle, although one may have not obtained the principle. In Graham's view this is self-contradictory (Graham 1992, 67). However, we should realize that, in CHENG Yi's statement, the first "principle" refers to the object of knowledge, while the second refers to knowledge of the object. Although the object is at the same time the subject (the mind reflecting upon itself), it is not contradictory at all if the subject does not know the object, that is, if the subject does not know itself.

16. In relation to that, Jean-Paul Sartre seems to agree with CHENG Yi when he argues that "to choose to be this or that is to affirm at the same time the value of what we choose, because we can never choose evil. We always choose the good, and nothing can be good for us without being good for all" (Sartre 1947, 20). In other words, when we decide to do something, we will always decide to do what we think are good things. Thus, if the thing we have done is wrong, our knowledge must be wrong too.

17. In this respect, another prominent Confucian scholar, Wing-tsit Chan, seems to concur when he comments that Cheng's statement "bears a striking resemblance to the Buddhist twofold formula of meditation and wisdom" (Chan 1963, 562). WEN Weiyao has a more balanced view but also thinks that intellectual knowledge "provides only the opportunity to elevate moral life, but is not necessarily the effort to realize this elevation" (Wen 1996, 159). I believe CHEN Lai comes closer to the truth when he states that, in CHENG Yi, "investigation of things is also a method of spiritual cultivation" (Chen 1991, 113).

18. This is also the view shared by CAI Fanglu (see Cai 1996, 114) and PANG Wanli (see Pang 1992, 170). The main problem with their view is that they have isolated some of CHENG Yi's statements arguing that "only after one knows can one practice" (*Yishu* 18; 187) from his other statements maintaining that knowledge can be obtained by handling human affairs. These apparently contradictory statements can be properly understood only if we realize that CHENG Yi refers here to the hermeneutic circle between knowing and doing, as I will discuss in my conclusion.

19. PAN Fu'en, for example, argues for this view: "If to understand the principle one has to investigate everything and have a broad knowledge, then one cannot say that all roads will lead to the country; similarly, if one only needs to have knowledge of the principle of one blade of grass or tree and then extend it to everything else, then it is superfluous to have a broad knowledge" (Pan 1996, 109).

20. Failure to see this distinction between the ideal situation and the actual situation also leads Peter Bol to think that CHENG Yi's understanding of *dao* is some immediate perception, perhaps like the Buddhist sudden enlightenment (see Bol 1992, 320–21). This view is echoed by Graham, who relates CHENG Yi's view to the Zen Satori (see Graham 1992, 78).

21. Although CHENG Yi uses *"jiao xiang yang ye,"* here translated as "mutual support," to explain the relationship between inner and external methods—to reflect upon one's own mind and investigate external things (see *Yishu* 2a; 34)—I believe this can generally apply to the relationships among all these different ways he mentioned.

22. A. C. Graham states that while CHENG Hao is more interested in examining one's own mind, CHENG Yi is more interested in investigating external things. This statement, in my view, should be modified to mean that CHENG Yi is more interested in investigating external things than CHENG Hao (not "than examining one's self"). But Graham is right to point out that "the two points of view are of course not incompatible" (Graham 1992, 75).

Appendix: Neo-Confucian Hermeneutics at Work: CHENG Yi's Philosophical Interpretation of *Analects* 8.9 and 17.3

1. A sample of representative English translations of this passage is as follows: "The Common people can be made to follow a path but not to understand it" (Lau 1979); "You can make the people follow the Way, but you can't make them understand it" (Hinton 1998); "The common people can be induced to travel along the way, but they cannot be induced to realize (*zhi* 知) it" (Ames and Rosemont 1998); "People can be made to sprout (produce, act, follow), they cannot be commissioned to know" (Pound 1956); "The common people can be made to follow it [the way]; they cannot be made to understand it" (Waley 1971); "The common people can be made to follow it, but they cannot be made to understand it" (Slingerland 2003); "The people may be made to follow a path of action, but they may not be made to understand it" (Legge 1971).

2. Here are some representative English translations of this passage: "It is only the most intelligent and the most stupid who are not susceptible to change" (Lau 1979); "Those of the loftiest wisdom and those of the basest ignorance: they alone never change" (Hinton 1998); "Only the most wise (*zhi* 知) and the most stupid do not move" (Ames and Rosemont 1998); "Only those of highest intelligence, and lowest simplicity do not shift" (Pound 1956); "It is only the very wisest and the very stupidest who cannot change" (Waley 1971); "Only the very wise and the very stupid do not change" (Slingerland 2003); "There are only the wise of the highest class, and the stupid of the lowest class, who cannot be changed" (Legge 1971).

3. See the interpretation in Qing dynasty scholar SHI You's 史佑 *Jingyi Zaji* 經義雜記 (Miscellaneous Notes on the Meanings of Classics), in Cheng 1990, 531.

4. See the comments by the Qing scholar Liu Baonan 劉寶南 (1791–1855) in his *Lunyu Zhengyi* 論語正義 (Correct Meanings of the *Analects*), in Cheng 1990, 532.

5. In one of the bamboo strips excavated at Guodian 郭店, *Respecting Virtue and Rightness* 尊德義—which some scholars speculate may have been written around Confucius's time—there is a related statement: "People may not be deluded" (strip no. 31, in Jingmen 1998, 174).

6. This, of course, does not mean that we absolutely cannot accept this interpretation, as Confucius or the *Analects* may indeed contradict itself. However, unless we cannot find a more plausible interpretation, as John B. Henderson points out, we should stick to the common commentarial assumption that classics are coherent. See Henderson 1991, 106.

7. Guo Moruo 郭沫若 (1897–1978) also thinks that, if we interpret *bu ke* as "not permitted to," then in this passage Confucius must be advocating a policy of keeping people in ignorance, but this is obviously incompatible with Confucius's persistent urge to teach people. Accordingly, Confucius should be understood as actually referring to the fact that people cannot be made to know it (see Guo 1996, 100).

8. Hou Wailu 侯外廬 (1930–1987) argues that this *Analects* passage shows that, for Confucius, common people do not have the capacity to have such knowledge (see Hou, et al. 1995, 1.169–170). Tu Weiming also does not think that Confucianism, like Daoism and Legalism, advocates a policy of keeping people in ignorance. Commenting on *Analects* 8.9, Tu claims that this "is primarily a lamentation and is not a basic Confucian policy" (Tu 2002b, 1.277).

9. Commenting on this passage, Wing-tsit Chan says, "Confucius was the first to pronounce this principle in Chinese history. Among his pupils there were commoners as well as nobles, and stupid people as well as intelligent ones" (Chan 1963, 44). I discussed this aspect of Confucius's teaching in Huang 2011b and 2013, chapter 4.

10. According to Cai Shangsi, although *Analects* 15.39 indeed claims that education should be provided for all without distinctions, this is something that Confucius did not follow. In addition to the limit he set on access to education in terms of property, Cai also claims that Confucius set a limit in terms of class, as Confucius said that "common people can be made to follow the way but cannot be made to understand it," and a limit in terms of sect, as he asked people "not to get along with those who follow different ways" (*Analects* 15.40). Thus, "although in appearance Confucius talks about education for all without any discrimination, in reality there is still discrimination" (Cai 1982, 193–94).

11. Cheng Yi also tells us that "in ancient times people started elementary learning (*xiaoxue* 小學) at the age of eight and great learning at the age of fifteen" (*Yishu* 15; 166). It is true that Cheng Yi himself does not follow this interpretation; commenting on this passage in his *Interpretation of the* Analects 論語解, he simply says that Confucius never refused to teach anyone who came with *li* (*yi li lai zhe* 以禮來者) (Jingshuo 6; 1144). It is not clear whether he means a gift or propriety by the word *li*

禮. It is worth noting, however, that CHEN Daqi 陳大齊 mentions the interpretation of *shu xiu* as a type of propriety: self-discipline (see Chen 1984, 280). This interpretation is also consistent with *Analects* 15.39.

12. Thus CHENG Yi states: "Common people are permitted to be enlightened but not to be made stupid, to be taught but not intimidated; to be followed but not forced; to be made to do things but not cheated" (*Yishu* 25; 319).

13. Along the same line, CHEN Daqi argues that, in order to make people do anything, it is also necessary for them to have some knowledge, the knowledge of how to do it. This is knowledge of what ZHU Xi means by *dangran*. They do not, however, need to have knowledge of why. This is knowledge of what ZHU Xi means by *suoyiran*. Common people have very limited intellectual abilities, so they can know the former but not the latter (see Chen 1996, 154).

14. In *Analects* 4.1 Confucius also says, "Of neighborhoods, humaneness (*ren*) is the most beautiful. How can a person be considered wise who, when having choices, does not settle in humaneness?"

15. Hall and Ames's translation of *zhi* 知 as "realize" has caught this sense of knowledge, as "to realize the *tao* [*dao*] is to experience, to interpret, and to influence the world in such a way as to reinforce, and where appropriate extend, a way of life established by one's cultural precursors" (Hall and Ames 1987, 227).

16. In developing his idea of getting it from oneself, CHENG Yi was also inspired by *Analects* 6.27: " 'Superior persons are broadly versed in learning and regulated by rules of propriety. Thus they will not overstep what is right.' This shows that they have not got it from themselves" (*Yishu* 6; 95). The passage is not attributed specifically to CHENG Yi. It is difficult to determine to whom it should be attributed because the idea of *zide* was advocated by both brothers. CHENG Hao, for example, also stated that "what is crucial in learning is getting it by oneself. . . . Therefore Confucius says that 'when I have pointed out one corner of a square to anyone and he does not come back with the other three, I will not point it out to him a second time'" (*Yishu* 11; 122). In CHENG Hao's view, only by interpreting this *Analects* passage in this way can it be made consistent with Confucius's self-description: "To teach without growing weary" (*Analects* 7.2, 7.34).

17. The passage is not attributed specifically to CHENG Yi. It is, however, consistent with other passages in which CHENG Yi talks about *zide*.

18. After discussing the same paragraph from the *Mencius*, Tu Wei-ming correctly points out that "while it is perfectly understandable that a respectable person may not be aware of the unrealizable potential in his nature, such as scientific, and artistic talents, it is inconceivable, in the Mencian sense, that a mature member of our society can be ignorant of his gems and, therefore, not be responsible for his acts as a moral agent" (Tu 1983, 222–23).

19. In order to make this three-grade theory of "Confucius" consistent with Mencius's theory of human nature as good, GU Tinglin 顧亭林 (1613–1682) argues that,

just as the nature of water is cold and yet there are still warm springs, so it is normal for heaven to give birth to people in the middle, and it is atypical to have wise people above and stupid people below. Mencius talks about normal people, while Confucius (in 17.3) talks about the atypical (in Cheng 1990, 1186).

20. The precise distinction between Mencus and Xunzi in their view of human nature is much more complicated than what this common generalization indicates (see Huang 2013b, 23–29).

21. On *Analects* 5.13, Tang Junyi 唐君毅 (1909–1978) argues that Confucius's view about the ways of heaven and human nature were rarely heard because before Confucius, the ways of heaven and human nature were considered to be in opposition, whereas Confucius did not regard them to be so. So Zigong is merely saying that Confucius rarely contrasted these two concepts, rather than that he hardly ever talked about them (Tang 1991, 32).

22. Tang Junyi also argues that Confucius holds the view that human nature is good: "Confucius says that humans are born with uprightness [*Analects* 6.19], that humaneness (*ren*) is here whenever I desire it [*Analects* 7.30], that a humane person can feel at home in humanness [*Analects* 4.2]. . . . So it is appropriate to think that he regards the human heart/mind as the place where good human nature resides. His claim that humans are relatively similar by nature is no different from Mencius's claims that 'things of the same kind are relatively similar' and that 'sages and I are of the same kind' (*Mencius*). They all mean that human nature is good" (Tang 1991, 31).

23. This passage is not specifically attributed to Cheng Yi, but it is consistent with other passages on *zibao* and *ziqi* that are attributed to him.

24. Pang Wanli also claims that "the two Chengs implicitly disagree with Confucius's claim that 'only the wise above and the stupid below do not change'" (Pang 1992, 147).

25. He also states that "while time is something that sages cannot go against, sages can certainly show us the way to change from ignorance to wisdom and from disorder to order" (*Yishu* 11; 122). Pan Fu'en 潘富恩 and Xu Yuqing 徐余慶 state that "Cheng Yi's 'principle of changeability' about the wise above and the stupid below refers to a one way change: the change of the stupid below to the wise above. In no time and under no condition will the wise above be changed to the stupid below" (Pan and Xu 1988, 356). This is understandable. On the one hand, if people are wise, they know that they cannot stop learning, and if so, they will not become stupid. On the other hand, if people stop learning, then they cannot be regarded as the wise above in the first place.

26. This passage is not specifically attributed to Cheng Yi. It is consistent with the view he clearly expressed in other passages. A similar passage is found at *Cuiyan* 1; 1188: "Wang Yanlin says: 'People can become good only because they have the sincere heart/mind to be so. It is only by being so that they can get it themselves. If they do not have the will, the good cannot be imposed upon them.' The master said: 'No. If we leave people alone and do not care about their unwillingness to become good, then

there are many people below the middle level who will give up on themselves and lack confidence. This is why sages emphasize education.'"

27. This passage is not specifically attributed to CHENG Yi. Some scholars attribute it to CHENG Hao.

28. Although this passage is not specifically attributed to CHENG Yi, a very similar passage is found in his commentary on the *Book of Changes* (*Zhouyi Chengshi Zhuan* 2; 831).

29. Lionard Shihlien Hsü argues that "since this lowest class of the people cannot be changed by learning or the teaching of virtue, such forceful methods as law and punishment must be used to rectify them, or, using the Confucian terminology, to 'bring them to the level of good people' [*Analects* 2.3]. In other words, law and the system of justice are to supplement political education, *li*, and moral discipline, in completing the function of rectification" (See Hsü 1975, 163).

Bibliography

Ackrill, J. L. 1980. "Aristotle on Eudaimonia." In A. O. Rorty, ed., *Essays on Aristotle's Ethics*. Berkeley: University of California Press.

Adams, Robert Merrihew. 1976. "Motive Utilitarianism." *Journal of Philosophy* 73, 467–481.

———. 2006. *A Theory of Virtue: Excellence in Being for the Good*. Oxford: Oxford University Press.

Allinson, Robert. 1990. "The Ethics of Confucianism and Christianity: The Delicate Balance." *Ching Feng* 33.3, 158–175.

American Law Institute. 2000. "The Insanity Defense." In Joel Feinberg and Jules Coleman, eds., *Philosophy of Law*, 6th ed. Belmont, CA: Wadsworth/Thompson Learning.

Ames, Roger T., and Henry Rosemont, Jr., trans. 1998. *The Analects of Confucius: A Philosophical Translation*. New York: Ballantine Books.

Analects. 1980. In *Translation and Annotations of the* Analects 論語譯注. By YANG Bojun 楊伯峻. Beijing 北京: Zhonghua Shuju 中華書局.

Annas, Julia. 1993. *The Morality of Happiness*. Oxford: Oxford University Press.

———. 2006. "Virtue Ethics." In David Copp, ed., *Oxford Handbook of Ethical Theory*. Oxford: Oxford University Press.

Anscombe, Elizabeth. 1958. "Modern Moral Philosophy." *Philosophy* 33, 1–19.

Aquinas, Thomas. 1952. *The Summa Theologica*. In *The Great Books of the Western World*, vols. 19–20. Chicago: University of Chicago Press.

———. 1993. *Commentary on Aristotle's Nicomachean Ethics*. Notre Dame: Dumb Ox Books.

Aristotle. 1915. *Ethica Nicomachea*; *Ethica Eudemia*; and *Magna Moralia*. In W. D. Ross, ed., *The Works of Aristotle*, vol. 9. Oxford: Oxford University Press.

Audi, Robert. 1979. "Weakness of Will and Practical Judgment." *Noûs* 13, 173–196.

———. 1989. "The Separation of Church and State and the Obligations of Citizenship." *Philosophy and Public Affairs* 20, 66–76.

———. 1990. "Weakness of Will and Rational Action." *Australasian Journal of Philosophy* 68, 270–281.

Augustine. 1952. *City of God*. In *Great Books of the Western World*, vol. 18. Chicago, London, and Toronto: Encyclopedia Britannica.

Baker, C. Edwin. 1985. "Sandel on Rawls." *University of Pennsylvania Law Review* 133, 868–928.

Baldwin, Jason. 2004. "Hume's Knave and the Interest of Justice." *Journal of History of Philosophy* 42, 277–296.

Bayles, Michael D. 1973. "The Complexity of 'Why Be Moral?'" *The Personalist* 54, 309–317.

Beck, Lewis White. 1960. *A Commentary on Kant's Critique of Practical Reason*. Chicago: University of Chicago Press.

Beitz, Charles R. 1989. *Political Equality: An Essay in Democratic Theory*. Princeton: Princeton University Press.

Benson, Mark A. 2005. "Conceptions of Self/No-Self and Modes of Connection: Comparative Soteriological Structures in Classical Chinese Thought." *Journal of Religious Ethics* 33, 293–331.

Bernstein, Richard. 1991. "Incommensurability and Otherness Revisited." In Eliot Deutsch, ed., *Culture and Modernity: East-West Philosophical Perspective*. Honolulu: University of Hawaii Press.

Bertram, B. C. R. 1976. "Kin Selection in Lions and in Evolution." In P. P. G. Bateson and R. A. Hinde, eds., *Growing Points in Ethology*. Cambridge: Cambridge University Press.

Bol, Peter. 1992. *This Culture of Ours: Intellectual Transitions in Tang and Sung China*. Stanford: Stanford University Press.

Boxill, Bernard. 1980. "How Injustice Pays." *Philosophy and Public Affairs* 9, 359–371.

Bradley, F. H. 1935. *Ethical Studies*. Oxford: Oxford University.

Broadie, Alexander, and Elizabeth M. Pybus. 1992. "Kant's Treatment of Animals." In Ruth F. Chadwich, ed., *Immanuel Kant: Critical Assessments*, vol. 3, *Kant's Moral and Political Philosophy*. London and New York: Routledge.

Browning, Don. 1992. "Altruism and Christian Love." *Zygon* 27, 421–436.

Bruce, J. P. 1922. *The Philosophy of Human Nature*. London: Methuen.

Buscemi, William 1993. "The Ironic Politics of Richard Rorty." *The Review of Politics* 55, 141–157.

Cai, Fanglu 蔡方鹿. 1996. *CHENG Hao and CHENG Yi and Chinese Culture* 程顥程頤與中國文化. Guiyang 貴陽: Guizhou Renmin Chubanshe 貴州人民出版社.

Cai, Shangsi 蔡尚思. 1982. *Confucius' System of Thought* 孔子思想體系. Shanghai 上海: Shanghai Renmin Chubanshe 上海人民出版社.

Chan, Wing-tsit (CHEN Rongjie). 1963. *A Source Book in Chinese Philosophy*. Ed. and trans. by Wing-tsit Chan. Princeton: Princeton University Press.

———. 1967. "Introduction." In *Reflections on Things at Hand*. Compiled by CHU Hsi and LÜ Tsu-ch'ien. Trans., with notes, by Wing-tsit Chan. New York: Columbia University Press.

Chang, Carsun. 1963. *The Development of Neo-Confucian Thought*, vol. 1. New Haven: College and University Press.

Charlton, William. 1935. *Weakness of Will*. Oxford: Basil Blackwell.

Chen, Daqi 陳大齊. 1970. *Collected Essays on Confucius' Doctrines* 孔子學說論集. Taipei 臺北: Zhengzhong Shuju 正中書局.

———. 1984. *Confucius' Doctrines* 孔子學說. Taipei 臺北: Zhengzhong Shuju 正中書局.

———. 1996. *A Subjective Interpretation of the Analects* 論語臆解. Taipei 臺北: Shangwu Yinshuguan 商務印書館.

Chen, Lai 陳來. 1991. *Song-Ming Neo-Confucianism* 宋明理學. Shenyang: Liaoning Education Press.

Chen, Rongjie (Wing-tsit Chan). 1991. "The Evolution of the Neo-Confucian Concept of *Li* as Principle 新儒學 "理" 之思想之演進." In *Essays on Chinese Philosophical Thoughts: Song and Ming Periods* 中國哲學思想論文集. Taibei 臺北: Shuiniu Chubanshe 水牛出版社.

———. 1996. *The Concept and History of Neo-Confucianism* 宋明理學的概念和歷史. Taipei 臺北: Institute of Chinese Literatures and Philosophy, Academia Sinica 中央研究院文哲研究所.

Chen, Zhongfan 陳鐘凡. 1996. *In Introduction to the Song Thought* 兩宋思想述評. Beijing 北京：Dongfang Chubanshe 東方出版社.

Cheng, Chung-ying. 1991. *New Dimensions of Confucian and Neo-Confucian Philosophy*. Albany: State University of New York Press.

———. "The Principle of Creativity in Confucius' Philosophy: On *Sheng* as *Li* and *Ren* as *Sheng* 孔子哲學中的創造性原則：生即理與仁即生." In *Essays from the Conference on the Occasion of Confucius' 2540th Birthday* 孔子誕辰2540周年紀念學術討論會論文集. Shanghai 上海: Sanlian Shudian 三聯出版社.

———. 1997. "On a Comprehensive Theory of *Xing* (Natuality) in Song-Ming Neo-Confucian Philosophy: A Critical and Integrative Development." *Philosophy East and West* 47, 33–47.

———. 2000. "Confucian Onto-Hermeneutics: Morality and Ontology." *Journal of Chinese Philosophy* 27, 33–68.

———. 2002. "Ultimate Origin, Ultimate Reality, and the Human Condition: Leibniz, Whitehead, and Zhu Xi." *Journal of Chinese Philosophy* 29, 93–119.

Cheng, Hao 程顥, and CHENG Yi 程頤. 2004. *Completed Works of the Two Chengs* 二程集, 2nd ed. Beijing 北京: Zhonghua Shuju 中華書局.

Cheng, Shude 程樹德. 1990. *Collected Commentaries on the Analects* 論語集釋. Beijing 北京: Zhonghua Shuju 中華書局.

Cohen, G. A. 2002. *If You're an Egalitarian, How Come You're So Rich?* Cambridge, MA: Harvard University Press.

Copp, David. 1997. "The Ring of Gyges: Overridingness and the Unity of Reason." *Social Philosophy and Policy* 14, 86–106.

Copp, David, and David Sobel. 2004. "Morality and Virtue: An Assessment of Some Recent Work in Virtue Ethics." *Ethics* 114, 514–554.

Cua, A. S. 2003a. "*Li*: Rites or Propriety." In A. S. Cua, ed., *Encyclopedia of Chinese Philosophy*. New York and London: Routledge.

———. 2003b. "Reason and Principle." In A. S. Cua, ed., *Encyclopedia of Chinese Philosophy*. New York: Routledge.

D'arcy, Martin Cyril. 1945. *The Mind and Heart of Love, Lion, and Unicorn: A Study in Eros and Agape*. London: Farber and Faber.

Dalh, Norman O. 1991. "Plato's Defense of Justice." *Philosophy and Phenomenological Research* 51, 809–834.

Dallmayr, Fred. 2003. "Confucianism and the Public Sphere: Five Relationships plus One?" *Dao: A Journal of Comparative Philosophy* 2, 193–212.

Dancy, Jonathan. 1993. *Moral Reason*. Oxford, UK, and Cambridge, US: Blackwell.

———. 2004. *Ethics without Principles*. Oxford: Oxford University Press.

———. 2009. "Moral Particularism." *The Stanford Encyclopedia of Philosophy* (Spring 2009 Edition). Ed. Edward N. Zalta. URL = <http://plato.stanford.edu/archives/spr2009/entries/moral-particularism/>.

Davidson, Donald. 1969. "How Is Weakness of the Will Possible?" In his *Essays on Actions and Events*. Oxford: Clarendon, 1980.

———. 1982. "Paradoxes of Irrationality." In Richard Wollheim and James Hopkins, eds., *Philosophical Essays on Freud*. Cambridge: Cambridge University Press.

Davis, W. H. 1991. "Why Be Moral?" *Philosophical Inquiry: International Quarterly* 13, 1–21.

Daxue, the. See *The Great Learning* in Chan 1963.

De Bary, Wm. Theodore. 1986. "Human Rites—An Essay on Confucianism and Human Rights." In Irene Eber, ed., *Confucianism: The Dynamics of Tradition*. London: Macmillan.

———. 1991. *Learning for One's Self: Essays on the Individual in Neo-Confucian Thought*. New York: Columbia University Press.

Demos, Raphael. 1964. "A Fallacy in Plato's *Republic?*" *The Philosophical Review* 73, 395–398.

Deng, Keming 鄧克銘. 1993. *The Development of the Concept of Li in Song Dynasty* 宋代理概念之發展. Taipei 臺北: Wenjin Chubanshe 文津出版社.

Donaldson, Thomas. 2008. "Globalization and Its Ethical Significance." In Fritz Allhoff and Anand J. Vaidya, eds., *Business in Ethical Focus: An Anthology*. Buffalo: Broadview.

Dorter, Kenneth. 1997. "Virtue, Knowledge, and Wisdom: Bypassing Self-Control." *Review of Metaphysics* 51, 313–343.

———. 2009. "Metaphysics and Morality in Neo-Confucianism and Greece: ZHU Xi, Plato, Aristotle, and Plotinus." *Dao: A Journal of Comparative Philosophy* 8, 255–276.

Fang, Litian 方立天. 1997. *Knowledge and Action in the History of Chinese Philosophy* 中國哲學史上的知行觀. Beijing 北京: Renmin Chubanshe 人民出版社.

Feng, Richang 馮日昌. 1991. "The Cheng Brothers' View on Investigation of Things and Extension of Knowledge 二程格物致知論." In XIANG Weixin 項維新 and LIU Zengfu 劉增福, eds., *Essays on Chinese Philosophical Thoughts: Song and Ming Periods* 中國哲學思想論集: 宋明篇. Taibei 臺北﹕Shuiniu Chubanshe 水牛出版社.

Feng, Youlan. 1981. *Collected Essays from the Hall of Three Pines* 三宋堂學術文集. Beijing: Beijing University Press.

———. 1995. *A New History of Chinese Philosophy* 新編中國哲學史, vol. 5. Beijing 北京: Renmin Chubanshe 人民出版社.

Fingarette, Herbert. 1972. *Confucius—The Secular as Sacred*. New York: Harper and Row.

Fletcher, Joseph. 1966. *Moral Responsibility: Situation Ethics at Work*. Louisville, KY: Westminster John Knox Press.

Foot, Philippa 2001. *Natural Goodness*. Oxford: Oxford University Press.

Frankfurt, Harry. 2003. *Reasons of Love*. Oxford: Oxford University Press.

Fu, Pei-jung. 2003. "Tian (T'ien): Heaven." In A. S. Cua, ed., *Encyclopedia of Chinese Philosophy*. New York: Routledge.

Fung, Yu-lan (FENG Youlan). 1953. *A History of Chinese Philosophy*, vol. 2. Princeton: Princeton University Press.

Gadamer, Hans-Georg. 1981. *Reason in the Age of Science*. Cambridge: MIT Press.

———. 1993. *Truth and Method*, trans. by Joel Weinsheimer and Donald G. Marshall. New York: Continuum.

Gauthier, David 1982. "Three against Justice: The Foole, the Sensible Knave, and the Lydian Shepherd." In *Midwest Studies in Philosophy* 7. Morris: University of Minnesota Press.

Gerson, Lloyd 1986. "Platonic Dualism." *Monist* 69, 352–369.

Gewirth, Alan. 1978. *Reason and Morality*. Chicago and London: University of Chicago Press.

———. 1980. "The Golden Rule Rationalized." *Midwest Studies in Philosophy* 3, 133–147.

Gosling, J. C. B. 1990. *Weakness of the Will*. London: Routledge.

Graham, A. C. 1992. *Two Chinese Philosophers*. LaSalle: Open Court.

Grandy, Richard. 1973. "Reference, Meaning, and Belief." *Journal of Philosophy* 70.14, 439–452.

Grant, Colin. 1996. "For the Love of God: Agape." *Journal of Religious Ethics* 24, 1–21.

Guo, Moruo 郭沫若. 1996. *Ten Critiques* 十批判書. Beijing 北京: Renmin Chubanshe 人民出版社.

Guthrie, W. K. C. 1975. *A History of Greek Philosophy*, vol. 2. Cambridge: Cambridge University Press.

Hall, David L., and Roger T. Ames. 1987. *Thinking through Confucius*. Albany: State University of New York Press.

Han, Yu. 1963. "An Inquiry on the Way." *Yuan Dao*. In Chan 1963.

Hare, R. M. 1963. *Freedom and Reason*. New York: Oxford University Press.

Harman, Gilbert. 2005. "Moral Particularism and Transduction." *Philosophical Issues* 15, 44–55.

Hegel, G. W. F. 1991. *Elements of Philosophy of Right*. Cambridge: Cambridge University Press.

Heidegger, Martin. 1962. *Being and Time*. New York: Harper and Row.

Henderson, John B. 1991. *Scripture, Canon, and Commentary: A Comparison of Confucian and Western Exegesis*. Princeton: Princeton University Press.

Heyward, Carter. 1989. *Touching Our Strength: The Erotic as Power and Love of God*. New York: Harper and Row.

Hill, Thomas, Jr. 2000. *Respect, Pluralism, and Justice: Kantian Perspective*. Oxford: Oxford University Press.

Hinton, David, trans. 1998. *The Analects*. Washington DC: Counterpoint.

Hobbes, Thomas. 1962. *Leviathan*. Ed. by Michael Oakeshott. New York: Collier Books.

———. 1998. *Leviathan*. Ed. by J. C. A. Gaskin. New York: Oxford University Press.

Höffe, Otfried. 1992. " 'Even a Nation of Devils Needs the State': The Dilemma of Natural Justice." In Howard Lloyd Williams, ed., *Essays on Kant's Political Philosophy*. Chicago: University of Chicago Press.

Hon, Tze-ki. 2003. "CHENG Hao" and "CHENG Yi." In A. S. Cua, ed., *Encyclopedia of Chinese Philosophy*. New York: Routledge.

Hosmer, LaRue Tone. 1994. "Why Be Moral? A Different Rational for Managers." *Business Ethics Quarterly* 4.2, 191–204.

———. 1997. "Why Be Moral?: A Reply to Shaw and Corvino." *Business Ethics Quarterly* 7.4, 137–143.

Hospers, John. 1961. *Human Conduct: An Introduction to the Problems of Ethics*. Ithaca: Cornell University Press.

Hou, Wailu 侯外廬, et. al. 1995. *A General History of Chinese Thought* 中國思想通史, vol. 1. Beijing 北京: Renmin Chubanshe 人民出版社.

———. 1997. *A History of Philosophy of Li from Song to Ming* 宋明理學史, vol. 1. Beijing 北京: Renmin Chubanshe 人民出版社.

House of Lords. 2000. "The M'Naghten Rules." In Joel Feinberg and Jules Coleman, eds., *Philosophy of Law*, 6th ed. Belmont, CA: Wadsworth/Thompson Learning.

Hsu, Fu-kuan. 1986. "CHU Hsi and Cheng Brothers." In Wing-tsit Chan, ed., *CHU Hsi and Neo-Confucianism*. Honolulu: University of Hawaii.

Hsü, Lionard Shihlien. 1975. *The Political Philosophy of Confucianism*. London: Curzon.

Hu, Shi. 1991. *Scholarly Works of Hu Shi: A History of Chinese Philosophy* 胡適學術著作集：中國哲學史, 2 vols. Beijing 北京: Zhonghua Shuju 中華書局.

Huang, Siu-Chi. 1999. *Essentials of neo-Confucianism: Eight Major Philosophers of the Song and Ming Periods*. Westport, CT: Greenwood.

Huang, Yong. 1995. "Religious Pluralism and Interfaith Dialogue." *International Journal for Philosophy of Religion* 37, 127–144.

———. 1996. "The Father of Modern Hermeneutics in a Postmodern Age: A Reinterpretation of Schleiermacher's Hermeneutics." *Philosophy Today* 40.2, 251–262.

———. 2000. "CHENG Yi's Neo-Confucian Hermeneutics of Tao." *Journal of Chinese Philosophy* 27, 69–92.

———. 2001. *Religious Goodness and Political Rightness: Beyond the Liberal-Communitarian Debate*. Harvard Theological Studies 49. Harrisburg: Trinity Press International.

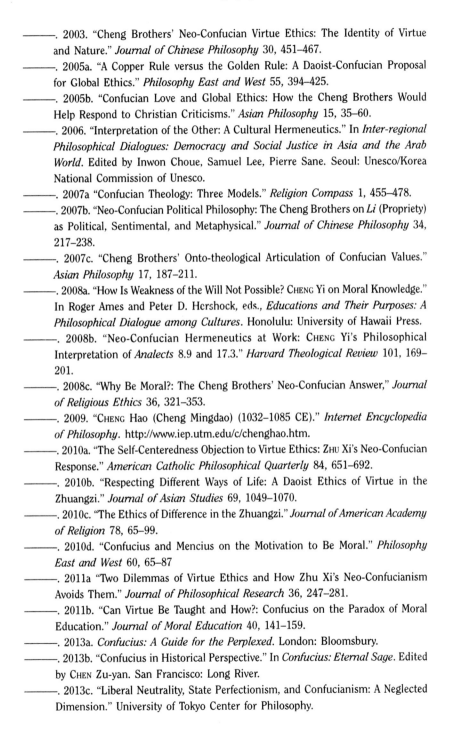

——. 2003. "Cheng Brothers' Neo-Confucian Virtue Ethics: The Identity of Virtue and Nature." *Journal of Chinese Philosophy* 30, 451–467.

——. 2005a. "A Copper Rule versus the Golden Rule: A Daoist-Confucian Proposal for Global Ethics." *Philosophy East and West* 55, 394–425.

——. 2005b. "Confucian Love and Global Ethics: How the Cheng Brothers Would Help Respond to Christian Criticisms." *Asian Philosophy* 15, 35–60.

——. 2006. "Interpretation of the Other: A Cultural Hermeneutics." In *Inter-regional Philosophical Dialogues: Democracy and Social Justice in Asia and the Arab World*. Edited by Inwon Choue, Samuel Lee, Pierre Sane. Seoul: Unesco/Korea National Commission of Unesco.

——. 2007a "Confucian Theology: Three Models." *Religion Compass* 1, 455–478.

——. 2007b. "Neo-Confucian Political Philosophy: The Cheng Brothers on *Li* (Propriety) as Political, Sentimental, and Metaphysical." *Journal of Chinese Philosophy* 34, 217–238.

——. 2007c. "Cheng Brothers' Onto-theological Articulation of Confucian Values." *Asian Philosophy* 17, 187–211.

——. 2008a. "How Is Weakness of the Will Not Possible? CHENG Yi on Moral Knowledge." In Roger Ames and Peter D. Hershock, eds., *Educations and Their Purposes: A Philosophical Dialogue among Cultures*. Honolulu: University of Hawaii Press.

——. 2008b. "Neo-Confucian Hermeneutics at Work: CHENG Yi's Philosophical Interpretation of *Analects* 8.9 and 17.3." *Harvard Theological Review* 101, 169–201.

——. 2008c. "Why Be Moral?: The Cheng Brothers' Neo-Confucian Answer," *Journal of Religious Ethics* 36, 321–353.

——. 2009. "CHENG Hao (Cheng Mingdao) (1032–1085 CE)." *Internet Encyclopedia of Philosophy*. http://www.iep.utm.edu/c/chenghao.htm.

——. 2010a. "The Self-Centeredness Objection to Virtue Ethics: ZHU Xi's Neo-Confucian Response." *American Catholic Philosophical Quarterly* 84, 651–692.

——. 2010b. "Respecting Different Ways of Life: A Daoist Ethics of Virtue in the Zhuangzi." *Journal of Asian Studies* 69, 1049–1070.

——. 2010c. "The Ethics of Difference in the Zhuangzi." *Journal of American Academy of Religion* 78, 65–99.

——. 2010d. "Confucius and Mencius on the Motivation to Be Moral." *Philosophy East and West* 60, 65–87

——. 2011a "Two Dilemmas of Virtue Ethics and How Zhu Xi's Neo-Confucianism Avoids Them." *Journal of Philosophical Research* 36, 247–281.

——. 2011b. "Can Virtue Be Taught and How?: Confucius on the Paradox of Moral Education." *Journal of Moral Education* 40, 141–159.

——. 2013a. *Confucius: A Guide for the Perplexed*. London: Bloomsbury.

——. 2013b. "Confucius in Historical Perspective." In *Confucius: Eternal Sage*. Edited by CHEN Zu-yan. San Francisco: Long River.

——. 2013c. "Liberal Neutrality, State Perfectionism, and Confucianism: A Neglected Dimension." University of Tokyo Center for Philosophy.

———. 2013d. "Between Generalism and Particularism: The Cheng Brothers' Neo-Confucian Virtue Ethics." In Stephen Angle and Michael Slote, eds., *Confucianism and Virtue Ethics*. London: Routledge.

———. 2013e. "How to Do Chinese Philosophy in A Western Philosophical Context: Introducing a Unique Approach to Chinese Philosophy." *Sinological Studies* 漢學研究 31, 117–150.

———. 2013f. "Virtue Ethics and Moral Responsibility: Confucian Conception of Moral Praise and Blame." *Journal of Chinese Philosophy* 40, 381–399.

———. 2014. "Toward a Benign Moral Relativism: From Agent/Critics-Centered to the Patient-Centered." In *Moral Relativism and Chinese Philosophy: David Wong and His Critics*. Edited by Yang XIAO and Yong HUANG, State University of New York Press.

———. Forthcoming. "The Patient Moral Relativism in the Zhuangzi." In Dennis Schilling and Richard King, eds., *Zhuang Zi: Ethics of Ease*, Harrassowitz.

Hume, David. 1957. *An Inquiry concerning the Principles of Morals*. New York: Liberal Arts.

———. 1978. *A Treatise of Human Nature*. Ed. by L. A. Selby-Bigge. Oxford: Oxford University Press.

Hurka, Thomas. 2001. *Virtue, Vice, and Value*. Oxford: Oxford University Press.

Hursthouse, Rosalind. 1999. *On Virtue Ethics*. Oxford: Oxford University Press.

———. 2004. "On the Grounding of the Virtue in Human Nature." In Jan Szaif, ed., *What Is Good for a Human Being?: Human Nature and Value*. Berlin and New York: Walter de Gruyter.

Ingen, John van. 1994. *Why Be Moral? The Egoistic Challenge*. New York: Peter Lang.

Irwin, Terence H. 1991. "The Structure of Aristotelian Happiness." *Ethics* 101, 382–391.

———. 1996. "Kant's Criticism of Eudaemonism." In Stephen Engstrom and Jennifer Whiting, eds., *Aristotle, Kant, and the Stoics: Rethinking Happiness and Duty*. Cambridge: Cambridge University Press.

Ivanhoe, P. J. 2002. *Ethics in the Confucian Tradition*. Indianapolis: Hackett.

———. 2008. "A Confucian Perspective on *Justice, Gender, and the Family*." A Paper Presented at the International Conference on "Virtue: East and West." The Chinese University of Hong Kong, May 20–22.

Jiang, Xinyan. 2000. "What Kind of Knowledge Does a Weak-Willed Person Have?—A Comparative Study of Aristotle and the Ch'eng-Chu School." *Philosophy East and West* 50, 242–253.

Jingmen Shi Bowuguan 荊門市博物館. 1998. *Bamboo Strips Excavated from the Chu Tombs at Guodian* 郭店楚墓竹簡. Beijing 北京: Wenwu chubanshe 文物出版社.

Kant, Immanuel 1956a. *Groundwork of the Metaphysic of Morals*. Trans. by H. J. Paton. New York: Harper and Row.

———. 1956b. *Critique of Practical Reason*. Trans. by Lewis White Beck. New York: Macmillan.

———. 1964a. *Doctrine of Virtue*. Ed. by M. Gregor, New York: Harper.

———. 1964b. *The Doctrine of Virtue: Part II of the Metaphysic of Morals*. Philadelphia: University of Pennsylvania Press.

———. 1965. *Critique of Pure Reason*. Trans. by Norman Kemp Smith. New York: St. Martin's.

Kaufman, Gordon. 1993. *In Face of Mystery: A Constructive Theology*. Cambridge: Harvard University Press.

Kong, Deming 孔德明. 1990. "Distinguishing Intention Independent of the Text and the Study of Confucius 離經辨志與孔子研究." In *Synthesis and Creation in Traditional Culture* 傳統文化的綜合與創新. Beijing: Jiaoyu Kexue Chubanshe 教育科學出版社.

Kraut, Richard. 1989. *Aristotle on the Human Good*. Princeton: Princeton University Press.

———. 1992. "The Defense of Justice in Plato's Republic." In Richard Kraut, ed.,*The Cambridge Companion to Plato*. Cambridge: Cambridge University Press.

———. 1998. "Egoism and Altruism." In *Routledge Encyclopedia of Philosophy*. New York and London: Routledge.

Kuhn, Thomas. 1976. "Theory-Change as Structure-Change; Comments on the Sneed Formalism." *Erkenntnis* 10, 179–199.

Küng, Hans. 1978. *On Being a Christian*. New York: Pocket Books.

———. 1989. "Confucianism: Ethical Humanism as Religion? A Christian Response." In Küng and Julia Ching, *Christianity and Chinese Religion*. New York: Doubleday.

Kupperman, Joel. 1981. "Confucian Ethics and Weakness of Will." *Journal of Chinese Philosophy* 8, 1–8.

Lao, Siguang 勞思光. 2003. *A New History of Chinese Philosophy* 新編中國哲學史, vol. 3a. Taibei 臺北: Sanmin Shuju 三民書局.

Lau, D. C., trans. 1979. *The Analects*. Middlesex, England: Penguin Books.

Lear, Gabriel Richardson. 2004. *Happy Lives and the Highest Good: An Essay on Aristotle's Nicomachean Ethics*. Princeton: Princeton University Press.

Legge, James, trans. 1971. *Confucius: Confucian Analects, The Great Learning, and The Doctrine of the Mean*. New York: Dover.

Lesses, Glenn. 1987. "Weakness, Reason, and the Divided Soul in Plato's *Republic*." *History of Philosophy Quarterly* 4, 147–161.

Lewis, Thomas A., Jonathan Wyn Schofer, Aaron Stalnaker, and Mark A. Benkson. 2005. "Anthropos and Ethos: Categories of Inquiry and Procedures of Comparison." *Journal of Religious Ethics* 33, 177–185.

Li, Chenyang. 2007. "Li as Cultural Grammar." *Philosophy East and West* 57, 311–329.

Li, Minghui 李明輝. 2001. *The Self-Transformation of Contemporary Confucianism* 當代儒學的自我轉化. Beijing 北京: Zhongguo Shehui Kexue Chubanshe 中國社會科學出版社.

Li, Rizhang 李日章. 1986. CHENG *Hao and* CHENG *Yi* 程顥程頤. Taibei 臺北: Dongda Tushu Gongsi 東大圖書公司.

Li, Zehou 李澤厚. 1999. *Reading the Analects Today* 論語今讀. Hong Kong 香港: Tiandi Tushu Gongsi 天地圖書公司.

Liji 禮記. 2004. In *Translation and Annotation of The Book of Rites* 禮記譯注, by YANG Tianyu 楊天宇. Shanghai 上海: Shanghai Guji Chubanshe 上海古籍出版社.

Liu, Xiaogan 劉笑敢. 2008a. "Between Two Orientations 掙扎遊走於兩種定向之間." In Liu Xiaogan, ed., *Orientations in Interpretations of Classics* 經典詮釋之定向. Guilin 桂林: Guangxi Shifan Daxue Chubanshe 廣西師範大學出版社.

———. 2008b. "The Unclarified Identity of Chinese Philosophy: Response to Discussions of Reverse Meaning Matching 中國哲學妾身未明? 關於'反向格義'之討論的回應." *Nanjing University Journal: Philosophy, Humanities and Social Sciences Edition* 南京大學學報哲學人文科學社會科學版 No. 2, 77–88.

———. 2009. *Interpretation and Orientation: A Study of Methodology of Chinese Philosophy* 詮釋與定向: 中國哲學研究方法之探究. Beijing: Shangwu Yinshuguan 商務印書館.

Locke, John. (n.d.). *An Essay concerning Human Understanding*. London: George Routledge and Sons.

Louden, Robert B. 1997. "Kant's Virtue Ethics." In Daniel Statman, ed., *Virtue Ethics: A Critical Reader*. Washington, DC: Georgetown University Press.

Lu, Lianzhang 蘆連章. 2001. *A Critical Biography of CHENG Hao and CHENG Yi* 程顥程頤評傳. Nanjing 南京: Nanjing Daxue Chubanshe 南京大學出版社.

Lü, Simian 呂思勉. 1996. *Outlines of Neo-Confucianism* 理學綱要. Beijing 北京: Dongfang Chubanshe 東方出版社.

MacIntyre, Alasdair. 1991. "Incommensurabillity, Truth, and the Conversation between Confucians and Aristotelians about the Virtues." In Eliot Deutsch, ed., *Culture and Modernity: East-West Philosophical Perspective*. Honolulu: University of Hawaii Press.

———. 2010. "Relativism, Power, and Philosophy." In Michael Krausz, ed., *Relativism: A Contemporary Anthology*. New York: Columbia University Press.

Mahoney, Timothy A. 1992. "Do Plato's Philosopher-Rulers Sacrifice Self-Interest to Justice?" *Phronesis* 37.3, 265–282.

McDowell, John. 1998a. "Comments on 'Some Rational Aspects of Incontinence' [by T. H. Irwin]." *Southern Journal of Philosophy*, suppl. 27, 89–102.

———. 1998b. *Mind, Value, and Reality*. Cambridge, MA: Harvard University Press.

McIntyre, Allison. 1990. "Is Akratic Action Always Irrational?" In Owen Flanagan and Amelie Rorty, eds., *Identity, Character, and Morality: Essays in Moral Psychology*. Cambridge, MA: MIT Press.

McKerlie, Dennis. 1991. "Friendship, Self-Love, and Concern for Others in Aristotle's Ethics." *Ancient Philosophy* 11, 85–101.

Melden, A. I. 1948. "Why Be Moral?" *The Journal of Philosophy* 45, 449–456.

Mencius. 2005. In *Translation and Annotation of the Mencius* 孟子譯註, by YANG Bojun 楊伯峻. Beijing: Zhonghua Shuju.

Meng, Peiyuan 蒙培元. 1989. *The System of Categories in Neo-Confucianism* 理學範疇系統. Beijing 北京: Renmin Chubanshe 人民出版社.

Midley, Mary. 1995. *Beast and Man*. London: Routledge.

Mill, John Stuart. 1972. *Utilitarianism, On Liberty, Consideration on Representative Government*. Ed. by H. B. Acton. London: Everyman's Library.

Morse, Stephen. 2003. "Inevitable Mens Rea." *Harvard Journal of Law and Public Policy* 27, 51–64.

Mou, Zongsan 牟宗三. 1990. *The Substance of Heart/Mind and the Substance of Nature* 心體與性體, 3 vols. Taibei 臺北: Zhengzhong Shuju 正中書局.

Mozi, The (Mo Tzu). In Chan 1963.

Murphy, Jeffrie. G. 1999. "A Paradox about the Justification of Punishment." In George Sher and Baruch A. Brody, eds., *Social and Political Philosophy: Contemporary Readings*. Orlando: Harcourt Brace College.

Needham, Joseph. 1956. *Science and Civilization in China*, vol. 2 of *History of Scientific Thought*. Cambridge: Cambridge University Press.

Neville, Robert Cummings. 1999. "Existential Conceptions of Love in Confucianism and Christianity." In Marko Zlomislic and David Goicoechea, eds., *Jen, Agape, Tao with Tu Wei-ming*. Binghamton: Global.

———. 2001a. *The Human Condition*. Albany: State University of New York Press.

———. 2001b. "Two Forms of Comparative Philosophy." *Dao: A Journal of Comparative Philosophy* 1, 1–13.

———. 2007. "A Comparison of Confucian and Christian Conceptions of Creativity." *Dao: A Journal of Comparative Philosophy* 6, 125–130.

Ni, Peimin. 2002. *Confucius*. Belmont, CA: Wadsworth.

Nielsen, Kai. 1989. *Why Be Moral*. Buffalo: Prometheus Books.

Nivison, David. 1980. "Mencius and Motivation." *Journal of American Academy of Religion* 47, 417–432.

Nussbaum, Martha C. 1994. *The Therapy of Desire: Theory and Practice in Hellenistic Ethics*. Princeton, NJ: Princeton University Press.

———. 1995. "Aristotle on Human Nature and the Foundation of Ethics." In J. E. J. Altham and Ross Harrison, eds., *World, Mind, and Ethics: Essays on the Ethical Philosophy of Bernard Williams*. Cambridge: Cambridge University Press.

Nygren, Anders. 1969. *Agape and Eros*. New York: Harper and Row.

O'Neill, Onora. 1989. "Kant after Virtue." In her *Constructions of Reason: Exploration of Kant's Practical Philosophy*. Cambridge: Cambridge University Press.

Okin, Susan Moller. 1989. *Justice, Gender, and the Family*. New York: Basic Books.

———. 2005. " 'Forty Acres and a Mule' for Women." *Politics, Philosophy and Economics* 4, 233–248.

Origen. 1957. *The Song of Songs: Commentary and Homilies*, trans. and annotated by R. P. Lawson. Westminster, MD: Newman.

Pan, Fu'en 潘富恩. 1996. *A Critical Biography of CHENG Hao and CHENG Yi* 程顥程頤評傳. Nanning: Guangxi Education.

Pan, Fu'en 潘富恩 and XU Yuqing 徐余慶. 1988. *A Study of CHENG Hao and CHENG Yi's Philosophy* 程顥程頤哲學研究. Shanghai 上海: Fudan Daxue Chubanshe 復旦大學出版社.

Pang-White, Ann. 2000. "The Fall of Humanity: Weakness of the Will and Moral Responsibility in the Later Augustine." *Medieval Philosophy and Theology* 9, 51–67.

———. 2003. "Augustine, *Akrasia*, and Manichaeism." *American Catholic Philosophical Quarterly* 77, 151–169.

Pang, Pu 龐樸. 1999. "Interpretation of *Analects* 8.9 使由使知解." *Guangming Ribao* 光明日報, October 22.

Pang, Wanli 龐萬里. 1992. *The Philosophical System of the CHENG Brothers* 二程的哲學體系. Beijing 北京: Beijing Hangtian Hangkong Daxue Chubanshe 北京航天航空大學出版.

Peng, Zhongde 彭忠德. 2000. "Also on *Analects* 8.9 也說 '民可使由之'章." *Guangming Ribao* 光明日報, May 16.

Plato. 1963a. *Protagoras*. In Edith Hamilton and Huntington Cairns, eds., *The Collected Dialogues of Plato*. Princeton: Princeton University Press.

———. 1963b. *Republic*. In Edith Hamilton and Huntington Cairns, eds., *The Collected Dialogues of Plato*. Princeton: Princeton University Press.

Pope, Stephen. 1994. *The Evolution of Altruism and the Ordering of Love*. Washington, DC: Georgetown University Press.

Postema, Gerald J. 1988. "Hume's Reply to the Sensible Knave." *History of Philosophical Quarterly* 5, 23–40.

Pound, Ezra, trans. 1956. *Confucian Analects*. London: Peter Owen Limited.

Pugmire, David. 1982. "Motivated Irrationality." *Proceedings of the Aristotelian Society* 56, 179–196.

Pybus, Elizabeth M., and Alexander Broadie. 1999. "Kant and the Maltreatment of Animals." In Ruth F. Chadwich, ed., *Immanuel Kant: Critical Assessments*, vol. 3, *Kant's Moral and Political Philosophy*. London and New York: Routledge.

Qian, Mu 錢穆. 2001. *An Introduction to Neo-Confucianism* 宋明理學概述. Taibei 臺北: Lantai Chubanshe 蘭臺出版社.

Rawls, John. 1996. *Political Liberalism*. New York: Columbia University Press.

———. 1997. "The Idea of Public Reason Revisited." *University of Chicago Law Review* 64.3, 765–807.

———. 1999. *A Theory of Justice*. Revised edition. Cambridge, MA: Harvard University Press.

Regan, Tom. 1999. "Broadie and Pybus on Kant." In Ruth F. Chadwich, ed., *Immanuel Kant: Critical Assessments*, vol. 3, *Kant's Moral and Political Philosophy*. London and New York: Routledge.

Rhodes, Rosamond. 1992. "Hobbes's Unreasonable Fool." *The Southern Journal of Philosophy* 30, 93–102.

Ridley, Mark, and Richard Dawkins. 1981. "Natural Selection and Altruism." In Philippe Rushton and Richard M. Sorretino, eds., *Altruism and Helping Behavior: Social, Personality, and Developmental Perspectives*. Hillsdale, NJ: Lawrence Erlbaum Associates.

Rorty, Richard. 1989. *Contingency, Irony, and Solidarity*. Cambridge: Cambridge University Press.

———. 1996. "Ambiguity of 'Rationality.'" *Constellations: An International Journal of Critical and Democratic Theory* 3, 73–82.

———. 1997. "Justice as a Large Loyalty." In Ron Bontekoe and Marietta Stepaniants, eds., *Justice and Democracy: Cross-Cultural Perspectives*. Honolulu: University of Hawaii Press.

———. 1998. *Truth and Progress: Philosophical Papers*. Cambridge: Cambridge University Press.

———. 1999. *Philosophy and Social Hope*. New York: Penguin Books.

———. 2000. "Is 'Cultural Recognition' a Useful Concept for Leftist Politics?" *Critical Horizons* 1, 7–20.

———. 2004. "Trapped between Kant and Dewey: The Current Situation of Moral Philosophy." In Natalie Brender and Lary Krasnoff, eds., *New Essays on the History of Autonomy: A Collection Honoring J. B. Schneewind*. Cambridge: Cambridge University Press.

Sachs, David. 1963. "A Fallacy in Plato's Republic." *The Philosophical Review* 72, 141–158.

Sandel, Michael. 1982. *Liberalism and the Limits of Justice*. Cambridge: Harvard University Press.

Santas, Gerasimos X. 1997. "Does Aristotle Have a Virtue Ethics?" In Daniel Statman, ed., *Virtue Ethics: A Critical Reader*. Washington, DC: Georgetown University Press.

Sartre, Jean-Paul. 1947. *Existentialism*. New York: Philosophical Library.

Scanlon, T. M. 1996. "Self-Anchored Morality." In J. B. Schneewind, ed. *Reason, Ethics, and Society*. Chicago and La Salle, Illinois: Open Court.

Schleiermacher, F. D. E. 1986. *Hermeneutics: The Handwritten Manuscripts*. Atlanta: Scholars.

Shaw, Bill, and John Corvino. 1996. "Hosmer and the 'Why Be Moral?' Question." *Business Ethics* 6, 373–383.

Shen, Vincent. 2002. "CHEN Daqi." In Antonio Cua, ed., *Encyclopedia of Chinese Philosophy*. New York and London: Routledge.

Shun, Kwong-loi. 2002. "*Ren* 仁 and *Li* in the *Analects*." In *Confucius and the Analects*. Oxford: Oxford University Press.

———. 2009. "Studying Confucian and Comparative Ethics: Methodological Reflections." *Journal of Chinese Philosophy*, 36, 455–478.

Silk, J. B., A. Samuels, and P. Rodman. 1981. "The Influences of Kinship, Rank, and Sex on Affiliation and Aggression between Adult Female and Immature Bonnet Macaques." *Behavior* 78, 111–77.

Sim, May. 2007. *Remastering Morals with Aristotle and Confucius*. Cambridge: Cambridge University Press.

Singer, Marcus. 1963. "The Golden Rule." *Philosophy: The Journal of the Royal Institute of Philosophy* 38, 293–314.

Slingerland, Edward. 2004a. "Conceptions of the Self in the *Zhuangzi*: Conceptual Metaphor Analysis and Comparative Thought." *Philosophy East and West* 54, 322–342.

———. 2004b. "Conceptual Metaphor Theory as Methodology for Comparative Religion." *Journal of American Academy of Religion* 72, 1–31.

Slingerland, Edward, trans. 2003. *Analects: With Selections from Traditional Commentaries*. Indianapolis and Cambridge: Hackett.

Slote, Michael. 1992. *From Morality to Virtue*. Oxford: Oxford University Press.

———. 2001. *Morals from Motives*. Oxford: Oxford University Press.

Smith, Michael. 2003. "Rational Capacities, or: How to Distinguish Recklessness, Weakness, and Compulsion." In Sarah Stroud and Christine Tappolet, eds., *Weakness of Will and Practical Irrationality*. Oxford: Clarendon.

Solomon, David. 1997. "Internal Objections to Virtue Ethics." In Daniel Statman, ed., *Virtue Ethics: A Critical Reader*. Washington, DC: Georgetown University Press.

Stalnaker, Aaron. 2006. *Overcoming Our Evil: Human Nature and Spiritual Exercises in Xunzi and Augustine*. Washington, DC: Georgetown University Press.

Statman, Daniel. 1997. "Introduction." In Daniel Statman, ed., *Virtue Ethics: A Critical Reader*. Washington, DC: Georgetown University Press.

Steward, Helen. 1998. "Akrasia." *Routledge Encyclopedia of Philosophy*. London and New York: Routledge.

Stocker, Michael. 1997. "The Schizophrenia of Modern Ethical Theories." In Roger Crisp and Michael Slote, eds., *Virtue Ethics*. Oxford: Oxford University Press.

Stout, Jeffrey. 1988. *Ethics after Babel: The Languages of Morals and Their Discontents*. Boston: Beacon.

Swanton, Christine. 2003. *Virtue Ethics: A Pluralistic View*. Oxford: Oxford University Press.

Tang, Junyi 唐君毅. 1966. *Introduction to Philosophy* 哲學概論, vol. 2. Jiulong 九龍: Mengshi Jiaoyu Jijin 蒙氏教育基金.

———. 1985. *On the Origin of Chinese Philosophy: Introduction* 中國哲學原論：導論篇. Taibei 臺北: Xuesheng Shuju 學生書局.

———. 1991. *On the Origin of Chinese Philosophy: Human Nature* 中國哲學原論：原性篇. Taipei 臺北: Xuesheng Shuju 學生書局.

Taylor, Charles. 1989. *The Sources of the Self: The Making of the Modern Identity*. Cambridge: Harvard University Press.

———. 1995. "A Most Peculiar Institution." In J. E. J. Altham and Ross Harrison, eds., *World, Mind, and Ethics: Essays on the Ethical Philosophy of Bernard Williams*. Cambridge: Cambridge University Press.

Thompson, Michael. 1998. "Representation of Life." In Rosalind Hursthouse, Gavin Lawrence, and Warren Quinn, eds., *Virtues and Reasons*. Oxford: Clarendon.

Tillich, Paul. 1960. *Love, Power, and Justice*. New York: Oxford University Press.

Toner, Christopher. 2006. "The Self-Centeredness Objection to Virtue Ethics." *Philosophy* 81: 595–617.

———. 2008. "Sorts of Naturalism: Requirements for a Successful Theory." *Metaphilosophy* 39.2: 220–250.

Toulmin, Stephen. 1964. *An Examination of the Place of Reason in Ethics*. Cambridge: Cambridge University Press.

Tu, Weiming. 1979. "The Creative Tension between *Jen* and *Li'* " and "*Li* as Process of Humanization." In his *Humanity and Self-Cultivation: Essays in Confucian Thought*. Berkeley: Asian Humanities.

———. 1983. "Akrasia and Self-Cultivation in Mencius." In Venant Cauchy, ed., *Philosophy and Culture*. Montreal: Ed-Montmorency.

———. 1995. "Happiness in the Confucian Way." In Leroy S. Rouner, ed., *In Pursuit of Happiness*. Notre Dame, Indiana: University of Notre Dame Press.

———. 1999. "Humanity as Embodied Love: Exploring Filial Piety in a Global Ethical Perspective." In Marko Zlomislic, ed., *Jen, Agape, Tao with Tu Wei-ming*. Binghamton: Global.

———. 2002. *Collected Works of Tu Weiming* 杜維明文集, 5 vols. Wuhan 武漢: Wuhan Chubanshe 武漢出版社.

———. 2007. "Creativity: A Confucian View." *Dao: A Journal of Comparative Philosophy* 6.2, 115–124.

Vacek, Edward Collins, S. J. 1996. "Love, Christian and Diverse: A Response to Colin Grant." *Journal of Religious Ethics* 24.1, 29–34.

van Norden, Bryan. 2007. *Virtue Ethics and Consequentialism in Early Chinese Philosophy*. Cambridge: Cambridge University Press.

Vlastos, Gregory. 1981. "Justice and Happiness in the *Republic*." In his *Platonic Studies*. Princeton: Princeton University Press.

Waley, Arthur, trans. 1971. *The Analects of Confucius*. London: George Allen and Unwin.

Walker, Arthur F. 1989. "The Problem of Weakness of Will." *Noûs* 23.5, 653–676.

Wang, Changming 王昌銘. 2004. "Understandings of *Analects* 8.9 對民可使由之的理解." *Language and Character Weekly* 語言文字周報, August 24.

Wang, Yangming. 1963. *Inquiry on the Great Learning*. In Wing-tsit Chan, ed. and trans., *A Source Book in Chinese Philosophy*. Princeton: Princeton University Press.

———. 1996. *Complete Works of Wang Yangming* 王陽明全集. Beijing 北京: Hongqi Chubanshe 紅旗出版社.

Watson, Gary. 1977. "Skepticism about Weakness of Will." *The Philosophical Review* 86.3, 316–339.

———. 1997. "On the Primacy of Character." In Daniel Statman, ed., *Virtue Ethics: A Critical Reader*. Washington, DC: Georgetown University Press.

Wen, Weiyao 溫偉耀. 1996. *The Way to Sagehood: A Study of the Cheng Brothers on Moral Cultivation* 成聖之道：北宋二程修養功夫論之研究. Taibei 臺北: Wenshizhe Chubanshe 文史哲出版社.

Wike, Victoria S. 1994. *Kant on Happiness in Ethics*. Albany: State University of New York Press.

Williams, Bernard. 1971. *Morality: An Introduction to Ethics*. New York: Harper.

———. 1985. *Ethics and the Limits of Philosophy*. Cambridge, MA: Harvard University Press.

———. 1995. "Replies." In J. E. J. Altham and Ross Harrison, eds., *World, Mind, and Ethics: Essays on the Ethical Philosophy of Bernard Williams*. Cambridge: Cambridge University Press.

Wittgenstein, Ludwig. 1958. *Philosophical Investigations*. New York: Macmillan.

Wong, David. 1989. "Universalism versus Love with Distinction." *Journal of Chinese Philosophy* 16, 251–272.

———. 1991. "Is There a Distinction between Reason and Emotion in Mencius?" *Philosophy East and West* 41, 31–44.

———. 2006. *Natural Morality: A Defense of Pluralistic Relativism*. Oxford: Oxford University.

———. 2009. "Comparative Philosophy: Chinese and Western." *The Stanford Encyclopedia of Philosophy*. Edward N. Zalta (ed.), URL = <http://plato.stanford.edu/archives/win2009/entries/comparphil-chiwes/>.

Wong, Waiying. 2003. "The Status of *li* in the Cheng Brothers' Philosophy." *Dao: A Journal of Comparative Philosophy* 3.1, 109–119.

Wu, Pi 吳丕. 2000. "On *Analects* 8.9 Again 再論儒家 '使民' 思想." *Guangming Ribao* 光明日報, June 3.

Xiao, Gongquan 蕭公權. 1999. *A History of Chinese Political Thought* 中國政治思想史. In *Modern Chinese Classics: Xiao Gongquan* 現代中國學術經典：蕭公權卷. Shijiazhuang 石家莊: Hebei Jiaoyu Chubanshe 河北教育出版社.

Xu, Fuguan 徐复觀. 1999. *A History of Chinese Theories of Human Nature: The Pre-Qin Period* 中國人性論史：先秦篇. Taipei 臺北: Shangwu Yingshuguan 商務印書館.

———. 2004a. *Collected Essays on Chinese Intellectual History* 中國思想史論文集. Shanghai 上海: Shanghai Shudian Chubanshe 上海書店出版社.

———. 2004b. *Second Collected Essays on Chinese Intellectual History* 中國思想史論文集續編. Shanghai 上海: Shanghai Shudian Chubanshe 上海書店出版社.

Xunzi 荀子. 1999. In *Library of Chinese Classics: Chinese and English*. Changsha 長沙: Hu'nan Renmin Chubanshe 湖南人民出版社, and Beijing 北京: Waiwen Chubanshe 外文出版社.

Yang, Bojun 楊伯峻. 1980. *Translation and Annotation of the Analects* 論語譯注. Beijing 北京: Zhonghua Shuju 中華書局.

Yang, Rongguo 楊榮國. 1973. *The Sage of the Reactionary Class: Confucius* 反動階級的聖人：孔子. Beijing 北京: Renmin chubanshe 人民出版社.

Yin, Zhenhuan 尹振環. 2000. "Do Not Misunderstand *Analects* 8.9 別誤解 '民不可使知之.'" *Guangming Ribao* 光明日報, July 18.

Yu, Jiyuan. 2007. *The Ethics of Confucius and Aristotle: Mirrors of Virtue*. New York and London: Routledge.

Yu, Zhihui 俞志慧. 1997. "Interpretation of *Analects* 8.9 《論語》泰伯 '民可使由之不可使知之' 章心解." *Kongmeng Yuekan* 孔孟學刊, No. 1.

Zhang, Zai 張載. 1978. *The Complete Works of ZHANG Zai* 張載集. Beijing 北京: Zhonghua Shuju 中華書局.

———. 2000. *Correcting Youthful Ignorance* 張子正蒙. Shanghai 上海: Shanghai Guji Chubanshe 上海古籍出版社.

Zhongyong 中庸. In *Liji*.

Zhou, Dunyi 周敦頤. 2000. *Penetrating the Book of Changes* 周子通書. Shanghai 上海: Shanghai Guji Chubanshe 上海古籍出版社.

Zhou, Qian 周乾. 2000. "Also on *Analects* 8.9 也論民可使由之." *Guangming Ribao* 光明日報, October 24.

Zhou, Yutong 周予同. 1996. *Collected Works on History of Chinese Hermeneutics* 中國經學史論著選集. Shanghai: Shanghai People's Press.

Zhu, Xi 朱熹. 1985. *Collected Annotations of the Analects* 論語集注. In *Four Books and Five Classics* 四書五經. Beijing北京: Zhongguo Shuju 中華書局.

———. 1997. *Classified Sayings of Zhuzi* 朱子語類. Wuhan 武漢: Yuelu Shuyuan 岳麓書院.

Zhu, Zhongming 朱忠明, and YE Yudian 葉玉殿. 1986. "On CHENG Yi's Doctrine of Investigating Things and Extending Knowledge 評二程的格物致知說." In *Collected Essays on the Thoughts of the Two Chengs* 《二程思想研究文集》. Zhenghou 鄭州: Henan Renmin Chubanshe 河南人民出版社.

Index